AF403424

The Nikon Camera in America,
1946–1953

The Nikon Camera in America, 1946–1953

MICHAEL WESCOTT LODER

Foreword by Robert J. Rotoloni

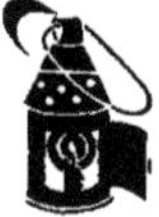

McFarland & Company, Inc., Publishers
Jefferson, North Carolina, and London

Unless credited otherwise, photographs are by the author.

Library of Congress Cataloguing-in-Publication Data

Loder, Michael Wescott.
The Nikon camera in America, 1946–1953 / Michael Wescott Loder ;
foreword by Robert J. Rotoloni.
p.   cm.
Includes bibliographical references and index.

ISBN 978-0-7864-3221-9
softcover : 50# alkaline paper ∞

1. Nihon Kogaku Kogyo Kabushiki Kaisha.   2. Nikon camera — History.
3. Camera industry — United States — History.   4. Photography — United
States — Equipment and supplies — History.   I. Title.
HD9708.5.C354N4966   2008   338.7'6814180973 — dc22   2007049205

British Library cataloguing data are available

©2008 Michael Wescott Loder. All rights reserved

*No part of this book may be reproduced or transmitted in any form
or by any means, electronic or mechanical, including photocopying
or recording, or by any information storage and retrieval system,
without permission in writing from the publisher.*

Cover photograph: A Nikon M from late 1950 or early 1951 with its
accessory lenses (James Kelly collection)

Manufactured in the United States of America

*McFarland & Company, Inc., Publishers
Box 611, Jefferson, North Carolina 28640
www.mcfarlandpub.com*

For Hans and Christiane,
and
Adolph and John

Thank you

Acknowledgments

I would like to thank several persons in particular who have given freely of their time and material in order to make this story correct and accurate. First I would like to acknowledge the personnel at the National Archives of the United States in College Park, Maryland, for their patience and help in finding and handling the many documents I had to locate there. Robert Rotoloni, president of the Nikon Historical Society, reviewed the manuscript and encouraged me again and again, even while in the midst of getting his own book on the Nikon rangefinder cameras finished. He also provided the foreword and many of the pictures and documents that I used to gain more knowledge of the Nikon Camera Company and Nippon Kogaku's early manufacturing problems. Many of these illustrations appeared previously in various issues of the *Nikon Journal* and I owe a special thanks to Bob for granting permission to reuse these, as well as my own writings that appeared in the *Journal*. A "thank you" goes to Mikio Itoh, Nikon, Inc.'s archivist in Tokyo, who also reviewed the manuscript and offered corrections and details. I would like to express gratitude to all the many members of the Nikon Historical Society (contact: Robert Rotoloni, President, P.O. Box 3213, Munster, Indiana 46321 USA) all over the world who gave freely of their knowledge and many of the images that appear in this book. This includes Hans Braakhuis, Jim Emmerson, Tony Hurst, James Kelly, Bill Kraus, Richard Lane, Ling Lee, Peter Lownds, Mike Symons and Nico van Dijk. A special thanks goes to Thede Loder for his willingness to locate and photograph Adolph Gasser and the Merchants Exchange Building in his own hometown of San Francisco. I would also like to thank David Douglas Duncan for his time, suggestions of sources and granting permission to use the picture of him that Jun Miki took in 1950. A thank you goes to Adriana Husta, widow of Danny Husta, for granting permission to use the pictures of the Ohi factory interior which her husband took in 1951, a thank you to Gerry Thompson for permission to use the picture of the PX waiting lines taken by her father and a special thanks to Shelley Mydans for granting permission to use the picture of her father and Duncan taken in Korea in 1950.

In addition to all the materials provided by the individuals above, the book also includes images provided by Time-Life/Getty Images and the Photography Collection, Harry Ransom Humanities Research Center, The University of Texas at Austin. I also must acknowledge the permission granted by the *New York Times* to quote extensively from Deschin's December 10, 1950, column on the Nikon.

An acknowledgment and thanks must go to my wife, Linda, and my library assistant, Rosanne Chesakis, for twice reading and proofing the manuscript prior to final submission. Then I need to expand that "thank you" to include the rest of my staff in the Ciletti Memorial Library at the Schuylkill Campus of Pennsylvania State University: my former colleague, Amy, and Mari, Vince and Susan for all their support in seeing this project to completion over these last few years.

Finally, I must express my gratitude to the late Adolph Gasser, and to John Gasser and Hans Liholm for generously sharing their memories, pictures and their life histories. And to Hans for his hospitality, willingness to review the manuscript (twice) and the use of his historic photographs and personal documents that help bring this period alive. But please note that while all of these individuals have done their upmost to insure that the narrative is as accurate as memories and documents allow, any remaining errors are my responsibility.

Table of Contents

Foreword by Robert J. Rotoloni

When I first began to research the history of Nippon Kogaku and their Nikon camera in 1971, the camera collecting world was a much different place. Back then, collectors and historians had little interest in Japanese cameras or the companies that made them. Precious little factual knowledge was available in the West about the mysterious Orient in any case, even though our knowledge of, and daily commerce with, the Far East was much greater than it had ever been before the end of World War Two. The language barrier added to the difficulties. Very little, if any, factual information about Nippon Kogaku's history was available in English, and getting Japanese writings translated was, and still is, extremely difficult and time consuming. Unlike European cameras whose literature could be easily translated from the original German, French, Italian, etc., the historian of things Japanese faced a very steep uphill challenge. Therefore, when I began, I had to depend on what was available in the English-language literature.

My initial source of information was the periodicals section of the Chicago Public Library where I was able to browse through nearly 15 years worth of every major photographic magazine published in the United States. It proved to be an excellent source of contemporary information about the Nikon camera and, to some degree, the manufacturer (Nippon Kogaku) and Japan's photo/optical industry. This source started me on my continuing quest for knowledge about Nippon Kogaku and the Nikon camera. Over the last three decades I have added information from many other sources from both sides of the Pacific. This includes factory records and interviews with many of the people who were involved with the design and production of the early Nikons. I have gained access to a great deal of Japanese literature and have had some of it translated over the years. In addition, I have had a tremendous amount of interaction with countless collectors all over the world. As a result, our knowledge today is absolutely massive compared to what it was 35 years ago.

However, the work of a historian is never really finished. Research is an endless educational process, and no one can ever really say they know it all, and that there is nothing left to learn. I know this first hand, for this spring, after 35 years of study, I received a manuscript and supporting documentation that touched on an aspect of the Nikon's history I did not know existed, let alone had access to. When Michael Wescott Loder first contacted me with his research, I realized that he had found and used an entirely original approach to determining the history of the Nikon! The result of that research is this book, which contains information that has never before been presented in such detail and completeness.

When Wes (as he is known to his friends) first explained to me what he was doing and showed me some of his materials, I immediately knew he was onto something that was not only important but also offered a new perspective to researching the Nikon. Over the years, I had gathered some knowledge concerning the role of General MacArthur and the GHQ and how it affected Nippon Kogaku. We knew about the relationship between MacArthur's people and the rebuilding of Japan's economy based on the Western model of capitalism. I was also aware of SCAP and its place in this rebuilding process. What I did not know was that a very detailed record of this interaction still existed and was housed in the National Archives. What Wes was able to learn from his research is literally mind-boggling in that it details, in some cases, a nearly day-to-day picture of what was going on in the immediate postwar years with Japan's optical industry and Nippon Kogaku in particular. I read his manuscript and gazed upon the material he had found in the archives with rapt attention for I was learning more with every paragraph and the turn of every page. For a historian, seeing new material that ties in with his or her own research and expands that knowledge is a true delight.

But Wes did not stop there. He went on to unearth more information about the first importer of the Nikon and the people involved than I thought existed. He learned when and where certain events occurred and even interviewed two of the major players in this part of the story. Wes made Overseas Finance & Trading come to life along with the roles played by Uno Lindholm, Hans Liholm and Adolph Gasser. Again, I knew "some" of what he writes of, but nowhere near the detail and accuracy. An amazing story.

Wes has not only brought to light a source of information never previously tapped by any writers concerned with the Nikon, but he has also distilled it down to an easy-to-follow yet highly detailed and enjoyable read. Not only will you learn a great deal about how the Nikon came to be (and how close it came to being stillborn), you will also walk away with a better knowledge of what the conditions were like in Japan during the immediate postwar years and how the "Japanese Economic Miracle" we all take for granted today started out so precariously. Since the world economy today is so entwined with that of Japan, this is very relevant history indeed. After pursuing this subject for 35 years and learning from so many sources, I thought that all that there was possible to learn had been found. Wes has proven me wrong. He has come up with a new approach and the result is a quantum leap in our knowledge of how the first Nikon camera came to be. Do we now know everything? Probably not. But I truly believe that Wes has uncovered the last great treasure trove of knowledge and all that will follow will simply be fine tuning of what you read here.

Robert J. Rotoloni is the founder and president of the Nikon Historical Society and editor and publisher of The Nikon Journal.

Preface

This book began as an attempt to locate a regulatory order that I was sure did not exist. Numerous recent sources I had read or accessed on the World Wide Web stated that the American Occupation of Japan authorities would not allow the first model of the Nikon camera to be exported due to its odd negative size of 24mm by 32mm. I did not believe this to be true. I had already read every primary source I could find on the early history of the Nikon while I was a graduate student at the University of Oregon back in the 1970s. None of these records mentioned a prohibition or ban on the export of Nikons. What these accounts did state was that first model Nikons went to the United States. But then the *importer* stopped taking shipments and told the manufacturer that it could not sell the cameras unless the format was changed. This was not the same as an Occupation order.

As I re-researched this period in photography's history, I realized that other half-truths and even outright falsehoods had accumulated around the early manufacture and exportation of the Nikon camera and its Nikkor lenses. Many accounts stated that it was not until 1954 that the Nikon officially made it to the United States. Any earlier arrivals had to be the result of accidents or purchases by G.I.s stationed in Japan. Yet this was plainly not true, as even a cursory examination of contemporary photographic magazines and their advertisements showed.

My quest for the truth soon evolved into a search for information as to what did happen. I became particularly curious about the Overseas Finance & Trading Company — a small firm run and owned by Swedes, but headquartered in San Francisco — that had been the early importer. The final stimulus to write came when I discovered that the two men most involved in the early importation of the Nikon and its first improvements were still alive and in good enough health to happily share with me their memories. These two men, Hans Liholm and Adolph Gasser, had gone to enormous lengths to make the Nikon a success in the period 1948–51 and yet, with no official acknowledgment appearing in any modern account, their contributions were being lost to history.

I have now worked in academic libraries for over thirty years. Before that became my chosen profession, I was a photographer. I happened into that vocation almost by accident. I had loved history since childhood and majored in it as an undergraduate but, with a four-year stint as an officer in the Air Force looming, I needed something else. I chose "Precision Photographic Services Officer" as my specialty. This led to an interest in still photography and Nikons. Between 1968 and 1973, my wife and I averaged better than a roll of film a week, and we assembled a wide selection of equipment. My natural historical curiosity in turn led to my finding out as much as I could about the equipment's genesis and the company that made them.

I read George Wright's *Nikon Manual*, and, later, while in graduate school, I located copies of the original articles on the Nikon and its Nikkor lenses that had appeared in major photographic magazines starting in 1950. None of these writings gave any indication that either the Nikon's manufacturer, Nippon Kogaku Kogyo Kabushiki Kaisha (or Nippon Kogaku K.K.), or the first importer, the Overseas Finance & Trading Company, had experienced any governmental interference or restrictions with bringing these cameras into the United States as early as 1949. I also read the stories of the later "discovery" of the Nikkor lenses and the Nikon camera, but at that time found them to be merely an interesting anecdote, the more colorful part of a success story, one often repeated but seldom placed into the context of its meaning for Japan, the world economy and future technology.

When I returned to this topic in 2003, I discovered that the first people to ask questions about the early Nikons were not historians, they were not even scholars. Rather, they were the latter-day camera collectors, those who loved the Nikon camera for what it was and what it represented. They asked questions, traded stories and tales and built a tradition largely based on oral histories and educated guesswork. These people were interested and concerned. They did want to know what had happened to the company and its products in the period from 1945 through 1953. Unfortunately, when these collectors started doing their research in the late 1970s and early 1980s, a great many difficulties stood in their way — difficulties which today can be overcome to a certain extent due to changes in communications and scholarly activity.

Part of the problems these amateur scholars faced was that almost all the documentation from this period resided in just three places. These locations were (1) the present-day Nikon Company itself in Tokyo, (2) its American distributor and (3) the files of the American Occupation authorities. All three of these locations posed difficulties. For a long time, the Nikon Company itself could not understand why anyone would be interested in what had happened during that period of the company's history. They neglected their records or lost them. Those that did exist were not readily available to American collectors because they were largely in Japanese.

From 1954 until 1982, the marketer and distributor of Nikon goods in North America was a company named "Nikon, Inc." which, from 1962, had been a subsidiary of Ehrenreich Photo-optical Industries. Its founder, Joseph P. Ehrenreich, was a major player in making the Nikon a success worldwide, but he actively promoted the impression that the history of the Nikon camera in North America began with his acquisition of the franchise in 1953. The efforts of the Overseas Finance & Trading Company and its successor, the

Nikon Camera Company, were ignored or even dismissed. Certainly, Ehrenreich made no effort to preserve the story of his commercial predecessors. It is even possible that much of the disinformation I was encountering had its origins in the self-serving publications that Ehrenreich sponsored.

The military occupation of Japan ran from 1945 until 1952 and encompassed almost the entire time period of this account. The Occupation came under the authority and control of "General Headquarters" (GHQ), and the "Supreme Commander for the Allied Forces" (SCAP). While the supreme commander was certainly General Douglas MacArthur for most of this period, "SCAP" was also the organization under MacArthur's command that directed the administration of Japan. The soldiers and civilians that actually ran SCAP poked their noses into every aspect of Japanese life. SCAP collected and maintained extensive records, but these remained classified and largely unavailable for scholarly use until the 1990s. Since then, these records have been declassified and moved to the National Archives of the United States where they are available for public research. The indexing of these files and the availability of that index on the World Wide Web have opened up this third source of information to any would-be scholar. While this has been a considerable advance, the index covers only file folder titles, which often reveal little of a folder's actual contents. In hand, the records, mostly carbon copies of correspondence, often prove to be contradictory, incomplete or misfiled. Still, for now, these precious records remain the finest primary resource available to American scholars for this important period in the Nikon's and Japan's history.

The following text, then, is my attempt to take these records and relate them to the efforts Nippon Kogaku K.K. was making to survive during the period 1945 through 1953. Combined with the stories that appeared in contemporary American publications, recent research and interviews with individuals still alive who were active in the importation business, I believe we finally have a history. It may still be incomplete, but all of it is truth, and that is all any reader might wish for. We hope that it will also serve as testimony to the individuals who made it happen.

Notes: Standard Japanese practice is to write personal names with the patronymic first, given name last — the opposite of Western linguistic practice. However, many Japanese names appear in American publications with patronymics last. For consistency and to avoid confusion, I have tried to follow the Western practice of placing family names last for all names.

Romanized Japanese spellings also vary greatly. For example, the main plant of Nippon Kogaku is spelled *Oi* in all the records of the Occupation, yet today, *Ohi* is the accepted spelling, and that is the spelling I have used in this account.

Portions of this book in slightly different form have appeared previously in issues of the *Nikon Journal*. This includes that part of the epilogue that covers the history of Ehrenreich Photo-optical Industries, the pictures of Hans Liholm's camera, the image taken with that camera and the pictures of Walter Gasser's camera.

Introduction:
A Meeting in San Francisco

No single incident that occurred during the American Armed Forces' Occupation of Japan was of greater importance to that country's postwar recovery than the discovery by the American photojournalists David Douglas Duncan and Horace Bristol of the quality of Nikkor lenses in June 1950. Without any attempt at exaggeration, we would state that if the superiority of Japanese optics had continued to remain unnoticed, the growth of an overseas market for Japanese precision and complex manufactured goods could have been seriously delayed for years or even been stifled. This statement includes not just Japanese photographic equipment, but any and all industrial products. The key to Japan's postwar economic — and political — recovery lay in its recreation of an overseas market for its manufacturers.[1] Yet in 1950, most American and other overseas merchants, and the American general public, held Japanese products in almost universal contempt. The immense positive publicity that the photographic and general news press gave to the Nikkor optics starting in December 1950 created a market and demand that has continued to grow to this present day. But it also caused importers and consumers to take a second look at all Japanese products, creating additional markets for everything from electronics to automobiles, all markets where today Japan is a major force.

The story of this discovery has been recounted many times. Like many good stories, it has a fairy-tale quality, with David Douglas Duncan — one of the great war photographers and photojournalists of the twentieth century — in the role of crown prince, suddenly finding that the princess he could not imagine existed was but a few miles away, waiting in a nearby factory for his appearance. That princess was the 85mm f2 Nikkor-P, an interchangeable lens that, mounted on his German-made Leica camera, outperformed the other lenses he had been using up to that point. But to retell that story now is to diminish the enormous efforts that hundreds of individuals had already put into both keeping the Nippon Kogaku company alive and creating a future for its products.

An event that was to have just as much of an effect on the future of Japanese photographic products, and the Nikon camera and its lenses, had actually taken place a year earlier and half a world away, and it did not involve any Japanese or American photojournalists.

Sometime in either late May or early June, 1949,* Hans W. Liholm, a young Swedish businessman living in San Francisco and operating the Overseas Finance & Trading Company, called on Adolph Gasser, owner of the General Camera Repair Shop located at 278 Post Street. He had left a camera off for Gasser's examination several days earlier and now was checking back to discover what Gasser thought of this new camera. His company had been importing the camera into the United States for several months and, not being a photographic technician himself, he wanted to know what an expert thought.

Liholm could not have picked a better person for this examination and analysis. Gasser had been repairing cameras and lenses for over twenty years. By 1949, General Camera Repair had six employees and was servicing almost all the local professionals. Gasser enjoyed a reputation for running the best photographic equipment repair facility on the West Coast and he was well known throughout the industry. But more important, Gasser also had an open and inquiring mind. For him, the fact that this new camera was engraved with "Made in Occupied Japan"† in prominent letters on the base plate did not play against it. He was more interested in the basic design, the parts used and the workmanship than in where it had been manufactured. In reporting his findings to Liholm, he placed them in the context of everything that was happening in the American photographic industry at that time. He also saw this camera as an opportunity for himself.[2]

Nippon Kogaku Kogyo Kabushiki Kaisha (the Japan Optical Industry Company, Limited, usually shortened to just Nippon Kogaku K.K. or Nippon Kogaku and hereafter usually referred to as NK for the words "Nippon Kogaku") had been attempting to create a quality 35mm interchangeable-lens camera for export since 1946. It had taken the company nearly two and a half years to design and complete prototypes, test them and begin manufacturing. It had not been an easy process. Even though this new camera's official start of production had been March 1948, fewer than four hundred of the new "Nikons" had passed inspection and left the factory. Liholm's company had imported as many as 72 of these new cameras[3] into the United States starting in February 1949, but so far neither Liholm nor anyone else had found many dealers willing to take a chance on selling what most regarded as Japanese junk. What could he do? What was keeping dealers from taking orders for this camera?

Gasser reassured Liholm and told him that the camera had "good points." In fact, overall, Gasser was impressed, but he advised against marketing the current version of the camera in the States. The biggest stumbling block that Gasser saw was the camera's format. The Eastman Kodak Company virtually controlled the film industry in the United States. Its

---

In interviews with both Hans Liholm and Adolph Gasser, neither one could remember the exact date of this visit.

†*The Japan Occupation authorities specified that all Japanese goods for export had to have this mark via SCAPIN #1535, released on February 20, 1947. SCAPIN #2061, released on December 5, 1949, allowed the alternative of either "Made in Japan" or just "Japan," but NK continued to use the longer "Occupied" label until at least April 1951, although the mark did shrink in size and move to less conspicuous locations on its products.*

processing machines for 35mm still film assumed a negative size of 1 by 1½ inch (24mm by 36mm). This new camera was using a frame size of 24mm by 32mm — a size promoted by the Japanese government. This meant that every frame advance moved the film just seven sprockets instead of the eight sprockets that a 36mm frame would require. As a result, the automatic film cutters in Kodak's machines would be slicing through negative frames instead of between. "You can't compete with Kodak. [It's like] trying to change the world,"[4] he told Liholm. If Nikon's manufacturer wanted to sell in the United States, it had to offer a camera that advanced the film eight sprockets on a wind.

What would be involved in changing this camera from 24 × 32 to 24 × 36? Liholm may not have understood all the enormous costs NK had already gone through to get a camera to a marketable state, but he did understand that NK simply did not have the resources or time to create a totally new body casting and shutter that would allow 24 × 36.

Gasser had taken the camera apart and knew what could be done. He now opened up the back, took off the back plate that separated the film plane from the shutter (held by four screws) and showed Liholm how it would be possible to change the shutter's gearing so that the advance would go eight sprockets. He also showed Liholm that by taking off one millimeter from each side of the film gate, the picture size could be expanded to 24 × 34 without having to create an entirely new body casting or shutter mechanism. The camera would still not be the 24 × 36 standard, but it might be close enough, and its negatives would not conflict with Kodak's machines.

Gasser pointed out other, more minor problems. The tripod socket was no more than a ⅜-inch stamping in the camera's baseplate. It was too thin and too shallow to be able to withstand any hard usage. Besides, it was not the American standard of ¼-inch. Gasser also felt that the film pressure plate was too flimsy and needed heavier duty blade springs to make it stiffer.

The meeting ended there. Liholm collected his camera and left, but not before Gasser had made it clear that he liked what he saw, and that if he could be of further help, he was available. Within months, the camera would change, and two years later, Gasser himself would be on his way to Japan to provide personal advice and help to the engineers and technicians of Nippon Kogaku.

These two events, a year and a world apart — one in San Francisco, one in Tokyo — were the pivotal encounters that would shape a company, an industry and a country's future. The narrative which follows provides the story and historical context for understanding what Nippon Kogaku was, what roles Hans Liholm, Adolph Gasser, David Douglas Duncan, Horace Bristol and others played, and how other historical events and the policies of the American Occupation authorities affected all that did happen.

1

Background: Nippon Kogaku's History to September 1945

For good or for ill, wars have a habit of causing great changes. The events covered in detail in this narrative actually had their beginnings over thirty years earlier with the outbreak of hostilities in Europe in 1914. Although Japan had made great strides prior to the First World War in its drive to become a modern, industrialized nation, it still lacked many of the necessary components needed to manufacture its own optical products.[1] German companies, such as Carl Zeiss and its Schott Glass Works, provided most of the optical glass used to make the few lenses needed for cameras. Other European and American companies made most of the dry plates and chemicals needed to make photographs and develop them. The actual formulæ and processes for making optical-quality glass were carefully guarded secrets of the various companies. Where secrets failed, patents followed, giving various German firms a near monopoly on the production of high-quality cameras and lenses. This meant high prices for a Japanese public increasingly interested in photography, but it did not approach a crisis until the war. Then the Allied blockade of Germany and Austria-Hungary effectively cut off all access to German optical goods.

While ordinary glasses containing either calcium (called "crown") or lead (called "flint") had been almost universally available for window panes, mirrors and containers since ancient times, the ability to manufacture glasses with predictable refractive indices for use in optical systems is a modern innovation. The discovery by Guinand, a Swiss glassmaker, that stirring new glass in its molten state resulted in a consistent, homogeneous product initiated the development of high-quality optics.[2] The concurrent development of photography, beginning with the experiments of the Wedgewood family, followed by the work of Niépce, Daguerre, Talbot and Herschel, quickly led to demands for better glasses for use in picture-taking lenses. A technological race ensued among various European countries and firms to develop new glass types and better manufacturing techniques.

Crude experimentation soon led to the use of mathematical formulæ based on Gauss's theories that made possible the prediction of the effects of combining lenses with varying surface curvatures. In the 1880s, the experiments of Ernst Abbe, working with Otto Schott and the Carl Zeiss Company in Jena, Germany, resulted in new glasses that contained barium, borates and phosphate. These ingredients, combined with ordinary flints and crowns, yielded far superior optics than had previously been possible. Starting with the "Protar," designed by Paul Rudolph and introduced by Zeiss in 1890, true "anastigmat" lenses with good corrections for all aberrations finally became available. So successful were the new Schott glasses and German designs based on these glasses that by 1900, virtually all optical glass was produced either by *Schott und Genossenor* or by two Guinard descendants, namely, Parra-Mantois in France and Chance Brothers in England.[3]

The Imperial Japanese Navy had already decided that superior optics were essential to reaching and holding a technical supremacy over its potential enemies. As early as 1894, it was installing Scottish-made Barr & Stroud rangefinders on its warships for use in fire control. The resulting superiority in gunnery that rangefinders gave to the Japanese navy were a major factor in its destruction of Russia's navy in the Tsushima Strait on 27 May 1905 — giving victory to Japan in the Russo-Japanese War. The Japanese army also saw optics as a means of gaining battlefield superiority. It established its own optical research laboratory in Tokyo in 1909, including a facility for repairing optical weapons.[4] The Imperial Navy followed suit and set up a separate research facility in the Tsukiji Arsenal in 1915. Faced with increasing war shortages, the Japanese government began to promote the expansion of a completely native glass industry.

But making immediate progress did not prove easy. Although the Japanese archipelago could provide most of the raw materials for making glass, every aspect of glass manufacturing had to be learned, from assembling the basic ingredients to making the ceramic vats and furnaces in which the various chemicals were mixed, melted and annealed. But the Japanese persisted, for the government had now made *jikyujisoku* or "self-sufficiency" a national goal.[5]

Perhaps hoping that a civilian firm might add to their own efforts, the Imperial Navy encouraged Koyata Iwasaki, president of the Mitsubishi *zaibatsu*, or financial group — and a graduate of Cambridge University — to create a new firm that would focus on optical equipment and optical glass products. Established on July 25, 1917, the new company, Nippon Kogaku, a fusion of Tokyo Keiki Seisaku Sho and Iwaki Glass, marked its birth with a gift of 2 million yen in financing from Mitsubishi.[6] The next month, this new firm would began work on its own facility in Oimachi in the Shinagawa District of West Tokyo with construction of works that included a factory covering over 51,000 square feet. In early 1918, NK would be joined by a third company, Fujii Lens Seizo-Sho, Japan's largest binocular manufacturer.

The oldest of the three concerns, Iwaki Glass Seizo-sho, had been a glass manufacturer since its founding in the early 1880s.[7] For much of the company's early history, it manufactured only plain sheet glass such as would have gone into window panes and other non-optical products. In 1914, it began to experiment with melting optical-quality glass and during the war the firm supplied the Japanese navy with mirrors for search lights. Only the small optical glass part of Iwaki Glass came into NK. The other part continues to this day as Asahi Techno Glass (ATG), specializing in glass for light bulbs, ceramics and other technical applications.

Tokyo Keiki Seisaku-sho also had its beginnings in the previous century, getting its start as a manufacturer of pressure gauges. From production of these it moved into nautical instruments, including compasses, depth sounders and other tools needed by the Imperial Navy. In 1913 it began to manufacture rangefinders. As with the case of Iwaki Glass, only the optical part of the company merged into NK. The other part, known today as Tokimec, still exists as an instrumentation manufacturer.

Founded in 1909, Fujii Lens was the largest of the three firms and the first optical company in Japan to make lenses for purposes other than spectacles. It had been established by Ryuzo Fujii, a former naval officer, in partnership with his brother, Kohzo, a chemist.

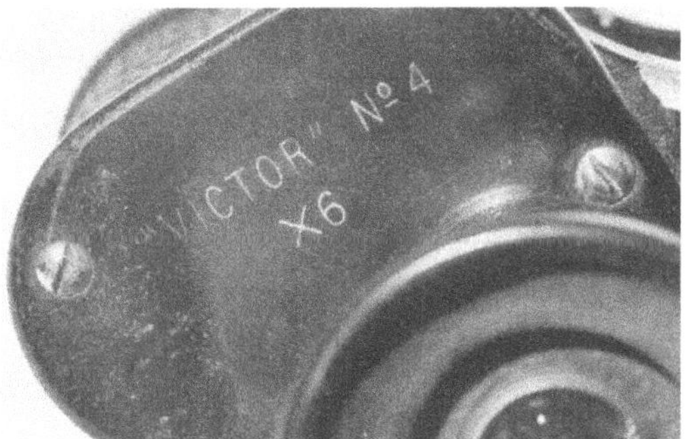

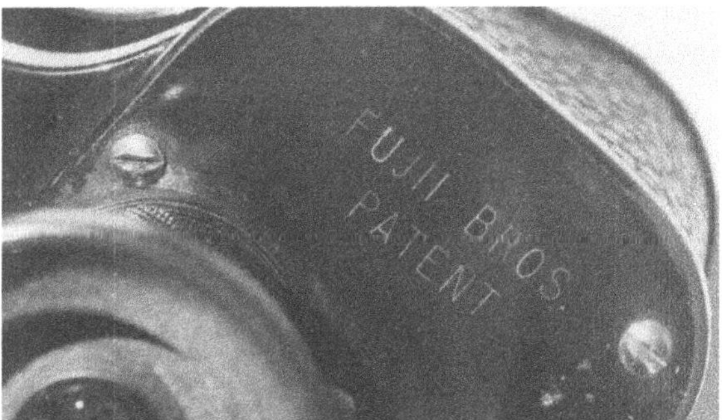

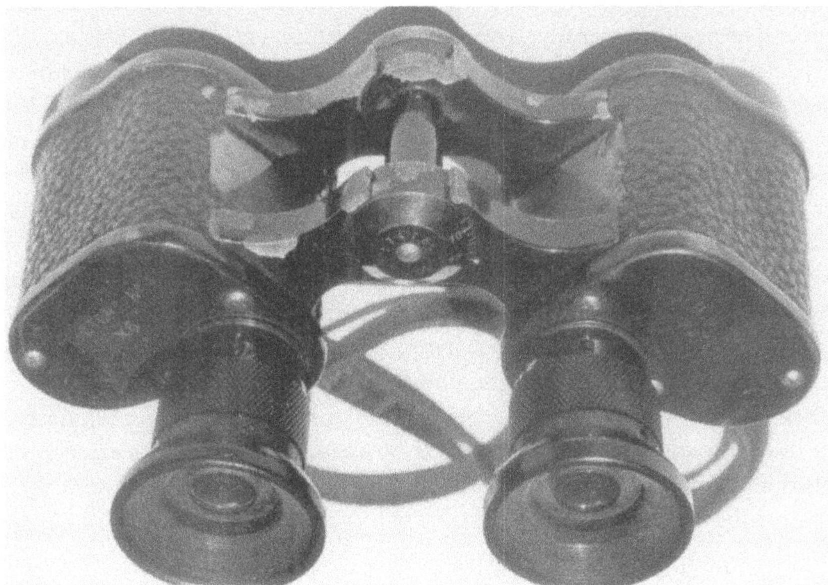

Pair of Victor binoculars manufactured by the Fujii Brothers, the immediate predecessor of Nippon Kogaku (Richard A. Lane photographs).

Ryuzo Fujii had studied optical design and manufacture in Germany at the turn of the twentieth century. After a year of research, the brothers built a new plant — called the "Shiba" plant — and equipped it with lens grinding and polishing machines and lathes imported from Germany. Soon they began fixing army optical equipment. By 1911, the company was making binoculars — the 8 × 20 "Victors" — selling most of them to the Japanese Imperial Army.[8] These were modeled on the British-made Ross binoculars and were the first prismatic units manufactured in Japan. The new Nippon Kogaku quickly took over the Fujii Company's binocular production and, by the end of the war, the new company had exported over 15,000 prism binoculars to England, France, the United States and Russia.[9]

From its very beginning, NK targeted its markets among industry, the military and the sciences. Domestic products, such as camera lenses, were not part of its agenda. Even in its first year of existence, it had begun work on rangefinders and periscopes, filling contract orders from the Imperial Navy. The combined company, registered on January 1, 1918, centered its production facilities in its new Oi [Ohi] plant. That same year it built its first furnace for optical glass production. A year later, the company invited eight German optical scientists and engineers to come and work in Tokyo on a five-year contract. Their names included Heinrich Acht, chief engineer and head of product design and drafting; Ernst Bernick, mechanical; Hermann Dillmann, optical computing; Max Lange, optical design; Albert Ruppert, prism grinding and polishing; Adolf Sadtler, lens grinding and polishing; Otto Stange, product design and drafting; and Kuet (or Karl) Weise, lens grinding and polishing. Considering the economic disaster that then gripped postwar Germany, this offer must have been particularly attractive. They may have been former Zeiss employees, although it is also possible that at least Acht had worked for Goerz. Two of these men, Lange and Sadtler, died while in Japan. All of the others, except Acht, returned to Germany at the end of their contracts. They trained Japanese engineers and technicians and helped the company to design optical equipment. During their stay, they helped redesign NK's binoculars based on Zeiss patterns and computed the first lenses for photography.* These new binocular types included the Luscar and Mikron models of 1921, and later the Orion 6 × 24 and Novar series. Heinrich Acht remained in Japan at the end of the five-year period, and he continued to work for the company until February 1928. Masao Nagaoka, who, later as the company's president, was to be of critical importance to NK's survival, joined the company as a chemist at this time.

Despite its having sponsored the formation of NK, the navy continued to run its own optical research center at the Tokyo Naval Arsenal until 1923, when that center was destroyed in the Great Kanto Earthquake that devastated Tokyo. The navy gave up, and its technical personnel transferred to NK, saving the company from financial collapse in the process. NK's factory had also suffered damage, but the navy provided funds for rebuilding the Ohi plant and the company was back in business by October. The army's arsenal and optical facilities had also suffered heavy damage, and it transferred much of its optical research to NK as well.

They may also have transmitted a little German culture. At the party celebrating the new contract with the Overseas Finance & Trading Company on April 25, 1950, the board members of NK entertained Hans Liholm by singing German popular songs.

NK was now endowed with the best knowledge concerning optics and optical production in the country, but the international naval limitations agreements previously signed in Washington in 1922 continued to cramp the Imperial Navy's plans for expansion and, with it, work for NK. For the rest of the decade, NK would struggle to stay in business. Despite this, research continued, particularly in the glass-manufacturing process. The scientists designed new, larger melting pots and developed new glass types. By the end of 1923, the company was able to manufacture 14 different glass types, and by the end of 1927, it was using new melting pots of its own design and had converted its furnaces to gas heat.

One of the last things Acht did before returning to Germany was to complete the design for a 500mm Cooke-type anastigmat lens called a "Flieger." This became NK's first photographic lens. The prototypes suffered from various sharpness problems, but after changing the triplet design, NK was able to provide satisfactory optics to the Japanese military. Acht also compiled a list of specifications for at least nine lenses varying in aperture and focal length. These ranged from as short as 75mm to the above-mentioned Flieger. Now it was the turn of the Japanese to travel to Europe. Starting in February 1928, one of the engineers Acht had trained, Kakuya Sunayama, inspected optical plants in Germany, England, France and the Netherlands. He returned seven months later and immediately started work on a Tessar-type optic called an "Anytar." The company planned to make the lens in a variety of focal lengths, but only the 120mm f4.5 lens actually reached production.[10] The initial design was not successful because NK had still not mastered the "annealing" technique whereby newly pressed glass blanks or disks are heated and then allowed to cool slowly under carefully controlled conditions over varying periods ranging from hours to months. Only in 1929, after many experiments and a switch to more consistent, electrically heated furnaces was NK to master the annealing procedure. The 120mm f4.5 Anytar lens would be offered in a German-made Compur shutter for the Konishi-made Lily Hand Camera. Three years later, in 1932, this same lens formula would appear with the name "Nikkor" — a label soon shared by all of NK's photographic lenses.

So far, much of NK's support had come from the military and was directed toward research into optical glass types and the glass-manufacturing process. This activity would soon increase and, before the end of the decade, it would become paramount. The naval limitations that resulted from the London Naval Conference of 1930 again relegated Japan to second-tier status relative to the British and American navies. The Naval General Staff found this to be unacceptable and pushed the government to grant a supplement that would increase the amount of money for research and technology development.[11] The Imperial Navy wanted to be able to dominate the entire Western Pacific — an area increasingly seen as Japan's own private pond. If the amount of tonnage that the Japanese navy could have was to be limited, then technology might be a way to offset that limitation. Better optics would be part of the answer.

With this increased funding, NK proceeded to grow throughout the 1930s with the Ohi plant and the adjacent Ohi Glass Factory taking on their final forms in 1933. A new building, designed by architect Toshiro Yamashita, and featuring three wings, numerous windows and external staircases, would be dedicated that year. The Ohi facility remains part of the company to this day, although from the 1990s on it would be used only for research and development projects. The company continued to send representatives abroad to try to learn more about the Germans' still carefully guarded secrets. Tsurayuki Yagi, later to become one of NK's vice presidents, spent nearly three years in Germany, much of this time working with Carl Zeiss. His studies became the design basis for the Imperial Navy's giant fire control rangefinders. The company also increased its research staff and the number of its experiments. Much of its glass went toward the manufacture of prisms that would be used in binoculars and periscopes — both important military tools — but more and more types of Nikkors began to appear.

In November 1933, a new company, Seiki Kogaku (Precision Optical) approached NK about the possibility of designing lenses for its new 35mm focal-plane shutter camera. The company had been recommended to the founders, Goro Yoshida and Saburo Uchida, by Uchida's older brother who had been a supervisor in one of NK's plants. Yoshida had been working on a prototype camera (named Kwanon) for over a year, but he had not yet solved all the problems of creating a linkage between the lens and a rangefinder that did not somehow violate one or

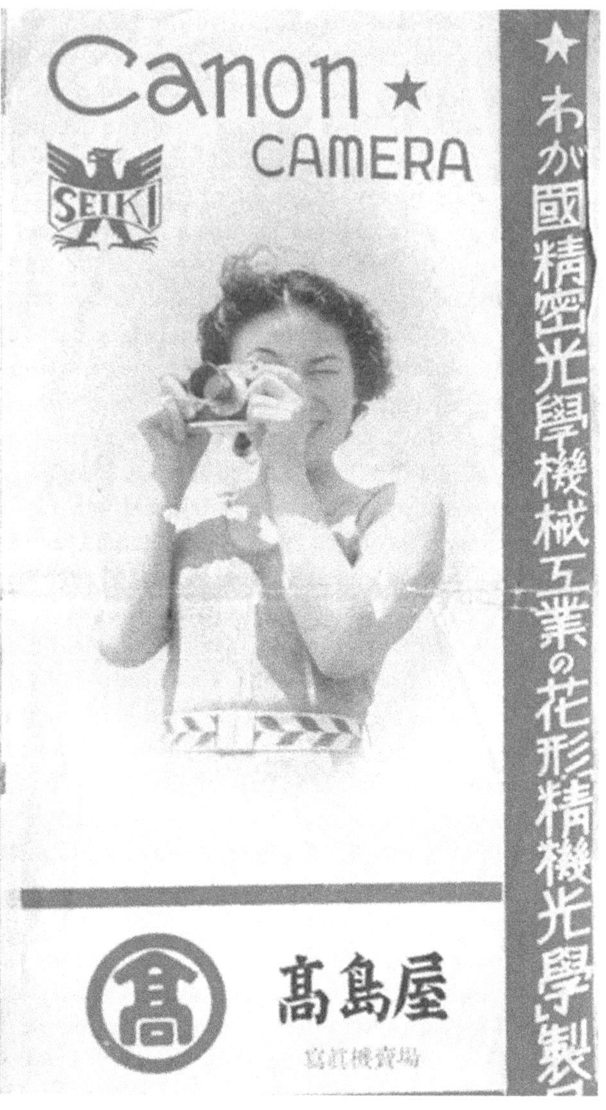

Cover of brochure for the new Hansa Canon of 1935 (courtesy Nikon Historical Society).

more of the patents that the German Leitz Company held. Leitz also held a patent for the placement of a viewfinder between two rangefinder windows, but Yoshida had been able to solve that problem by having a spring-loaded finder pop-up above the rangefinder housing when in use. NK agreed to help, but then offered to provide the lens for the new camera as well. Kakuya Sunayama had designed a 50mm f3.5 Nikkor several years earlier, and he saw this new camera as an opportunity to make use of his design efforts. By the time the Hansa Canon appeared for sale in 1935, it not only would come with a 50mm f3.5 Nikkor lens, but its rangefinder mechanism, pop-up viewfinder and lens focusing mount

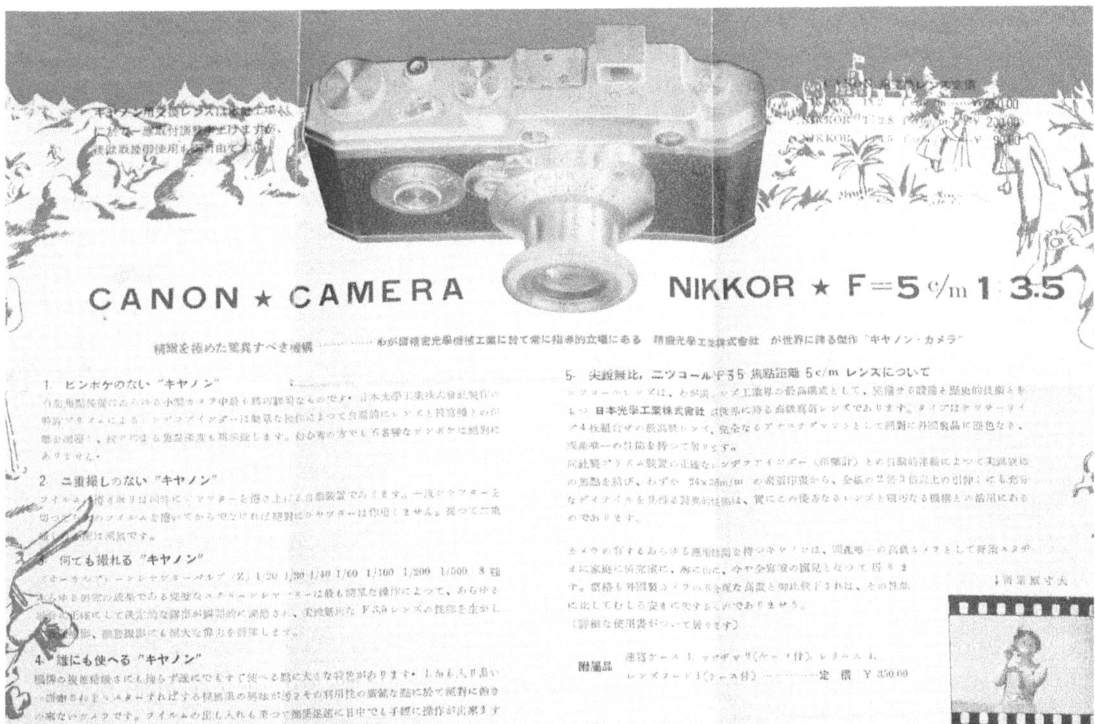

Advertising brochure put out in 1935 by the Seiki Kogaku Company for their new Hansa Canon 35mm camera. Its normal lens was supplied by Nippon Kogaku. What the ad does not mention is that NK also designed and manufactured the focusing mount, viewfinder and rangefinder mechanisms (brochure courtesy the Nikon Historical Society).

would also be products of NK.* These were all manufactured in NK's facilities, then added to the new cameras after the shutters were installed in the Canon factory. Like the Leica's rival, the Zeiss-made Contax, the focusing mount designed by Eiichi Yamanaka was built in and only the barrel-mounted optics were interchangeable.

In designing the 50mm f3.5 Nikkor, Sunayama had copied the Zeiss Tessar design closely. However, its quality did not match that of the equivalent Elmar lens from Leitz,[12] and he reworked the design. Eventually, he would design a total of four different 50mm lenses for the Canon with maximum apertures ranging from f4.5 to f2. The 50mm f2 Nikkor-H was a copy of the Sonnar lens pioneered by Zeiss in 1902. The company also prototyped a 70mm f3.5 lens, a 50mm f1.5 lens and other longer focal lengths for 35mm cameras. In 1940, Seiki Kogaku, already showing a tendency toward manufacturing a multitude of models, would introduce the "Canon Jr." This viewfinder-only, 35mm camera lacked slow speeds and instead of using the elaborate mount that NK was providing, it featured a simpler interchangeable 39mm thread. This camera also came with Nikkor lenses.

Seiki Kogaku also manufactured a folding rangefinder camera using 2¼ roll film in the 1930s. Called the Seica, it came with a Nikkor lens as well, in this case a 7.5 cm f4.5 in a German-made Compur shutter.

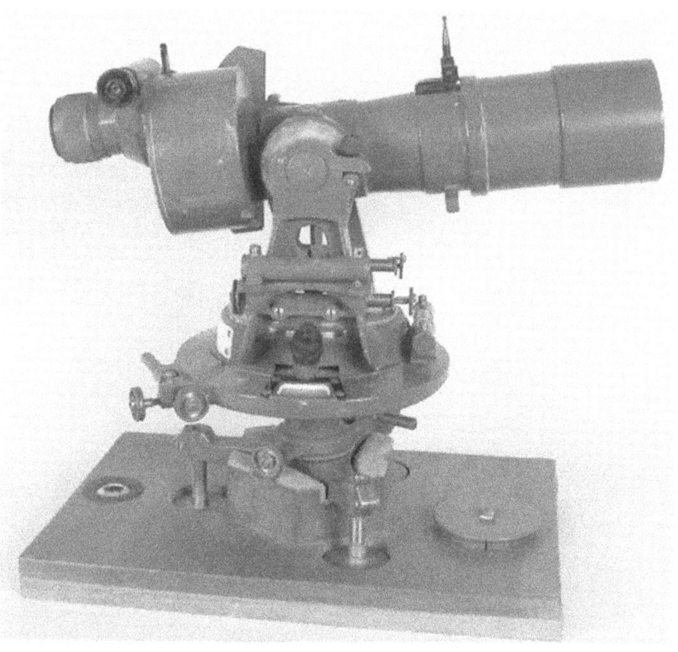

NK military ordinance: An artillary theodolite from 1932 (Mike H. Symons photograph).

By now NK was manufacturing microscopes under the "JOICO" and "Nikko"* label and had continued to offer binoculars under the "Mikron" and "Orion" names. It was also marketing a range of surveying instruments (such as transits and levels), telescopes and industrial measuring instruments, but as Japan's war efforts accelerated, production of these domestic products declined, and then disappeared. In return for its total commitment to the war effort, NK received many government contracts and began expanding at an enormous rate.

The navy was determined to make itself optically independent of any foreign suppliers. It did not quite succeed. Even though NK now could manufacture a wide range of glass types, both crown and flint, it still could not match the range of the Germans. The Japanese would import "about 200,000 pounds of optical glass from Schott in 1939–1944."[13] Much of this glass would be shipped on rafts towed by submarines in order to escape the Allied blockade.

Throughout the war, NK kept adding new plants and hiring more employees [See Appendix II for a complete list of NK's wartime plants]. In 1940 it had 7,585 workers, and by 1943, close to 16,000.[14] It was manufacturing periscopes for submarines and binocular periscopes for use in trenches. It was supplying thousands of binocular sets to both the army and the navy. The bomb sights on the navy's carrier bombers were NK products.[15] The first such telescopic units were copies of German and British designs, but they were soon replaced by more sophisticated reflector types, including the Army Type 100, which NK also made. Later in the war, as the skills of pilots deteriorated due to inexperience, NK manufactured "Type 2" telescopic sights for the navy. Modeled on bomb sights that had come out of German Heinkel bombers that Japan had purchased before the war, they used a rotating prism and a gyro-stabilized inclinometer that were easier to set and control.[16] NK was also making cameras for use by artillery units as well as aerial cameras and lenses for the air forces.

The first company logo consisted of the outline of a three-sided prism. "Nikko" in roman script became a feature of a new company logo in 1930. This logo also added the outline of a lens on top of the prism. NK dropped the use of the word "Nikko" for its products and went with the revised, better-known logo featuring the company name and location (Nippon Kogaku Tokyo)—all in roman script—after World War II.

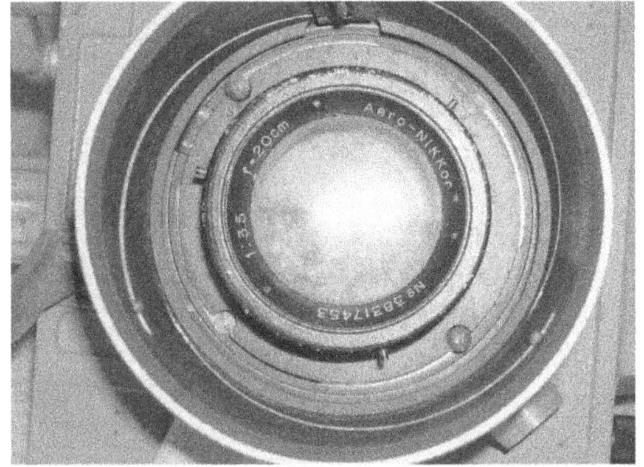

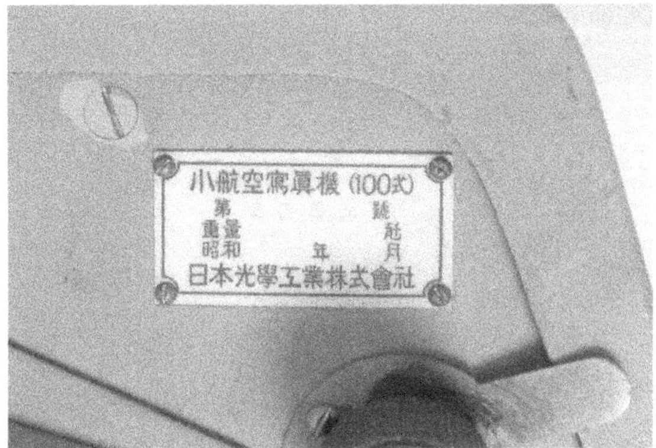

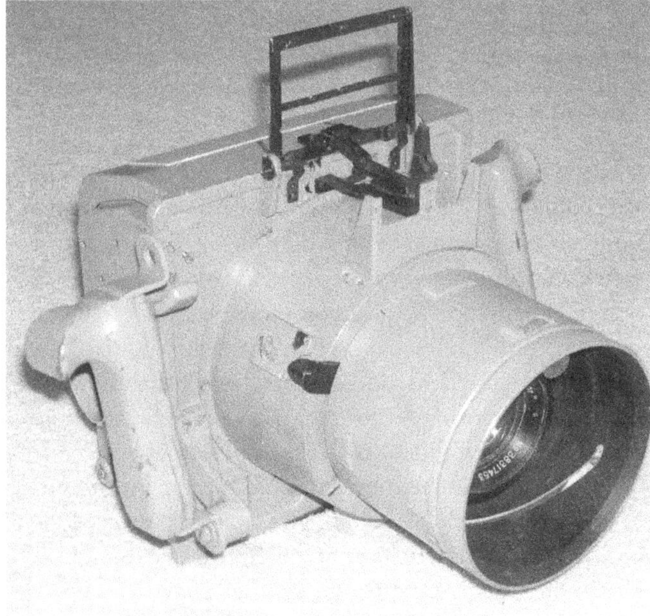

A Nippon Kogaku–made aerial camera from World War II, complete with 200mm Aerial-Nikkor lens (Bill Kraus photographs).

NK modeled its aerial cameras on well-known European and American designs, including the Fairchild K-8.[17]

Of all its wartime products, the company remained proudest of its rangefinders. These were absolutely critical both for sighting in artillery and naval guns and for fire control. The bigger the guns and the farther their range, the longer the base of the rangefinders had to be. The rangefinders NK manufactured for the battleships *Yamato* and *Musashi*, each some 15 meters in length, were the largest in the world.[18]* NK had started work on these rangefinders in 1936 after the failure of the second London Naval Limitation Conference. The *Yamato* and the *Musashi*, at 70,000 tons and each mounting 18.1 inch guns in their three main turrets, were the largest battleships ever built. NK would recall its optical achievements during the war more than six years later when Eichi Yamanaka, then chief of the Business Section, would be quoted as saying: "Perhaps in the future we will resume production of our excellent artillery rangefinders and submarine periscopes."[19]

The research into manufacturing periscopes for submarines was another area where NK would make major technological advances. Determined to create periscopes with the

**By the middle of World War II, the Allies were using radar for fire control on ships. The Japanese, with little knowledge of radar, developed superior optics instead.*

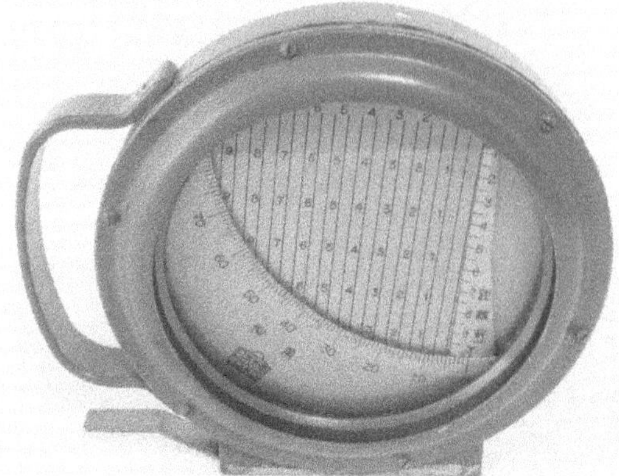

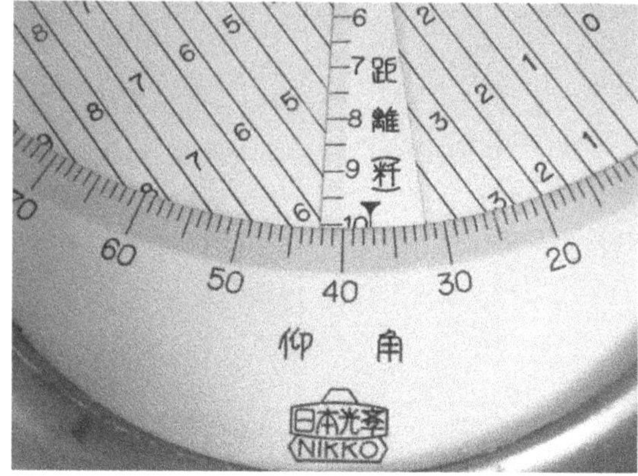

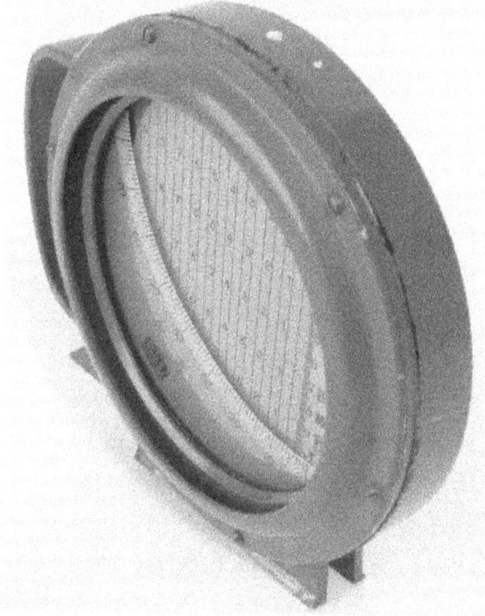

NK manufactured pendulum altimeter from World War II. Pendulum altimeters were mounted on anti-aircraft ship rangefinders. This is a naval version painted green/gray (Richard A. Lane photographs).

smallest possible diameter in order to cut down on the detectable wake the scope's tube would leave, NK used a series of relay lenses to pipe light down the ten-meter tubes. Unfortunately, this resulted in so much light loss that their periscopes were almost unusable except in broad daylight. This is not what the Imperial Navy wanted. The best times to use periscopes were at dawn and dusk when their wakes were harder to spot. The company turned to experimenting with lens coatings — an area only recently pioneered and patented by Zeiss and the American optical firm of Bausch & Lomb. The company successfully used evaporated coatings of cryolite, a double fluoride of sodium and aluminum — a technique it would transfer to all its optics after the war.[20]

By late 1944, the company had expanded to a point of near unmanageability with the navy and the government in almost total control. It had locations all over Tokyo, as well as two plants in the Nagano Prefecture. It had grown to over 16,000 employees with more than a thousand working in administration alone. This level of operations could not be sustained, and as the supplies of raw materials declined in 1945, NK's production slowed. Immediately after the surrender on the 15th of August, all operations came to a halt, and with the future of Japan and NK in limbo, the company's management ordered all of its locations* to close and all of its workers to leave and wait on events.

---

*The number of facilities that NK was operating during the war varied, and different sources quote different figures. The same goes for the maximum number of workers that NK employed. Company records refer to 23 plants, but the SCAP records refer to only 16 or 17. A portion of the Ohi plant was bombed and burned. A section of the Kawasaki plant was bombed and destroyed with loss of life and injuries. None of the other NK locations appear to have been damaged. See Appendix II for the fates of the various factory locations.

2

The Genesis of the Nikon:
A Company in Search of a Product

In September 1945, with the surrender complete, the management of Nippon Kogaku had to confront a new order. Prior to 1937, 70 percent of its production had gone to Japan's army and navy; after 1937, this had grown to 100 percent.[1] All this was gone, but NK still existed. Now it had to figure out what it had to do to keep on existing. Over the next four years, NK would not only have to reinvent itself as a company, but also survive desperate economic conditions and threats to its existence coming from both the Japanese government and the Occupation authorities. The development of the Nikon camera during this period must be seen within the context of these difficult conditions, as well as within the context of worldwide photographic activities and camera manufacturing.

The Situation in 1945–1946 and the Move to Camera Manufacture

On October 16, 1945, the new Economic Division of the United States Eighth Army issued what appears to be the first of several directives to the company. In this letter, "Jap Optical Ind, Co, Ltd" was permitted to "immediately start production of ... Spectacles, Binoculars ... Photographic lenses ... Microscopes and magnifying glasses ... Measuring and surveying instruments ... Clinical and Scientific glass ... Crucible and other fireproof materials."[2] The annex that listed these products assigned values in yen to each category. Whereas binoculars and microscopes promised returns of ¥415,000 and ¥410,000, respectively, photographic lenses were only assigned a value of ¥25,000 — the lowest value of any category. Cameras do not make the list at all. It is noteworthy that all these products, with the possible exception of binoculars, were products made for a domestic market. Neither NK nor the Occupation authorities had yet begun to consider exports.

The directions to the company from the Americans continued to be favorable until the end of the year. A directive for the "Shiojiri"[spelling varies in Occupation accounts] factory permitted the company to "manufacture the items you have hitherto handled."[3]

The company had already responded to the new era by forming the first of 15 committees to prepare a strategic plan for the company's survival and regrowth. This group, the "Committee to Deal with the Post-War Market," presented two reports to management on September 20th and September 29, 1945, listing 38 potential products. Neither report mentions cameras as a potential product. The idea of manufacturing cameras may have surfaced in these early meetings, but was then dropped. This is understandable. NK had no history of making cameras for a civilian market.[4]

The arrival of thousands of American soldiers (along with smaller contingents of troops from Britain, Australia and India) changed the equation quickly. Whatever negative attitudes these foreigners might have felt toward their former enemies, they showed an appreciation for Japanese optical weaponry. Its quality had been recognized during the war, and was acknowledged by Samuel Morrison in his epic *History of United States Naval Operations in World War II*. "Two other classes of materials in which the Japanese had a definite

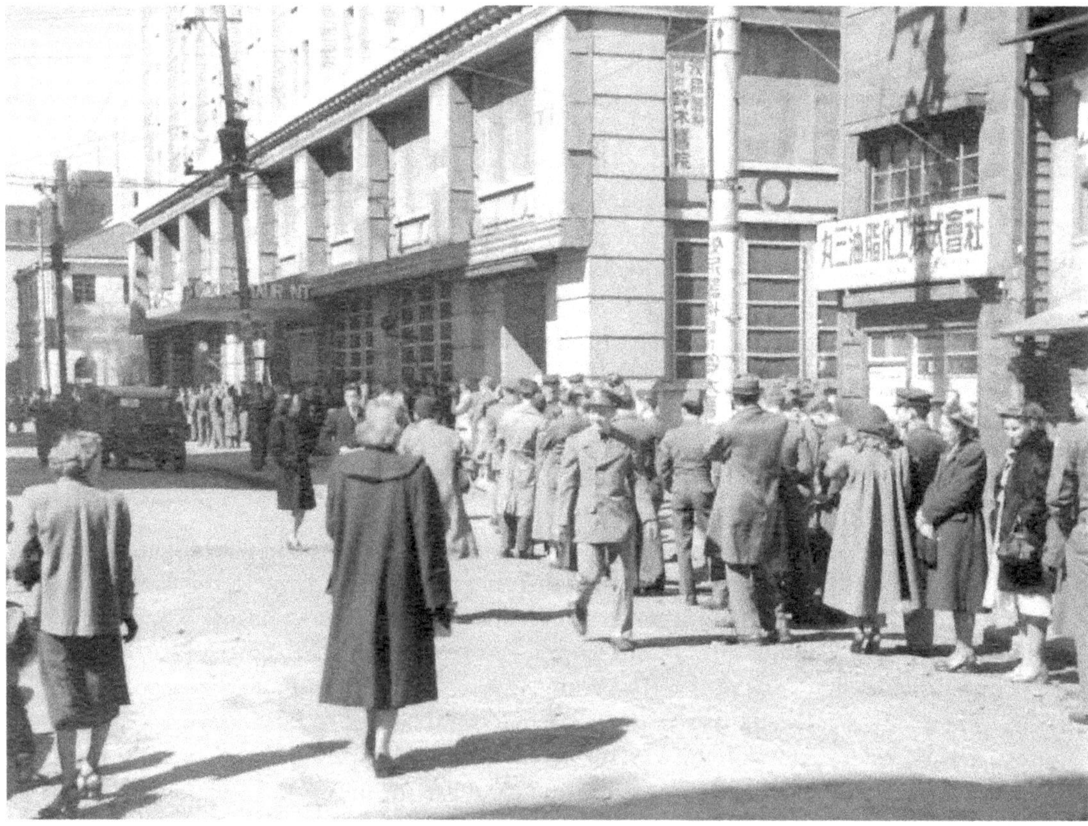

Lines outside the PX located in the Ginza branch of the Matsuya department store in 1948 (Edward Kelleher photograph).

superiority were pyrotechnics and optics. ... their binoculars were so much better, especially for night work, as to be eagerly sought after by American officers and bluejackets."[5] G.I.s stripped planes, ships and barracks of binoculars, telescopes, rangefinders and gunsights and any other transportable optical equipment they could carry off before their destruction as war material.

While an American soldier's pay was low, it was far higher than any amount that employed Japanese workers enjoyed at that time. The G.I.s had limited opportunities for spending the money they had, spending a lot of it on alcoholic beverages, prostitutes and cheap souvenirs. However, as the war trophy supply disappeared, the soldiers and sailors — particularly the better-paid officers — began to show an interest in new Japanese optical goods, buying locally made binoculars and cameras as quickly as they appeared in the military exchanges (PXs) — general merchandise shops where military personnel and their dependents could buy or order almost anything from pins and sewing needles to telescopes — often at prices far lower than in stateside stores.[6] One such army officer, Major Edward Kelleher, described how he waited outside the PX located in the Ginza branch of the Matsuya department store in 1948 for seven hours in order to buy the Japanese-made 35mm camera that he used throughout his stay in Japan. He remarked that "The store always had long lines and remained quite popular with the occupying forces."[7]

General Headquarters (GHQ) for the Occupation Forces had quickly begun to encourage these optical purchases, both as a spur to the Japanese civilian economy and as a means of depleting the Americans' pockets — since money spent on optics would not be available to spend on booze. NK took note of this interest and by the beginning of the new year had added "camera production" to its list of potential civilian products.

NK called back 1,725 employees[8] and reopened the Ohi plant* in November 1945. Workers immediately began manufacturing opera glasses and binoculars on a limited basis. This was the easiest approach to take since conversion of binoculars from a military product to a civilian product involved little more than changing the label on a box, and the company had the setups and raw materials on hand. By April 1946, the company would be selling as many binoculars as it could make to the American Occupation forces. It began closing up and disposing of its other locations, concentrating its machinery at the Ohi plant. By mid–1946, all but one of the other locations had been closed. The company continued to use the Shiojiri factory, located in the Prefecture of Nagano.

The decision to focus NK's resources on the Ohi facilities made sense. From its first inception, Ohi had been designed and built as an optical manufacturing facility. The glass works, absolutely critical to NK's future, were at Ohi. Most of the products that might be of use in a civilian market had been made at Ohi. The retention of the Shiojiri plant is a bit harder to explain, and it receives little mention in historical accounts of NK. Originally a silk manufacturing facility, NK bought the building in 1943 as part of its continuing war expansion. The location then had two appealing features: located near the mountains north of Tokyo, it was not subject to the bombing that increasingly threatened the company's other locations in the greater Tokyo area. In addition, the plant's proximity to forests gave

---

As mentioned earlier, NK actually had two plants at Ohi: the Oi factory and the Oi glass factory.

the company a source for the various hardwoods that NK needed for manufacturing instrument cases, tripods and mountings. Immediately after the war, the plant became a farm implement manufacturing facility. This activity did not last long, and the Shiojiri work-force soon returned to manufacturing instrument cases. Eventually it assembled instruments as well, particularly microscopes, before closing in August 1950.[9]

The company was now embarked on a course that would take it into strange waters. It had been an all-powerful company producing over 80 percent of all of Japan's optical glass. The demands of the military for optical goods had been insatiable. The company had never had to market or promote its goods. The military specified, bought and used. Its 28 years of experience gave the company a strong sense of seniority, knowledge and strength, but in reality, neither management nor the workers had any idea what they were getting into. Their self-confident ignorance was almost to be the company's undoing.

If NK knew little about what it had to do to become a successful and profitable company selling to the private sector, the American Occupation authorities brought their own well-meaning, if dangerous, agenda to the table. Foremost was the need to demolish Japan as an industrial, military power. Edwin Pauley, reparations commissioner for Japan (and Germany), visited Japan in the fall of 1945 and on the 18th of December his mission presented its findings to U.S. president Harry S. Truman. The U.S. State Department, in turn, forwarded its recommendations to the Far Eastern Commission. Part of this report called for the dismantling of virtually all of Japan's factories that had been used to support its war effort — including aircraft factories, machine-manufacturing plants and arsenals. The mission also saw the *Zaibatsu*[10] — the "gigantic financier families" that controlled much of Japan's industries — as major contributors to Japan's martial attitude and recommended that they be dissolved.[11] Machinery, heavy industrial equipment and even half of Japan's electrical power capacity were to be removed and given to Japan's major war-time victims — notably the Philippines and China. On January 20, 1946, GHQ began setting aside plants for reparations. By August 1947, over 500 facilities would share this fate. Nippon Kogaku could only wait and hope that it would not be included.

At its peak, NK had employed over 16,000 workers.* Approximately 1,800 had been rehired when the company resumed limited production in December 1945. Many of its former workers promptly set up their own optical shops to make items for the Occupation forces. During the war, Seiki Kogaku (Canon) had been using NK facilities as part of its support for the war effort. When that company returned to using just its own factory, it took many of NK's discharged workers with it.[12] In a sense, NK had sowed the seeds of its own competition. Yet the company retained a feeling of obligation and friendship toward many of these former workers. It also needed to get rid of as much excess machinery as it could in order to downsize its equipment inventory to a more realistic level. It began selling off its unneeded facilities and "loaned" machinery to former employees with the understanding that these friends would care for (and use) the equipment until NK needed it

The president of NK, M. Nagaoka, gives different figures in his report to the Holding Company Liquidation Commission. On pages 1 and 2, he states that at the company's height in 1945, it was operating 20 plants plus a central administrative unit and it employed over 23,000 workers. After the war, it closed all but two plants and discharged 93 percent of its workforce. He also noted that in 1945, the company was operating 4,141 machines!

again. The company shuffled this equipment around, moving in some units from the other factories and moving some of the original Ohi equipment out. By May 1946 it was apparent that NK would never be in a position to use much of this loaned or stockpiled equipment and it began applying to the SCAP (Supreme Commander for Allied Powers)* authorities to sell off its surplus. This manufacturing equipment included lathes, drill presses, tapping machines, gear cutting machines, surface grinders and other machines for shaping and cutting metal.

By December 1946, NK still had too many machines. For example, on December 15, 1946, NK reported to SCAP that of the original 268 lathes at the Ohi plant, it had lent out 198, retaining only 51 for production. But it had also brought in an additional 201 lathes from other locations. So it actually had 298 lathes at the Ohi plant, but had 41 in storage and really only needed 247. Confusing? Yes, and a headache for both the Occupation authorities and the company as it tried to keep track of and figure out uses for a huge inventory.[13]

The company was back in the optical equipment manufacturing business, but as late as May 1946, binoculars and opera glasses remained the only finished retail products it could show on the Japanese Optical Production Chart that SCAP was carefully preparing each month. Part of the problem was power. Tokyo's electrical grid was in such bad shape that the government would not let NK run any of its electrical furnaces, which, in turn, meant that the company could not melt any new optical glass. For nearly two years, the company had to make do with the glass stocks that it had on hand at the end of the war.

Still, the figures for those items the company could make do not look too bad, with 652 binocular sets and 704 opera glasses making it out the door in May 1946. In June, the figures are much the same with 590 binoculars produced and 747 opera glasses. The number dropped to 448 binoculars in July and 355 opera glasses, but in August, production picked up again with figures of 964 for binoculars and 1,750 for opera glasses.[14] Compared to other Japanese optical firms, NK was making a lot of binoculars and selling a lot as well. To put these numbers in perspective, only Tokyo Kogaku Kikai K.K. was producing more in either of these categories. But NK was not going to be able to survive or grow on binocular sales alone. The company needed more retail products, particularly products for overseas export. Exports meant cash, money needed to purchase food to feed the company's employees and their families. Making optical products for export was no longer just essential; now it was the official policy of SCAP. To encourage this focus, exports were given tax-free status while any domestic sales had to include an additional 120 percent excise tax.[15]

Trouble now came from another quarter. SCAP had taken note of NK's shifting around of machinery and rental agreements and decided to take a closer look at this company that had been the military's number one supplier of optical equipment. On October 26, 1946, Second Lt. James Morrison issued a report accusing the company of deliberately violating GHQ directives concerning the restriction of sales of capital assets.[16] On November 13, 1946, Asst. Adjutant General, Lt. Colonel R. Shafer confirmed the designation of NK as a

---

As noted in the preface, "SCAP" not only meant General Douglas MacArthur, the head of the Occupation Forces, but also the entire administration that worked under him.

"privately-owned munitions plant"— to be effective on December 21, 1946 — and therefore subject to reparations. SCAP took control of the closed but still-owned "Shimada" plant immediately, and began making plans for the dismantling of the company's equipment for shipment abroad.[17]

This could only mean the end of Nippon Kogaku. Desperate, the company enlisted the help of the Ministry of Commerce and Industry to come to its defense. The ministry promptly did so with a three-page letter to the headquarters for the Tokyo-Kanagawa Military Government District. "The nature and object of this particular company," the writer pleaded, "are entirely peaceful and its activities as suppliers to the military were only for the period when their pressure and demands on the Company were overwhelming and compulsory."[18] The writer went on to point out that Nippon Kogaku's products were only optical goods and were "not purely fighting weapons." One wonders how much this anonymous writer had to bite his tongue when one considers such "optical goods" as gun rangefinders, submarine periscopes, aerial bomb sights and officers' binoculars. In any case, the SCAP authorities were not buying.

The ministry made a better case when it pointed out that many of NK's products were unique and if the company lost its machines, much of Japan's capacity for manufacturing precision instruments would be lost. Optical goods were "comparatively high valued" and most of the materials for making them could "be obtained in the country ... [and would] make lucrative export goods for Japan."

The writer then followed up his plea with a projection of products for 1947. Again, optimism was the rule, with projected production of a new camera set at 300 per month starting in March and increasing to 400 per month by August. Other products for domestic sales were coming on line, including printing lenses, scientific instruments, reflecting mirrors, surveying instruments, microscopes, cine-talkie lenses and ophthalmic lenses.* Indeed, the company was sure that it could meet over 37 percent of the demand for surveying instruments and over 33 percent of the demand for microscopes. Their projection for cameras was more modest. The monthly production of 300 would only meet 5.8 percent of the projected national demand.[19]

The letter was not enough. On April 29, 1947, Colonel Shafer signed a directive that all dispersed machinery would be placed under the control of Military Government teams. The wheels of change would, however, move slowly. On July 7, 1947, the Occupation authorities were in receipt of another letter — this time signed by Haru Seimiya of the Commerce and Industry Section — asking that NK be allowed to continue to use the machinery in place at the Ohi plants until the time would come for its removal, thus allowing "...peaceful commodities [to be] ... produced for the purpose of the stabilization of the national livelihood and reconstruction of a new peaceful Japan."[20]

The reparations program was never as complete, nor did it progress as quickly as the potential recipients of the material hoped or demanded. The collapse of the Nationalist

---

Spectacles receive little mention in histories of NK, but the company made many of these for the domestic market— as Nikon, Inc. still does today. Unfortunately, the return on spectacles was small and the company saw little cash income from their sales during this period.

Chinese government and the coming of the Cold War would change the Occupation authorities' attitude toward reparations and bring an end to material transfer as a means of meeting them. NK never actually lost any of its equipment to reparations, but for the next three years, much of its machinery would be locked up in an unused part of the main Ohi plant while the company struggled to make do with the equipment it did possess. Much of the surviving SCAP paperwork from this period deals with the Occupation personnel taking inventory and inspecting equipment for reparations to make sure that the machinery was still onsite and available for shipment abroad. At the same time, much of the NK administration's time was spent trying to convince SCAP to let the company use that same equipment in meeting the growing demands for its products. For example, a letter to the commanding officer of the Chiba Military Government Team dated July 7, 1947, gives December 21, 1946, as the date that NK was designated as a "Reparation factory,"[21] but then gives June 9, 1947, as the date the company had to have its inventory of machinery ready. The July letter (from Haru Seimiya of the Committee of the Liaison Office) asks that NK be allowed to continue to use the machinery in place for "peaceful purposes." Apparently the permission was granted.

If the authorities in the Economic and Scientific Section concerned with reparations were to act as the "bad cops" in their efforts to transform Japan's industries, the staff of Scientific and Technical Division within that section gradually emerged as the "good cop." The precipitous destruction of five cyclotrons in November 1945 by the U.S. Army had been denounced by scientists worldwide.[22] In response to that criticism, the army actively recruited civilian scientists to fill many of the ranks in the Scientific and Technical Division. These men and women tended to be more sympathetic both toward the plight of their fellow scientists and toward those industries that were closely connected to scientific research.

Perhaps noting this, the company board decided that a scientist with no business or military background would be the best public face they could don at this critical stage in the company's existence. NK's president had been Yoshio Hatano. He had headed the company since the 1930s and led NK to achieving the largest size and profitability it had yet experienced — and to its downfall. In May 1946, he had been replaced by Hideo Araki, a businessman who had started with Mitsubishi before coming to NK in 1935.[23] But in January 1947, Araki would, in turn, be replaced when NK's board appointed Dr. Masao Nagaoka, a scientist and head of NK's Glass Works Division, to be its new president. A chemist with a high reputation in Japan's academic and scientific communities, Nagaoka had been born in 1897, a son of Hantaro Nagaoka, a world-renowned physicist. He had earned his doctorate from Tokyo University before joining NK, where he had become an expert on the various glass formulæ that NK had developed and which were one of the company's greatest strengths.

Nagaoka brought a sharp, inquisitive and intellectual mind to the position, one that never stopped questioning and looking for better answers. His fluent knowledge in English also proved to be an asset in the company's negotiations both with the SCAP authorities and the exporters that he would have to deal with in the next few years. He remained the president of NK through the 1950s, moving from president to board chairman in 1959 before finally retiring in 1961.* He would also serve as president of the Japan Optical Glass Industry Association, the Japan Optical Industries Association and the Japan Telescope Industries Association. He would use his position in these societies to relentlessly push the manufacturers to achieve higher and higher standards.[24]

The real winner during this period was the Shiojiri factory in Nagano. In 1946, the facility had reopened and began producing thrashers, weeders and other farming implements. However, the company was able to convince the authorities that this plant had never been a "private owned munitions plant," and its machinery was therefore not subject to reparations, even though NK as a whole was. In 1947 the workers resumed the manufacture of telescopes, tripods and microscope stands, along with such nonoptical goods as knives and can openers (!).[25] Of interest is that the president's report shows more female workers (53) than male (48)—perhaps a reflection of both the rural setting and labor availability. Tripods were the most important product—a result of Shiojiri's proximity to wood sources—and the plant was seen only as an auxiliary facility to the main operations at Ohi. As the overseas demand for binoculars continued to grow, the company scaled back on domestic market–oriented microscope production and transfered some of the binocular assembling to the Shiojiri location. The Shiojiri workers' salaries averaged 20 percent lower than those of the Ohi workers, gaining savings for NK. The company had to cut costs where it could. The fiscal picture was not looking good, and it would soon get worse.

Designing Cameras for a Civilian Market

Even as early as the fall of 1945, many of NK's employees were asking if the company could get into the camera manufacturing business. The reorganized company added a fourth group to its section on machine design within the Division of Design. This group was to handle "matters concerning the designing of cameras and projectors."[26]

Tatsuhiko Arakawa in his article on the birth of the Nikon that appeared in the *Nikon Journal* has nicely summarized the problems the company now faced.[27] While the company had a record of experience in working with cameras in its efforts to design and manufacture the lenses, viewfinder and rangefinder mechanisms for the Hansa Canon 35mm camera, all the workers who had been involved with that project were no longer with the company. Many, in fact, were now working for Seiki Kogaku—soon to rename itself the Canon Camera Company. No one currently working in the company had any experience with building, marketing or distributing cameras. To make things worse, none of the company's employees were even "long time enthusiasts or connoisseurs."[28] Still, management was not to be deterred. Was this not Nippon Kogaku, the largest and greatest of Japanese optical firms?

The design group met on April 4, 1946, under the leadership of Masahiko Fuketa and decided that the company would "manufacture two kinds of cameras: a twin-lens reflex and

He was replaced by Hiroshi Shirahama, vice president for much of this period and also a person of critical importance to NK's survival.

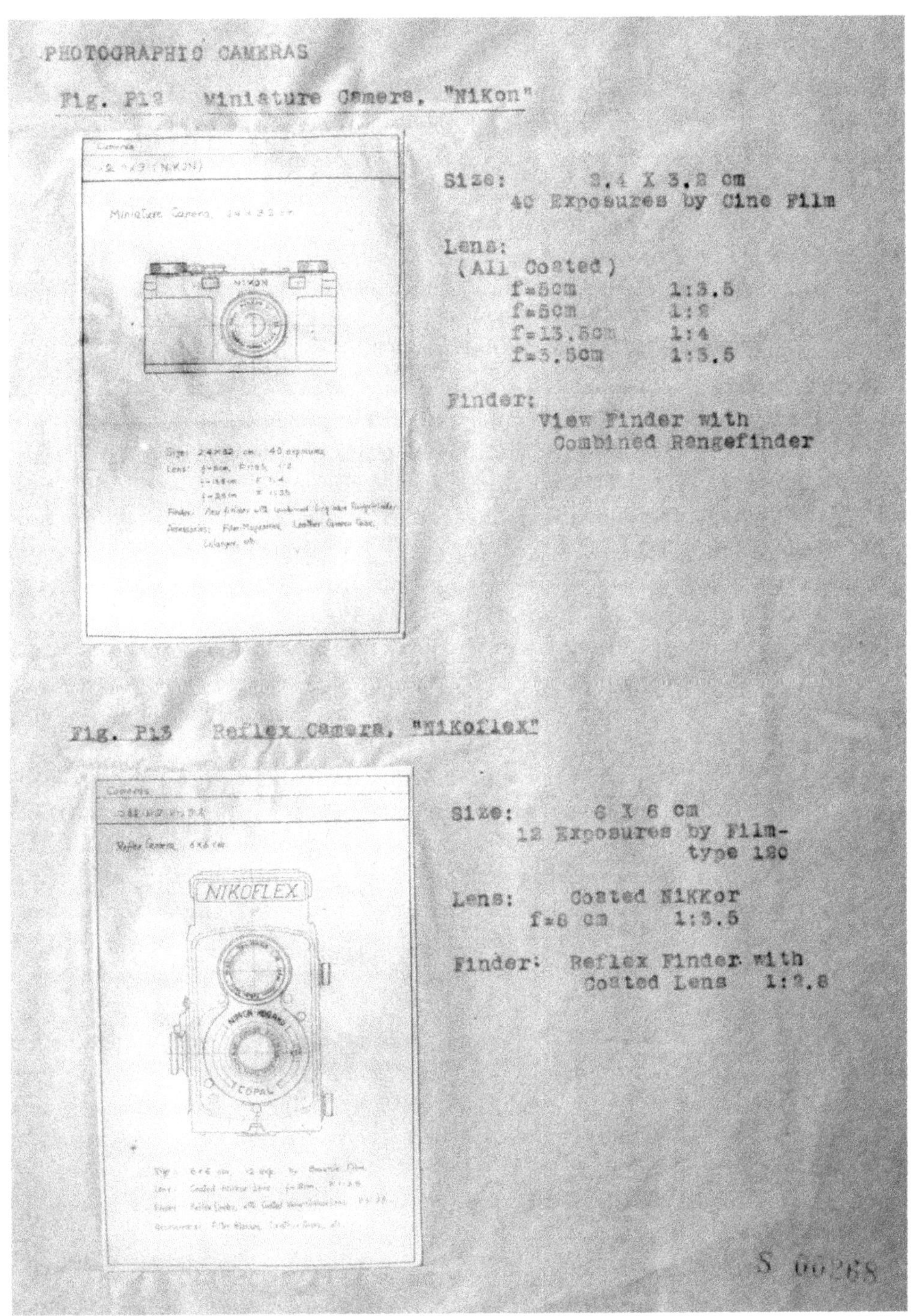

The yet-to-be born cameras of 1947. A page from a report prepared by Nippon Kogaku for the Occupation authorities illustrating every one of the company's products, past and current. The yet-to-be manufactured Nikon appears here along with the soon-to-be-stillborn Nikoflex. While the specs for the Nikon list four lenses, the 35mm wide angle would not actually see production until 1950 (National Archives).

a small size, high-quality camera."[29] The previous February, Minoru Takahashi, a technician in the Ohi factory, had been given a Canon 35mm camera and told to disassemble it and make a complete set of drawings of all parts. It took him two months to complete this task. Immediately, the design committee moved ahead with plans to build and test samples of its new cameras with the goal of having them ready for manufacture and marketing by December 1946! Prototype production order number 6FT for 20 of the small 35mm cameras went out in April. Two months later, the first production order, number 6FB, followed.

In reviewing what was happening, one might be tempted to assume that the blind were leading the deaf. How could this company hope to succeed with its combination of ignorance and overconfidence? How could they have expected to have two cameras — or even one — ready for the market in eight months when it had taken two months just to make drawings of a camera that had already been built? An answer might be found in reviewing the strengths that NK now brought to this endeavor as well as taking a look at its possible competition.

Even in its reduced circumstances, NK remained the 800-pound gorilla among the various Japanese optical manufacturers. On June 25, 1946, as part of its ongoing evaluation of Japan's industries, the Research and Statistics Division of the Economic and Scientific Section of GHQ-SCAP released its "Special Report No. 10: Camera Production in Japan."[30] This report lists 16 camera-manufacturing companies that accounted for "95% of present production capacity." Of these 16 firms, all but three were characterized as "of medium to small size." NK was the only company neither family-owned nor single-person owned. At this point, NK had yet to produce a single camera, yet it is on the list — because it had promised to produce as many as 4,800 cameras in 1947! Another comparison: the largest Japanese camera manufacturer at that time was Konishi Roku Shashin Kogyo K.K. Its expected output for just 1946 was 34,488 cameras — a total production number that NK would not reach until 1954! Yet the company (Konica) had a capital of only ¥16,500,000, which does not sound too bad until one realizes that NK's capital at that same time was ¥50,000,000 (fully paid up).

The "Special Report No. 10" exists in two versions. The final report limited its narrative to only two pages out of a total of seven. While the final report stated that the various camera manufacturers expected to be able to produce 85,000 units in 1946, it indicated that "due to the bad food situation and other factors adversely affecting production, only 75% of the ... production estimate may be realized."[31] Even though NK was the largest optical company, it was being affected by food and power shortages in the same way as all Japanese manufacturers.

The draft runs to 15 pages and includes some revealing commentary — both good and bad. The report states: "...compared with foreign types of medium quality, it becomes apparent that there are differences, especially as to mechanical performance, but it is safe to assume that these handicaps will be overcome soon. ...optical calculation of lenses and their manufacture by the larger firms leaves little to be desired, although they do not invent new lens constructions."[32] The final paragraph of the draft — on page 15 — is unusually prophetic, but it expressed the old assumptions as to what the Japanese were capable of doing still held sway: "Although in 1946 the production of cameras in Japan does not yet play a very important role in the economy ... some years hence, Japan will possibly export hundreds of thousands of them, becoming a challenge to other camera exporting countries. However, as in the past, the Japanese camera industry will certainly not be leading in novelties, but will be able to copy the best designs of the world efficiently."[33]

NK still accounted for over 80 percent of all optical and quality glass production. Virtually all the other camera manufacturers were dependent on NK as a source for either glass or the finished optics they would mount in their products. The company had already designed and manufactured a full range of normal lenses for the 35mm format. It had a comprehensive range of glass formulæ to draw on. NK was also the only manufacturer able to supply lenses with apertures of either f2 or f1.5. Lenses for its new cameras were not going to be a problem. When the demand came, the company would also be able to prove that its engineers could be original and fully capable of generating their own ideas and designs.

The international situation was promising as well. German companies, particularly Carl Zeiss, had held a near monopoly on high-quality optics before the war. But by 1945, Zeiss's factories were damaged or destroyed, its employees scattered and divided between several occupation zones. Soon an entire plant for manufacturing the famous Zeiss Contax would be on its way to Kiev in the Ukraine along with many German technicians as part of the reparations that the Soviet Union was taking. The Contax and the Leica were still the standards, but neither camera was going to be readily available in the same quantities as that of 1939 for quite some time. Leitz had survived the war intact and was able to resume production of its Leica IIIc in short order, but it would not reach the high quality it had insisted on before the war until the late 1940s. West German Zeiss re-formed as a new company in Stuttgart and began manufacturing its new Contax IIa in 1949. East German Zeiss never did return to making rangefinder cameras, nor did it ever regain the quality standards the prewar Zeiss firm had maintained.

Eastman Kodak had made an attempt to compete directly against the Germans with its Ektra camera in 1941. But its engineers were unable to design a jam-proof focal plane shutter and production had been put on hold with the coming of the war. An expensive and eccentric design, the Ektra was to prove an even greater marketing failure than the Edsel, and the company abandoned its only American-made effort at a top-of-the-line professional 35 soon after the war.*

Amateur photo enthusiasts in the United States were increasingly turning to 35mm film as their format of choice. Just as computer clubs would briefly be the rage in the late 1970s, "camera clubs" were attracting thousands of photographers who met weekly or monthly in small groups to share darkroom facilities, hear guest lecturers and discuss the latest and best in techniques and equipment. Almost all these aspiring amateurs were working in the smaller, more economical 35mm and 2¼ square formats. Most professionals still insisted on using 4 × 5 press cameras for newspaper and commercial work, but the new

---

The Foton, Bell & Howell's 1948 35mm camera, aimed at professionals and deep-pocketed Americans was also to prove an expensive failure.

glamour figure was the war correspondent and photojournalist — and those brave heroes used 35mm Leicas or Contaxes.

Color was also a growing factor in the 35mm success story. In 1946, most picture-taking families were still making do with folding, roll film cameras that yielded black and white negatives just large enough not to require an enlarger for making prints. But color was the future. Americans liked color slides for putting on shows for their friends and for themselves, and color slides meant 35mm. The American Argus Camera Corporation sold millions of its Argus A and Argus C3 cameras based on that desire. Herein lay an opening. American manufacturers were filling the need at the low end, but the market for a quality 35mm camera with a reasonable price was wide open. If any manufacturer could get such a product into the hands of consumers before the German camera industry had reclaimed its dominant position, that company might be able to capture and hang onto enough market share to succeed.

Other external factors had to be considered. NK had a tradition of manufacturing high-quality products because that is what its customers (the government, the navy, the army) had demanded. But most Japanese consumer goods for export prior to the war and during the Occupation period were little better than junk. Exterior finishes often lent a quality appearance, but internal workings were crudely finished and assembled, and many items soon broke and could not be repaired. Most prewar American goods that had found their way to Japan had been of mediocre quality, and the Japanese, believing that price was the only American standard, had responded by making the most inexpensive products they could. Cheap goods resulted, but this had, in turn, created a poor impression of all Japanese products.

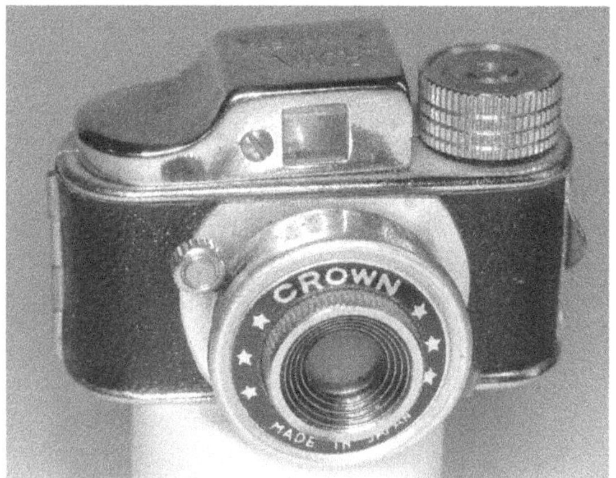
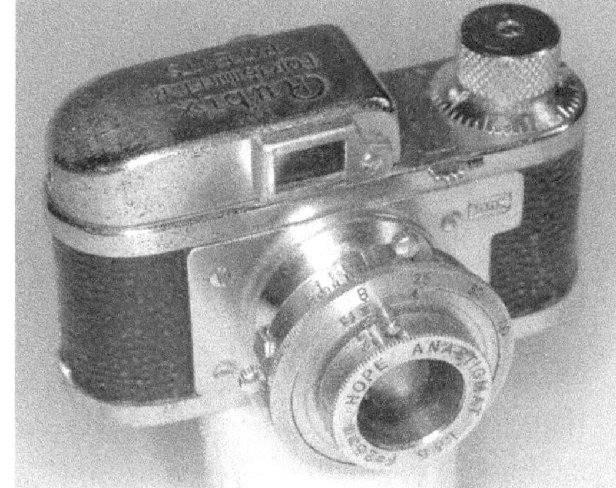

Two examples of the "Hit" type cameras. The Japanese made and sold thousands of these little 17.5mm film cameras to both their own people and to American soldiers and sailers. Dozens and dozens of different names adorned the face or top plates, but regardless of the name, all operated pretty much the same and had the same marginal quality. The Rubix on the right above, with its three shutter speeds plus B and Leica-like detailing, is perhaps a little better than most of the cameras of this type (Jim Emmerson photographs).

Among the most notorious of postwar products were the little "Hit" type* still cameras. Manufactured by hand in little, one-or-two room shops, stamped out of sheet metal and equipped with one-element lenses, simple shutters and crude finders, most of these tiny cameras took still pictures on 17.5mm film.[34] The Japanese public bought thousands of these because that was all most could afford. G.I.s bought thousands too, but soon discovered that the cameras seldom lasted for more than a few rolls of film, and their lenses produced only crude images. If NK was to sell its products overseas, the company would have to battle this reinforced reputation just to get into camera shops. Its camera had to be of high quality throughout and have no features that might prejudice a shopping public.

Another problem would soon come to the forefront. NK could make glass and it had access to a wide range of machinable metals such as brass, aluminum alloy and phosphor-bronze used for gears, helicals and body castings, but the special steels needed to make reliable springs were a more difficult item, one that the company would soon be struggling with.

The New Nikon's Features and Their International Bases

In examining this new camera that NK was soon to present to the public, a knowledgeable photographer in 1946 would immediately have noted a number of familiar features, yet noticed an element of strangeness. This would be due to the camera's combining features from both Zeiss's Contax and the Leica. Externally, the Nikon looked very much like a Contax II; internally, its features were almost pure Leica. To understand how the engineers arrived at that design, one must understand the history of the German 35mm rangefinder camera and the design challenges and decisions that engineers in that country had already dealt with 15 years earlier.

The Leica was the first, and for many years the only, still camera that used 35mm, double-sprocketed movie film in a double frame (1 inch by 1½ inch, or 24 × 36mm) format.[†35] It has been argued, and some do to this day, that the 1:1.5 aspect ratio results in a picture that is too wide in the landscape view or too tall when viewed vertically. Certainly a full negative will not fill an entire sheet of 8 × 10 or 5 × 7 photographic paper. Nevertheless, that was the format that Oskar Barnack chose back in 1912 when he designed the first Leica prototype and that was the format that Leitz company used when it began to manufacture in 1926. When other German camera manufacturers also began to make 35mm cameras, most followed the Leica pattern. Eastman Kodak gave 35mm film and the 1 × 1.5 format its influential blessing with the introduction of the Retina series of 35mm cameras in 1934 and by offering 35mm film in preloaded magazines holding enough film for either 20 or 36 exposures.

Except for the rare model B, all commercial Leicas used a cloth, double-curtain, self-capping focal plane shutter. Other cloth focal plane shutters were available, such as those

From the name of one of the best-known brands.

†The first camera to use double-frame 35mm film remains controversial. Follow endnote for source.

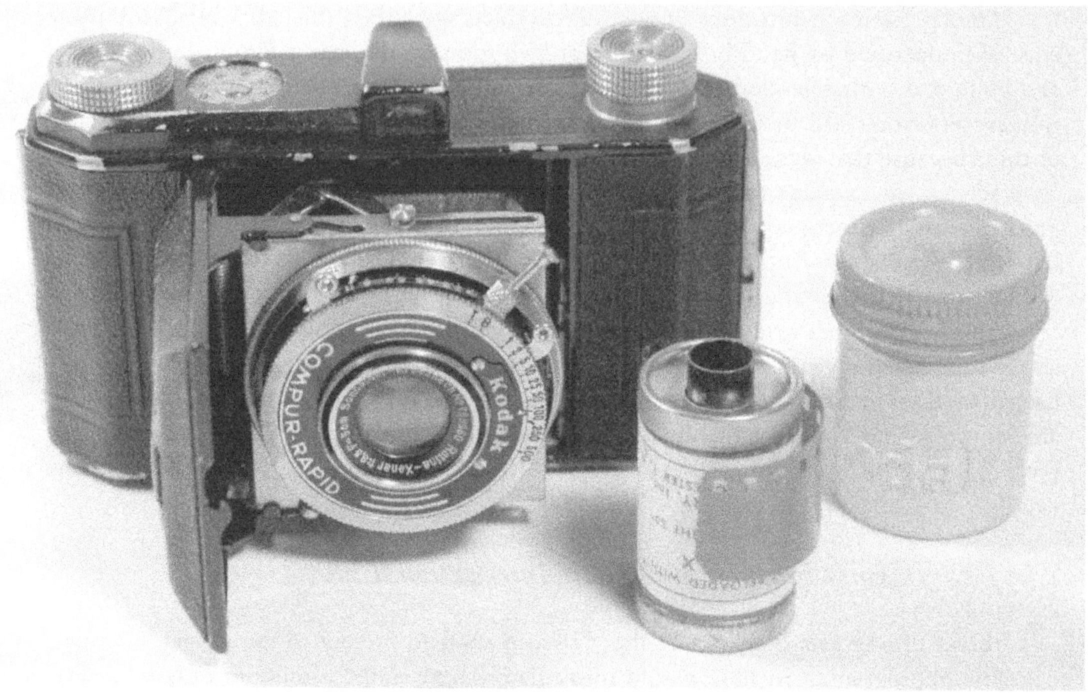

Eastman Kodak and the Retina Camera. The Eastman Kodak Company's decision to market its own 35mm cameras provided legitimacy for the use of that film in still photography and for the 24 × 36 format. Prior to 1934, 35mm camera owners had to buy their own movie film roll ends and load their own cartridges. When it introduced the Retina camera — manufactured by the former Nagel Camerawerk in Germany — Kodak began selling 35mm film in preloaded magazines that yielded 36 exposures per roll.

The Kodak Retina in this illustration is a type 119, manufactured from 1936 to 1939. It was the third model in what would become the Retina I series. The Eastman magazine in the foreground still holds its original roll of Plus X, rated at only ASA 50 and using a highly flammable cellulose nitrate base.

found on the Graflex and Speed Graphic 4 × 5 cameras, but exposure on those cameras came from selecting a combination of openings and curtain speeds, and required that a dark slide be in place whenever the shutter was tensioned since the shutter was not self-capping. The Leitz design had several immediate advantages over other types of shutters. It was relatively simple to manufacture, dependable and consistent. Its design made the film advance and the shutter cocking one, connected operation — thereby preventing unintentional double exposures. Advancing the film pulled both the film and the shutter curtain in the same direction and the same distance. Since the first curtain always traveled at the same speed, the clockwork mechanism needed to control only the timing of the second curtain's release. When the second curtain started its travel approximately $\frac{1}{20}$ of a second after the lead curtain, the full frame would receive exposure. Higher shutter speeds resulted from the following curtain releasing before the first curtain had reached the end of its run, producing a part-frame opening that traveled across the film. The narrower this opening, the shorter the exposure. Later, Leitz would add slower speeds governed with a separate clockwork mechanism that held back the second curtain from starting its travel. An additional dial on the front of the camera was used to set these speeds that allowed exposures up to a second in length.

The Leica's shutter gave lens designers the maximum flexibility since the size and position of an interlens shutter did not have to be taken into account. When interchangeable lenses became important, the shutter was out of the way, giving these engineers the freedom to design and mount lenses of almost any focal length.

The cloth focal plane shutter also allowed Leitz to build every part of its camera in house. Two German instrument companies, Compur and Prontor, had largely perfected the interlens leaf shutter by the early 1920s. By standardizing the design and using mass production, these companies were able to turn out thousands of reliable, quality shutter assemblies cheaply. These shutters were to prove irresistible sirens for many German camera manufacturers, who were willing to compromise lens and camera design in order to avoid the expense of developing and manufacturing their own shutters. Since Leitz had patented every possible aspect of their shutter, potential competitors wishing to build a similar rangefinder 35mm camera really had only two choices: either use an interlens leaf shutter or start from scratch and build something sufficiently different that it could pass through the patent gauntlet that Leitz had constructed.

Carl Zeiss, through its photographic division of Zeiss Ikon, was the only German firm willing — and probably had the technical and financial resources — to attempt such a direct challenge in a 35mm rangefinder camera. But by the time the Contax I camera entered the marketplace in 1932, Leitz had already sold thousands of Leicas and moved up to a model offering both a coupled rangefinder for focusing and a full range of interchangeable lenses. Again, the rangefinder mechanism that Leitz incorporated into the Leica was simple, straightforward and dependable, yet readily adjustable for accuracy if it got out of alignment. A housing fronted with two additional windows took in two magnified views of the subject. A mirrored prism behind the righthand window deflected that image at 90 degrees over to another semi-silvered prism that brought the two window images together. A simple, spring-loaded lever attached to the righthand prism. This ran from the prism to connect to another lever that took a position immediately behind the lens mount. Pressure from a ring extending out of the back of the mounted lens moved that lever back and forth as the lens was focused in and out, causing the images gathered through the two windows to separate or come together to form one image. Rangefinders were in common use on cameras, but again, Leitz was able to patent its elegant coupling mechanism, forcing its competition to explore other approaches.

The third feature of the Leica that was to cause trouble for competitors was its lens mount. The interchangeable lenses that Leitz offered mounted using a 39mm screw-in thread. The mount was the same for all its lenses, but the rangefinder coupling cam that projected out of the back of each lens had to be cut and angled differently for each focal length so that the rangefinder always focused in terms of the standard lens that the rangefinder was designed for. Again, patents protected this feature as well.

Zeiss was determined to offer a new 35mm, interchangeable lens rangefinder camera that would offer all the same features as the Leica — and more. It would have a full range of shutter speeds in a focal-plane shutter and have full rangefinder coupling for all its wide range of lenses. It took Zeiss several tries but with its second version, the Contax II of 1936, Zeiss had a winner. The Contax offered all its shutter speeds on one dial that did not rotate during exposure, a large, bright, combined rangefinder-viewfinder, a bayonet mount for its superb lenses and a completely removable back instead of the removable bottom that Leicas used. By the beginning of World War II, the Contax had caught up to and passed the Leica in sales.

But despite a high reputation and handling characteristics as good as or better than the Leica's, the Contax did not lend itself to imitation. Everything about the camera was more complicated than the Leica. This was partly due to the patent restrictions around which Zeiss engineers had been forced to design. But another reason for the camera's complexity was that the Contax was the product of a committee, and its features reflected the design decisions of a giant company aiming to cover all possibilities. Oskar Barnack designed almost all of the original Leicas himself and for himself. As a result, the camera reflected the philosophy and vision of one man. The Contax was a company's vision, with every aspect of its product potential playing into the design.

These then were the two professional-level 35mm rangefinder cameras that NK engineers, principally Masahito Fuketa* and Hiroshi Shirahama, had to draw on in designing their new camera. As noted above, an NK engineer had already taken a Canon camera apart and made up drawings of every part and function. Now the company had to create new working drawings for their own design.

One of the biggest trophies that the victorious Allies took from the Germans were their patents. Every part of the Leica or Contax, including shutters, rangefinder couplings, lens designs, even optical formulæ, were now freely available for American manufacturers to use. Whether the Japanese also had the permission to use these ideas is not as clear, but the still-prostrate German manufacturers were not in a position to challenge their former ally's use of their patents. NK could pick and choose the best ideas from either company. And this is what NK did. In the process of doing so, the NK designers made several significant decisions that would have important consequences for the future success of their camera.

Apparently, the engineers liked the overall shape and design of the Contax better than that of the Leica, although the new camera would be smaller and closer to the Leica in size. It would have the cut corners of the Contax instead of the rounded ends of a Leica. This was also a design feature of the Canons — cameras much closer in design and spirit to the Leicas. Second, they lifted the fully removable back off the Contax, copying it almost exactly. Indeed, looking up at the back of the new camera, one could easily confuse it with a Contax. They also sheathed the new camera in leather instead of the rougher, more durable, leatherlike vulcanite material that the Leica used. Deciding that the double-bayonet mount of the Contax would help differentiate their camera from the many Leica copies appearing

---

Fuketa would later become a company vice president and a member of its board. He would have a hand in the design of all the Nikon cameras through the Nikon F of 1959. The "F" associated with NK's reflex 35mm cameras honors Fuketa.

in Japan and make it superior for quick interchangeability of lenses, they decided to use that mount, despite the higher manufacturing costs, together with the projecting escutcheon that the Contax mount demanded.*[36] The third feature borrowed from the Contax was the combined rangefinder-viewfinder — a feature also found on the postwar Canons. As a result, the new camera looked externally a lot like a compact Contax II.

However, the interior mechanisms were almost all straight out of a Leica. The new camera had a cloth, horizontally traveling focal plane shutter that, spring for spring and gear for gear, was right out of a Leica — or a Canon, for that matter. This was really the only possible decision NK could have made. The Contax shutter, with its vertically traveling curtains built of brass slats assembled like a roll-top desk, and its complex gearing that coupled a horizontal film movement with a vertical-traveling shutter was beyond the manufacturing abilities of any Japanese company at that time.

The Contax's rangefinder-viewfinder system incorporated a bar prism that ran the length of the camera to act as a light-pipe to carry the righthand image across the interior of the camera to the viewfinder at the left end of the camera. This gave a brighter image for focusing, but it took a lot of room and added noticeably to the camera's weight. The rangefinder's pivoting prism connected directly to a finger wheel on the top front of the camera. Turning the edge of the finger wheel rotated both the prism and, via gears, the focusing mount for a normal lens, which was built into the camera's lens mount. Again, a sophisticated system almost impossible to get out of alignment but expensive and complicated to build.

NK wanted to use the Contax mount, but it simply could not duplicate its coupling mechanism. The company's solution was ingenious, but would be an endless source of controversy in the future. NK duplicated the Leica's focusing rangefinder mechanism almost exactly, the only change the combining of the rangefinder-viewfinder window for one-point focusing and viewing. The focusing helical for the normal lens was shaped at its rear to match the same action as the rangefinder coupling cam on a Leitz lens. A spring-loaded lever bore against this surface and rotated the rangefinder prism. The camera still had a finger wheel for focusing the normal lens in the same place as a Contax, but this wheel connected only with the focusing mount. The rangefinder focusing took its guidance directly from the back of the lens helical.

This is where the problem came in. Because the Leica-type rangefinder coupling took its information directly from the cam on the back of the internal focusing mount — instead of via gears connected to the focusing mount — the pitch of the Nikon helical had to be modified slightly in order to focus a normal lens accurately from infinity to the three-foot closest point. This did not seem to be a major issue in 1946. The difference between a Contax's focusing and a Nikon's at the closest focus amounted to less than an inch and even the depth of focus on a 50mm f2 lens covered that difference wide open. Indeed, NK's engineers may not have even been aware of the difference initially. But faster lenses and longer focal length lenses were going to be a problem. A Nikkor telephoto lens set at infinity would

Apparently Motoichi Mori, NK's chief engineer during much of this period (?), actively advocated manufacturing a Nikon with a thread mount at least through August 1951.

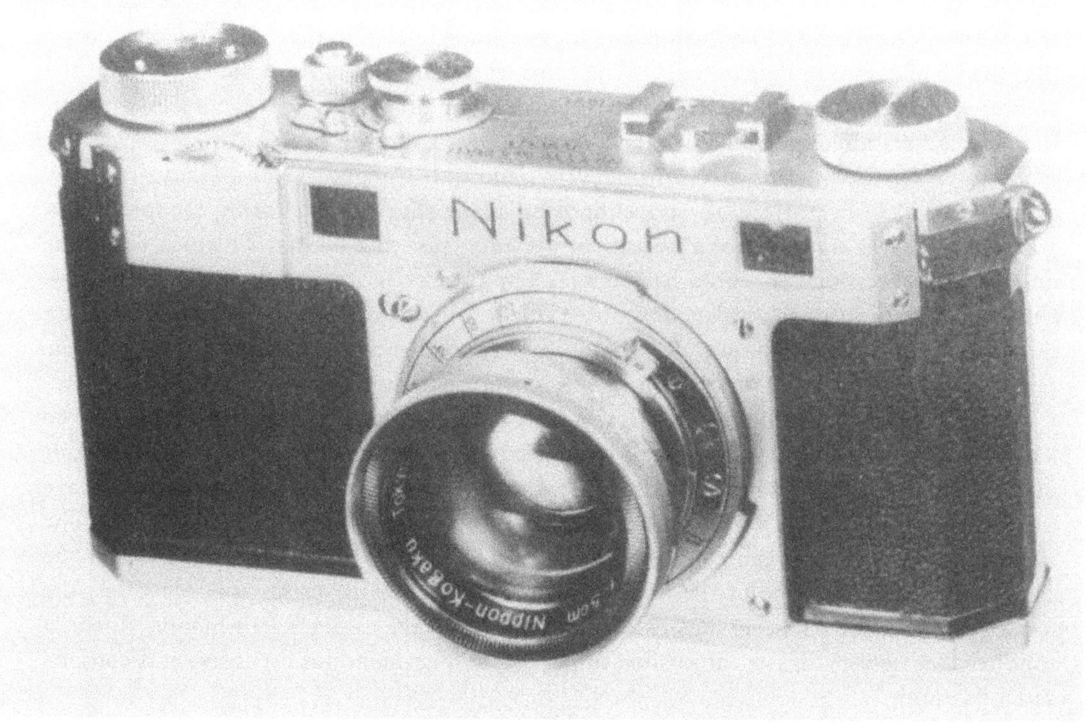

Portrait of the first Nikon camera. This is one of the pictures that Nippon Kogaku used in its early advertisements and appears to be camera number 6097, one of the prototypes. Note the eight screws securing the front plate. These would be reduced to only six screws between camera numbers 60952 and 60969. The company name appears as text on the top cover instead of the NK logo, another feature of the prototypes (courtesy Nikon Historical Society).

yield sharp results on either a Contax or a Nikon because the mounts were the same, but if one depended on the rangefinder, the difference in helical pitch would result in increasingly out-of-focus pictures the closer the lens was focused.

The engineers made one other novel design decision. Because of the front escutcheon, they could not fit a slow shutter speed dial on the front of the camera like the Leica and its direct imitators did. Instead, the engineers combined the fast and slow speed dials one above the other on top of the camera conveniently set right in front of the shutter release.

So far, the designers had made a series of decisions that took the best ideas from both of the top brands and combined them in an original way that would certainly differentiate their product from all its potential competitors and do so in a positive way. But the designers made one more decision that was to prove almost fatal to the company's future.

In the summer of 1946, NK still saw its new camera as a product for both domestic and overseas markets. The Japanese government was then promoting a modification of the 35mm format that would expose a frame of 24mm by 32mm. To encourage this frame size, the Ministry of Education specified that projectors for Japanese schools would use this size.[37] Almost all of NK's former products had gone to the government, and it is possible that the designers saw this governmental support as close to a directive. The 24 × 32 format (sometimes called the "nippon" format) had a certain appeal. As already noted, this meant that the film advanced only seven sprockets for each frame instead of the standard eight. This, in turn, meant an extra four or five frames on every 36-exposure roll of film — not an inconsiderable savings for the impoverished Japanese. These negatives also fit 8 × 10 sheets of paper with less negative or paper loss.

Several other Japanese 35mm camera manufacturers would also shape their cameras around this format. The Chiyoda Kogaku Seiko Company's first 35mm camera, the Minolta 35 of 1947,* would use this format, as did the Olympus 35 I, the first camera from the Olympus Optical Company, a manufacturer that had its start making microscopes. Others included the Minion 35 and the little-known and inexpensive Opema.

Confident that their new camera would be ready for manufacturing in short order, the company issued production orders in June 1946, even though the design had not been finalized.

Solving Problems and Assembling Pieces for a Camera in Difficult Times

In the meantime, the 2¼ square format roll-film twin-lens reflex that was to be the company's other flagship camera had run into trouble. To be called a "Nikoflex," the camera was an out-and-out copy of the successful German-made Rolleiflex and Rolleicord cameras then popular with both professionals and amateurs. The Research and Design Department team had pushed ahead with the Nikoflex and, on July 25, publicly showed mockups of the new camera. But the company's lack of experience with interlens leaf-shutters was now to be the camera's undoing. Designing either an inexpensive Prontor-type shutter, or a more-expensive Compur-type shutter was simply not possible without the purchase of new press tools. This was not going to happen, and the company reluctantly decided to put the Nikoflex on hold and focus its attention on the development of its 35mm camera.[†38]

The other issue NK settled that summer was giving a name to this new 35mm camera. Various names were considered. The most likely contender was "Nikkorette," referring to a contraction of the company's name and "ette" to signify small size. But the name did not catch on and the stronger name "Nikon" was settled on by September. That month the

---

*Like the Nikon, Chiayoda Kogaku would modify its focal-plane shutter, interchangeable lens 35 to a 24 × 35.5 format in 1949 using the same technique used to create the Nikon M. The Minolta 35 never was a big seller in the United States and remained substantially the same through a production period that ran into the mid–1950s.

†The use of roll film may also have been a factor. On page 87 of Baird, The Japanese Camera, he reports that domestic film supplies were so short that SCAP banned all sales of roll film sizes in order to leave enough materials for making medically needed X-ray film. While the ban did not last long and did not affect sales for export, it may have primed NK's interest in 35mm as an acceptable format for both domestic and foreign sales.

design department finished its work. The company set up space in the metal-working department of the Ohi factory for production and issued production dates and goals — even though not a single prototype had yet been built.*

The need for export sales was increasingly driving the company's thinking. Exports meant cash; exports meant food and resources needed to buy raw materials. NK needed exports in order to survive and it needed them badly.

In 1947, almost all exports still left the country in only two ways: through either the *Boeki Kodan* (modern spelling is *Boheki Kodan*) or the CPO. The *Boeki Kodan* (Trade Corporations) were government-sponsored organizations that undertook to receive, market and ship goods to overseas markets. They continued to be almost the only means that any Japanese firm had to get their goods out of the country until the spring of 1949 when the Occupation authorities ordered the government to abolish all but the *Boeki Kodan* that purchased goods for the government itself.† The timing of this abolition is significant for it gave an opening for private companies, such as the Overseas Finance & Trading Company, to take over the function that the *Boeki Kodan* had performed.

The CPO was the "Central Purchasing Office" for the military and citizen Occupation exchange system. At that point, the CPO figured it could sell any cameras it could get — provided they met the CPO's standards for quality.

With a big market available, NK pressed ahead. The workers began building the 20 prototypes called for while at the same time they proceeded with manufacturing parts for the projected first production runs. It took them until November to get just two prototypes assembled and it took another year for the last prototype to get finished. One of these 20 failed to work at all, so the first camera off the first production run (Order 6FB-1), number 60921, was substituted. These first cameras suffered from light leaks and various mechanical problems, particularly with the shutters. As each problem was addressed, all the cameras on the production lines had to be modified to correct the errors being found.

The engineer in charge of the testing, Minoru Takahashi — the same person who had made the drawings of the Canon — ran vibration tests and tests for heat and cold resistance with the first four prototypes. The slow speeds did not hold up well, and the governor had to be modified. The workers had to learn to be more careful and the metal in the shafts and springs needed to be improved. Still, Takahashi was not satisfied and, after the second tests, he added a radial ball bearing to the main shaft that adjusted the curtain travel. The company received its first new camera patent for this innovation.§39

If the camera part of the business was not getting off the ground, the demand for optical glass was once more growing, as were the demands for NK's lenses. With G.I.s buying

---

The company considered September 1946 as the month the design was finalized and, following its then standard practice, set 6091 as the start of the camera's serial numbers. "6" = 1946, "09" = September. 1946 was also the year 2006 of the Japanese calendar.

†*The SCAPIN #1926/4 dated March 5, 1949, provided for the dissolution of the* Boeki Kodan *and their replacement with private contractors for nongovernment goods.*

§*Camera #6095 was the first of the prototypes to contain this ball bearing. In all, NK would be issued at least nine new patents relating to the Nikon camera between 1948 and 1950.*

Ξxhibit 1

No. ____

<table>
<tr><td colspan="4" align="center">6FT-1 の 完成 経過 Completion Log</td></tr>
<tr><td colspan="4" align="center">1947 November   1948 April
22.11. ～ 23. 4.</td></tr>
<tr><td colspan="4">6FT-1   小型カメラ試作   20 台   Small camera Trial Production Quantity</td></tr>
<tr><td colspan="4">(『完成記入台帳』による) This record is based on the full account of produc</td></tr>
<tr><td>完成年月日
Completion YmD</td><td>完成数量
Completed Qty</td><td>ボディ番号
Body #</td><td></td></tr>
<tr><td>1947 22.11.18.
november 18</td><td>1</td><td>No. 60911</td><td>第1次試験に使用
Used in the first testing</td></tr>
<tr><td>22.11.24.</td><td>1</td><td>No. 6094</td><td>第1次試験に使用
Used in the first testing</td></tr>
<tr><td>22.12.17.</td><td>1</td><td>No. 6096</td><td></td></tr>
<tr><td>22.12.22.</td><td>1</td><td>No. 60913</td><td></td></tr>
<tr><td>23. 2.13.</td><td>1</td><td>No. 6095</td><td>第3次試験に使用 Used in the 3rd testing
(RS-4ベアリング使用)
Rs-4 bearing was used</td></tr>
<tr><td>23. 2.18.</td><td>3</td><td></td><td></td></tr>
<tr><td>23. 2.25.</td><td>2</td><td></td><td></td></tr>
<tr><td>23. 2.29.</td><td>2</td><td></td><td></td></tr>
<tr><td>23. 3.12.</td><td>1</td><td></td><td>6FB-1の1台を起した分 No.60921
22.12.9.シャッタ試験報告</td></tr>
<tr><td>23. 4. 5.</td><td>5</td><td></td><td></td></tr>
<tr><td>23. 4.30.</td><td>2</td><td></td><td></td></tr>
</table>

Nippon Kogaku's record of some of the tests of the Nikon prototypes (courtesy Nikon Historical Society).

its cameras as fast as it could make them, Canon, in turn, was purchasing 50mm f3.5 Nikkors and a bit later, 50mm f2 Nikkors from NK to go on its improved models. The Canon Camera Company was making progress. As mentioned in the previous chapter, in 1939 it had added a cheaper, interchangeable lens camera to its line that was aimed at the low end domestic market. Instead of using the elaborate bayonet-mount system that NK had designed for the first Canons, this series used what was called the "J" mount. Like the Leica, it used a 39mm thread mount, but in order to avoid patent infringement charges, the thread pitch was different. Attempting to mount a Leitz lens on a "J" mount Canon or visa versa would result in stripped threads. Immediately after the war, Canon modified this mount to what is generally called the "J-slop" mount. Closer to the Leica's thread in pitch, it allowed either "J" mount or Leica mount lenses to go on. In 1945–46, Canon had been so strapped for cash that it could not afford the moroccan leather needed to cover its cameras. Instead, it substituted embossed black paper. But with the model SII, Canon was able to go to a high-quality finish and a mount that exactly duplicated the Leica thread. The NK-designed mount for the Hansa Canon from 1935 was gone and forgotten. Soon, the company also added a rotating prism in its viewfinder that allowed two additional magnifications, duplicating the view of longer lenses and giving more rangefinder focusing accuracy.

Up until early 1947, all the lenses for these Canons were Nikkors. In February 1946, NK had begun making and supplying camera lenses once more to meet the demands from Canon and other growing camera companies. SCAP production figures give only 11 lenses for that month. But by October the number would reach a high of 176. In November the number slipped to 101 and by February 1947 the number would be down to 43.[40]

Part of the reason for this drop was that NK did not have enough quality optical glass of the correct types to make all the lenses its customers needed. It also was trying to preserve some of these optics for its own new camera. This was particularly a problem with the 50mm f2 Nikkor. At least two of its six elements required barium glass types that had been supplied by the Schott Glass Works before and during the war. After it had exhausted those stocks, NK redesigned the lens formula to use glass types it did have on hand. This series (starting with serial number 7081) would be the lenses that came as standard equipment on most of the first Nikons (a few came with lenses in the 609XXX series). In 1948, once more able to melt its own glass, NK was finally able to manufacture all the glass types this lens needed and redesigned and upgraded the 50mm f2 Nikkor again. These lenses came with serial numbers starting with either 8061 or 8111.

But by 1947, the Canon Company had given up on NK and purchased its own lens grinding and finishing machines and begun to make and sell its own "Serenar" lenses. NK was still making photographic lenses, but it had to find other manufacturers who needed them — or get its own camera out the door.

As noted earlier, NK had started applying coatings to periscope prisms and relay lenses for submarines during World War II. In April 1946, the company transferred this technology to its camera lenses. At first they used cryolite, but shifted to using magnesium fluoride in 1948 [or 1949] after getting permission to purchase vacuum pumps needed for that process.*

Lens coatings had first appeared in 1892 following the discovery by the English lens designer, Dennis Taylor, that old lenses with tarnished surfaces transmitted more light than clear ones.[41] He duplicated this effect by dipping lenses in a solution of ammonium sulfide and nitric acid. Zeiss and the American firm of Bausch & Lomb developed the technique further in the 1930s.

Each air-to-glass surface of an uncoated glass element in a lens can reflect as much as 10 percent of the light falling on its surface. This scattered light degrades sharpness through increased flare and, in multiple-element lenses, reduces considerably the amount of light reaching film or a viewer. Symmetrical Gaussian optics with multiple air-to-glass surfaces theoretically promised the best corrections and sharpness, but the eight or more air-to-glass surfaces in these designs reduced transmitted light to levels that few optical manufacturers were willing to accept prior to the widespread use of lens coatings. As a result, the best high-speed lenses for 35mm cameras had been Zeiss's Sonnars, optics based on the Tessar with six or seven elements but having only six air-glass surfaces.

Coatings set at one-fourth the wavelength of light in the visible spectrum could reduce the 10 percent loss to less than 1 percent and yield better sharpness in the bargain. Early single-layer coatings could be computed for only one wave length. Usually this was green in color since that lies in the middle of the visual spectrum. This is why most early coated lenses have a distinct purple tinge, the result of reflecting back red and blue, the colors at opposite ends from the middle green. To point out its new coatings, NK started engraving a red-filled "c" on the beauty ring of all its lenses. These early coatings were soft and easily scratched, so they were applied only to inner glass surfaces. The front outside surfaces remained uncoated.

While the company was working on its camera and trying to make ends meet with its binoculars, the design department was developing new optics for 35mm, 2¼ × 2¼ cameras and for 8mm movie cameras. The first lenses for 35mm were "normals." As noted, NK had resumed supplying 50mm lenses with maximum apertures of either f3.5 or f2 for the Canon camera. Following the pattern already set by Leitz, both of these lenses were nominally two inches in focal length (51.6mm), but again following the German pattern, they were engraved "f = 5cm." Zeiss normals were supposedly slightly longer, which might have caused a focus problem, except that even with the best quality controls, finished focal lengths varied by as much as a half a millimeter plus or minus.

This supposed difference between Zeiss "normals" and Leitz/Nikkor "normals" has been cited by several sources, including NK itself, as the reason for the difference in the helical pitch between the Contax mounts and the Nikon mounts. Note, however, that John Wolbarst in his June 1951 report on the Nikon, reported that the actual precise focal lengths of the two 50mm f1.4 Nikkors tested were 52.05mm and 51.92mm. The 50mm f1.5 Zeiss Sonnar used for comparison had a focal length of 52.07mm.[42] In actual practice, such differences were meaningless.

Special permission to purchase vacuum pumps from the Tokuda Company was granted by SCAP on June 13, 1949. The pumps were "To be used for coating of lenses or binoculars and cameras."

The 50mm f3.5 Nikkor-Q* was a four element design that duplicated Zeiss's Tessar or Leitz's Elmar, depending on one's point of view. The 50mm f2 Nikkor-H was a close copy of the six-element Zeiss Sonnar of the same focal length and aperture designed by L. Bertele. Zeiss optical designs were the best in the business in 1945, and NK wisely followed their designs for most of their early lenses. In addition to these lenses, NK copied the Zeiss 50mm f1.5 Sonnar and the 135mm f4 Sonnar telephoto, but came up with a simpler design for its 85mm f2 telephoto. A team that included Masahiko Fuketa prototyped an original 50mm f1.8 Nikkor using a nearly symmetrical Gaussian six-element design, but, due to glass shortages, it was delayed and never saw production.[43] The company's final design was a 35mm f3.5 W-Nikkor wide angle. Zeiss had made an excellent 35mm wide-angle before the war, the 35mm f2.8 Biogon, but NK decided to go with a Tessar formula with a more modest maximum aperture.

For the still not-quite-dead Nikoflex, NK designed an 80mm f3.5 Nikkor normal "taking" lens that could be paired with an 80mm f3.2 Nikkor viewing lens. NK later sold many of these lenses to the Aires Company, which used them in its twin-lens reflex, the Airesflex. Nikkors of 80mm and 75mm also ended up on other Japanese-made 2¼ square cameras, including the Beautyflex. For the popular amateur 8mm movie format, NK designed a 13mm f1.9 "normal" Ciné-Nikkor and a 38mm f1.9 Ciné Nikkor telephoto. Both of these lenses came in the standard ⅝-inch "D" mount that almost all 8mm movie cameras used. For now, all these accessory lens designs, for the Nikon, Leica thread cameras and movie cameras, would be put on hold until the market for such lenses had grown.

Reaching for Quality and Production

On December 24, 1946, NK's secretary had forwarded a "program of production" to the Economic and Scientific Section, GHQ, SCAP, in which he confidently predicted that "Production Schedule (Jan.–Sept. 1947) will show very clearly the great improvement that the company is going to achieve in the coming year both in variety and the nature of the products."[44]

In reality, the next 21 months, from January 1947 through September 1948, were to be the most difficult time in the history of both Nippon Kogaku and its new camera. The high hopes that the company had for its newest product were to be tested and brought low numerous times. NK had projected that by March 1947 it would be producing 300 cameras per month, yet by the end of August 1948 it had managed to finish only 200 cameras — virtually all of them manufactured between March and August 1948.

**Unlike German optics, which tended to sport a multitude of names, all of NK's lenses had been called "Nikkor" since the early 1930s, but NK did take to adding special prefixes or suffixes to the Nikkor name. Special-purpose lenses, such as the Nikkors for movie cameras and the Apochromatic process lenses, gained a prefix that identified their intended specific use, i.e. Ciné Nikkor and Apo Nikkor. Wide-angle lenses for the rangefinder cameras were all just "W-Nikkors." But all other lenses for cameras had a suffix that indicated the number of glass elements in the lenses. In this case, the "Q" indicates a lens with four elements. The 85mm Nikkor-P had five elements, both the 50mm f1.5 and the later f1.4 Nikkor-S had seven elements, the 135mm f4 and later f3.5 Nikkor-Q had four elements and the 50mm f2 Nikkor-H had six.*

What had gone wrong? Actually, almost everything. The company's faith in itself and its understanding of quality control were both initially misplaced. Manufacturing a precision 35mm camera proved far more difficult than anyone in the company had ever imagined, and economic problems that all Japanese manufacturers were struggling with continued to take their toll. As noted earlier, the company had already issued four production orders by September 1946 even though not a single prototype had been built or proofed. To quote the Nikon Company's official history *Forty Years*:

> The trial plans for the Nikon were completed in September 1946, and production
> began right away. However, many inadequacies were found in all parts, and revisions
> were made one after another. In the meantime, mass production went ahead without
> waiting to solve the problems, and the people at the production site started to get
> confused about how to deal with [different versions of] the plans.*

Here were teams of workers trying to manufacture parts based on drawings for a camera that still did not physically exist! The "final" drawings were actually anything but final, and changes had to be made continuously. Needless to say, the workers became thoroughly confused, not knowing which drawing or instructions to use as revision after revision piled up. The workers had great difficulty getting even the prototypes finished and did not get the last ones done until November 1947. As these trial cameras were completed, they were tested and the newer ones modified. Finally, in April 1948, over a year after the original tests were supposed to have been concluded, the tests were said to be complete and the go-ahead granted for the production of marketable cameras. In reality, hardly any problems had been solved. The shutters were still giving problems, the lens helicals were not accurate enough and other mechanical parts were not being built to high enough standards.

Shortages of certain materials continued to be part of the problem. "Goat skin, piano cord, spring steel and raw rubber..."[45] remained in short supply. Even silk of the proper thinness and quality for the shutter curtains proved difficult to locate with some being supplied by an umbrella manufacturer![46] Stamping out and chroming the brass coverplates proved difficult and expensive. Unable or unwilling to bear the expense of creating a precision die-cast mold for the basic body casting, the engineers decided to go ahead with a sandcast mold instead. While this saved the cost of having a metal mold made, the resulting sandcast bodies were heavier than die-cast bodies would have been, and they required extensive hand fitting (including the grinding out of the groove into which the back would fit) to bring them to the same tolerances that die-cast parts would have enjoyed right out of the mold.

The more exotic glass types remained in short supply, limiting NK's ability to experiment with new lens designs and affecting the manufacture of the optical components. As noted earlier, NK was not allowed to fire its furnaces until the fall of 1947 due to both fuel and electrical postwar shortages. Until then, the company had to depend on stocks of optical glass left over from the war. When NK did receive permission to resume glass

---

As quoted in translation in Arakawa, "Birth of the Nikon," 3. Arakawa was not a designer. He worked in the sales office, but he was a member of the original design team. See Endnote 51.

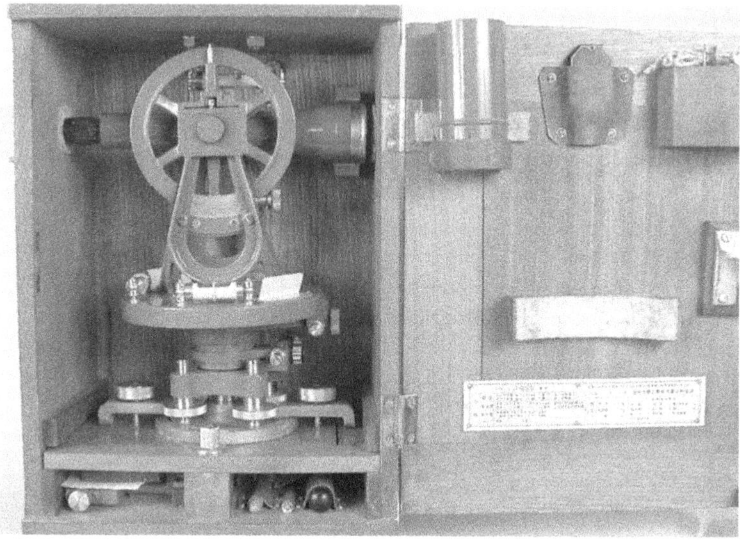

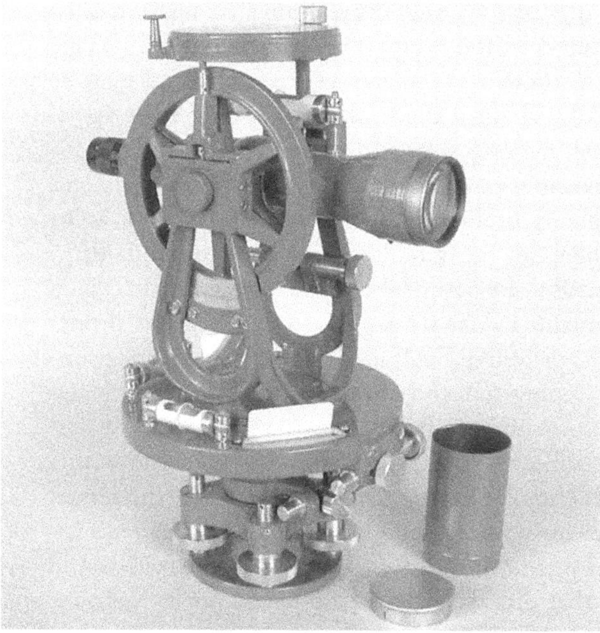

manufacture, it was only on a limited basis. Not until late 1948 was the glass shortage to ease.

Cash flow also continued to be a problem. NK was in a position to manufacture high-quality scientific equipment as well as lenses for use in the graphic arts industry, but these were domestic products. Few Japanese companies could afford to purchase such items, and when they did, they wanted to use barter instead of paying in scarce yen. For example, NK projected a regular production of printing lenses of 30 per month in 1947. In reality, NK could only wait for orders to come in. When they did come in, the company would put together a temporary team to fill the order, then shut down the production line until a new order was received. The company was able to do this because production was still based on batch units and not on an assembly line. A team assigned to a project would split up the processes among the members and each would work either individually or collectively on a product until it was ready to go out the

A Model G-II Transit Theodolite from 1951. A precision-made instrument similar to the military transits NK had made before and during the war, the G-II was comparable in quality, accuracy and workmanship with any equivalent unit then made in either the United States or Europe. While other, smaller Japanese optical companies were concentrating on producing high-demand, profitable products, such as binoculars and cameras, NK persisted in offering the widest range of optical products, even instruments such as transits for which there was little or no demand in postwar Japan or overseas. SCAP records indicate a total NK production of only 578 transits between March 1948 and April 1951. This particular unit would have been among the last made during that period (Mike H. Symons photographs).

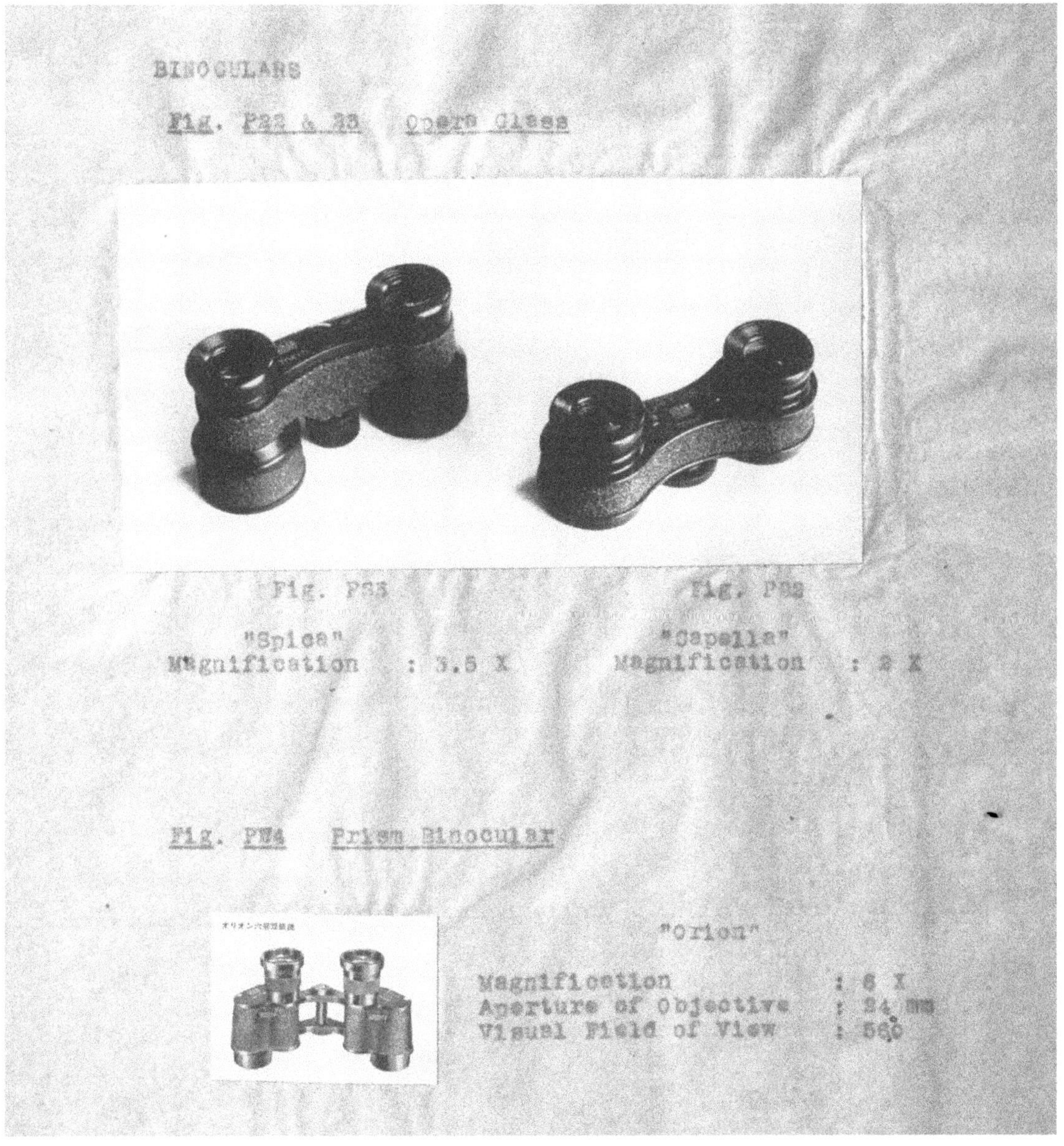

Another page from the report illustrating all of NK's products prepared for SCAP. The Spica and Capella opera glasses and the Orion binoculars were all sold in the military exchanges (National Archives).

door. In any case, the product runs were so small during this period that it is doubtful that an assembly line would have made sense. For example, it is estimated that NK manufactured fewer than 600 of its high-quality transit theodolite, the G-II model, during the three years (1948–51) of its production and availability.

Binoculars remained the only product generating a strong cash flow. At first, each type

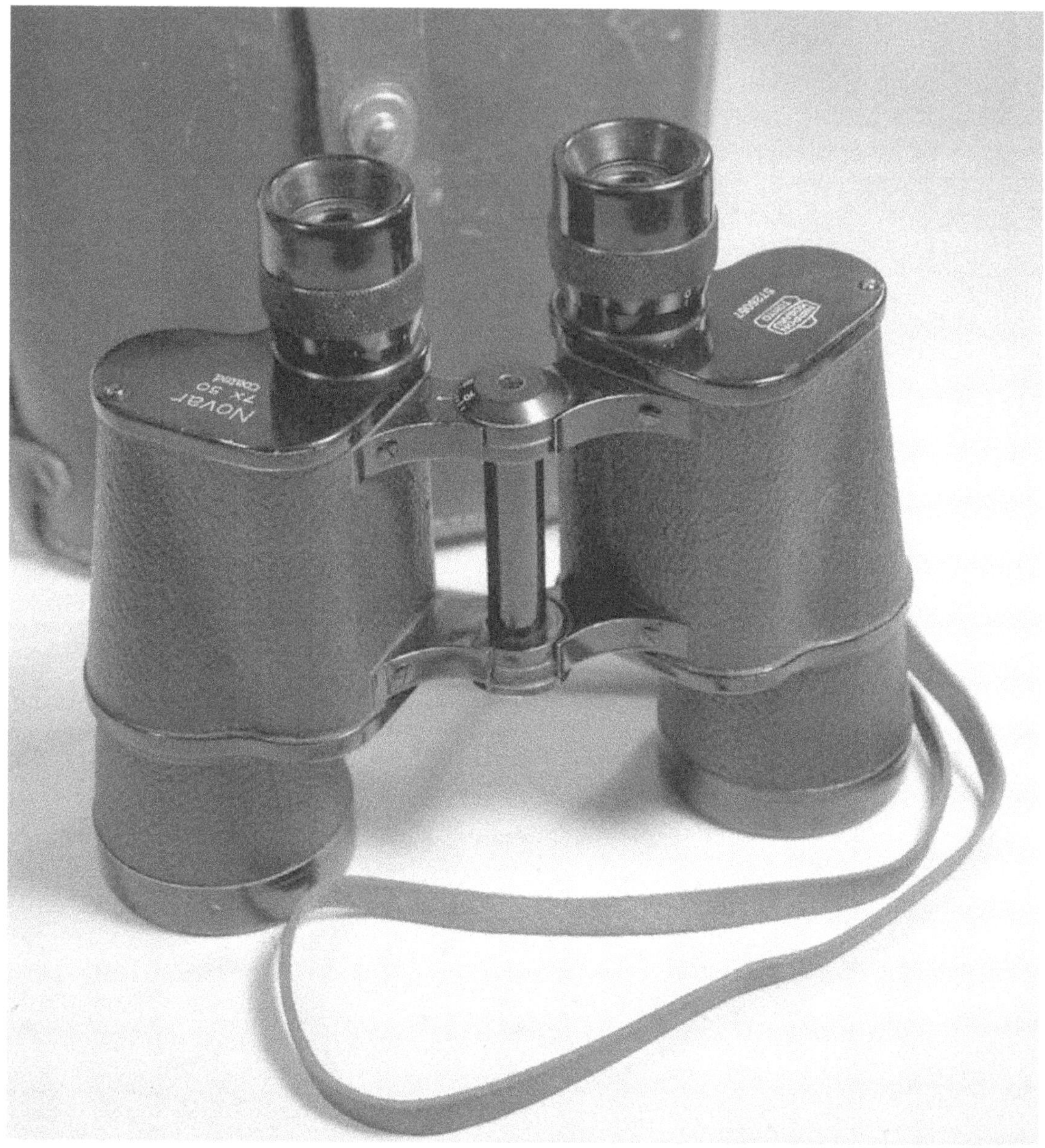

Novar Binoculars. A pair of Nippon Kogaku–manufactured 7X 50 Novar binoculars. (The first post-war Novars were labelled 7X 49.) An almost exact replica of the standard military and naval issue binoculars from World War II, NK produced and sold over 38,000 pairs of Novars between 1946 and 1951, almost all to American service personnel stationed in Japan. While the exterior finish on this sample is somewhat crude, the view and focus remain perfect, even after over 55 years. NK continued to manufacture 7X 50s using almost this same pattern until at least the early 1970s. The Novars all had individual eyepiece focusing (IF). Most later units sold with center focusing, although IF remained an option. NK later promoted these as "Tropic" or "Marine" binoculars because IF allowed better protection against moisture.

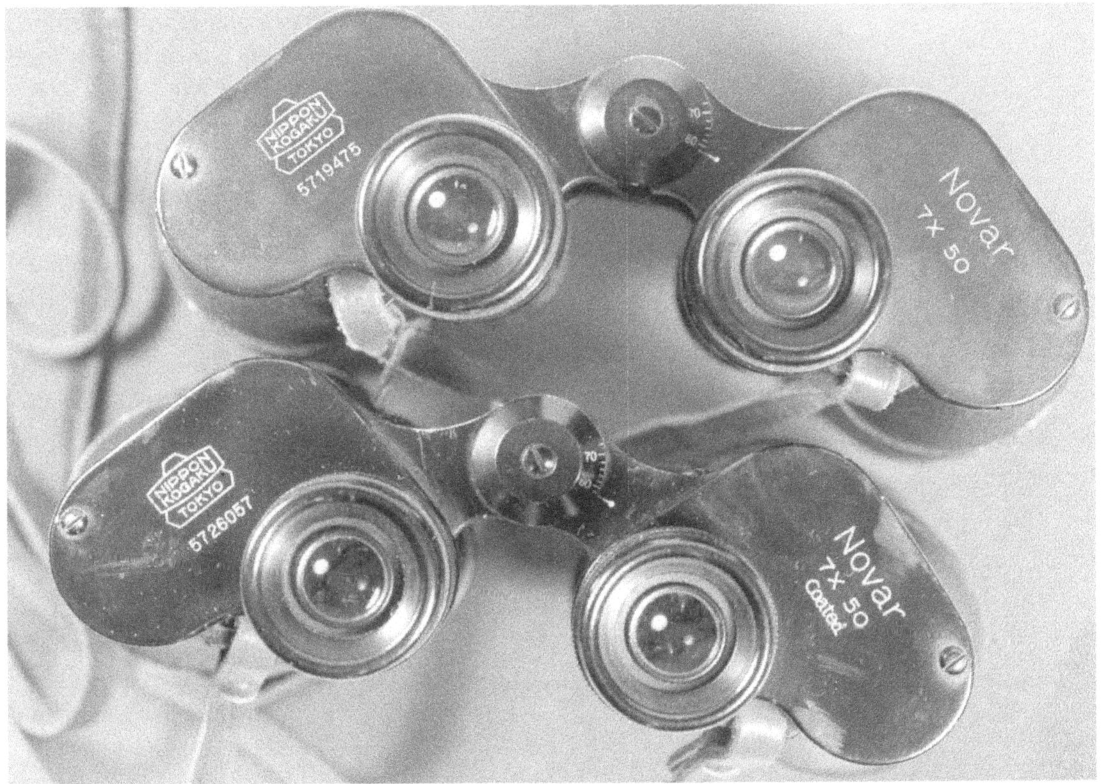

Early and late Novars, both MIOJ. The optics in the earlier pair are still uncoated.

of binocular had its own trademarked name, of which the most prominent were the Novar, Mikron, Orion, Shiki, Spica and Capella. The Novars were 7 × 49 (later 7 × 50) standard units similar to binoculars used by the Japanese navy and army during the war. They received early approval from GHQ for "export" to the military exchanges and were popular optical purchases by G.I.s. From January 1947 to February 1948, NK manufactured 5,624 Novars, of which it delivered 4,750 for export. Almost all of these were sold through the military exchange stores. Only Tokyo Kogaku's "Pride" sold more units. Most of the Orions NK sold were compact 6 × 26 units based on a 6 × 24 military design that dated back to the 1930s and closely resembled the Victors that the Fujii Optical Company had manufactured before the creation of NK. These also proved popular, although on a much lower scale. A total of 1,852 of these were exported during this same period.

The soldiers also bought opera glasses — small, inexpensive, nonprismatic glasses such as the 4× Shiki, 3.5× Spica and the 2× Capella — mainly as souvenirs, since it was not likely any would ever be used in a theater or at a race track. In 1946, twice as many opera glasses were going out the door as binoculars, but soon other Japanese optical companies began manufacturing opera glasses — inferior to NK's, but selling at an even lower price. NK, committed to maintaining quality, could not compete. As a result, NK's more lucrative

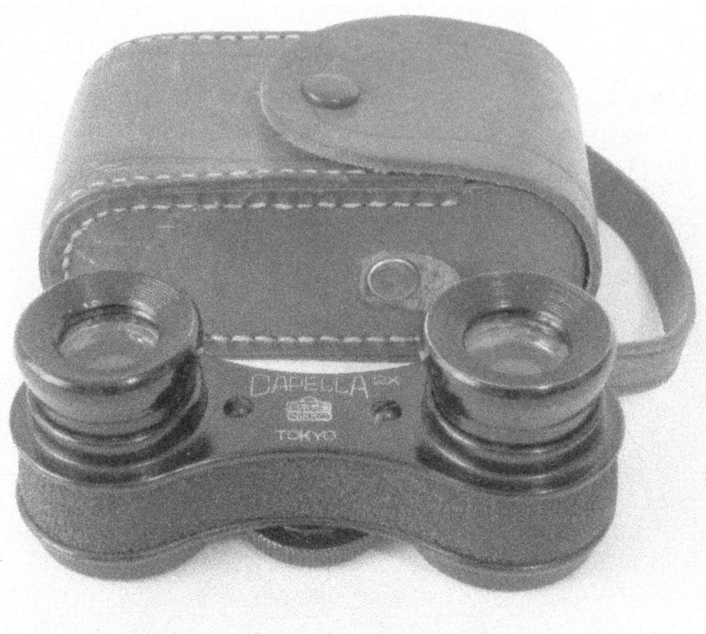

A pair of NK-made Capella 2X power opera glasses with case (Richard A. Lane photograph).

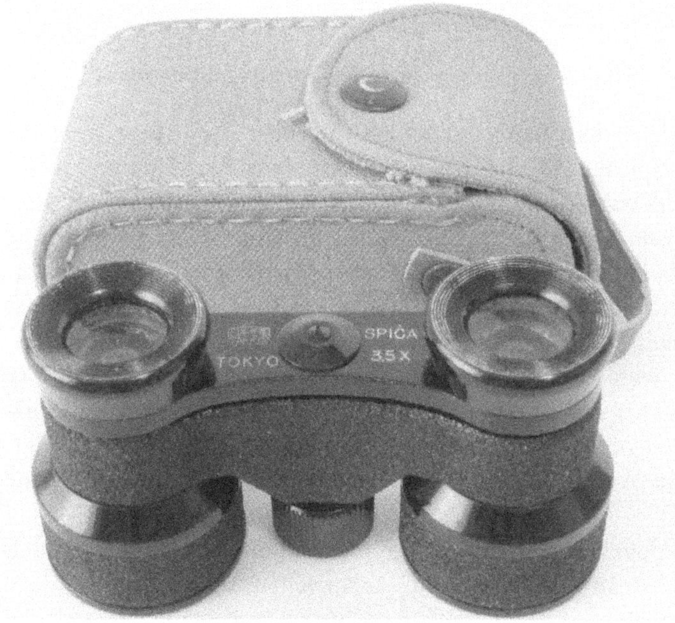

A pair of NK-made Spica 3.5X power opera glasses with case. NK made most of the Capella and Spica glasses in the immediate postwar period before the "Made in Occupied Japan" inscription became a requirement. As a result, only a few have that marking (Richard A. Lane photograph).

binocular numbers soon overtook the numbers for opera glasses, and NK ceased their production in November 1946.

The tiny six-power prismatic Mikrons with their polished chrome finishes and zippered leather pouches proved popular as well. Many of the pouches came with pink silk linings and silver-painted exteriors, evidence that women were the intended users. Eventually NK would use the Mikron name on all its binoculars, a practice that continued until 1959.

If the Nikon camera continued to be unavailable, the sale of Nikkor lenses to other Japanese camera manufacturers was growing. The Nippon Camera Company was once more manufacturing an interchangeable-lens 35mm rangefinder camera. Their product, the Nicca Camera—first manufactured as the Nippon in 1940—duplicated the Leica IIIa so closely that even a knowledgeable photographer might be fooled at 15 feet. The camera was well made, if

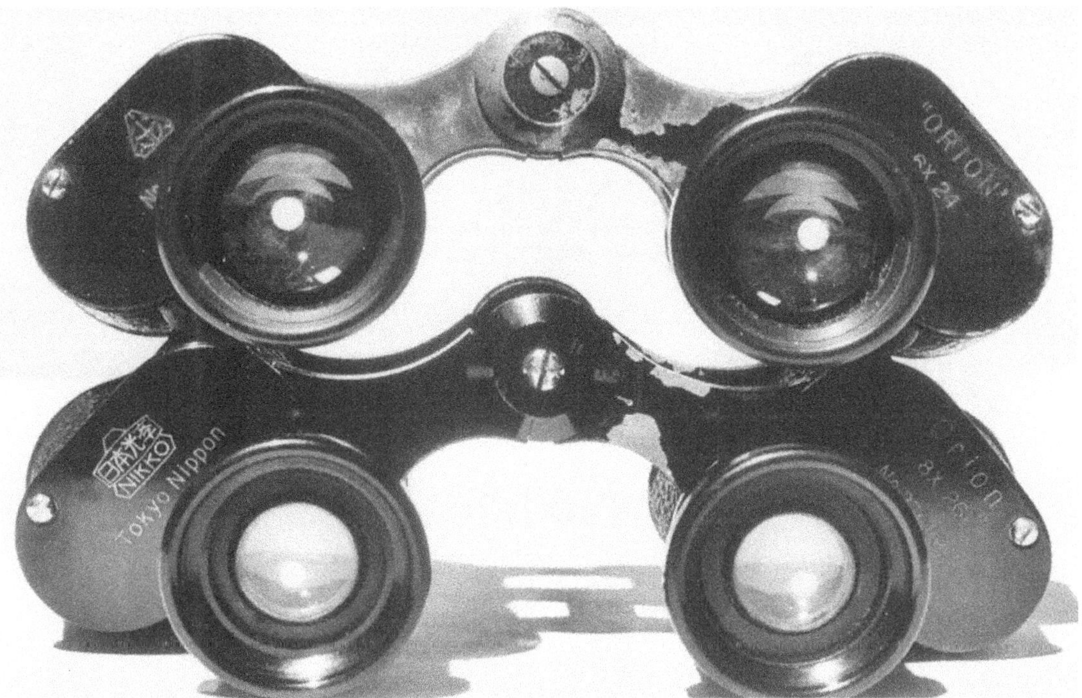

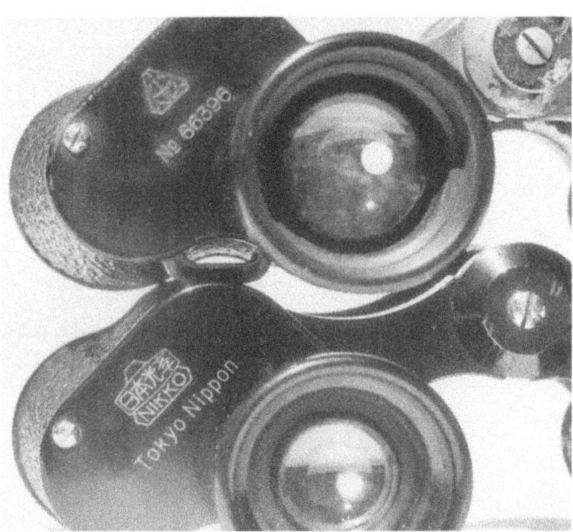

Orion Binoculars. Prewar and early Occupation-period 6 × 24 Orion binoculars (note the early logos). Most Orions went to the Japanese military prior to the end of the war. While popular items with the Occupation forces, their sales did not come near to matching those of the larger, more-modern Novars (Richard A. Lane photographs).

initially cruder than a Leica. Throughout its production life, all Niccas came with Nikkor lenses. Since the Nicca used the 39mm Leica thread mount, this meant that NK would have to be manufacturing all its rangefinder-coupled lenses in at least two mounts: Leica-thread and Contax bayonet.*

By the fall of 1947, the Nikon Camera was still not in production, but rumors of its

Although the Nicca improved over the years, it never did quite get away from the Leica IIIa design. Its sales failed during the changeover to single-lens reflexes in the late 1950s and, during the economic downturn in 1958–59, Yashica bought out the company in order to gain a facility that could manufacture focal plane shutters. Shortly afterward, in October 1959, NK discontinued offering lenses in the Leica thread mount. Niccas still have a reputation as being among the best "Leica copies" that were made in Japan.

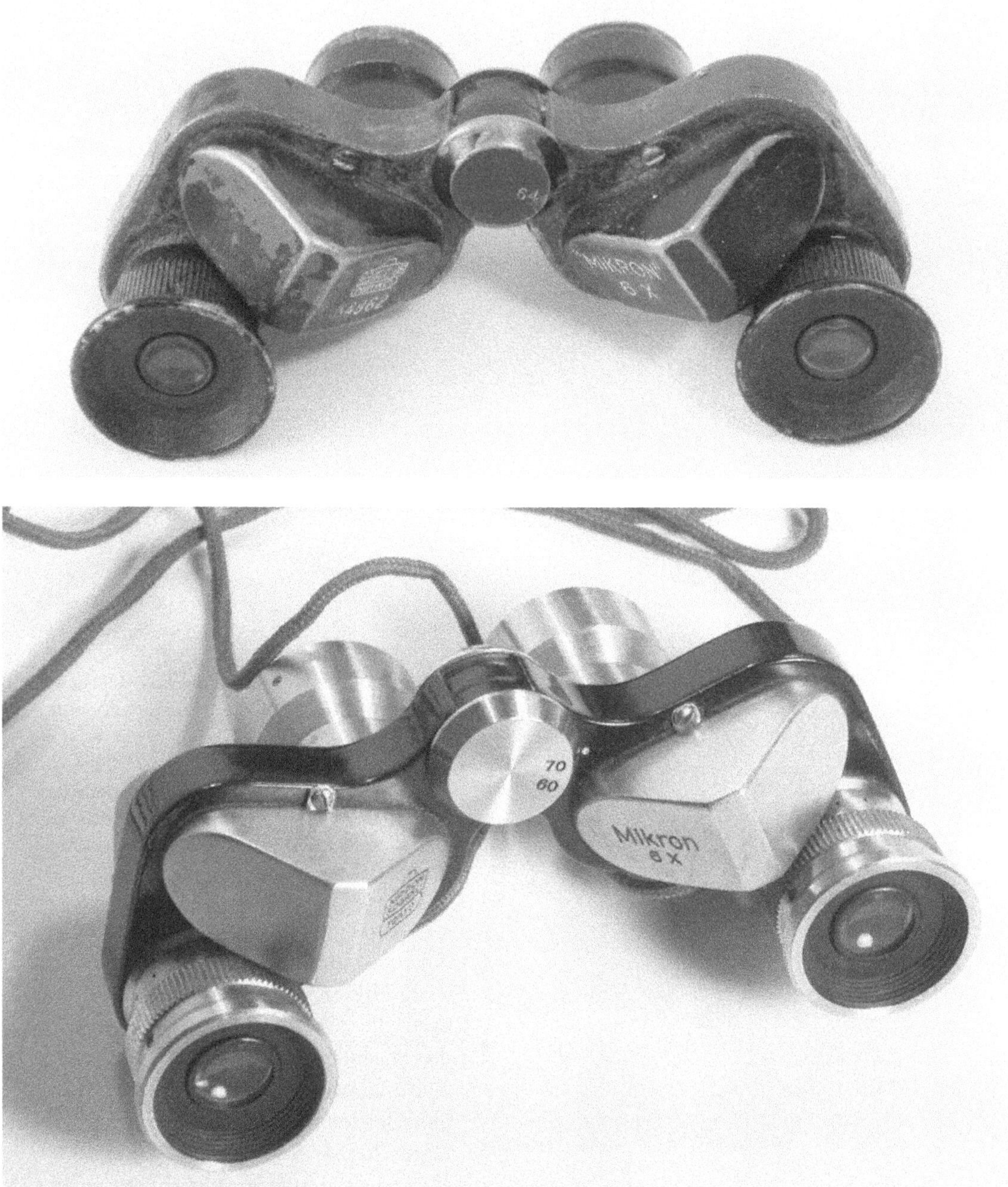

Two different 6X Mikrons. The black-painted pair is from the immediate postwar period. The stainless steel and chrome pair dates from early 1950 and is a nice example of the quality that NK was by then achieving. Compact, inexpensive, but of high quality, the all-metal Mikrons proved highly popular. By the end of the Occupation, NK would be labeling all its binoculars except the Novars as "Mikrons," dropping names such as Orion and Opplem (Richard A. Lane photographs).

existence had spread throughout Japan's optical industry. Many people, both inside and outside the company, were looking forward to the camera's availability, certain that a new product from NK could only help the reputation of Japan's photographic products. In October, NK took out an advertisement in the *Kouga Monthly* in which it announced its new camera — if not to the world — at least to a Japanese public. The most important feature that this advertisement touted was that it was using the "24 × 32mm" format.

An additional problem was now looming for NK. GHQ believed that the *zaibatsu*, the closely held industrial and banking giants that controlled almost all of Japan's major industries, had been important contributors to the militarization of Japan in the first half of the twentieth century. Although NK was a publicly traded corporation, over 43 percent of its shares were held by the Mitsubishi *Zaibatsu*. NK's history prior to World War II might be taken as proof of that close relationship, for the company had been assembled by the Mitsubishi Group specifically to provide the navy with a domestic source of optical equipment.

SCAP intended to dissolve these cartels and their companies, and set about doing that in 1947. So, even if NK was to survive the removal of equipment for reparations, it might not survive the loss of financial support and stability that being part of the Mitsubishi *Zaibatsu* gave it.

Again, what the right hand threatened to take away, the left hand granted. All through 1947, SCAP officials were making visits to the Ohi and Shiojiri plants, poking around, counting machines and labelling ones for reparations, and making sure that machines already set aside were being kept well greased so that they would not deteriorate while awaiting overseas shipment. At the same time, the company's finances were being reviewed by other SCAP officials as they prepared to break up the parent cartel *and* NK. Simultaneously, NK was seeking permission to use machinery set aside, but essential to its operations. It also kept up a steady correspondence with SCAP in which it continued to paint a rosy picture of how its products would soon be contributing to the revival of Japan's domestic economy and pleading with SCAP not to move ahead with the dissolution of the company.

Perhaps the most significant piece of correspondence from this period is the document that the company's new president, Dr. Masao Nagaoka, prepared for the Holding Company Liquidation Commission and which he delivered on March 8, 1948.[47]

In his report, he recounted the company's proud history and its attempts since the war to act as a good corporate citizen. His most important point was that if SCAP was to discourage production of this company "...decrease of exports, attended with a rise in prices [would result]. Thus an adverse effect to the cause of culturalization of this community and upon export trade will result in more loss than gain. It may be mentioned incidentally that the majority of the company's products are available for exportation and will more frequently be intended for foreign markets, leaving the domestic demands to the exploitation by competitors." Dr. Nagaoka went on to point out that NK could hardly be monopolistic due to the very nature of the optical industries. His points included: (1) While large investments were needed to develop the glass-smelting operations, even small shops with minimal capitalization could compete in the manufacture of eyeglass spectacles and simpler telescopes. (2) The optical industry was old and well established with glass and lens formulæ well known, precluding the use of a few patents to strangle competition. (3) NK had been big, but its expansion in the 1930s and during the war had been via expansion of its own facilities — not by taking over and eliminating rivals. (4) NK had always been only an optical firm. It would not be expanding into other products and industries and therefore pose a threat to other companies.

Dr. Nagaoka's statement was followed by a statement from the chief representative of the workers' union, who, while maintaining that management's statements were one-sided, nevertheless, backed up the position of the company. He joined in pointing out that NK did not have a monopoly on the production of optical glass and affirmed that the workers' jobs contributed to the democratic development of postwar Japan.

The report concludes with a list of the trademarked names that were part of NK's assets in 1948. While names like "Nikkor" (photographic lenses) and "Nikon" (Hand camera 35mm film) remain to this day, other names (Luscar, Mikron, Hermes, Capella, Spica, Nikoflex, Orion, Novar, etc.) are today lost to history, a record of a time when every NK product had a different name, a time before one product was to take over an entire company.

Although the parent Mitsubishi *Zaibatsu* was temporarily dissolved, most were not,[48] and in time the commission would conclude that while NK was the dominant force among Japanese optical companies, it did not control production and it was not preventing "the advance of other competition companies."[49] As discussed earlier, the growing political and economic crisis both in Japan and overseas was soon to change the entire attitude of GHQ, reshaping its purpose. As Robert A. Fearey reported in 1950, the goals of the first two years had been "liquidation of the war (demobilization, disarmament, repatriation, trial of war criminals, etc.) and the introduction of a democratic political, social and economic structure." By the end of 1947 these tasks had been largely completed and the Occupation had entered "...new phase ... in which the primary concern of the Occupation authorities became the acceleration of economic recovery and the consolidation and assimilation of the reforms introduced in the previous phase."[50] In reality, the reforms had helped Japan make giant strides toward becoming a more democratic society, but they were not putting food on Japanese tables. Further destruction of Japan's economic and industrial structure could only increase the threat of starvation and engender support for a growing leftist movement. The Allies had envisioned an occupation lasting a year or two, at most. The country would then get on with making its way, with the Japanese solving their own problems and with minimal aid from the United States. By December 1947, Japan's industrial output remained at only 45 percent of what it had been in 1934 and there were now 15 million more people — and growing rapidly. Inflation, particularly in wages, was driving up the cost of Japanese goods. Without its empire to guarantee both a source of raw materials and a ready market for its manufactured goods, Japan was having to sell to an open market, which was largely hostile to Japanese products. Japan could no longer compete on price alone. Products had to start showing some originality as well. In addition, the country had to figure out ways to generate the hard currency needed to buy the raw materials from abroad that were so essential to much of its manufacturing efforts. (Note that during this period, finished cotton goods were Japan's most important export product, yet all the raw cotton it needed to make these goods had to be imported, mostly from the United States.)

Unwilling to supply large amounts of aid to Japan indefinitely, on May 12, 1948, the Americans announced their intention to discontinue support for the reparations program. Although the SCAP teams would continue to monitor equipment that had been set aside for shipment abroad, NK had escaped the fate many other companies had suffered, and pricing reforms later in 1948 would make Japanese goods, particularly optical goods, more competitive both at home and overseas. The demand for optical glass was also beginning to expand and by July 1948, the company received permission to expand their production numbers for cameras from 300 per month to 500 per month. The quota for telescopes and scientific instruments — still mostly aimed at a domestic market — would be increased to 50 per month in each category. Binoculars and microscopes, the largest product categories after optical glass, were not affected by this change and continued to be the company's most important products.

One wonders if the engineers in charge of the camera project really believed that they had finished testing the prototypes in March 1948, or whether they simply decided to go ahead and start "regular" production to satisfy the demands of management. Certainly the camera was beginning to look like a never-show. It was already over a year late to market and NK's first ads were five months old. Nevertheless, March 1948 is generally regarded as the beginning of production of the Nikon camera, even though the records indicate that eight* cameras actually made it off the production line the previous month. All that spring and summer, the factory workers slowly continued to assemble cameras, some equipped with the 50mm f2 Nikkor lens, some equipped with the less expensive 50mm f3.5 Nikkor lens. Packed with a leather ever-ready case and instructions in pale yellow-striped boxes, the new cameras appeared to be of high quality.

Having decided that their camera was ready, NK had to figure out where and how to market it. Export was by now the obvious answer, but the company knew virtually nothing about selling overseas. Their earliest brochures are a reflection of this hesitation and confusion. Published in English, but still displaying the old Kanji characters and "Nikko" in its logo, the first "feature" the brochure mentions is the 24 × 32 format, which it states is a "More convenient form for picture trimming with the least waste of negative material."[51] The language indicates export, but this feature could appeal only to a domestic market.

The company was expected to use the *Boeki Kodan* for exporting and, unsure of proceeding on its own, NK entered into an agreement with the *Boeki Kodan* to supply that organization with 200 Nikons, 100 would be equipped with the f2 Nikkor and 100 would be equipped with the f3.5 Nikkor.

With a firm order in hand, the company concentrated its resources and had the necessary number ready for inspection in July. Only 70 passed the inspection and even these had enough defects that Arakawa indicates that the passing should have been "provisional"[52] Somehow the company managed to complete the 200 contracted cameras by

---

Numbers, numbers, numbers. Determining the actual dates and numbers for these early Nikons is an endless source of confusion and argument. In reality, no one seems to be able to agree on when the first production cameras made it off the line and how many were produced during this period. The SCAP report of "Actual Production and Distribution of Cameras" lists nine Nikons available for export as of March 31, 1948.

September 5, 1948. A total of 70 of these cameras were finished in the weeks of August 16 through 29 alone. Perhaps exhausted by this effort, NK would not complete another camera until September 19. That week, NK delivered the 200 promised Nikons to the *Boeki Kodan*. As it proved, these would be the only Nikons that NK ever sold through the trade corporation. The 100 50mm f3.5 Nikkors that went with half these cameras were almost the entire production run of that lens in the Nikon mount, making that formula one of the rarest of all Nikkors.

The 50mm f3.5 lens for the 35mm format had been the most common lens for the Leica cameras. Leitz would sell thousands of 50mm f3.5 Elmars. Zeiss also offered either a 50mm f3.5 or 2.8 Tessar as their entry level normal lens. The Elmar continued to sell well on Leicas all the way into the early 1950s. Yet only the very first Nikons ever came with an f3.5 lens. Why? Two answers: price and speed. The 3.5 normal lens was the least expensive lens and therefore the easiest way to purchase a Leica or a Contax. The Leica was selling on its name. For thousands of customers, the name was what was important, not the speed of the lens, and, because the Leica was expensive, going with a less costly lens still allowed customers to get the name they wanted. However, in 1948, the Nikon had no reputation. The company quickly discovered that if the name on the front of the camera meant nothing, the speed of the normal lens did. Customers were willing to take a risk and buy a Nikon because it offered the speed of an f2 lens. Export production records show only

| Manufacturer | Name of Camera | Preced- | For the Week | | Stock on | Stock at | Export | Remarks |
			Production	Export	Sunday	Boeki Kodan	Sales ('47–Oct. '48)	
Takachiho Optical Co., Ltd.	Olympus Chrome Six I	61	31	1 (IE301 USA)	91	0	21	
"	" II	2	2	0	4	0	0	
"	Olympus 35 I	23	0	1 (IE301 USA)	22	0	2	
Fuji Photo Film Co., Ltd.	Fujica Six IA	6	60	0	66	0	0	
"	" IB	2	0	0	2	0	0	
"	" IC	247	0	0	247	200	0	
Tokyo Optical Co., Ltd.	Minion III	338	0	0	338	78	407	
"	Minion 35 A	22	0	0	22	0	0	
Japan Optical Co., Ltd.	Nikon F/2.0	108	2	6 (Sample for Export)	110	100	10	
"	" F/3.5	100	0	20 (For Hongkong)	80	80	20	
Chowa Optical Co., Ltd.	Leotax	134	12	0	146	18	40	
"	Semi Leotax	208	27	0	235	50	54	
Kuribayashi Camera Works	Petri I	249	40	0	289	238	32	

Record of the first Sale and Export of the Nikon Camera. The SCAP camera and lens production record for "Japan Optical" for the week of October 18 to 24 1948, the *Boeki Kodan* shipped 20 Nikons to Hong Kong. Another 30 would follow the next week. All of these were equipped with the f3.5 Nikkor lens (National Archives).

123 50mm f3.5 Nikkors ever left the factory on a Nikon and none were sold separately. However, the company did make many more of this lens type in the Leica thread mount for Canons and later Niccas.

As good as its promise that it could sell the new camera, in late October 1948 the *Boeki Kodan* shipped 20 Nikons to Hong Kong for sale in that British crown colony. A week later it shipped out another 30. These would be the first Nikon Cameras sold.* Finally, two years after the camera's design had been approved, the Nikon camera was out in the world and in camera shops for customers to examine and purchase.

The result of this interaction was almost immediate and disastrous. One by one the new cameras started coming back from Hong Kong with jammed or erratic shutters, scratched film or loose helicals. In the end, many of these first 50 cameras would fail. The fate of these returned Nikons was to be sad. Placed in storage at Ohi, most were eventually destroyed to avoid the high inventory taxes all Japanese companies then had to pay. While the *Boeki Kodan* did eventually sell all but 70 of the 200 Nikons it had received, NK never dealt with the *Boeki Kodan* again. Whether this initial bad experience was a factor or whether the increasingly negative attitude of SCAP toward the *Boeki Kodan* was more important is difficult to determine. For whatever reason, NK decided that it would develop its own overseas markets and sales.

From October through the new year, NK engineers continued to struggle, trying to cure the problems that were plaguing their camera. Instead of concentrating on further sales, the company began sending out samples of its camera to the United States and elsewhere, inviting and urgently seeking feedback.

Sometime in the autumn of 1948, one of these new Nikons arrived in the camera repair shops of the Eastman Kodak Company in Rochester, New York. The technician there, R. A. Marjoram, examined this new camera (#609194),† disassembled it and then wrote a report on what he had found. This report[53] gives considerable insight into both the quality and the technology that was possible in Japan at that time, but it also points to many of the problems NK was facing. Sluggish grease, poor-quality coatings on the shutter curtains, low-grade metals and poor fitting parts were among the problems Marjoram listed. Soon his report was circulating among various dealers and would-be dealers throughout the United States — discouraging many from taking on a chancy product.

From September through the end of January 1949, NK would assemble 135 additional cameras beyond the 200 it had sent to the *Boeki Kodan*, completing its first production order for 300 cameras (#s609021–609320). Forty-two of these would leave the factory as "Samples." The *Boeki Kodan* sold another 40 of the cameras it had in stock: 20 went to Bangkok, Thailand, in early December and another 20 went to Singapore in mid–December, but NK itself would not sell any.

Perhaps feeling that it had done as much as it could with its new camera, perhaps

---

In e-mail correspondence with Robert Rotoloni (December 11, 2003), he expressed the belief that these cameras were actually sold through the trade house of Jardin Matheson, an international conglomerate still based in Hong Kong that had gotten its start in the opium trade.

†*Nikon #609194 is now in the collection of the International Museum of Photography at George Eastman House.*

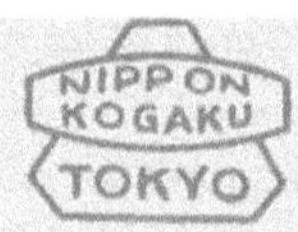

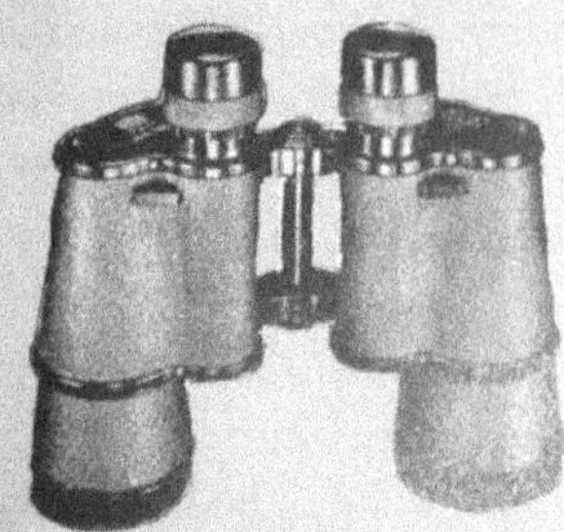

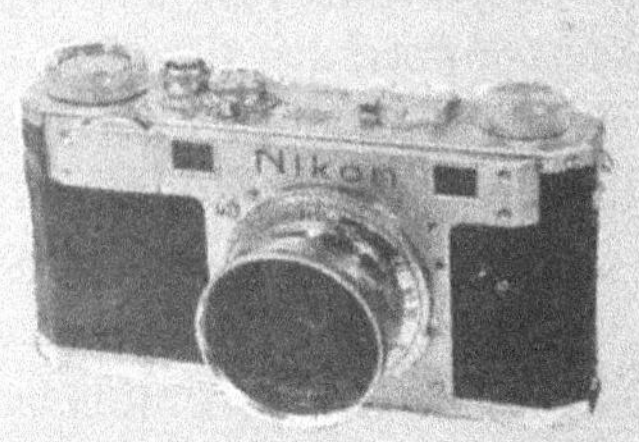

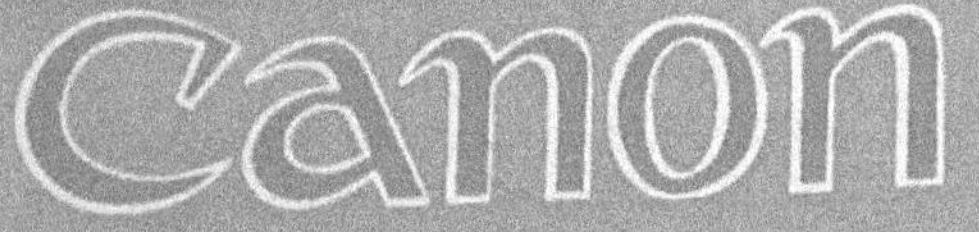

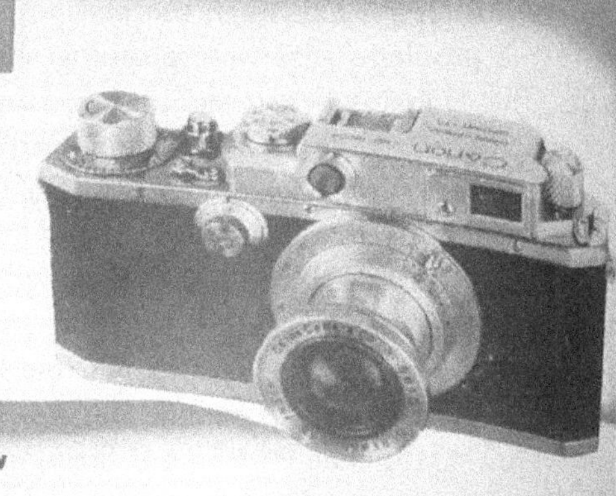

Top: "Japan Optical Co." advertisement for Novar binoculars and the Nikon camera that appeared in the English-language *Oriental Economist*'s publication *Japan's Export Industries* in 1949. Note the crude logo. This is one of only two camera advertisements in that book to appear in color. The other is for the Canon. The camera in the picture is a very early production unit, or one of the late prototypes. Note that it has eight screws securing the front escutcheon plate (The *Oriental Economist*, 1949). *Bottom*: The Canon ad from the same publication. Canon was (and is today) the Nikon's most important Japanese-made rival (The *Oriental Economist*, 1949).

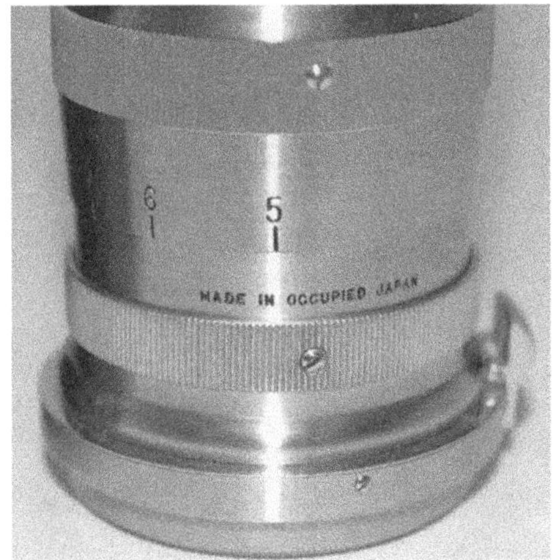
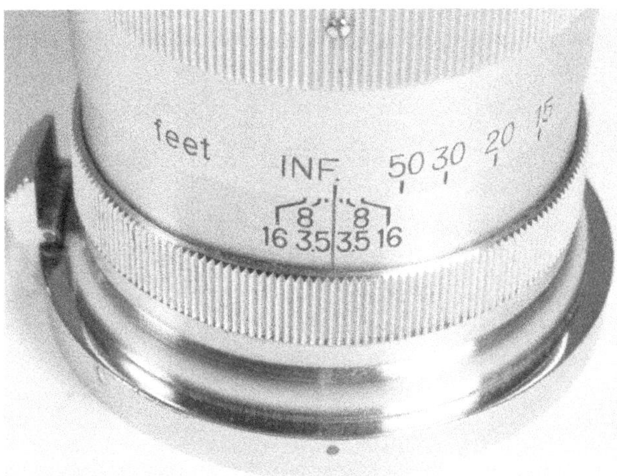

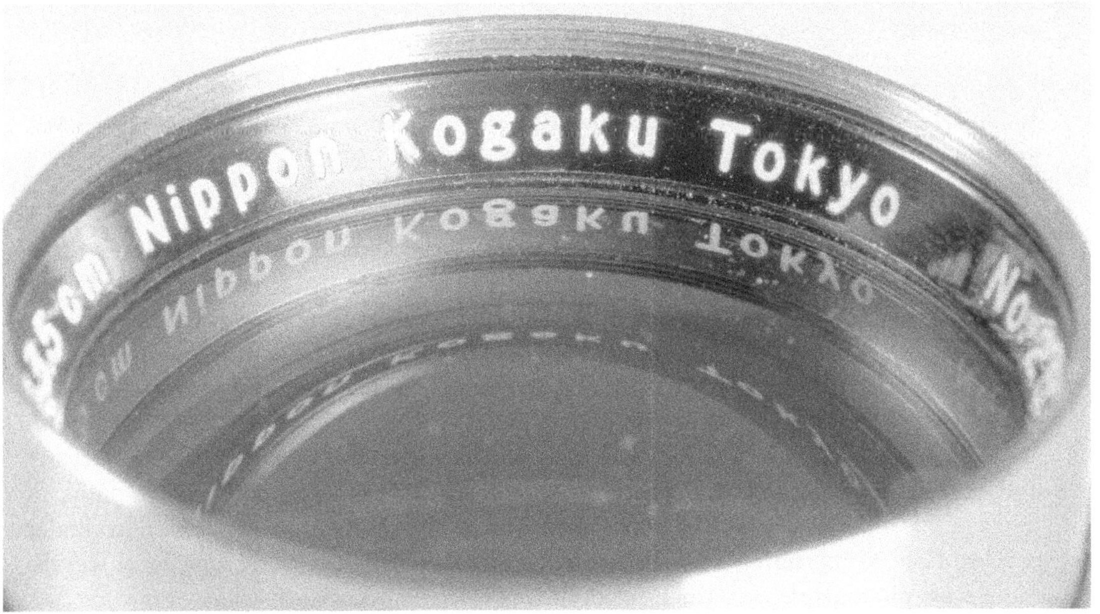

A 135mm f4 Nikkor from 1948–49 and a 135mm f3.5 Nikkor from 1951. The 13.5cm f4 Nikkor was the first accessory lens that NK made available for its new camera. It would become obsolete with the introduction of the faster 135mm f3.5 Nikkor in December 1950 and be discontinued in early 1951. Note that the beauty ring identification labels on both these lenses are engraved "Nippon Kogaku Tokyo." NK would replace the "Tokyo" with "Japan" on lens beauty rings in mid to late 1951. Note also the prominent "Made in Occupied Japan" engraved on the 135mm f4's lens barrel. NK continued to use the MIOJ mark well into 1951, even though less onerous "Made in Japan" or just "Japan" had been authorized in December 1949. However, the mark did eventually move to a barely noticeable engraving on the rangefinder connecting ring on the rear of the lens. Note the differences in the finishes of the two lenses. The f3.5 Nikkor with its sharper milling and smaller screws is a much-better finished product than the cruder f4 Nikkor on the left. Also note the depth of field marks go only to f16. None of the early Nikkors had smaller than f16 stops.

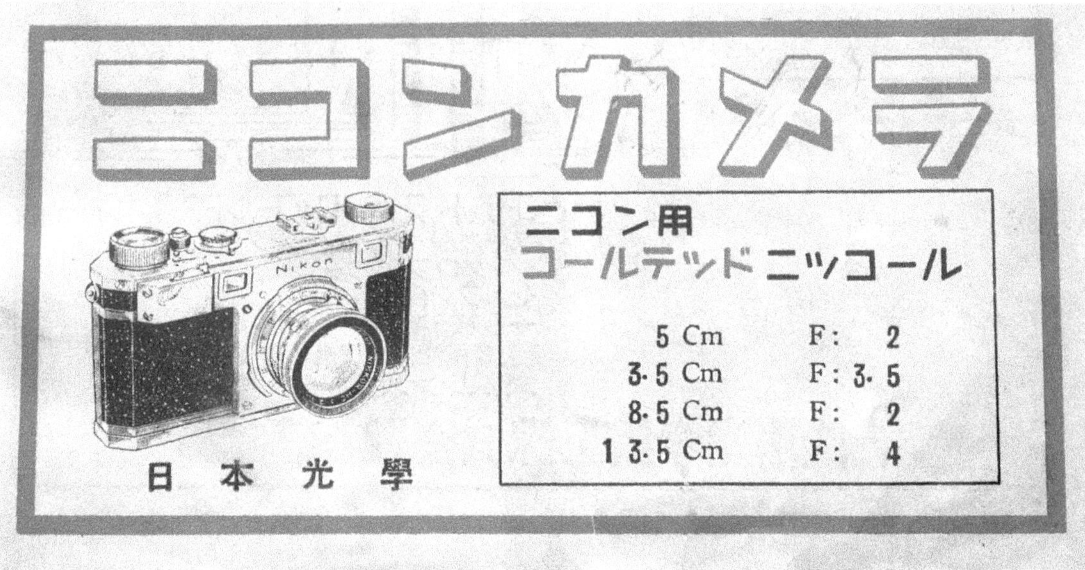

Another early advertisement for the Nikon camera. This may date from early 1950 when the 3.5cm wide-angle Nikkor was finally in production and the 5cm f3.5 had been dropped. The camera in the illustration is one of the early prototypes (courtesy Nikon Historical Society).

feeling that there might now be a market for additional lenses for what was, after all, an interchangeable lens camera NK in November began to offer its 135mm f4 Nikkor-Q in the Nikon mount. An exact duplicate of the fine 135mm Zeiss Sonnar lens of the same maximum aperture, the lens later sold well in both the Nikon and the Leica thread mount. Looking for any sales it could get, the company even made at least one copy of this lens in a mount for the Exakta single-lens reflex.

Why was the 135mm the first accessory focal length that NK chose to manufacture? Today, when most photographers think of interchangeable rangefinder 35s, they think in terms of high-speed normals and wide-angle lenses. The greater difficulty that rangefinder cameras have with framing and compensating for parallax when using long focal lengths cause most photographers to reach for their single-lens reflex.

A very different attitude prevailed in 1948. Wide-angle lenses were few and difficult for optical firms to design in such a way that pictures did not show noticeable light falloff at the edges. Telephoto lenses were simpler. Besides, getting closer was what people wanted to do. Candid and informal pictures were becoming the rage in 35mm and what better way than with a telephoto lens? Almost all camera manufacturers accepted 135 mm as the maximum focal length that the rangefinder could handle and still give some focusing accuracy.

By January 1949, NK finally had its newest product, the Nikon camera, in production and was exporting small numbers, mostly to Asian markets. The period of September 1945 through August 1948 had been the most difficult the company would ever experience. But if it could build an overseas market, it might be able to survive and grow. The question NK now had to face was how.

3

Creating an Overseas Market

Use of the *Boeki Kodan* had not proved very successful. With the trade corporations' dissolutions approaching, Nippon Kogaku had to confront the dilemma of how it was to continue to market and sell its products aboard. Finding a satisfactory overseas partner would remain the company's greatest concern until April 1950 when NK signed exclusive exportation agreements with two Swedish-owned exporting-importing companies. These two companies won the contracts because of the individuals involved, their abilities and their connections. Their actions and what they meant for NK's future and the Nikon camera are explained in this chapter.

Lindholm, Liholm and Gasser: The Three Most Important Players

Japan had been reopened to foreign trade in August 1947, but every would-be entrant seeking permission to negotiate trade agreements came only after getting permission from SCAP. And as John Gunther pointed out in his observant book on contemporary Japan, all were labeled as "traders" whether they were bankers, merchants, attorneys or professors.[1] Their numbers were limited, they could only stay in certain hotels and they paid much higher prices for everything than did military personnel. The only compensation any of these pioneers received was that they paid no local taxes. Until 1950, if they were American, they paid no American income tax on Japanese income either. SCAP wanted control and it was rightfully concerned about carpetbaggers and black marketers taking advantage of the postwar situation. MacArthur did not want anyone, particularly the communists, ever to be able to say that the Americans were exploiting the Japanese.

The SCAP records in the National Archives retain the paperwork for all the hundreds of "traders" that applied to SCAP for permission to reside and work in Japan. Many were representatives of book publishers, anxious to gain permission to publish Japanese-language versions of popular books.

Among these files is one for Horace Bristol, an American photojournalist who had worked for Time-Life before the war. He arrived in Tokyo on assignment for *Fortune* and decided he wanted to stay. His files* are an excellent example of the problems that all "traders" probably encountered as he sought permission both to get paid in dollars instead of yen (which could not be reconverted) and to enter into contracts with Japanese publishers. Bristol was living and writing in Japan, trying to sell his pictures and photographic services to Japanese publishers. SCAP denied him permission to do so because "...if correspondents are permitted to sell their material to Japanese publishers, it would be similar to granting any member of the occupation the right to sell their services to Japanese in Japan."[2] Bristol would reword his request and in May 1949, SCAP granted him permission to "Enter into contractual agreements with Japanese publishers for the use of literary material owned outright by the licensee...."[3] Bristol would still be in Tokyo a year later, writing about Japan and other Far East locations and taking pictures there for publications. His presence would be one of the key factors in what would happen in June 1950.

None of NK's personnel had been able to travel abroad since before the war. Nor had it been possible until 1948 due to SCAP regulations that actively discouraged Japanese nationals from leaving their country. In addition, the cash resources necessary to pay for such travel remained in critically short supply. As a result, NK had little idea what overseas markets were really like. So, to get started on direct overseas sales, it made contact with a Japanese national recently returned home from Stockholm named Shigero Sakai.*

Sakai had spent the war in Sweden where he worked as a go-between for Japanese companies and their German and Swedish counterparts. Much of his work involved procurement of various raw materials and finished goods that Japan itself could not supply, but which it needed for its war effort. With an English wife and himself conversant in English, Sakai moved easily in the European world. While in Sweden, he made the acquaintance of a businessman named Uno Lindholm.§

Lindholm was what Americans a generation ago would have called a high-class "wheeler-dealer." Adolph Gasser in an interview characterized Lindholm's business practices as "He would find out you needed a locomotive engine, sell you one, then go out and find the engine, buy it and deliver it to you." Lindholm thrived on contacts and bargains. He maintained no "accounts receivable" or inventory, relying for his successes on acting as a quick-action–reaction middleman via his various import-export brokerage firms, particularly his Stockholm-based company, the Western Trading Company, located on the prestigious Kungsgatan (King's Street).

The National Archives holds six folders on Bristol [ARC #s 321669, 321670, 322322, 322386, 322589, 322590].

†*Modern references to Sakai indicate that his given name was "Noae," but his own business card clearly shows that his given name was "Shigero," and that is what I use here.*

§*Except where noted, most of the information in this chapter is based on extensive interviews with Adolph Gasser and Hans Liholm conducted in 2003–05.*

For a business person such as Lindholm, postwar Japan looked like it could be a lucrative market indeed, and in 1948 he traveled to Japan where he touched bases with his old friend, Sakai. Sakai was by now operating in Japan on a basis similar to what he had been doing in Sweden: acting as an independent contractor and middleman between various Japanese companies and overseas importers. Sakai's exact role remains a bit of a mystery. He did not work for Nippon Kogaku. Both Hans Liholm and Nikon's archivist, Mikio Itoh, insisted that Sakai was working for Lindholm and Western Trading at this time. But Dr. Nagaoka, NK's president, and Sakai's own card identified him as the "Director" of the "Far East Mercantile Co." Gasser believed that Sakai worked for himself and was NK's "export manager." Whatever his status, Sakai would certainly act as the godfather for all of Lindholm's Japanese contracts over the next several years.

Sakai and Nagaoka had been middle school classmates and had remained friends. As a result, Sakai was well aware of NK's products. In fact, he had been in negotiations to export NK's products since the previous year, and by the spring of 1948 the "Manhattan Novelty Corporation, New York, the Allen Rhode & Co., Maryland, Foreign Trade Promoters, New York and E.L. Heymanson & Co., Australia"[4] had all expressed an interest in the new camera. Both Manhattan Novelty and Allen Rhode were already importing NK's binoculars, so adding the new Nikon to their product lines would have been a natural.

Sakai showed a sample of the new Nikon to Lindholm, who immediately decided that this was a product *he* wanted to sell, and that the United States would be the best place to do it. Accordingly, on his return trip home he stopped in San Francisco where on April 18, he hired a young Swedish citizen resident in the United States named Hans Werner Liholm to be the manager of a new company for North America.

Carl Liholm, Hans's father, also worked in the import-export business. His mother was German, but Hans's parents were divorced. Hans and his older brother had spent part of their earliest years in Germany before permanently settling with their father in Stockholm in the early 1930s. Liholm completed his schooling in Sweden at the Sigtunastiftelens Humanistiska Läroverk, graduating on VE day (May 8) in 1945 at the age of 20. He was offered a scholarship to attend the old and famous Lund University by its dean who had conducted the verbal examinations on graduation day. Instead, he applied to the Stockholms Handelshögskola where he scored 33 points (a very high score) on their entrance evaluation. "We could never refuse you," he was told, but the school officials recommended that he get some work experience first.

Accordingly, Liholm signed on as an all-around trainee with the Aktiebolaget Göteborg Bank. He soon moved into the foreign banking department where, within a month, his linguistic skills (he then spoke four languages — Swedish, German, French and English), knowledge of modern business practices and hard work led him to achieve the same productivity as many veterans who had been in that department for decades. As the Swedish economy began booming in the postwar period, Liholm prospered. Told that he was "Doing as good as any of our senior employees," Liholm suggested a deal: "If working like a senior, why not get paid as such? And would you please consider after an additional year or so in your foreign banking department, to get me a job in one of your correspondent banks

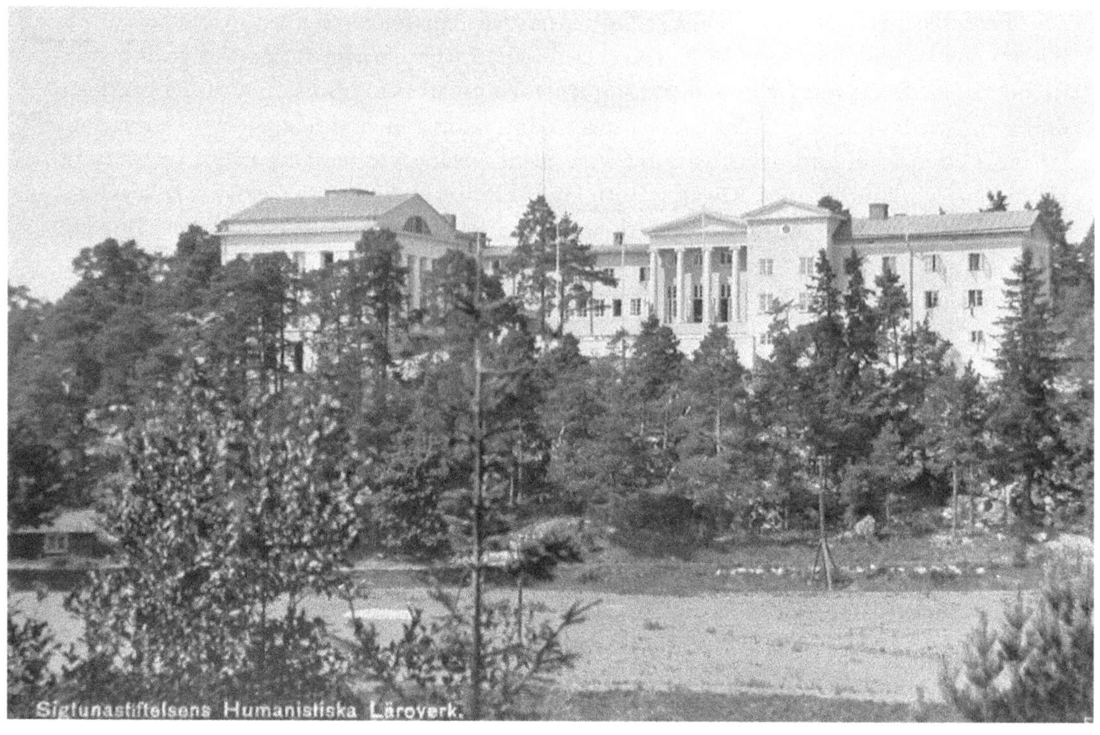

The *Sigtunastiftelsens Humanistiska Läroverk* where Hans Liholm attended high school and from which he graduated on VE day (May 8) in 1945 (photographer unknown, courtesy Hans W. Liholm).

in the United States, preferably San Francisco." The bank agreed, and Liholm stayed with them until the spring of 1947 when he left for the United States.

For Liholm, this was a dream come true. He shipped over in a converted Liberty ship, earning his way by painting and chipping paint en route. Arriving in San Francisco, he went to work for the Bank of America. He also took courses at the American Institute of Banking, picking up an understanding of American commercial law that would prove useful in his importation negotiations later.

Being in the same line of business, Carl Liholm knew Uno Lindholm personally. Learning of the entrepreneur's plans for developing an office and business in the Bay area, he recommended his son to Lindholm. When Lindholm stopped in San Francisco in April 1948, and met the young Liholm, he hired him to set up and manage this American sister company to Western Trading. Liholm, in turn, had Ken Ferguson, a prominent lawyer he knew through his bank work, register the new company with its headquarters in San Francisco. The company was to be called the Overseas Finance and Trading Company (usually referred to as OFITRA). Uno Lindholm was to be president; Ferguson was to be vice president and Liholm would be secretary, treasurer and manager. Or, as he explained it, "I was to do all the dirty work." Ferguson was never active in the company's operations. The company started as one office, staffed by Liholm, a secretary and a part-time bookkeeper. Soon it started importing NK binoculars and other optical goods and marketing them throughout the country. Still, selling the new camera to Americans was a primary goal for both OFI-TRA and NK from the very beginning.

Certainly Lindholm's timing was perfect. More and more American companies were getting interested in NK's more popular products. On February 8, 1949, NK was able to report to the minister of commerce and industry that it had a contract to deliver 1,500 pairs of binoculars to the J.M. Dinken Company in New York.[5] This would have been in addition to shipments it was already making to the companies mentioned previously. To meet this demand, NK was transferring part of its binocular production out to the Shiojiri plant and cutting back monthly microscope production at that location by half (from 200 to 100) in order to free up space.

Hans Liholm was apparently not working entirely alone in getting the new OFITRA and its contracts with Japan going. In the spring of 1949, Lindholm had another one of his agents, Arkadi M. Grekow [or Grekof] in Tokyo working on nonphotographic deals. Grekow and his wife secured permission from SCAP to come to Tokyo under both the "Western Trading" and the OFITRA masthead, and by that July he was arranging to barter

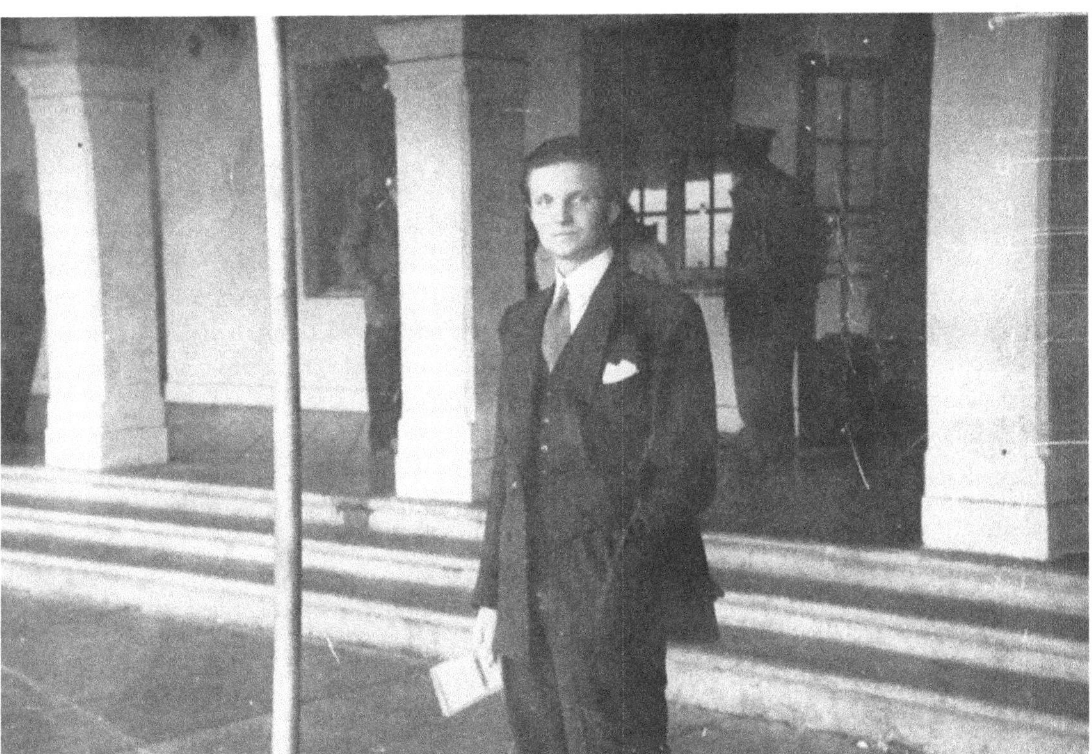

Hans Liholm in San Francisco in 1948. Uno Lindholm's inscription on the back reads: "I *San Francisco en morgon kl 5 a.m. fredagen* [Friday] *18/6 1948 Uno Lindholm.*" This was the day when Lindholm met Hans Liholm and began the organization of the Overseas Finance & Trading Company. Liholm was standing just outside Lindholm's hotel (Uno Lindholm photograph, courtesy Hans W. Liholm).

ZURICH   STOCKHOLM   TOKYO

OVERSEAS FINANCE & TRADING COMPANY INC

SAN FRANCISCO, 4

H. W. LIHOLM   465 CALIFORNIA STREET
SECRETARY-TREASURER   YUKON 2-3491

OFITRA's simple business card from 1948. Note that this card gives Liholm's title as "Secretary-Treasurer." In reality, he ran the whole business in San Francisco and "got to do the dirty work." His personal card identified him more accurately as "Manager" of the Overseas Finance & Trading Company (courtesy Hans W. Liholm).

the delivery of $197,000 worth of grade 9 sisal hemp for making rope to Japan in exchange for a delivery of Japanese steel to Brazil. In due course, Soares de Olveira & Cia delivered 2453 bales to Kobe on 11 August 1949.[6] Apparently the quality of the fiber did not meet the specified grade in many cases, resulting in letters back and forth to adjust the payments. While this had nothing to do with the Nikon, it appears to be typical of the way Lindholm operated and the way bartering was used for most trade transactions then occurring with Japan. It also appears typical of the free use that Lindholm made of various company names, first using one, then the other as the occasion or need arose.

Liholm and OFITRA (S.F.) were not just acting as a Japanese goods importer either. Liholm noted that during his time with the company, he also imported and attempted to market a number of Swedish inventions including "a high quality slide rule, a non screw tube cap, [and] a fishing reel."[7] Apparently none of these ideas pressed on Liholm by the ever-hopeful Lindholm were successful.

In the meantime, Liholm was in contact with Sakai and NK's management. In early 1949, Dr. Nagaoka got special permission from SCAP to fly to the United States to meet with the various importers who were selling his company's products. He first flew to San Francisco where he met and interviewed Liholm. Liholm picked Nagaoka up at the airport and lodged him in the Fairmont Hotel. The two conferred for several days before Nagaoka flew on to New York City where he met with other would-be importers. Liholm, young and with only a small company to offer, had his work cut out convincing Nagaoka that OFITRA could make things happen for NK. But apparently the interview went well because in February 1949, NK shipped 24 Nikons—12 with the f2 lens, 12 with the f3.5 lens—to the United States. The *Boeki Kodan* supplied the cameras with the f3.5 lens and NK supplied the cameras with the

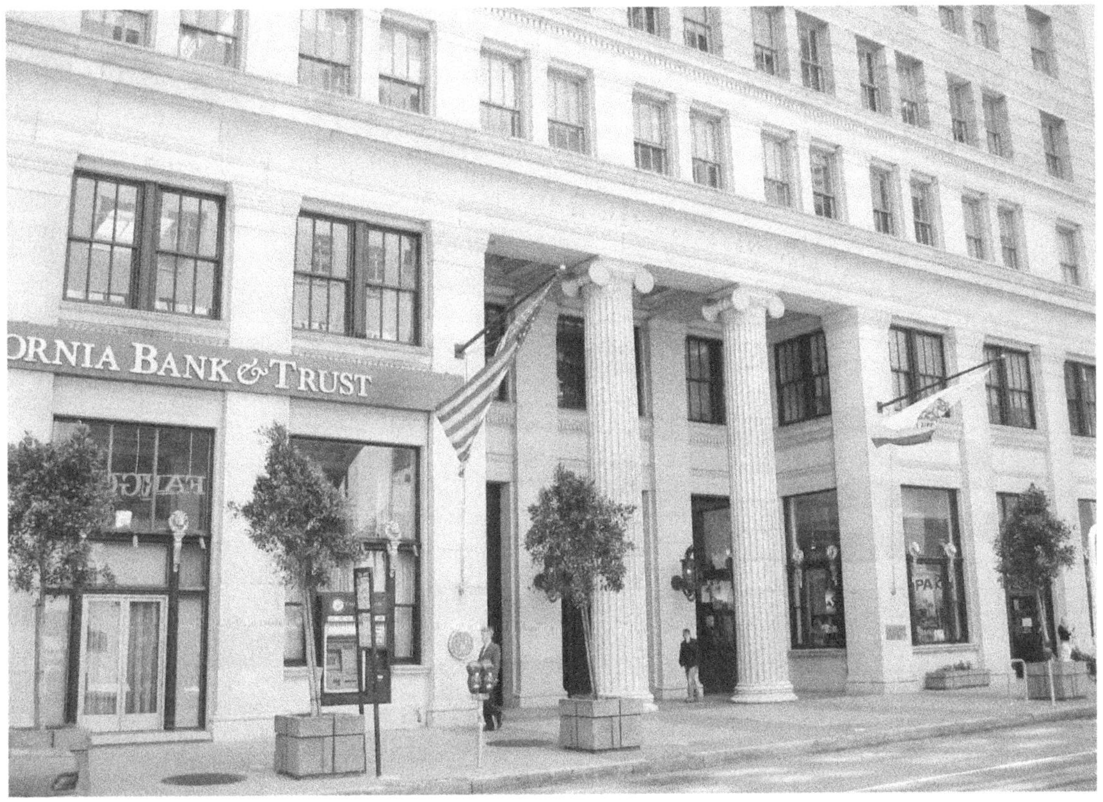

Where it all began: The Merchant's Exchange Building on California Street in downtown San Francisco. The Overseas Finance & Trading Company had offices here from its founding in 1948 through 1951 (Theodore C. Loder IV photograph).

f2 lens directly.* In March, an additional 17 cameras followed and in April another 27 traveled by ship to America. Between February and May 30, NK exported a total of 72 Nikons to the United States — not counting the many samples that also went to America. OFITRA received all 72. But the May shipment was to be the last. What happened? The answer appears to be the camera that Adolph Gasser examined in his shop.

Liholm characterized himself as only an "informed amateur" when it came to photography, but he had certainly entered into the importation of NK's products professionally. Since setting up OFITRA, he had received and successfully marketed hundreds of NK's binoculars. He learned about a report on the Nikon that was supposed to be of help in selling the camera to dealers and ordered a copy. It is possible that this was a copy of the Marjoram report. Whether it was or not, it proved to be a huge disappointment, for all the report did was point out the camera's problems. Again and again, Liholm approached dealers, asking only that they at least look at the camera and give it a chance. Few doors

In the end, the last 26 Nikons with the f3.5 lens all went to India in one shipment in late March. The 70 f2 Nikons still with the Boeki Kodan *returned to NK with termination of the* Boeki Kodan *in May 1949.*

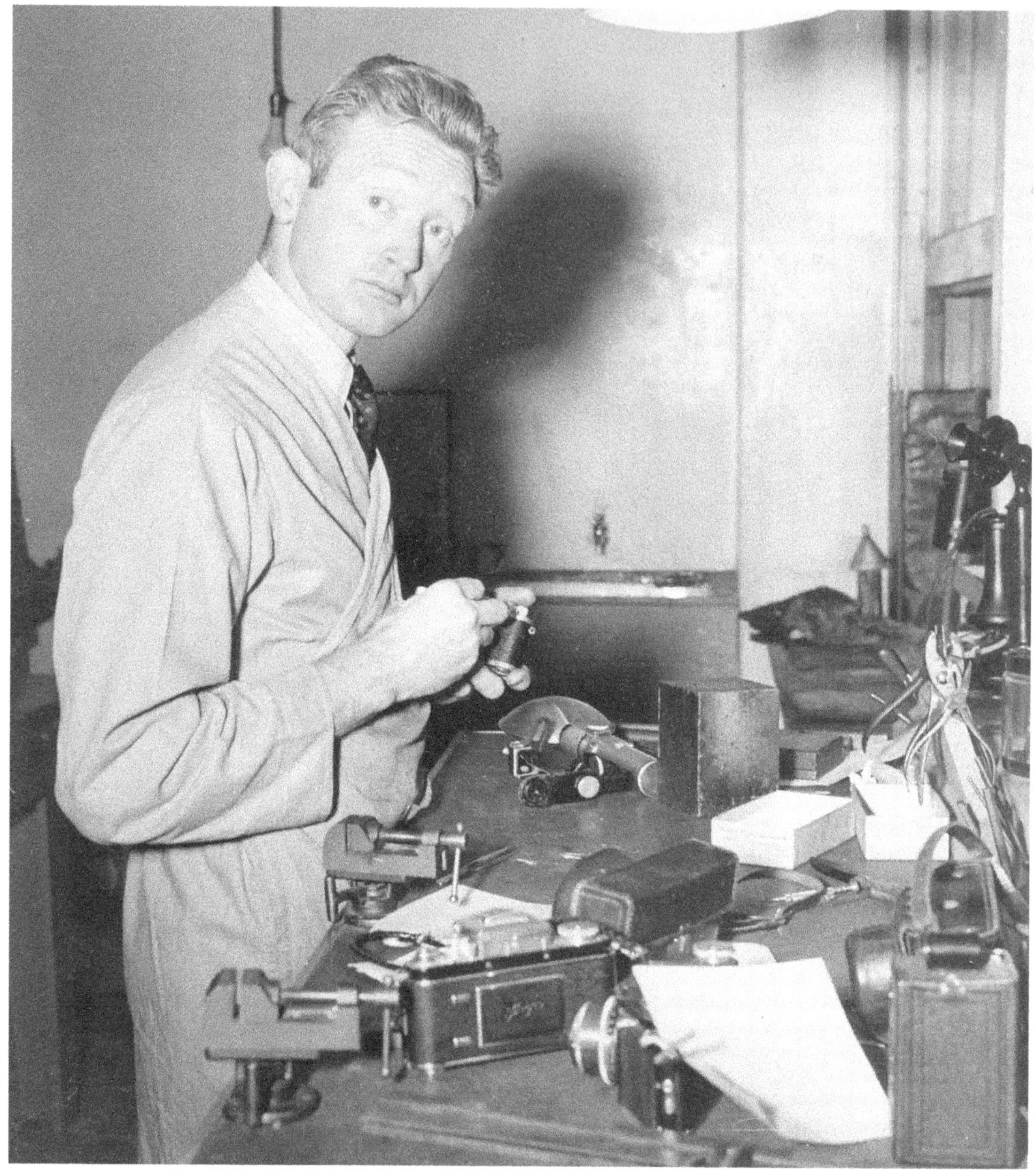

A young camera repairman: Adolph Gasser sometime in the 1930s (photograph courtesy of John Gasser).

opened. Reactions varied from "Get that Japanese junk out of here" to "Leave us alone." Realizing that he needed some kind of service organization that could repair and guarantee the Nikon locally, Liholm began searching for someone who could inspect the incoming cameras and provide expert technical advice. He soon contacted the one person whom everyone agreed would set him straight: Adolph Gasser.

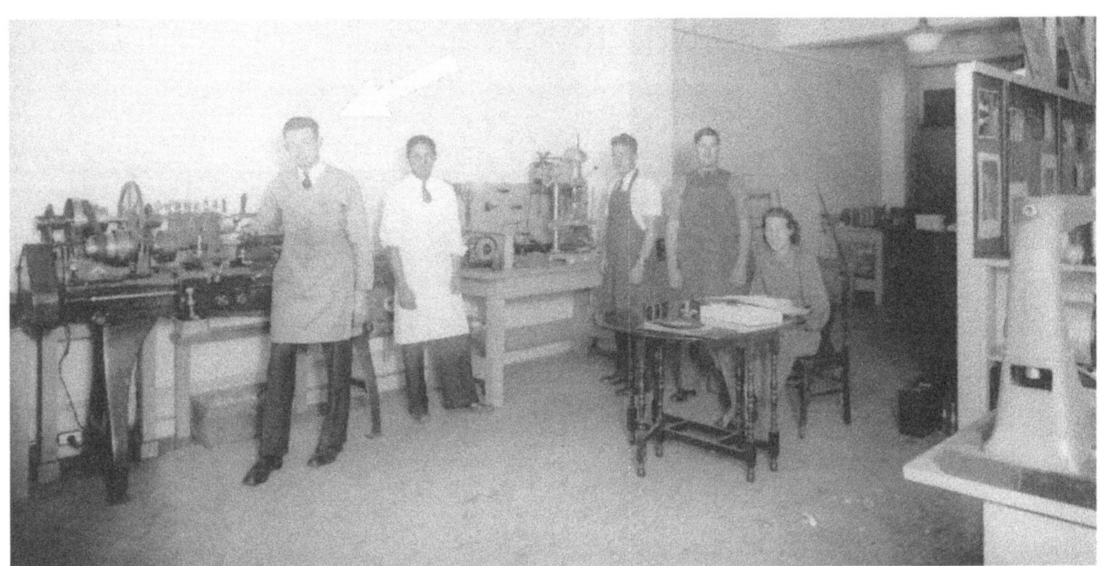

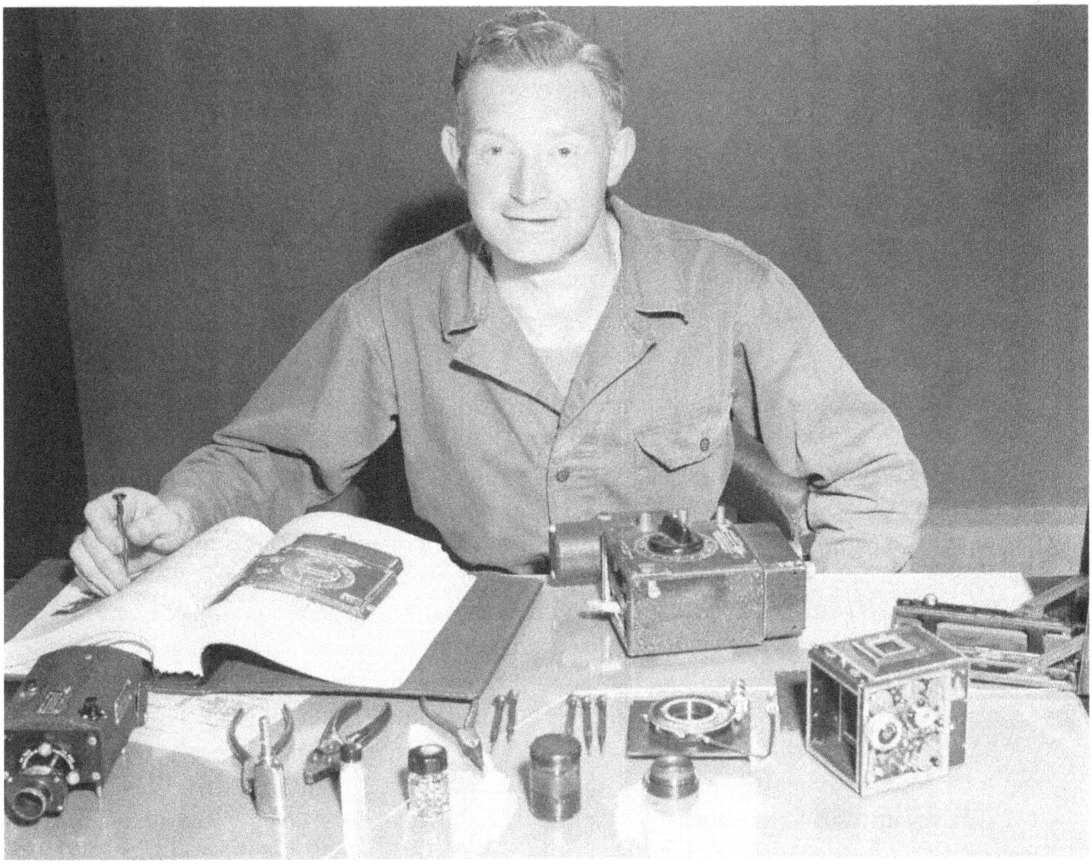

Top: The interior of General Camera Repair, San Francisco, in 1939. The arrow points to Adolph Gasser standing on the left. *Above*: Adolph Gasser seated with the tools of his trade in Colorado Springs (photographs courtesy John Gasser).

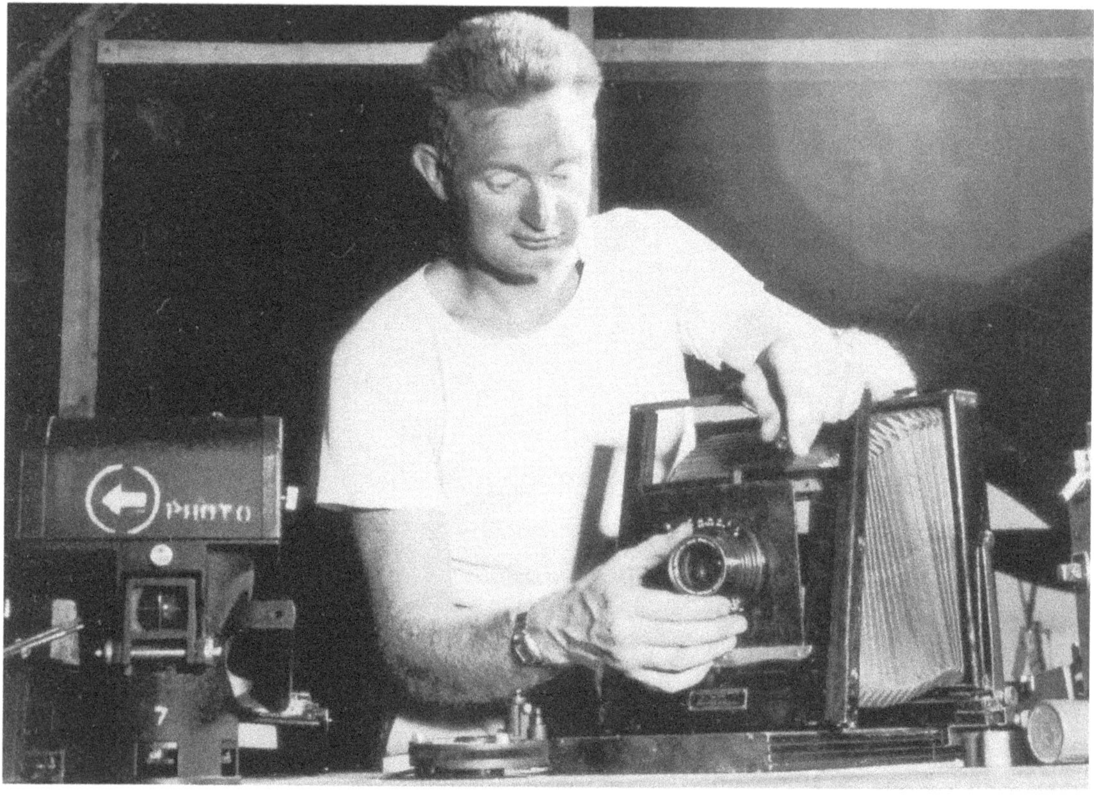

Corporal Gasser at his work bench at Wendover Air Force Base, Salt Lake City (photograph courtesy John Gasser).

Gasser was a San Francisco native. He had graduated from the Rochambeau Polytechnic High School in 1929. With the Great Depression starting and his parents divorced, there were no funds for furthering his education, so Gasser took an apprenticeship as a camera repairman at Charman's Camera Works. He worked there for two years, earning $12.50 a week while continuing to live with his mother. He described how "Ten dollars went to his mother [for room and board], 50 cents went in the bank" and "the rest I could use for pleasure." After two years at Charman's he switched and took a job with Charman's rival where he worked another 18 months. He then took a position at Haloid, a company that made photographic paper in competition with Photostat. By 1937 he had saved the enormous sum of $700 and he decided to get married and set up his own camera repair business. He was then 26 years old.

Although his business prospered, by 1943 Gasser was not a happy man. He was having some marital difficulties and with the war in full swing, he felt that he had to do his part. He volunteered for the Army Air Corps. By some fluke, he was rated as a camera repair technician and assigned to Colorado Springs where he came under the command of an officer named Jerome Ossip. Captain Ossip may have been rated as a photo officer, but he knew next to nothing about photography. He quickly figured out that Gasser did, so when the unit in Colorado Springs was broken up, he made sure that Gasser went with him to

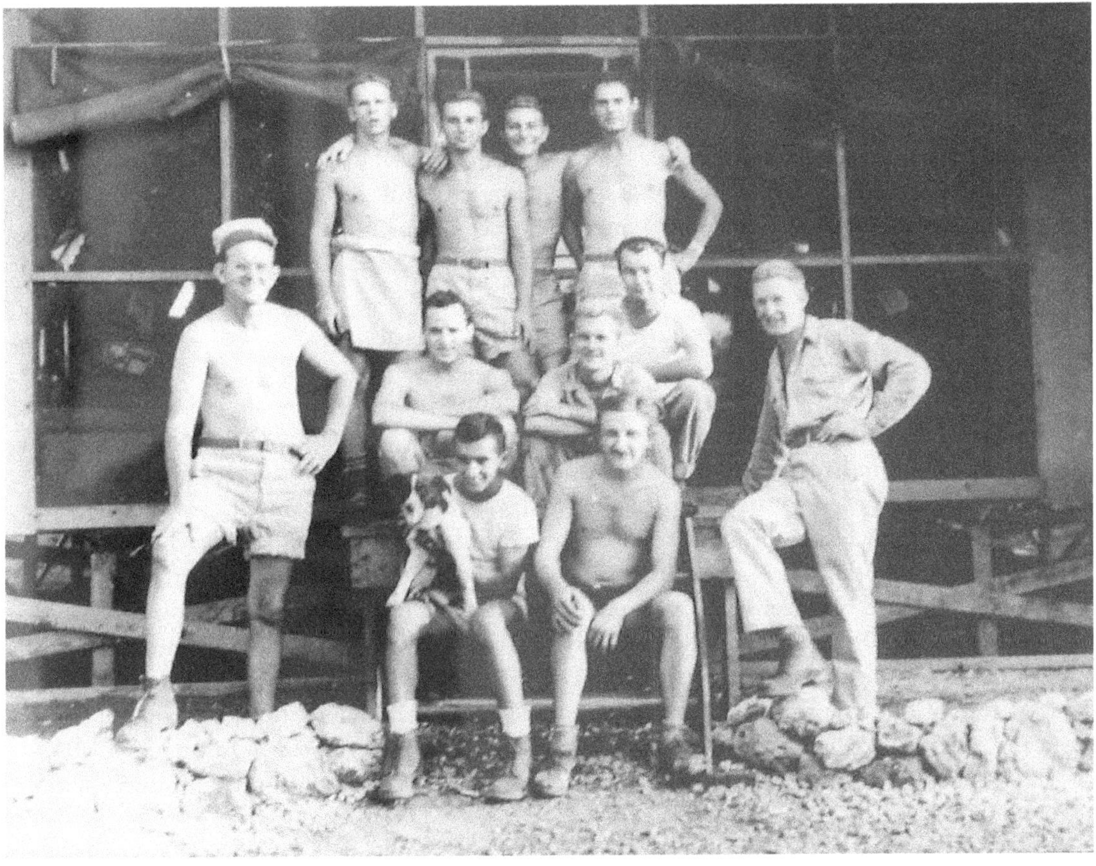

Adolph Gasser (standing right with hand on hip) with fellow members of the 509th Composite Group on Tinian Island in 1945. Thirty-one years old at the time, Adolph was proud that he could easily keep up with the younger airmen (photographer unknown, courtesy John Gasser).

his new assignment with the 509th Composite Group being organized at Wendover Air Base near Salt Lake City. From there, they would travel by boat to the small island of Tinian, located three miles away from Saipan in the Marianas.

Tinian had been an important Japanese base, but the navy and marines had captured it in July 1944, and the Americans had since turned it into a major air facility located a "mere" 1,500 miles from Tokyo. The 509th was flying the big, new B-29 bombers with their polished aluminum hulls. Assigned to the 390th Air Service Group, Gasser shared Quonset huts with four other men right next to the runway where they spent their time repairing and maintaining aerial cameras and loading and unloading film magazines. They would mount these cameras in the planes and unload the film when the planes returned from their bombing runs over Japan. On August 6, 1945, Gasser handed a K20 aerial camera to Staff Sergeant George Caron, the tail gunner of the B-29 named the Enola Gay as it prepared to leave for its mission over the Japanese city of Hiroshima. Caron insisted that he knew "nothing about photography" but Gasser showed him how to sight the camera, shoot it and advance the film, and told him he would do fine. Caron used that camera to take the widely published picture of the mushroom cloud resulting from the atomic bomb dropped that day.

At the war's end, Gasser was reassigned to Roswell Air Base in New Mexico where he shortly arranged his own discharge. He returned to San Francisco and reopened his shop. By 1949, he had the largest and best shop in the city. But he was also looking for other opportunities. He saw in this new camera one such opportunity.

Modification of the Nikon Camera

Taking Gasser's advice to heart, Liholm reported back to Sakai and Nagaoka on the problems that Gasser had detailed [see introduction], and requested that NK redesign the camera.[8] Liholm had only sold about 25 Nikons up to that point, and it remains unclear as to what happened to the other cameras he had received. What was clear was that OFI-TRA would not be accepting any more cameras unless changes were made. To emphasize that point, Liholm told Nagaoka that "It can't be sold" with the 24 × 32 format.

NK had to decide what it wanted to do. If the United States was going to be cool to its camera, then the camera would have to change. Gasser had already provided NK with the simple solution to the company's dilemma. He may even have modified one or more of the Nikons to the 24 × 34 format himself. Liholm, in turn, sent one of those cameras back to Japan to show the NK engineers what Gasser meant. On August 4, 1949, NK swallowed its pride, accepted the American recommendations, stopped production and retooled.

Supposedly, 738 of the first model Nikon had been built, with the 20 prototypes bringing the total up to 758 (or 759, depending on where #60921 falls). In reality, that total never existed. The SCAP export production records indicate that 592 made it out of the factory and into marketing, and that is probably the more accurate figure [See Appendix 1]. Scores of the new cameras never worked, were never offered for sale and later destroyed. Except for 12 shipped to Vancouver, Canada, at the last minute, the 154 plus unsold cameras still at the Ohi plant in August were converted to the next model. (These all received new top plates and backs and the replaced parts were discarded, so those model I serial numbers are gone. It is possible that over 200 Nikons ended up being converted.) The *Boeki Kodan* had sold 130 of the Nikons it had received. Except for 78 samples, NK sold the rest through its own sales efforts. Hong Kong, with a total of 233 sales, received by far the most. The United States was next with 72. India with 26 and Canada with 25 were next. Belgium, Singapore and Bangkok each took 20. Sweden got two. Only nine went to domestic sales, all institutions: The government bought four in May and a university, a laboratory and a hospital bought a total of five in June.

Overall, the first Nikon camera could receive only a grade of "C" at best. Although Majoram admitted that the camera he examined was among the best he had seen come out of Japan, this was damning with faint praise. The basic design was good, the ideas expressed in the camera were good, but the execution was simply not up to the standard that an American buying public expected — even from Japan. NK needed to produce a camera that was reliable and easy to fix.

The Nikon production had never even gotten close to the 300 or 400 per month NK had predicted. The months of January and May 1949, with runs of 108 and 86, respectively, were the best of a sorry lot. Still, the news was not all bad. The company was trying and it was learning from every sample report and every broken, returned camera. Dr. Nagaoka, with a scientist's zeal for facts and data, kept insisting that every rejected camera had to be investigated. The company had to know what it was doing wrong in order to get it right. Comparing a late production run Nikon I with a prototype or one of the cameras from the beginning of production makes the differences in quality, particularly internally, immediately apparent. The later cameras look better and handle better. Further improvement would soon come with the next model.

The accessory lenses for their 35mm camera were one area still with untapped potential. NK had started production of the 135mm f4 the previous November as already noted. Following the pattern already established with their camera, NK began marketing this lens by shipping out samples in January 1949 when it had over 100 of the new optic on hand. In April it began exporting this lens to the United States. It also began manufacturing its 85mm f2 Nikkor. In May, four 135mm Nikkors went to the United States along with two of the new 85s. More sample shipments continued throughout that summer. If NK's personnel did not know much about camera mechanics, they did know optics. When the demand was there, they could manufacture lenses a lot faster and in greater numbers than they could cameras.

It also understood what it had to do to make its lenses more competitive. On August 15, it was petitioning Tokyo's Civil Affairs Team for permission to remodel parts of the Ohi plant to allow installation and conversion of machines used in making lens barrels. By installing and powering lathes so that they spun at 1,200 RPM instead of only 800 RPM, the displacement of the spindles could be reduced from 50mm to 32mm and the eccentricity of the barrels and other machined parts could be reduced from $\frac{1}{100}$ of a millimeter to $\frac{3}{1000}$ of a millimeter.[9] Quality was increasingly the name of the game and NK was determined to get there.

The biggest change that NK made to its camera in 1949 was the modification of the gearing and film gate to allow a standard advance and a wider picture. The gap between frames was still wider than a standard 24 × 36 camera, but once a transparency was placed in a slide mount, it would hardly be noticeable.

The designers took the opportunity to make other changes and improvements. Following Gasser's recommendations, they deepened the tripod mount and inserted a $\frac{3}{8}$-inch thread chrome-brass bushing. This, in turn, received a quarter-inch threaded bushing locked in place with a set screw. A permanently mounted film takeup spool that removed a lot of the fumble-finger work of loading film became standard, replacing the easily lost or dropped separate spool the first Nikons had featured. A raised frame appeared on the removable backs marking the place for an oversized, reinforced pressure plate. Perhaps as a sign of Japan's growing confidence in itself, the "Made in Occupied Japan" engraving that had appeared so prominently on the bases of the first cameras slowly shrank. In another year it would move to an almost unnoticeable stamp in the leather on the camera's back.

NK resumed camera production in late August 1949, and in October it began releasing its new and improved camera. To make sure that dealers and customers would be able to tell the new model from the old model, all the remaining top plates were pulled out and the letter "M" was engraved before every serial number.* This then became the "Nikon M" and this was the camera that would bring NK fame and, ultimately, fortune.

Into Winter 1950, the Ciné Nikkor and Cash Flow at Last

Export sales of the new model camera remained nonexistent during the fall of 1949. NK continued to produce an average of 20 to 50 new cameras a month, but it appears that both NK and OFITRA were working on other plans. These would soon bear fruit.

One of the problems that had still not been overcome was the apparent unwillingness of the CPO (Central Purchasing Office) to accept the Nikon for sale in the military exchanges. It is not clear who was making that decision, but the 24 × 32 format of the former Nikon may have been the problem. What confuses this issue is that several sources state that the GHQ or SCAP would not "permit export of the Nikon I, and the CPO hesitated to place the order."[10] Since virtually all the first model Nikons that were sold *were* exports, these statements cannot be correct as written. But another interpretation is possible. Sales to the CPO for the military exchanges were considered "exports" (and were just as free of excise taxes as the "exports" to Hong Kong or the United States). While SCAP may not have concerned itself with what types of cameras were headed to the United States, it would certainly have been concerned with the cameras that were going into the PXs for soldiers to buy. Despite an extensive search of both the SCAPINs (regulations issued by SCAP to control Japanese business activities) and the SCAP records in the National Archives, we have found no order forbidding either the overseas export or the sale of 24 × 32 cameras in the exchanges. In 2004, Nikon archivist Mikio Itoh admitted to the author that Nikon, Inc. did not have a written record of such a ban.[11] No contemporary records mention such a ban. OFITRA was the organization rejecting export of the Nikon to the United States — not GHQ. This does not mean that such an order did not exist. It just means that it may not be locatable at present. For whatever reason, the first model Nikon did not sell in the military exchanges nor, apparently, did many of the other 24 × 32 format cameras of that period. (The Minolta 35, also a 24 × 32 format camera, did sell in the PXs.) CPO sales were where the money was. NK was heavily dependent for its very existence on its

---

Apparently the company ordered at least 4,000 top plates for its new cameras with numbers running from 6091 to 6094000. When the company finally used up all these plates, it ordered more but soon decided not to bother to add the "M" to the new serial number series. Only Nikons as high as 6094125 have been found with the "M" suffix.

Various theories have been advanced explaining what the M stood for. "Modified" is usually the accepted term. Others have suggested that the "M" points out that the camera's format was midway in width between the "L" or Leica format of 24 × 36 and the "N" or Nippon format of 24 × 32, but it would be highly unlikely that NK would have wanted to point out that their camera was still not the standard size.

- 4 -

Shipment of 15,000 pieces of these
movie camera lenses will be made to
the Overseas Finance Company within
this year, and a contract covering
60,000 to 70,000 is under way.

9. Proposed changes in manufacturing facilities:

No change is planned in manufacturing facilities.
Shuffle in production setting and advanced manufacturing skill and efficiency in management will
combine to take care of the proposed increasing manufacture.

10. Expenditures with respect to conversion:

No expenditures to be incurred.

11. Plan and location at which to continue production
after removal of reparations equipment:

Should reparations removal be enforced, the
Company would completely lose its production facilities
because its entire factories are held on reparation.

However, the Company would strive to continue its
operation with some changes in production items if
necessary, resulting from difficulty in duplicating
some high accuracy machines.

NIPPON KOGAKU KOGYO K.K.

M. Nagaoka, President

Documentation of Liholm's First Big Success. Part of a letter President Nagaoka sent to the minister of international trade and industry on October 20, 1949, noting the deal with OFITRA that would allow the sale of thousands of Ciné Nikkors (National Archives).

binocular sales to the CPO. Canon was making and selling hundreds of its cameras to the CPO. If NK's camera was to survive, the company had to get it into those stores.

In the meantime, Liholm was working on other ideas. The American market for the Nikon camera still did not look good, but OFITRA was now firmly and completely committed to NK for its future existence. Liholm began looking at the company's other products. NK's binoculars were proving successful, but several importers were bringing these in. Liholm wanted something that he could handle exclusively. He found it in NK's 13mm f1.9 Ciné Nikkor.

In another letter in the continuing series addressed to government authorities — this time to the minister of international trade and industry dated October 20, 1949 — NK once more requested permission to expand its product numbers. Among these requests was one for increasing production levels from 3,000 to 4,000 and up to 7,000 for photographic lenses. Like NK's earlier requests, this appears wildly optimistic until one reads the last note that followed. "8mm lenses F:1.9, F:1.5 for movie cameras are made exclusively for export as a new promising item in this line. Shipment of 15,000 pieces of these movie camera lenses will be made to the Overseas Finance Company within this year, and a contract covering 60,000 to 70,000 is under way."[12] This is the earliest record in the SCAP archives connecting OFITRA with NK. Following the Lindholm pattern of doing business, Liholm had negotiated a one-time contract with the Revere Movie Camera Company for 15,000 13mm f1.9 Ciné Nikkor lenses to go on some of its 8mm movie cameras.

At that time, Chicago was an important American center for photographic equipment manufacture. Home of Revere Camera and the Wollensak lens company (among others), the Windy City would see a lot of inexpensive cameras and lenses go out to American buyers before the Japanese finally put most of these companies out of business in the late 1950s and early 1960s. Revere Camera manufactured a wide range of 8mm and 16mm amateur and advanced amateur movie cameras and movie projectors. With cast aluminum bodies and spring-wound motors, their cameras were similar in appearance to the highly regarded Bell & Howell movie cameras, felt solid in the hand and yielded competent home movies for thousands of American families. Most of their 8mm movie cameras came with 13mm f2.5 Wollensak Raptar lenses. The faster Ciné Nikkors that would now be available for their cameras went on the more expensive models, particularly the Model B63s, which sported a three-lens turret.*

Liholm's deal with Revere was to prove to be a critical move for both OFITRA and NK. Liholm made the sale by loaning a 13mm Ciné Nikkor to Harry Mazur, a well-known professional freelance photographer based in Los Angeles. Mazur used the lens to make movies of a variety of subjects, including a night shot of the Camel cigarette billboard in Times Square, New York City. Mazur and Liholm then made an appointment to meet with Sam Briskin, president and founder of the Revere Camera Company.† They showed the movies to Briskin and two technicians. Briskin was impressed and eventually agreed in a written contract to take the 15,000 Ciné Nikkors.

Determined to gain NK's confidence, Liholm took the process one step further. Knowing how strapped for cash NK was, he arranged a line of credit through friends at the Bank of America so that NK would have cash to draw on to cover the manufacturing costs of the lenses.

Only one hurdle remained. Revere, well aware of the reputation of Japanese goods,

*Briskin sold the Revere Camera Company to 3M in 1960. The company was still selling Revere-brand digital cameras and batteries to fit them in 2006.

†A self-made man, Briskin had come to America from Kiev in the Ukraine in 1914 at age 17. He also founded Wollensak Recorders and Opticals, the manufacturer of the Raptor lenses. He became one of Chicago's leading philanthropists before his death in 1961.

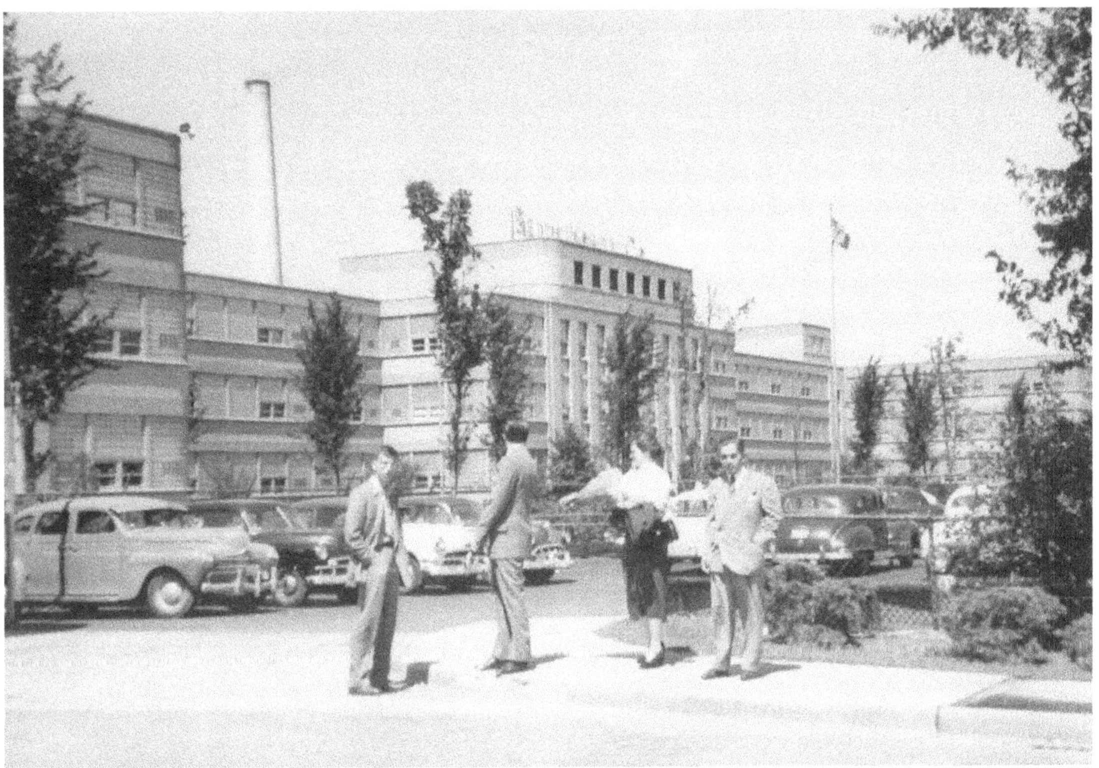

The outside of the Revere Camera Company factory as it appeared in 1949. The identity of the three men is not known for certain, but Liholm may be the taller man in the middle with his head turned away. The woman standing in the foreground is Barbro Nyberg, Liholm's companion and later his first wife (photographer unknown, courtesy Hans W. Liholm).

did not want the lenses to show any indication as to their place of origin. NK, proud of its name and product, was equally insistent that "Nippon Kogaku" had to be on its lenses. Finally, NK agreed to restrict the NK logo to the rear lens caps and add the name "Revere" to the lens inscription. Revere was delighted. Once they received the lenses, they promptly mounted the lenses on their cameras, discarding the rear caps in the process.

By December 1949, NK had produced 3,550 of these lenses and immediately shipped 2,550 of them to the United States. Over the next half year, NK would churn out another 24,450 of these little lenses in "D" mount. In the end, NK made 28,000 13mm Ciné Nikkors during the Occupation period and Revere bought every one. While it only took in seven dollars per lens, multiply this by the sheer numbers produced and one can understand the big difference in cash flow that this one deal yielded for both OFITRA and NK. NK was still having trouble getting as many as 50 cameras built in a month, but it could produce thousands of lenses of good quality when the sales were there to drive the production — and when cash was available to pay the workers.

In addition to the Ciné Nikkor contract, OFITRA was working out a deal to take over the importation of NK's vertexometer (lensmeter or lensometer) into the United States.

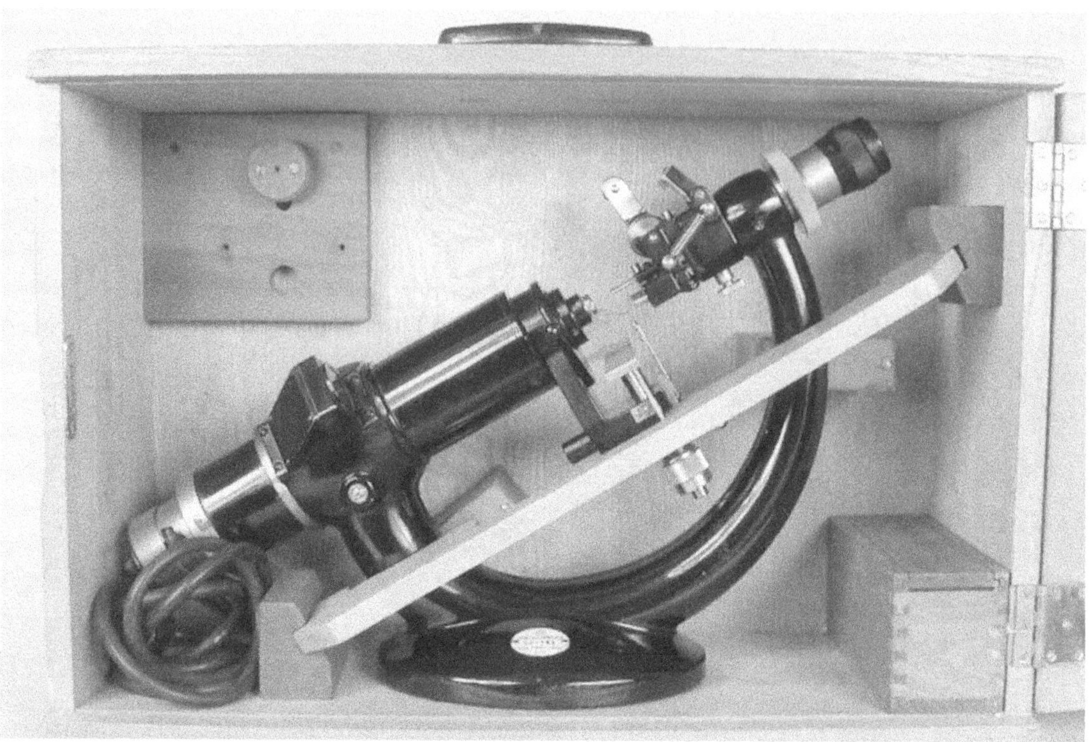

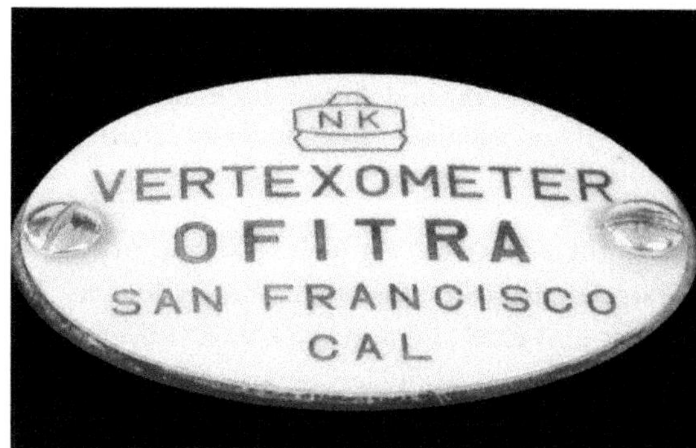

An early Occupation period Nippon Kogaku-made vertexometer in its wooden storage case. This is one of the hundreds of vertexometers (or lensometers) OFITRA imported between 1949 and 1951. Note the prominent "OFITRA" label on the instrument's base. Opticians use lensometers to measure the strength and correction of eye glass lenses. Liholm's successful marketing of this device helped build a market for NK's professional optical instruments (Mike H. Symons photographs).

Lensmeters were (and are) optical measuring instruments used by opticians to measure the strength and correction of eye glass lenses. They are the most fundamental of all instruments that optometrists and opticians use every day in their business. Until 1949, their production and sale had been virtually a monopoly of the Rochester-based Bausch & Lomb Optical Company (B&L), which had been charging a monopoly-level price for their product. The same letter of October 20 mentioned above indicates that both the Grey International Corporation of New York and B.J. Grossman & Associates in Chicago were sharing the importation of a total of 500 lensmeters with OFITRA, but Liholm had plans to take another 2,000 lensmeters in the spring of 1950 and he soon beat out his American competitors.

OFITRA was able to bring in simpler-to-operate NK lensmeters and sell them at a price close to half of what B&L had been charging. Not only did these sales also aid NK's cash flow, but they helped build NK's reputation for making fine optical goods among American professional workers.* Other precision optical products, notably microscopes, process lenses, transits and levels would soon follow. If NK still did not have a market for its camera in America, OFITRA could find a market for its other optical products.

According to Liholm and Gasser, Bausch & Lomb Optical was furious at this loss in a lucrative market it had considered exclusively its own. When NK products began to appear in American advertisements under the name of the "Japan Optical Company," B&L brought suit against OFITRA in federal court charging that the use of the word "optical" was an infringement of its registered trademark. OFITRA promptly dropped the anglicized version of Nippon Kogaku. This is why ads in 1951 refer to the "Japan Optical Company" but later ads do not.

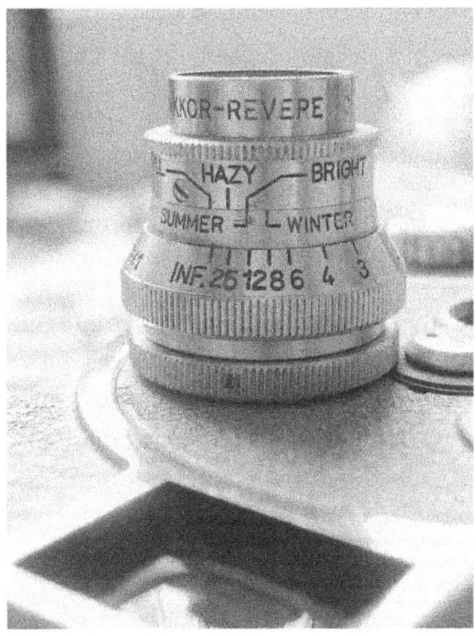

One of the thousands of 13mm f1.9 Ciné Nikkors that Nippon Kogaku provided for the Revere Camera Company in 1949–50 (Nico van Dijk photograph).

But B&L was not satisfied. Determined to rid itself of NK completely, it continued its suit, maintaining that since "Kogaku" was just the Japanese word for "Optical," it should be banned as well. In a decision finally handed down in federal court in 1956, this proposition was firmly rejected. "The applicant must disclaim the wording that appears in the mark, not a translated version which is not technically part of the mark."[13] Owning a trademarked name in one language gave no rights to that same meaning in another language.

In an interesting side note to this period in NK's history, a "Reparations Inspection Check Sheet" dated October 24, 1949,[14] records that NK now had permission to use 884 machines — a considerably higher total than the fewer than 300 it had been permitted to use in 1946. A note, handwritten at the bottom of the report, adds that the building and its fence had recently suffered "minor typhoon damage" but that the "Plant will pay burden cost for repairs."

A month later, S. Tanaka, the chief of the Procurement and Reparation Division of the International Trade and Enterprise Bureau, Ministry of International Trade and Industry, forwarded the request for the increased lens production to GHQ.† In this letter, Tanaka expanded on NK's progress toward becoming a good corporate citizen in the new democratic Japan, noting that:

This same letter lists the approval of GHQ/SCAP for the production of up to 500 cameras per month.

†*As was typical, requests for changes had to go through the Japanese government but then had to get GHQ's final approval.*

This is the biggest optical industry plant in this country and has the superior techniques; it enjoys the facilities which can conduct an integrated work from the melting of glass to the finishing course as products while, on the other hand, it takes pride in its long history of operation. To make this plant operate its function means to preserve the techniques of the highest degree in the optical industry in this country; it is the prime importance to let it continue the business.

Considered from the purport outlined above, this application contributes much to the rehabilitation of Japanese economy and further it is clear that the other facilities cannot attempt the production; therefore, we entreat you to give the permission for the production of the amount[s] applied above to this plant.[15]

Apparently, only the application for this increase had to be submitted in order for NK to go ahead with its increase in production of both instruments and lenses because the final approval from the Economic and Scientific Section of GHQ/SCAP did not come until January 3, 1950.

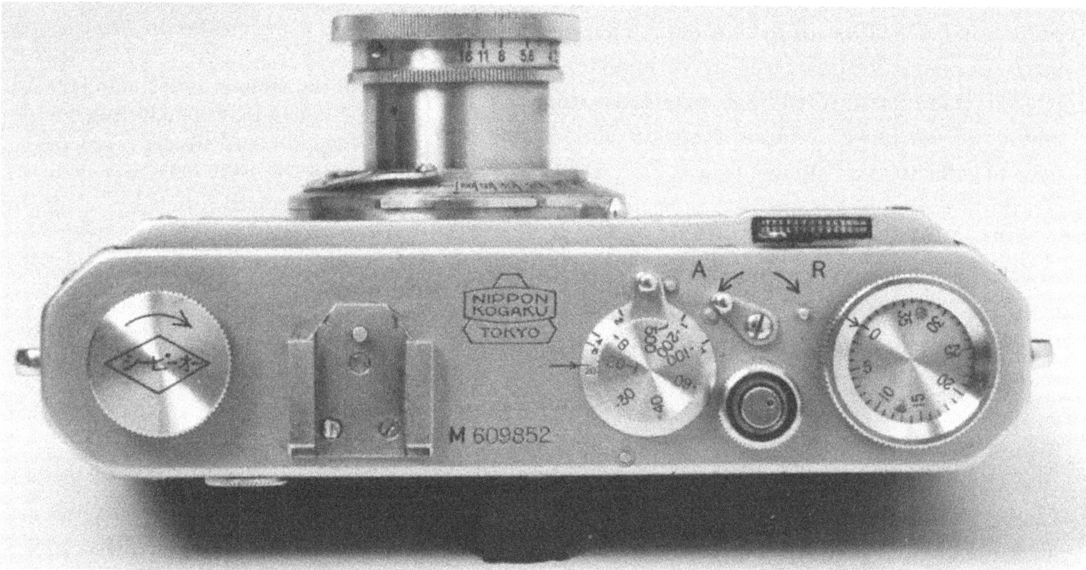

The CPO Nikon. The American military exchange stores were the most lucative market for all Japanese camera manufacturers during the Occupation period. A Central Purchasing Office (CPO) acquired camera equipment and other Japanese manufactured goods from marketing agencies and, in turn, distributed these goods to the various post exchanges, base exchanges and ships' stores. With one exception, Nippon Kogaku made no sales of its camera or lenses to the CPO until April 1950 when the Overseas Finance & Trading Company took over the marketing.

The exception was a Nikon M that SCAP records indicate was shipped to the CPO in January 1950. It is possible that the early Nikon M pictured here is that camera. The serial number (M609852) is correct for that time period. Note the prominent diamond engraved on the rewind knob. Within that diamond appear the Japanese characters that would translate to "CPO!"

No other Nikon has been found with this unique marking. This camera was owned at one time by Burt Rubin, later Jose Wu Chang (Jose Wu Chang photograph, courtesy Nikon Historical Society).

If Liholm's efforts to help NK break into the American optical market were showing some success, his efforts to market the redesigned Nikon camera were still at a standstill. Samples continued to go out, but the only sales that SCAP's Export Records show through the end of the year were eight cameras to Burma and 14 to "E.B."

But Liholm was able to provide one extra service for the redesigned camera. NK could not locate a native steel wire of sufficient high quality for making the springs that the shutter required. Liholm sent the company samples of American wire. These too were rejected. Liholm then contacted Uno Lindholm who had Western Trading provide Swedish piano wire. This proved to be of the necessary quality, and NK used it in the camera's shutters from then on.

In December 1949, Lindholm decided to push for more trade with Japan. He sent one of his confidants, Ludvig Hagberg, the manager of the Western Trading Company office in Stockholm, to Tokyo. Like OFITRA/S.F., Western Trading operated out of a small corporate headquarters in Stockholm. Hagberg was to set up the importation of "special foods and nourishments, dairy products and special milk products for children"[16] marketed by Guigoz Ltd of Vuadens, Switzerland. These products were to be sold only to foreign residents. Apparently this venture was to prove unsuccessful due to problems with handling the foreign exchange, but in a few months, Hagberg's name would show up again in SCAP files, this time relating to NK.

In January, Western Trading scored with a sale of 100 Nikon Ms to Switzerland — possibly as a result of the work of a man named von Levinski, Lindholm's representative in that country. Other Nikon Ms were starting to trickle out of Japan. Two went to Canada, five to "Siam" and four left as "invisibles." (SCAP's export reports give no clue as to what "invisibles" meant.) NK also made 18 domestic sales. As before, these went to "government, hospital and university" locations. Among this mix of shipments the smallest one was the most important. NK delivered one Nikon with an f2 lens to the CPO. Perhaps this was just a sample, or a trial shipment. The Nikon was still not on the CPO's list of cameras that could be sold in the military exchanges.*

In February 1950 sales were still moving slowly. Six cameras went to Venezuela and "invisible" got another four. NK also shipped four 135mm Nikkors and two 85mm Nikkors to Venezuela. Of greater significance than this small trickle to South America was the addition of cameras equipped with the long-delayed 50mm f1.5 Nikkor-S. NK now was offering a camera with a normal lens as fast as any manufacturer was offering anywhere.

Spring 1950, the First Market Breakthrough and Two Contracts

In the meantime, Liholm and Gasser maintained their contacts. As a result of their growing confidence in each other, at some point that fall or early winter, the enthusiastic Gasser volunteered to go to New York to test reactions to the Nikon and its lenses and try to line up endorsements.

It is possible that this was Nikon #609852, the only camera found so far with "CPO" engraved on its rewind knob. Certainly the number and timing would be correct.

Using the contacts he had built up through his business, Gasser traveled to New York City in December 1949 or January 1950 (Neither Gasser nor Liholm could remember the date of this trip, but Liholm did remember that it was in winter because Gasser did not own a winter coat and Liholm loaned him his.)* There Gasser met with Mitch Bagdonowicz (Bagdanovitch or Bagdanovitz, the spelling varies.) of the Eastern Optical Testing Laboratories, located at 49 West 19th Street. He convinced Mitch to test sample Nikkor lenses. Mitch was impressed and would later state that he felt that the Nikkors were "as good or better than the Zeiss lenses." He met with Frank Scherschel, assistant picture editor of *Life* magazine, and he met with Albert Levin, who would soon become the camera's first East Coast "salesman." Levin was already handling the little Ricoh-made "Steky," one of the better-quality, inexpensive 16mm Japanese still cameras then being manufactured, and other photographic lines, but the Nikon would be the first 35mm camera he would sell.[17]

Finally, Gasser visited Martin Forscher, owner and proprietor of Professional Camera Repair Service located at 37 West 47th Street. Marty ran the best-known camera repair shop on the East Coast. For Gasser, meeting him was like "meeting a brother." They spoke the same language of cameras and lenses. Gasser was able to persuade Forscher's shop to act as the repair and service center for Nikons on the East Coast. A year later, these experts would be ready to create a chorus of endorsements that OFITRA and Gasser could draw on to help build the Nikon's reputation.

With this rudimentary sales and service system in place for Liholm to call on, Gasser returned to San Francisco, and Liholm resumed marketing Nikons in the United States. In March, OFITRA received 20 cameras and ten accessory lenses. Twelve of these were Nikon Ms with 50mm f3.5 Nikkors — the last cameras that would ship with that slower lens. Most of these cameras were sold to professionals in the Bay area — photographers willing to take a chance on an unknown product based on their trust in Gasser's judgment.

The 50mm f1.5 Nikkor lens that shipped on three of the cameras was a newly available product, first marketed the previous month. Again, NK optical engineers had closely copied the best formula available, the 50mm f1.5 Sonnar, and now they could claim to offer the fastest normal lens of any Japanese manufacturer. Like the 50mm f3.5 Nikkor, this lens would have only a short production life. Nippon Kogaku's first true high-speed lens, it only stopped down to f11 and still took what had been the Zeiss standard filter screw-in attachment size of 40.5mm. As with the other introductions, most of the first cameras with this lens went out as samples or "invisibles."

The winds of change were blowing across Japan. The Japan of spring 1950 was a far different place than the Japan of spring 1946. A devastated country that had been on the verge of mass starvation was now a nation with a renewed sense of purpose and self-confidence. While many workers remained underemployed, and incomes remained tight for both companies and individuals, the reforms of 1946–47 had yielded to pragmatic measures aimed more at recovery than change. The textile, porcelain and shipbuilding industries were growing and domestic orders for goods were up.

OFITRA was also growing. Liholm had started with a small office in the prominently

Or maybe even as late as November 1950, although that date seems less probable.

located Merchants Exchange Building near the corner of Montgomery and California streets. By 1950, the business had grown to the point where OFITRA moved to a suite of rooms in another part of the same building. His staff also began to grow. His first hiring was Arne Rosengren, another Swede who had lived in San Francisco for a number of years and knew the area better than Liholm. He served as Liholm's office manager and assistant and remained with the Nikon Camera Company after Liholm left.

Jack Bennett was one of Liholm's first salesmen. He had extensive knowledge of the optometric end of the business and helped Liholm negotiate many of the early sales of the vertexometers, particularly through the House of Vision in Chicago. He lasted only a short time with the company. Liholm fired him over loyalty issues after discovering that he had gone through Liholm's desk while Liholm was away.

The staff included at least two other men, one a salesman with an expertise in binoculars, the other a Filipino who acted as warehouse manager and driver. OFITRA owned a former Railway Express truck, which the company used to pick up shipments at the docks as they cleared customs. As the imports grew, Liholm rented a basement room in the Merchants Exchange building that had a combination lock on the door. Equipment could be sorted, tested and inventoried there before being shipped to customers.

Liholm had also been joined by Barbro Nyberg, a young Swedish dancer he had known in Stockholm before leaving for America. She wrote that she was coming to visit him, but as Liholm ruefully remembered, "When she got off the ship* with seventeen pieces of luggage, I knew she was not coming for just a visit." She stayed with Liholm and married him a year later. They would part in 1951 after he became ill in Europe and shortly thereafter divorced.

Sensing that the time was now right, Uno Lindholm decided to make a pitch for selling all of NK's products to the CPO with his companies as the middlemen. His Stockholm manager, Ludvig Hagberg, was still in Japan trying unsuccessfully to set up the food import deal he had first proposed the previous fall. Now Lindholm, through Hagberg, writing under both the Western Trading and the Overseas Finance & Trading letterhead, made the first pitch to the head of the Foreign Investment Board on March 30, 1950.* In this letter, he pointed out that "Being closely connected in business with Japan Optical Co. Ltd. for export through the Western Trading Co., Ltd., I want to sell their articles in Japan as well."[18] He admitted that his earlier plans to import goods into Japan had fallen through, and now he asked SCAP to "...kindly grant me a license to sell Japanese Optical goods to Army personnel and holders of O.S.S. cards in dollars."[19]

As with previous such requests, apparently just asking was sufficient to get the ball rolling because in April 1950 "CPO" suddenly became NK's biggest buyer of the Nikon camera and its lenses. NK "exported" 111 Nikons that month. CPO accounted for 57 of that total (The United States with 15, Sweden with ten, "Invisible" with 22 and "Sample" with seven accounted for the rest.) CPO also got a good share of the accessory lenses. Many of

---

The Swedish passenger liner Gripsholm.

†*Where was Sakai? Perhaps Lindholm felt that an approach from a non–Japanese trader would have a better chance of succeeding. Perhaps Lindholm trusted Hagberg more.*

The Nikon Camera in America, 1946–1953

SHIGERU SAKAI

KYOKUTO BOEKI KAISHA, LTD.
(FAR EAST MERCANTILE CO.)

ROOM NO. 696
MARUNOUCHI BLDG.
TOKYO, JAPAN

Mr. H. W. Liholm
introducing Mr. S. Sakai
director of Far East Trading Comp.
and one of my best & oldest
friends since the middle school
course.

M. NAGAOKA
DIRECTOR & PRESIDENT

Nippon Kogaku Kogyo K. K.
5447. Oi Morimae-cho,
Shinagawa-ku Tokyo.

Telephones:
Omori (06) { 2 1 1 1 - 5
             { 3 1 1 1 - 5

Sakai's own business card and the personally annotated business card of Dr. Nagaoka, president of Nippon Kogaku (both sides), which Sakai presented to Hans Liholm upon Liholm's arrival in Japan in April 1950. The annotation provides a reason for Sakai's success in gaining marketing and negotiation leverage with Nippon Kogaku during this period (cards courtesy Hans W. Liholm).

these went out in the Leica thread mount. With so few of its own camera sold and so many Leica and Leica-mount camera owners, NK had to follow the market that existed.

The next month, the company sold another 76 Nikons. This time, half went to Venezuela, but the CPO still took another 15 and another ten Nikkor lenses. These numbers might appear pitiful, but after months of seeing nothing but samples and "invisibles" going out the door, these cash sales in dollars were welcome. As a final touch of cream, OFITRA was still selling the 13mm Ciné Nikkors to Revere at a rate of 2,000 per month.

With the doors to the CPO open, it was now Hans Liholm's turn to push for an exclusive contract for North America. In April 1950, he flew to Japan with a stop in Anchorage, Alaska, traveling in a four-engine Constellation and arriving at Haneda Airport on the 8th. He checked into the Yashima Hotel, located in the Nihonbashi District of Tokyo ("Not

***Opposite*: Hans Liholm's passport from 1950: identity page and page fixing his date of entry into Japan as 8 April 1950 and his date of departure as May 4, 1950. It had taken him nearly a month to negotiate the export agreement for OFITRA with Nippon Kogaku (courtesy Hans W. Liholm).**

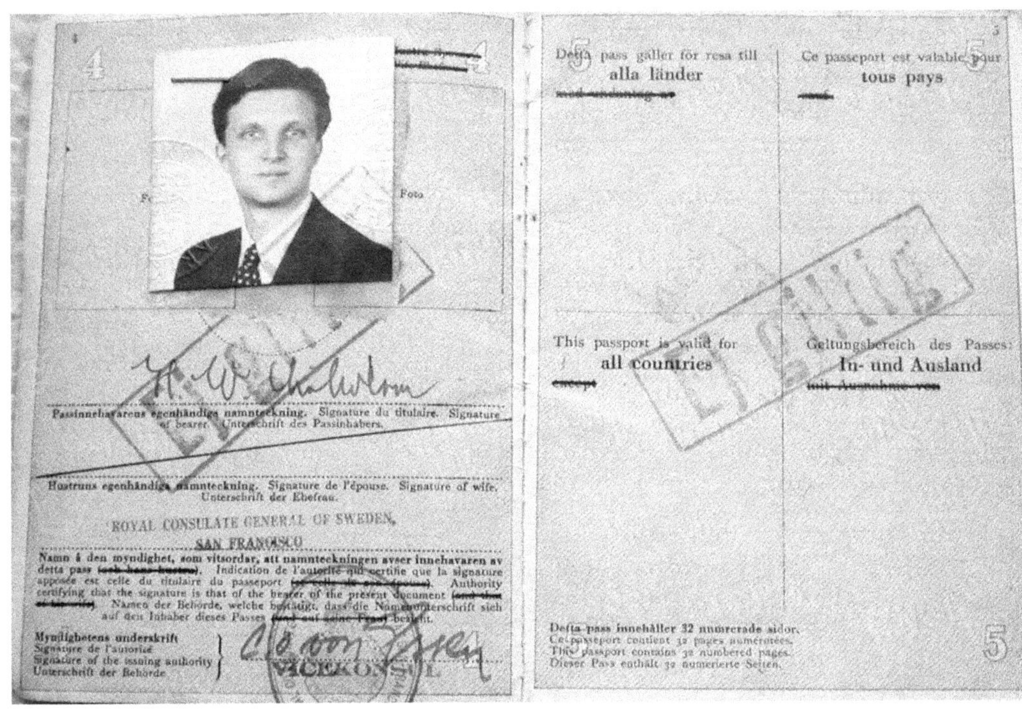
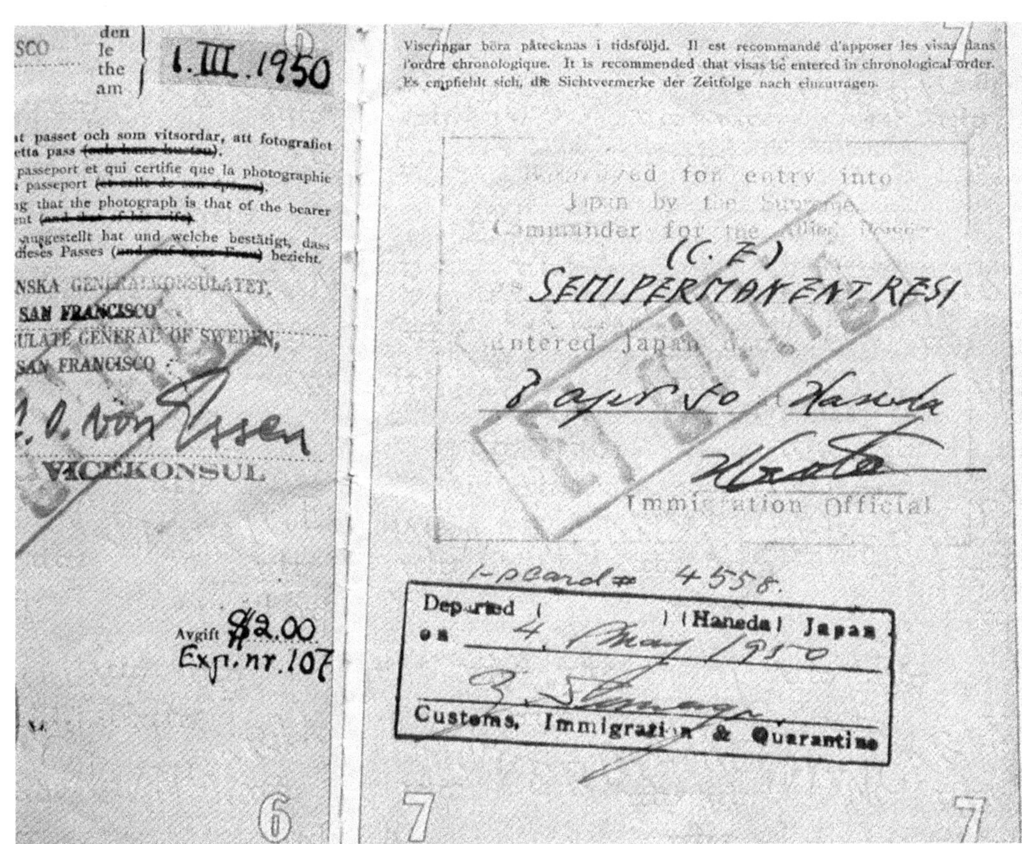

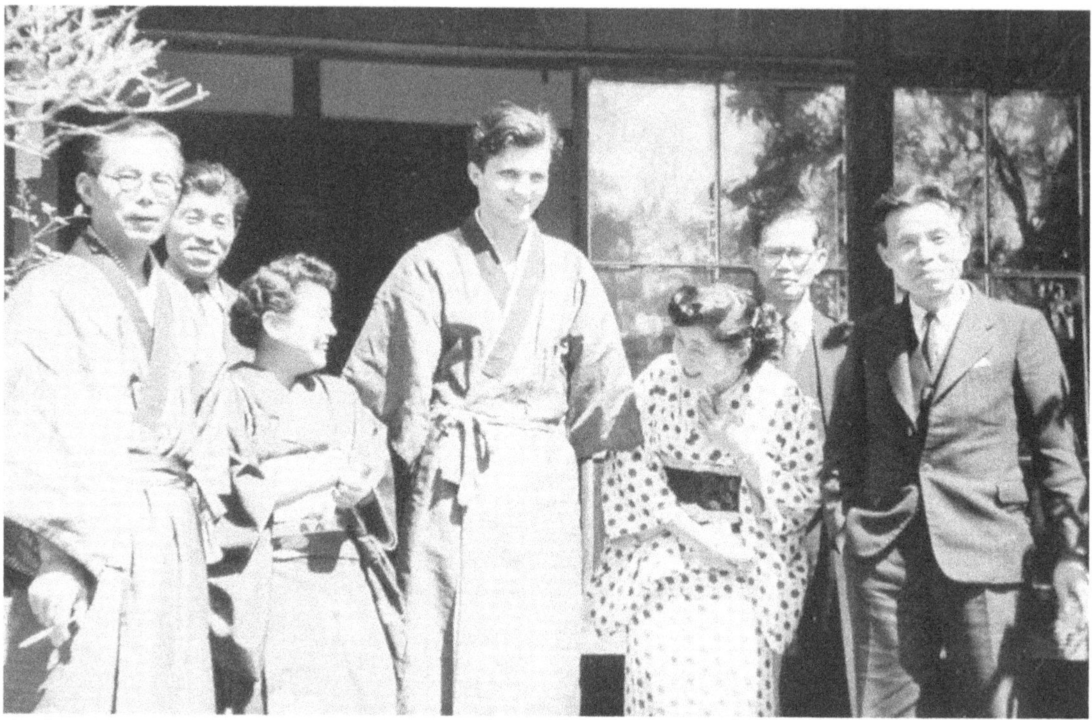

The young Hans Liholm at a country inn in April 1950. Shigeru [Noae] Sakai is the person wearing a kimono to the far left. The other two men on the right worked for NK, but Liholm could no longer identify them, but Yoshiro Iwata of the Nikon Corporation indicated that the person to the far right is Kinjiro Fukai, a "director of the inspection division within NK." Second from right, wearing glasses, is Yoshio Yamanac, a director of "development and researching division of glasses in NK." The man second from left remains unidentified. The caption on the back (written by Liholm's mother) reads: "Mein junge in Tokid." The kimono Liholm is wearing was a gift from his hosts. When he received it, it was so short it barely covered his knees, but one of his hosts added extra cloth to bring it down to the correct length (photographer unknown, courtesy Hans W. Liholm).

one of the best hotels, but nice enough," according to Liholm). Except for relaxing weekend retreats at "country inns," he resided there for his entire stay in Japan.

Shigero Sakai soon came to call, presenting one of Nagaoka's calling cards with Sakai's name on it identifying him as "One of my best & oldest friends since middle school course."[20] Liholm had been carrying on an extensive correspondence with Sakai, but this was their first meeting. Sakai, "Our man in Tokyo,"* would serve as Liholm's host, escort and translator during Liholm's entire stay. Western Trading's Ludvig Hagberg joined them and negotiations with NK's board began.

The three would meet with President Nagaoka, NK's board and other managers, particularly Noboru Hamashima — then in charge of exports — on an almost daily basis. In interviews, Liholm indicated that these talks began almost as soon as he arrived in Japan.

*As Lindholm defined Sakai to Liholm.

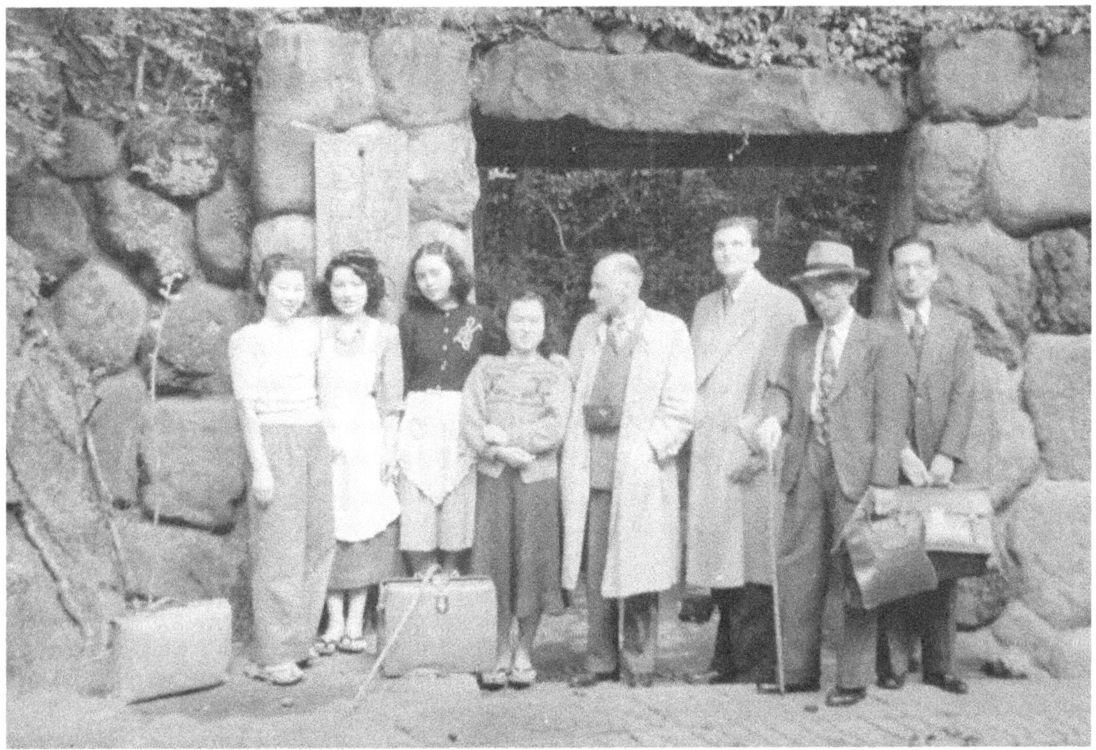

Ludvig Hagberg, manager for Western Trading Company, and Hans Liholm at a country inn near Tokyo in April 1950. "*Hagi-san*" stands in the middle with a new Nikon camera "on his belly." Liholm is standing behind, third from right. Second from right is Hiroshi Shirahama, then the vice president for Research and Development, and further over Sanetoshi Kuratsuji, Nippon Kogaku's sales manager. Note the bulging briefcases. Liholm did not identify the four young women. It is possible they worked at the "country inn" where Hagberg, Liholm and the men from Nippon Kogaku were staying. Note the aprons. Also note that with exception of the *monpe* pantaloons worn by the woman to the far left and thong sandals, all four women are in Western dress and they all have permanents (photographer unknown, courtesy Hans W. Liholm).

But in a dinner speech* that Dr. Nagaoka gave on April 24, he indicated that Liholm, Hagberg and Sakai had been "inspecting our factory and in business talks" for three days.[21] However long the actual negotiations lasted, the Japanese were impressed with Liholm, Nagaoka remarking that "Apparently, he [Liholm] has no time for rest. He devotes all his time for the sake of our mutual business."[22] Recalling these sessions, Liholm expressed his enormous respect for Nagaoka. He was "Very knowledgeable, open-minded, sharp, noticeably a scholar and working at a higher intellectual level. [He] was very committed to his company. Explain and he understood."

**Nagaoka remarked that "American people don't feed you too many dishes," so this was just a "tempura party." Tempura are selections of fresh fish, shellfish or vegetables, dipped in batter, deep-fried and served immediately with various sauces on the side.*

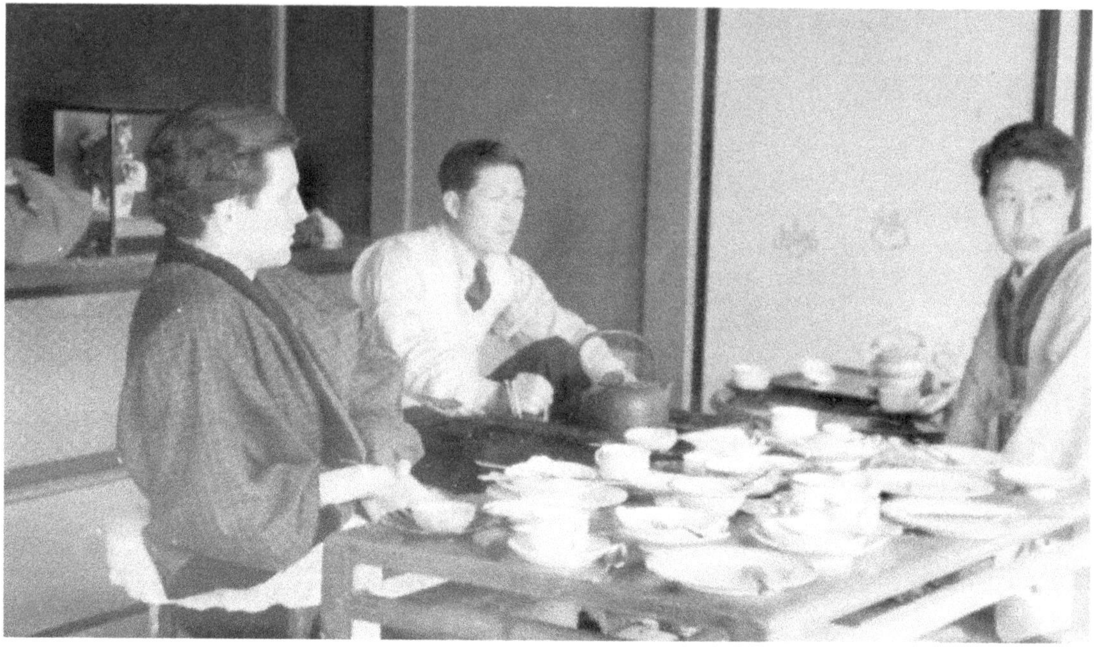

Hans Liholm (left) at lunch in kimono. His ability to kneel comfortably was an asset in his negotiations and meetings. The man in the middle is unidentified, but the woman was Shigeru Sakai's companion (photographer unknown, courtesy Hans W. Liholm).

All of the Japanese had many, many questions for Liholm. When Liholm asked questions, Sakai would translate, then the board members would discuss their answer for a long time. The meetings lasted for hours with lunches being served in lacquered boxes. Taken on a tour of the Ohi factory, Liholm was told that 12,000 people were dependent on his ability to successfully sell NK products, particularly the Nikon to Americans. Could he do it?

Liholm felt the pressure. Japan's poverty was still enormous. Traveling in a car through Tokyo, it was obvious to Liholm that many people were starving. Not only was food still in short supply, but many drugs remained unobtainable. Before he left for Japan, Sakai had sent Liholm a long list of medicines to bring with him for Sakai's own use and the use of Sakai's companion who was in poor health.

NK wanted to reach an agreement, but remained unsure as to whether granting an exclusive contract to the young Liholm and his OFITRA was the best and wisest course to take. Liholm, in turn, was nervous, "Scared to death," by the idea of so many people being dependent on OFITRA's ability to market NK's camera successfully. He knew how much prejudice there was against Japanese products in the United States, and how many cheap products the Nikon would be competing against. Getting and granting a contract involved a lot of trust.

The two Swedes, Hagberg and Liholm, one young and tall, one older and short, got along well.* The Japanese liked Hagberg too, and called him *"Hagi-san,"* perhaps because he was totally bald. Liholm liked having Hagberg along whenever he met NK officials,

Liholm referred to Hagberg as a "nice old man."

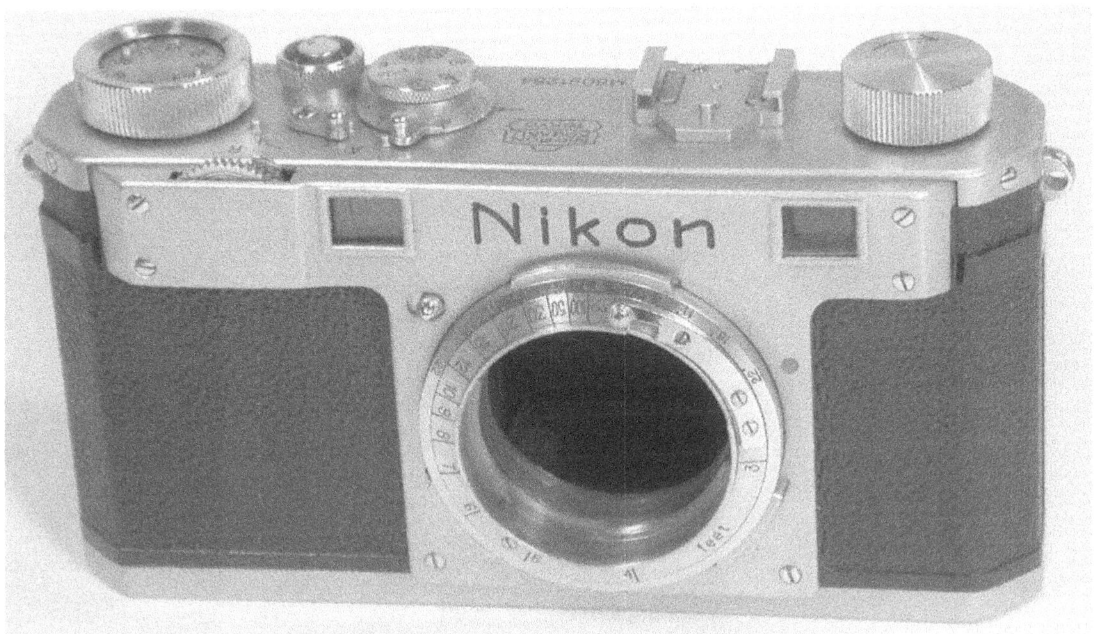

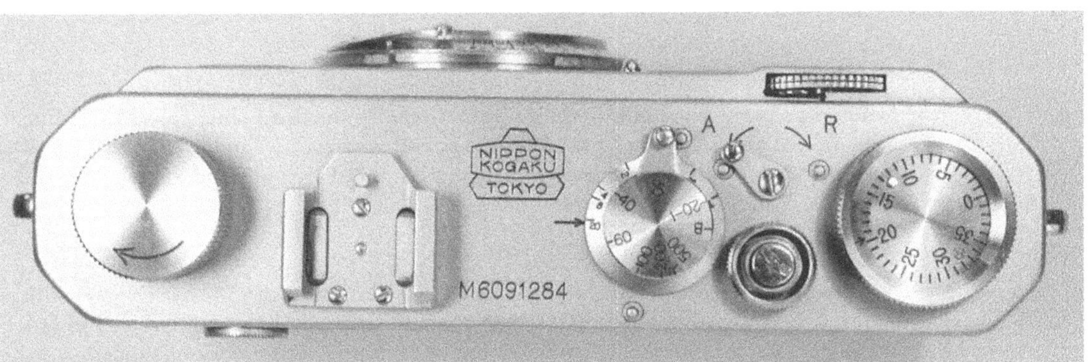

The Nikon M camera that Dr. Masao Nagaoka gave to Hans Liholm in April 1950 when Liholm came to Tokyo to negotiate the contract that gave OFITRA exclusive import rights to all NK products for North America. Only the camera remains. The normal lens and two accessory lenses were lost many years ago. Externally, this camera appears similar to the first model Nikon. Internally, there are many differences, particularly the widening of the film gate to 34mm.

In the camera was an exposed but rewound roll of Kodak Plus X film. The film was obviously very old since the magazine ends were uncrimped. Nevertheless, careful processing allowed a few of the images to survive. On the next page is one of them.

remarking that "of our Japanese friends never showing up fewer than 10 or 12 at any meeting." but Liholm handled virtually all the negotiations for OFITRA.

NK's management was not conversant with American business "boardroom" practices, but all the Japanese Liholm met were very polite and gracious. Thinking back, he suggested in his second interview that perhaps [being Swedish] he was more sensitive than "hardened

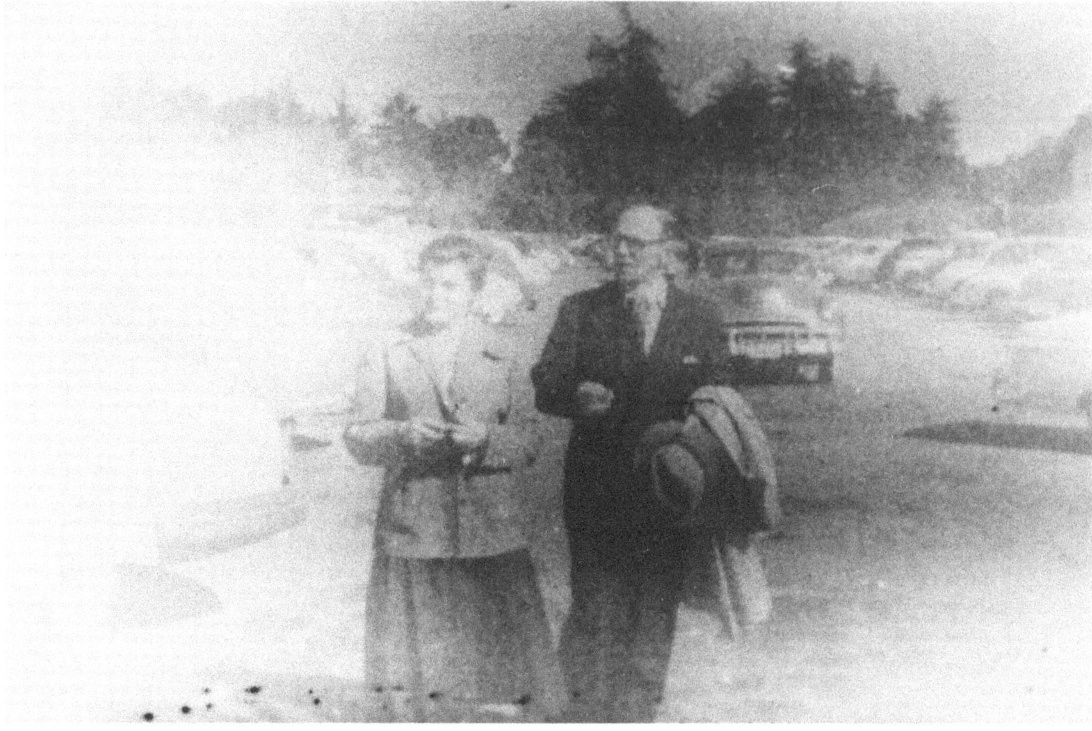

Barbro Nyberg, Liholm's companion and first wife, somewhere in the San Francisco area standing with Olof Dahlin, an inventor of a new kind of tube cap, and whom Uno Lindholm, president of OFITRA, sent to America (at OFITRA's expense) in hopes that Liholm would find a market for the man's invention (Hans W. Liholm photograph).

Opposite, top: A camera about to take on the world: A Nikon M from late 1950 or early 1951 with its accessory lenses. Left to right: the 135mm f4 Nikkor with its lens hood, first marketed in late 1948, the 85mm f2 Nikkor, first marketed in the spring of 1949 and to the right of the lens caps, the 35mm f3.5 W-Nikkor, first marketed in the spring of 1950. On the camera is mounted a variframe finder, an essential accessory for framing all the auxiliary lenses. Note the chain attached to the finder. This goes to a magnifier that fits over the camera's eyepiece, increasing the camera view to life size and vastly increasing focusing accuracy. On the camera is a contemporary 50mm f2 Nikkor.

After five years of development and early attempts at manufacturing and marketing amidst the enormous difficulties of postwar Japan, the Nikon and its lenses were about to take on the premier 35mm camera manufacturers of the world — with quality and features equal to those available from any manufacturer. It would do so with the help of a number of Americans: importers, photojournalists and newswriters (James Kelly collection).

Opposite, bottom: The porcelain peach that Dr. Nagaoka gave Hans Liholm on April 26, 1950, at the successful conclusion of the negotiations that gave the Overseas Finance & Trading Company the exclusive right to import all Nippon Kogaku products into North America. The peach was the only decoration in Nippon Kogaku's board room and had been manufactured by the same company that provided china for the emperor (courtesy Hans W. Liholm).

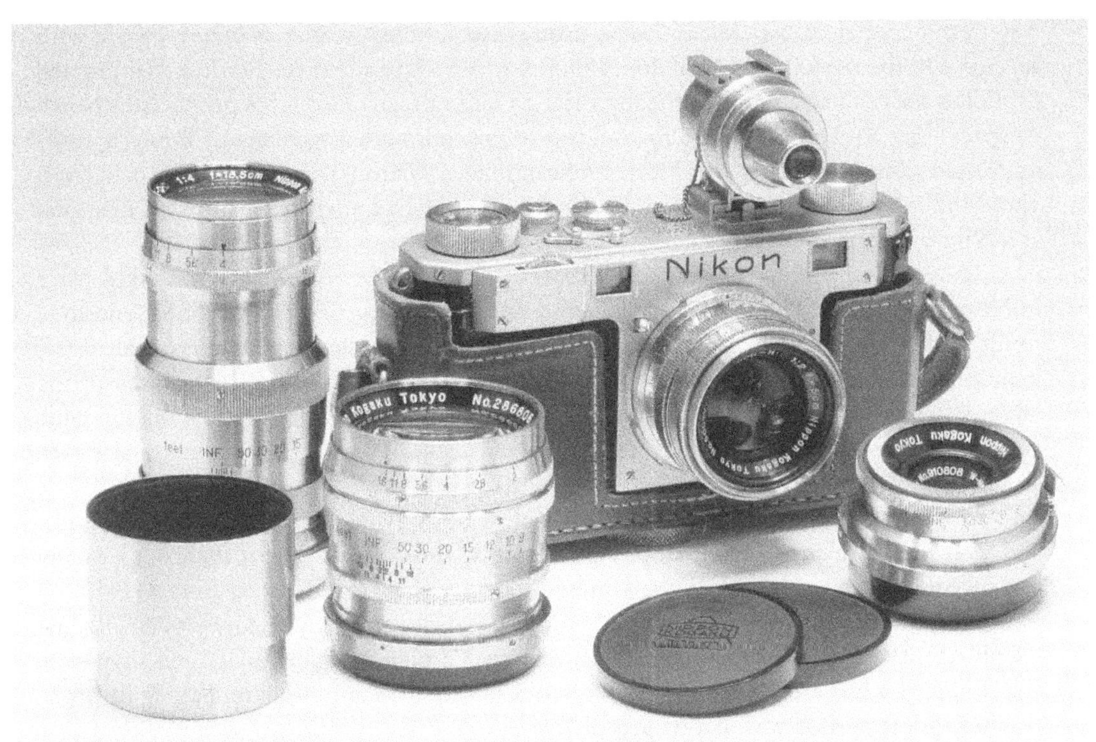

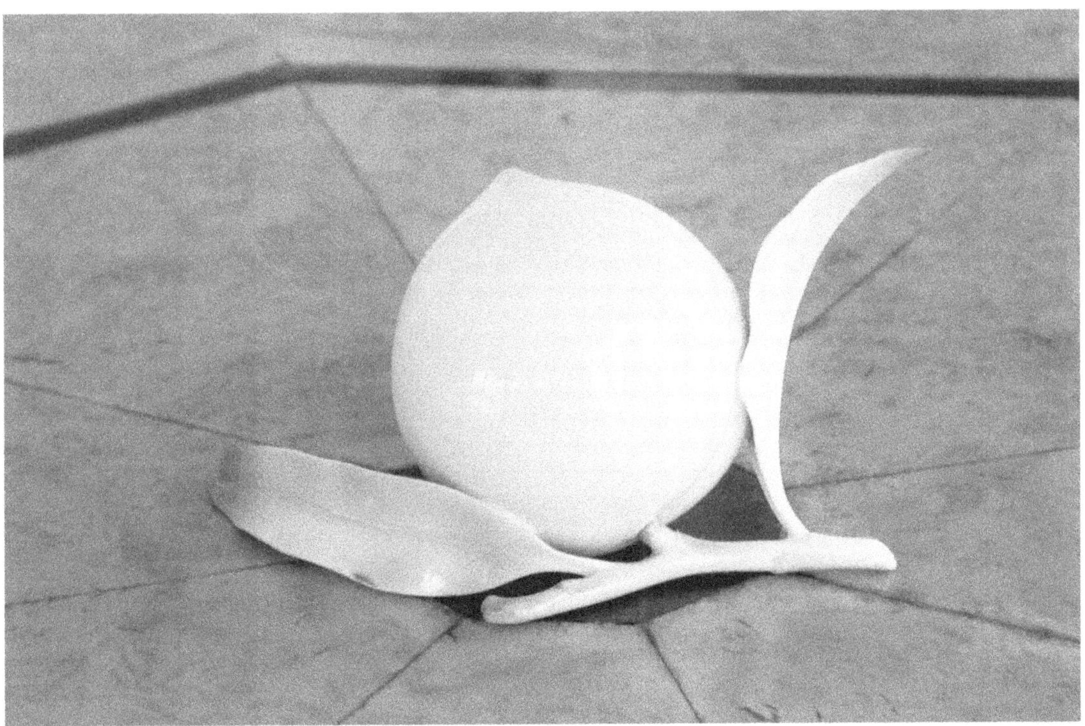

American negotiators" would have been. In any case, Liholm's work was to be crowned with success. On the morning of April 26, 1950, following a late-night celebration, NK granted OFITRA the exclusive rights to the importation and sales of all of NK's products in North America. [See Appendix III for a the full text of the contractual agreement.] Western Trading would gain similar rights on May 1 for Scandinavia. Through the work of his managers, Uno Lindholm had finally achieved the arrangement he had envisioned since his first look at a Nikon camera two years earlier.

The contract signing would end on a special note. All the negotiations had taken place in NK's boardroom. The room was plain and without any furnishings except for one large round table ("like Arthur's round table") and a dozen or more chairs. The room's only ornamentation was a porcelain, almost-white peach and leaves that sat in the middle of the table. After the signing of the contract, Dr. Nagaoka lifted the china peach off the table and presented it to Liholm to "take back to Barbro." Liholm has kept and cherished it ever since.

Thrilled and triumphant, Liholm left Tokyo on May 4. This time he headed south and west to return to America, stopping in Burma, India, Iraq, Egypt, France, Germany and Sweden. He arrived back in the United States via New York City on June 8, 1950.

Most of the pieces were now in place for NK and its camera. The company finally had a high-quality product that compared well with any camera being manufactured anywhere. In OFITRA, it had an importer in the United States totally committed to making its products sell. All it needed was market acceptance.

4

The "Discovery" of the Nikkor
(and What Immediately Followed)

If one sees Hans Liholm and Adolph Gasser as equivalents to John the Baptist — men preparing the way for those who would come later — then the American photojournalists who started using and endorsing the Nikkor lenses and the Nikon camera in the summer of 1950 were the evangelists who created the believers. OFITRA provided the means of getting NK's products into the hands of buyers. David Douglas Duncan, Horace Bristol, Jacob Deschin and the others covered here were the men who brought the buyers to OFITRA.

Two Photographers Encounter an Unknown Lens

A native of Whittier, California, Horace Bristol had taken up photography at an early age. By the 1930s he had his own business and had become closely associated with many photographers in the "*f*64" group* working in the San Francisco area, including Ansel Adams and Edward Weston. He worked closely with Dorothea Lange in her documentary work and, in 1937, *Life* hired him as one of its first photographers. That winter he traveled with John Steinbeck throughout the Central Valley of California, taking pictures of the recent immigrants who had been forced off the Great Plains by the dust bowl conditions and the Great Depression. That investigative tour became the basis for Steinbeck's novel *The Grapes of Wrath*, and Bristol's pictures were used in a photographic essay in *Life* on that book and the movie that followed in 1939–40.[1]

In 1942, Bristol was one of five photographers whom Edward Steichen hired and had

Never a formal organization, the photographers active in the group promoted sharply focused images that ran counter to the soft, romantic images then the standard for most commercial landscapes and portraits.

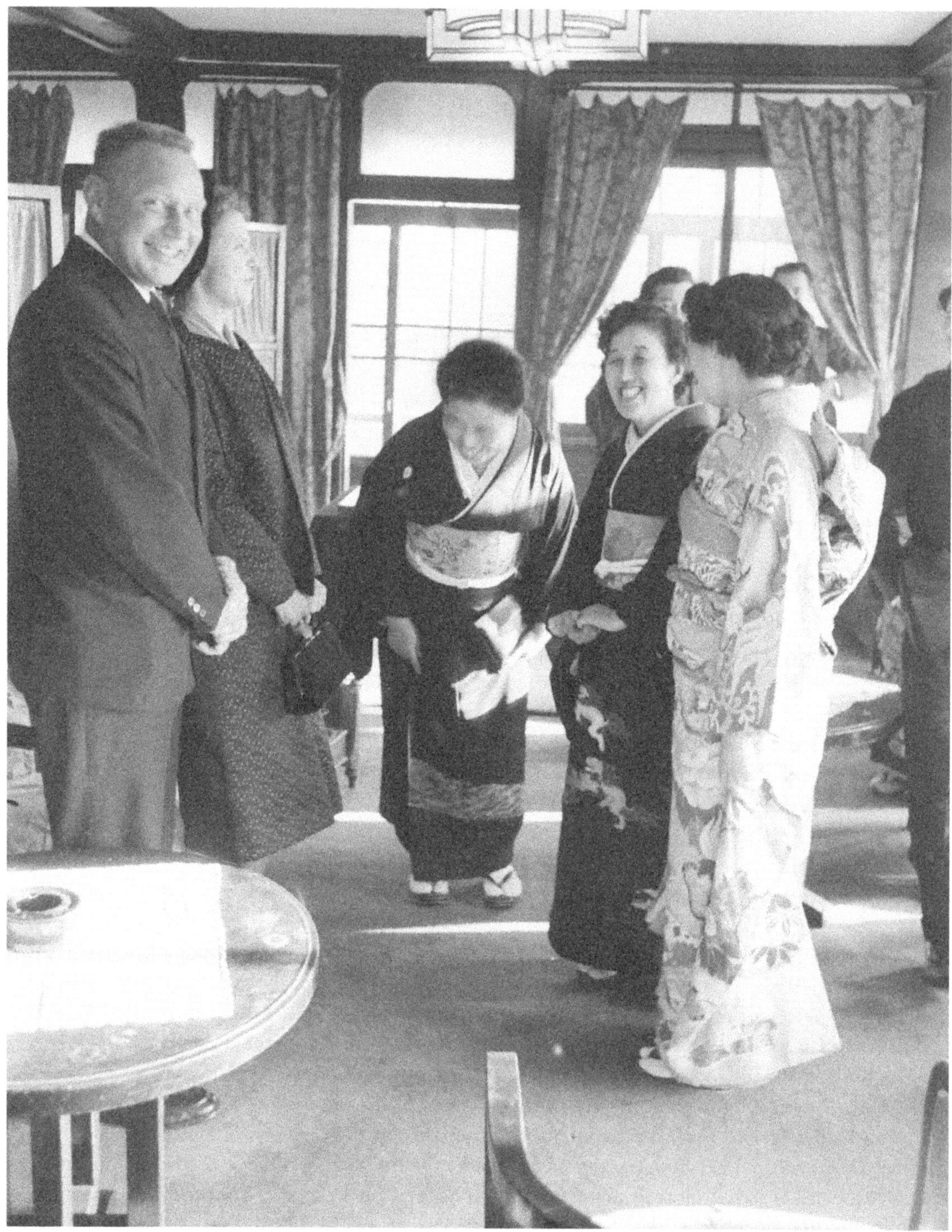

Horace Bristol is the happy man on the left standing with his wife and beaming at the photographer in February 1953. The occasion was the meeting of his son's future in-laws in the days prior to the traditional Shinto wedding ceremony (Michael Rougier, photograph. Copyright Time & Life Pictures/Getty Images. Used with permission).

commissioned in the navy to document the work of naval aviation. He served on aircraft carriers in the Pacific campaigns until 1945. Discharged, he accepted an assignment for *Fortune*— an older magazine in the Luce empire of publications that included *Time* and *Life*— that took him to Tokyo. There, he fell in love with Japan, its culture and its people, and, after the end of his direct work with *Fortune*, decided to stay, along with his American wife and son.

By June 1950, with his resident "trader" status established, Horace Bristol had set up his own freelance photo and publishing business in Tokyo—a little company called the "East-West Photo Agency." He built a small darkroom for his own use which just happened to be across the hall from the offices occupied by *Life*'s Tokyo bureau. As the American photo correspondent on-location, one familiar with both the language and the culture, Bristol and his lab quickly became a magnet for every American photojournalist visiting Japan.

That month, one of the Americans visiting Bristol's lab was a photojournalist named David Douglas Duncan — on an assignment to take pictures of Japanese art for *Life*. For a person who had already been in one war as a combat photographer and would, in time, become one of the most famous visual documenters of two other wars, the idea that Duncan was in Tokyo to photograph art ceramics at the Ueno National Museum may seem a bit odd, but Duncan had already led such a varied life that it is possible to imagine that he could have photographed anything (and he did).

A native of Kansas City, Missouri, Duncan had been active in the outdoors, including becoming an Eagle Scout. He first attended the University of Arizona before moving to the University of Miami from which he graduated in 1938 with a dual degree in zoology and Spanish. Throughout the Depression he had worked as an "amateur" professional, getting pictures published in newspapers and magazines and learning picture-taking and layout skills. By 1941, he could claim credit for a *Life* cover and work appearing in the *National Geographic* magazine, as well as numerous pages in newspapers.

In 1943 Duncan enlisted in the U.S. Marines and, after earning a commission as a second lieutenant, worked his way through the Solomon Islands as a combat photographer. Assigned to the South Pacific Combat Air Transport Command (SCAT), Duncan somehow managed to get himself into almost every theater and type of plane, learning survival skills, along with visual skills that would soon allow him to capture the kind of pictures of soldiers, marines and violent action that still define combat for two generations of American readers.[2]

During that war, Duncan had made the acquaintance of Jay Eyerman, *Life*'s chief photographer. In March 1946, Eyerman, in turn, introduced the discharged Duncan to Wilson Hicks, then the executive editor of *Life*. Hicks promptly hired Duncan as "...our latest Life photographer."[3] Since that date, Duncan had traveled widely on assignment. He had been in India, eastern Europe, Turkey, the Middle East and Africa. Perhaps Japan was just another country in a long and growing list of places where Duncan had worked.

These two American ex-servicemen, Horace Bristol and David Douglas Duncan, were now to become the major players who would take the stage in an event for which hundreds of technicians and businessmen like Liholm, Gasser, Nagaoka, Fuketa and Sakai had been making the arrangements. Like many good stories with multiple observers and retellers, several versions exist concerning what happened next, with each of the principals seeming to recall the events in slightly different order and with different details, usually casting themselves into the central role in the process.

Jun Miki was Time-Life's only Japanese contract photographer at that time. He had been serving as Duncan's assistant for the last four weeks as Duncan traveled throughout Japan. "I carried his bag, loaded his cameras & cleaned his lenses," he explained in a 1990 interview. He related one version:

> ... One day, Mr. MURI,[Murai] Ryuichi, a professional photographer came to Life to see his friend.
>
> As he had an unfamiliar lens, I asked him to show it. It was the Nikkor 85mmf/2 lens. I borrowed it and took snap shots of Mr. Duncan, saying, "This is Japanese Sonner[sic]."
>
> "Oh, Japanese Sonner. Where is Japanese Cadillac?" laughed he with a tone of kidding the imitation paradise Japan.
>
> I made an enlarged print of 8 × 10 in. (approx. 20 × 25 cm) from the negative just taken and showed it to him, saying, "The picture is taken well even with Japanese Sonner."
>
> Upon looking at the picture, his countenance changed at once. With taking out a magnifier, "Amazing! It's very sharp! Whose product is it? Let's go to this company right away. Contact them, please," said he in rapid succession."[4]

Arthur Goldsmith, in his retelling of this story, adds more details.[5] Muri was using a Nicca, the 35mm Leica lookalike camera made by the Nippon Camera Company that NK was supplying all the lenses for. The friend he was visiting was another Japanese photographer named Takamasa Inamura — who was then working for Bristol's East-West Photo Agency. Miki borrowed the 85mm Nikkor from Muri, put it on a Leica IIIf, showed the lens to Duncan, who was standing in the hall between the *Life* office and Bristol's lab and took a picture of Duncan.

Duncan, in turn, remembered his words at that moment as "What the hell are you doing, Miki? You're wasting your time." Apparently Duncan's reaction was

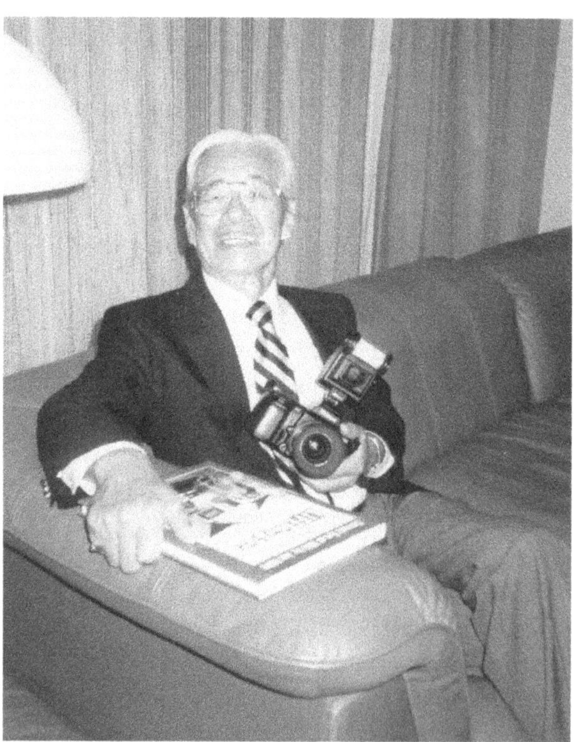

Jun Miki in 1990. Picture take by Peter Lownds while Miki was visiting in the Netherlands. By then Miki had become one of the most respected, elder photojournalists in Japan (Peter Lownds photograph, courtesy Nikon Historical Society).

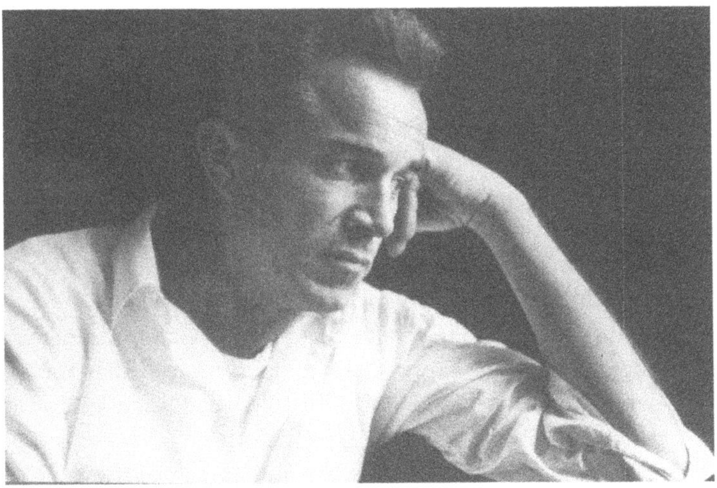

The Photographer, David Douglas Duncan, in *Life*'s bureau headquarters in Toyko, June 1950. This is one of the pictures taken by Jun Miki with an 85mm f2 Nikkor that got Duncan and Horace Bristol interested in Nippon Kogaku's lenses (Jun Miki photograph. Photography Collection, Harry Ransom Humanities Research Center, University of Texas at Austin).

not just because it was a Japanese lens, but also because it was evening and the outside light was failing.[6]

Bristol's memories also differed. "He had a camera with a big, rather heavy-looking 85mm lens on it. I asked him, 'What have you got there?' and he said, 'I've got a new Japanese lens that['s] really very sharp.' I said, 'I don't believe it.' Remember, at the time, we were all using German lenses exclusively. 'No, it really is,' he insisted. 'Here—you try it yourself."[7]

Bristol did. He loaded a camera and took a series of pictures of the view out their window, which happened to contain lots of details of windows, buildings and vertical and horizontal lines. Bristol developed the film and examined the results. Impressed, he took the negatives across the hall to the *Life* office where he showed the results to the dumbfounded Duncan.

Whichever version of the story one believes—whether it was a portrait shot of Duncan that he saw the next day in a print or negatives that same day taken by Bristol, the results were the same. Duncan was impressed, so impressed that he immediately wanted to go visit the factory where the Nikkor lenses were being made.

As Bristol noted, all the photojournalists at that point were using German lenses, primarily Zeiss or Leitz optics on their Contaxes or Leicas. Before the war, these lenses had been heavy but sturdily built, with indestructible, heavily chromed barrels holding what were state-of-the-art designs. Since the end of the war, the Germans had been in a continuous struggle to get back up to their prewar standards while at the same time incorporating the new technology of lens coatings and the use of lighter alloy metals. It was only in 1949 that West German Zeiss had been able to get its new version of the Contax, the IIa, into production. Leitz had just started to market an updated version of its Leica, the IIIf. Despite these recent advances, most photographers were still using equipment that predated the war, or had been built in the late 1940s when the German companies were still struggling. Duncan was still using the recently discontinued Leica IIIc. Bristol was still using prewar Contax IIs or IIIs. Their personal standards reflected their use of lenses that may not have been either the latest or the best that Leitz or Zeiss could offer. This is not to denigrate the Nikkors that these men were seeing for the first time. The Nikkors were good;

they were better optically than anything Duncan or Bristol had seen, but their quality had come as a result of a lot of hard work and steady improvements on the part of all of NK's workers. Zeiss and Leitz would improve their lenses over time, regaining or surpassing their own prewar standards, but they were never quite able to get past the Nikkors during the period when the Nikon rangefinder cameras were made.

Regardless of which story is truth (and slightly different other versions developed later), all the participants agreed on what happened next: Miki located and contacted his friend, Dr. Nagaoka, and the next day, Bristol and Duncan hired a taxi cab and rode over to NK's Ohi factory. According to Duncan,[8] before they went, Bristol or Duncan asked if any other Japanese company was making comparable lenses. They were told that the Canon Camera Company did. Either Bristol or Miki phoned the Canon factory but were told that they were "too busy" to meet with the two Americans. That brushoff would put Canon behind Nikon in terms of prestige throughout the 35mm rangefinder era.

At the Ohi factory, Dr. Nagaoka received them and took them on a tour of the facilities. Returning later with their own camera equipment, Duncan and Bristol had their lenses tested on NK's own optical benches and, set in the company's projection test equipment, compared the results with newly finished Nikkors picked at random off the production line. Impressed, Duncan postponed his work on Japanese art for a week to do more testing. All the Nikkors did well, particularly the 50mm f1.5 and the 85mm and 135mm. The new, simpler and slower 35mm W-Nikkor made less of an impression. Duncan and Bristol compared notes, and Duncan proceeded to buy a set of Nikkors in thread mount for his Leicas. Upon request, NK modified the coupling cams on Nikkor telephotos to match the Contax, and Bristol bought a set of Nikkors too.

The final question was what to do with the now redundant German lenses that Duncan and Bristol still owned. Regardless of how much better the Nikkors might have been, Leitz or Zeiss optics were valuable and almost impossible to obtain items in Tokyo. Rather than suddenly "flood" the market, Duncan and Bristol agreed between themselves to slowly outlet their surplus so as to not "...break the market."[9] And they did.

Duncan and Bristol completed their lens research on a Friday. That next Sunday, the 25th of June, the North Korean army swept across the 38th parallel in an attempt to engulf its southern sister country suddenly and quickly. Duncan reacted immediately. He shipped out for Korea at once, "beating the Marines" to the peninsula. He took with him two Leicas, one equipped with a 50mm f1.5 Nikkor and the other with a 135mm f4 Nikkor. During the first two weeks, Duncan scouted the rapidly retreating front line, met General MacArthur briefly and flew a combat sortie in an Air Force F-80 jet. Attaching himself to a marine platoon, which welcomed the veteran as one of their own, Duncan began taking scores of pictures trying to give a "...story which is timeless nameless dateless wordless story which very simply quietly says 'This is war.'"[10]

Within days, a second *Life* photographer who had just left Tokyo, Carl Mydans, would be also headed for Korea. He had been *Life*'s Tokyo bureau chief for three years, gone back to the United States, heard about the war and was promptly on his way back to Japan at General MacArthur's specific request. Encouraged by Duncan, he too got one of the unrestricted tours of the Ohi plant courtesy of Dr. Nagaoka, and before he headed to

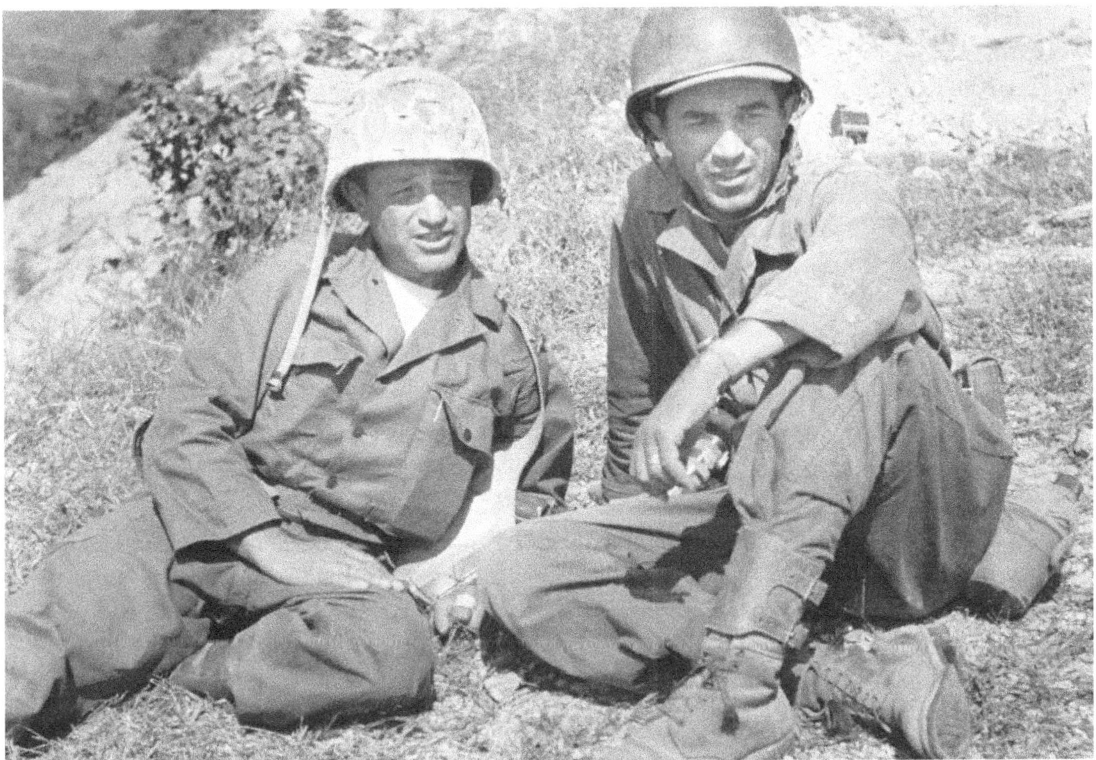

Carl Mydans and David Douglas Duncan seated together somewhere in Korea in 1950. Duncan wears his Leicas with Nikkor lenses around his neck. The soldier who took the picture used Mydans's camera (photographer unknown. Photography Collection. Harry Ransom Humanities Research Center, University of Texas at Austin).

Korea, he equipped himself with a full set of Nikkors for his Contaxes plus a Nikon camera. Instead of getting a 135mm f4 Nikkor as Duncan had done, NK provided him with a premarket sample of their new 135mm f3.5 Nikkor. Still just a prototype, this lens would not go public until the end of the year when it immediately became a favorite of all the professionals.

Mydans had gotten his start working for the Farm Security Administration shooting many of the same types of pictures of poverty and people struggling to find jobs and hold onto their dignity that Bristol had in his work for *Life*. He had been the fifth photographer hired by *Life* and had served as roving correspondent-reporter before the war. He and his wife, Shelley, also a correspondent for *Life*, had been caught in Manila in the Philippines at the outbreak of World War II. Interred for 21 months, they had been repatriated as prisoners of war. Mydans then covered the war in Italy and southern France before returning to Luzon on MacArthur's own ship.[11]

Mydans was followed by more *Life* photographers, including John Dominis and Howard Sochurek and later Hank Walker. As each one disembarked from his plane in Haneda, Bristol, now firmly established in his role of matchmaker, would take them immediately to the Ohi factory before they even had a chance to get to the Tokyo Press Club.* Dominis and Sochurek also bought Nikkors. Walker decided to leave the equipment he had brought with him with Bristol and left for Korea with a new all–NK outfit. Soon all of these men were sending back films to New York that had the lab technicians and editors talking. Duncan and Mydans were shooting the sharpest and best negatives *Life's* staff had ever seen. (According to Miki, *Life* sent Duncan a cable asking him why he was using a [4 × 5] "plate camera.")[12] What was happening? What were *Life's* photojournalists doing? What were these Nikkor lenses and what was this Nikon camera anyway?

How the Nikkors Were Different

What was it that these photographers, technicians and editors saw in 1950 that put the Nikkor lenses ahead of their contemporaries? One explanation could be that the Nikkors were not so much better as different.

Often the quality of photographic optics lies not so much in their technical details — statistics that measure dry "number of lines per millimeter" resolution or contrast — but often in the more subjective areas of appearance of sharpness, evenness of coverage and color balance. A photographer and a publisher may prefer certain photographs — and therefore the cameras and lenses that made those pictures — not because a lens is "sharper," but because of the combined effect that all of the lens's characteristics bring together to focus an image on film. Even today, the photographs that can result from using Leitz lenses have certain distinct color and tonal qualities that are quite different from the renderings of Nikkor lenses or Canon lenses, or other manufacturers.

Part of the reason for the success of the Nikkors in 1950 and afterward was due to the real quality of their lenses, but they were also successful because of the choices that NK engineers and designers made in the creation of the Nikkors. None of these factors were necessarily apparent from looking at the lenses' exteriors. Photographers found out these qualities by using the lenses and later by testing them.

Certainly the earliest Nikkors did not exude a high sense of quality the way the best products of West German Zeiss or Leitz, or even some of the more minor German companies did. Prewar German lenses had been made almost entirely of brass and other heavy alloys, such as phosphor-bronze (often used in focusing helicals). Nickel alloy and black-paint finishes had given way to shinier, more durable, polished or brushed chrome finishes that by 1940 had come to symbolize quality lenses for 35mm. This perception had been reinforced by the initial offerings coming out of the Russian occupied zone in eastern Germany and from most American manufacturers. Lenses for the Argus cameras and the lenses from Carl Zeiss–Jena were manufactured with inexpensive, unpainted aluminum-clad mounts that quickly lost their finishes. These lenses looked and felt cheap.

In their attempt to offer both the look and the feel of quality (and use up some of the

---

Ironically, by 1951 Bristol would shift over to using almost nothing but Canon Serenar lenses. See Tokyo on a Three Day Pass.

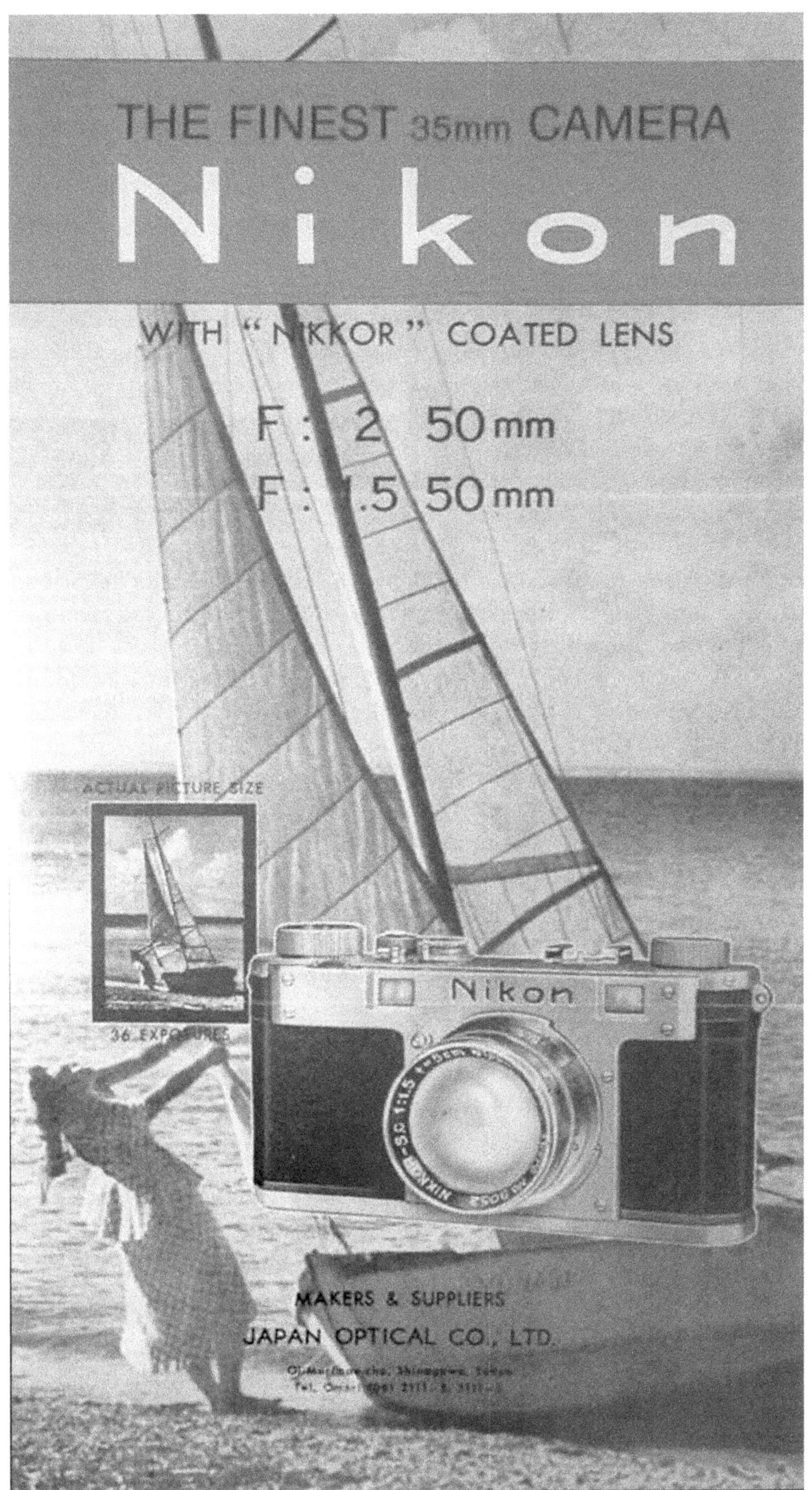

Cover of one of the brochures for the Nikon M published in 1950.

readily available brass being recycled from shell and bullet casings), NK built their early Nikkors around heavily chromed brass helicals, rings and mountings. This gave a "feel" of quality, but the cruder engravings and milled focusing rings and diaphragms, the coarsely finished and threaded screws and the hand-filed and fitted rangefinder cams could not have been very confidence-inspiring.

But by mid–1950, NK's machine work had improved considerably. Engraved letterings were smaller and better formed, screws were also smaller and better made. Late-Occupation Nikkors looked and felt good in the hand. They were still considerably heavier than the latest lenses coming out of Germany, which increasingly were using aluminum alloys for the outer rings and sheathings, but in appearance, they were a close match to most German lenses in that period.

Other factors combined with this basic quality appearance and feel. Of perhaps greatest importance was the glass that NK was using. First and foremost an optical firm, NK had a firm control over the making of all its glass. It was an area of their greatest advances and pride.

One of the biggest problems that the prewar Schott Glass Works had struggled with was how to minimize the bubbles that always seemed to result from the melting and mixing of batches of glass. Zeiss had even set one of its optical melting plants on a barge in the Elbe River in an attempt to use the surrounding water to buffer vibrations during melts. Dealers had become so used to seeing tiny bubbles in lens elements that they tried to make a virtue of a defect by stating that such bubbles marked the best-quality optical glasses. Yet from the beginning, NK's glasses were almost free of such defects. The company went to great lengths, even in the worst days of 1946, to insure that only the best pieces of glass were used in its own products — sometimes rejecting as much as 70 percent of a melt to get that quality. One of the major reasons NK never sold its 50mm f1.8 Nikkor was that it did not have enough quality stocks of the right type of glass.

A second major factor was that NK's engineers had been able both to use the best of the German designs and to do so in combination with the 80 or more glass types that the company could mix or match to its own needs. Speed was a selling point, and as the technicians (using lots of time on abacuses) tweaked the lens formulæ, they realized that lens coatings were giving them more options in design. The soon-to-be-released 50mm f1.4 was not much different from the 50mm f1.5, and, in terms of actual light transmission, it hardly gave any gain at all, but its value as a sales point cannot be overemphasized. The 135mm f3.5 Nikkor was only one-third of a stop gain over the old 135mm f4 Nikkor and Sonnar, and it was a bigger and heavier lens, but it included improvements that all users quickly noticed. Zeiss's designs, in a sense, remained stuck in its past. NK was aiming for a future.

The final factor in the perception of the Nikkors' quality lay in decisions that the technicians made that affected the actual pictures that the Nikkors recorded. NK did this in two ways: by setting the optimum distance at the closest focusing point and by emphasizing resolution over contrast at the wider apertures. If these two factors sound like a bit of sleight of hand, they were, but this generally meant sharper (although not necessarily crisper) pictures.

A lens can be computed to yield its best resolution at only one distance. Moving away from the setting can result only in a gradual lowering of resolution. This is why general purpose lenses computed for work at 20 feet to infinity never produce the sharp closeups that simpler lenses computed for such work seem to be able to achieve. Leitz had computed its lenses to yield their highest resolution at infinity. While there was nothing wrong with that decision, it meant that at closer distances, their lenses were not performing as well at the very point when details were becoming important. The Nikkors were designed to yield their highest resolution up close (one meter according to some, 13 feet according to others). This probably could not be discerned in a landscape shot of a misty mountain, but it could certainly make a difference when shooting pictures of individuals or closeups. Such pictures looked sharper because they were.

Generally lenses give their best performances closed down two or three stops. Wide-open, flare and aperture-affected aberrations conspire to destroy contrast and resolution. The Nikkors did no better than anyone else's lenses at infinity and wide open, but they did very well close up and wide open because they were optimized for that combination.[13]

These last items were subtle factors, but as magazines experimented with how far they could actually blow up 35mm negatives to the point where they were offering double spreads across the oversized pages of *Life* or *Look*, such factors became purchase breakers.

Summer and Fall 1950

While NK was enjoying this unexpected demand resulting from the outbreak of war, the story of OFITRA/Western Trading's relationship was continuing as a series of new challenges for both NK and Lindholm's combo of companies. On May 16, as a follow up to Liholm's successful negotiations, the Ministry of Finance within the Japanese government had issued its license to OFITRA to sell NK products to Occupation personnel. On May 19, Arkadi Grekow, once more in Japan and acting for OFITRA, requested that the chief of the Foreign Investment Board GHQ/SCAP issue its license to go with the one OFITRA had received from the government.

It is unclear as to whether this was follow-up paperwork to the request initiated earlier by Hagberg for Western Trading. Whatever, Grekow failed to pass security. His check sheet contained "derogatory information."[14] His request was turned down on July 5.

The potential for widespread corruption had been a continuing shadow hanging over Japan throughout the Occupation. The Japanese placed a high value on honor, but with low salaries the norm, and a bureaucratic system that took months to get things done, what could a trader do? In a business operational climate where every single action, from ordering a new machine to export licenses, had to receive a government approval — and where every government action had to have SCAP's approval — the temptation to smooth or expedite the flow of paperwork with a "bonus" must have been enormous. The Japanese already had an expression for the process that contractors had to go through in order to get locally issued building permits from SCAP: the "'three P's: petitions, parties and presents."[15] Apparently, Grekow had accused a department of SCAP of such corruption and now his remarks had come back to haunt him. Grekow protested and an investigation ensued.

The follow-up report stated that back on December 16, 1948 [possibly at a party?] Grekow "charged that no business deal could be arranged through the Foreign Trade Section, ESS, SCAP, unless someone was given a bonus. He also charged that a Lieutenant Colonel would not approve the export of fifty (50) locomotives until the price of one locomotive was promised him as a bonus."[16] Interviewed, Grekow denied the allegations. A Lieutenant Kor insisted that Grekow had made the remarks in front of his and Grekow's wives. However, it was now impossible to confront Lieutenant Kor because of Kor's value as a liaison officer with an important Russian mission. Grekow's wife denied that he ever said anything "...about dishonest practices."[17]

The whole matter dissolved into a kind of "He said — she said" argument from which the investigators could draw no conclusion. The security personnel recommended that the case be closed. On July 12, Major General Alonzo Fox, deputy chief of staff for GHQ, reviewed the records and, possibly deciding that the whole business was silly, or that Grekow by now had been put in his place, directed that Grekow and OFITRA get its license. On July 17, a humbler Grekow submitted his last letter and got his permit.

Uno Lindholm, through his personally owned companies, would now appear to have crossed a last hurdle in his dream to create an exclusive importing arrangement that featured the products from the largest optical producer in Japan. But the Japanese government was not through. On November 16, 1950, L.N. Salwin, chief of the Anti-Trust and Control Branch ESS/FTP, GHQ/SCAP received charges against NK from M. Ikenega, the director of the Commercial Division of the Fair Trade Commission. Using laws passed during the height of the reform activities of 1947, Ikenega accused NK, OFITRA and Western Trading of violating the law prohibiting private monopolies. The basis for these charges were the very contracts that Liholm and Hagberg had worked so hard to obtain and which had reached their final form only that previous spring. Suddenly aware that OFITRA had gained exclusive rights to import all NK products into North America and that NK had granted similar rights to Western Trading Company for Scandinavia, the government now decided that these exclusive contracts would result in a "restraint of trade"[18] and constituted a monopoly arrangement. The SCAP records do not include any additional paperwork on these charges. Whatever the results were, they must have been favorable toward OFITRA, because Lindholm's creations would continue to enjoy exclusive rights to import NK products for another three years.

NK's exports proceeded to grow all that summer. The CPO took only 25 cameras and 40 accessory lenses in June, but in July, the CPO took 182 cameras. Of these 118 were equipped with the 50mm f1.5 lens. OFITRA also imported nine cameras into the United States. An additional 76 lenses went to the exchange stores that month. August showed lower numbers with only 100 cameras reaching the military. Again, all but a few were cameras with the f1.5 lens.

Production had been keeping up with exports, but in September it slowed as NK began transitioning to a new high-speed normal lens, the 50mm f1.4 Nikkor. The company made 20 cameras with that lens that month and 14 of them promptly went to the CPO. A month later, they were shipping 76 of this combo to the CPO. Now offering the fastest normal lens in the world for 35mm, NK knew it had a winner, and it was doing all it could to get its camera out with the new lens. Strangely enough, the 50mm f1.5 Nikkor was not quite dead. It remained in production for another two months before quietly disappearing from NK's production reports.

In the meantime, Adolph Gasser was providing advice to NK's engineers on further improvements they could make to their camera and lenses. The company was then experimenting with adding clickstops to lenses, but the engineers were not sure how to do so while keeping the cost down. According to Gasser, this was a "big issue" with the company at that time. Writing to Sakai and NK, he advised them to "Keep it simple" with grooves in the lens underneath the aperture rings and a small ball bearing held in with a clip that would slide over and engage each groove in turn. NK would start to incorporate such click stops in its lenses with the new 50mm f1.4 Nikkor.

With flash — both electronic and bulbs — growing in importance, every camera manufacturer was trying to figure out ways to add and "arm a circuit" to their cameras that would fire a flash in sync with a shutter. Gasser designed a way to add a flash circuit to the Nikon which would become standard on the Nikon later that fall.[19] He remarked, a little ruefully, that he "took out a patent" on his design but never made any money on it.

Gasser also sent NK samples of an oil lubricant that had been developed by Shell Oil for the U.S. Air Force for use in aerial camera shutters and diaphragms. Because this oil was stable and highly resistant to the effects of extreme cold, Gasser was able to convince NK to start using it in the helicals, diaphragms and shutters in place of the heavy grease that had compensated for poor precision in the earliest Nikons. Whether it was due to this oil or NK's increasing quality, the resistance of the newer cameras to freeze up in cold weather was soon to pay dividends in building the Nikon's reputation.

While these problems were being solved and encouraging sales figures were being recorded, that August the final piece in the puzzle of how to build NK's products in the most efficient way fell into place. The American armed forces needed local photographic repair facilities, particularly for aerial cameras and other photographic equipment getting shot up, damaged or worn out in Korea. The U.S. Air Force contracted with NK to do those repairs. NK was once more in the business of supporting a military service. American technicians moved into the plant to supervise and check the work that NK's workers were doing. They did not like the quality control system that NK had been using at all.

While NK had always believed in and emphasized the importance of quality, until that August, quality inspections had been carried out by a separate division within the company. The inspectors did not actually get to check new cameras or lenses until they were ready to go to market. This may not have been much of a problem with lenses since only a few mechanical parts had to be checked and testings of resolution, element centering and coating uniformity could best be done on finished optics, but this had been a real problem with the more complex Nikons. By the time a camera reached the inspectors, if something did not work, or did not work properly, determining where the problem lay often meant disassembling an entire camera. Back in 1948 or early 1949, resources had been in such short supply that hundreds of new cameras had ended up being set aside rather than fixed.

The Americans used, and they demanded that NK use, a process called "Continuous Quality Control" for the company's contract work. Every repair was to be broken down into steps. A technician was not to move forward to a new step in the repair process until the previous step had been finished and the work in that step had been inspected and approved. A similar approach was being advanced by the American statistician Dr. W. Edwards Deming, who was in Japan at that time, and whose lectures NK engineers attended.[20] Here was the answer to NK's quality control problems. Once the Inspection Division understood what the Americans were doing and wanted, the company quickly incorporated continuous quality control routines into all its own processes. This change paid quick dividends. The final inspections had been a bottleneck with perfectly good cameras held up while the inspection teams worked their way through cameras that were not. Now with little problems being caught at an easily correctable point in the process, the final inspections were to become almost a formality as Mr. Watanabe or Mr. Koakimoto signed each card that went with every lens or camera that left the factory stating "This lens has passed the test" or "This article has passed the test."

A somewhat apocryphal story has come down concerning Watanabe and NK's inspection standards during this period. Two American sailors had ordered Nikkor lenses and, as was possible at this time, they stopped by the Ohi factory to pick them up. They toured the factory and eventually found themselves in the inspection room where Nikkors were receiving their final approval prior to shipment to marketing. The two described watching several men testing lenses with various equipment. The last person in the line was having trouble with one lens. He checked it one way, then another, all the while shaking his head in disapproval. Suddenly, he set the lens down on the table, picked up a hammer and with one blow shattered the lens's glass. Then he tossed the offending optic into a barrel before moving on to the next lens. Amazed, the two sailors checked out the barrel's contents. It was over half full of destroyed lenses![21]

Military necessity also got NK out of a postwar strike* on August 21.[22] Discovering the plant idle, army inspectors complained and had the Labor Section of Kanto Civil Affairs order the workers back to their jobs. The inspectors then wrote up the union because the strikers had hung numerous paper banners above the machinery. This was a fire hazard and threatened the buildings and machinery, particularly equipment still encased in heavy grease for reparations. The days when SCAP's mission was to reform and bring a liberal democracy to Japan were over. Prosperity and a strong economy to help in the fight against communism were now the priorities.[23]

The Deschin Article

David Douglas Duncan was in Korea by June 27, 1950, less than three days after the start of the invasion. A week later he was taking pictures from the cockpit of an attacking U.S. Air Force jet fighter. He was on hand to meet the U.S. Marines when they arrived to lead the first offensive out of the Pusan Perimeter. His photo essay covering a marine assault on "No-name Ridge" quickly gained him praise and publicity. He flew to New York in

The strike was apparently precipitated by NK's plan to close the Shiojiri plant.

September where he met briefly with *Life*'s editors before returning to Korea that fall. One of the things he had to explain was how he was managing to get sharper images than the editors were used to seeing.

Duncan would be with the marines at Inch'on and stay with them in their drive toward the first liberation of Seoul. He would be back with the U.S. Marines again when the Communist Chinese armies poured across the Chinese border into North Korea, and he would suffer and walk with these men in their fighting retreat around the Changjin Reservoir and down to the coast at Hungnam in December. He would be the last American to leave North Korea on Christmas Eve, 1950, wading out to a Higgins boat that had waited for him to get just a few more shots of the soldiers and marines evacuating.*[24]

By that November, the various news services and news magazines all had photographers in the field. As Bristol spread the word and these war correspondents talked among themselves, more and more bought Nikkors and used them. They included Michael James with the *New York Times*, John Rich of NBS, George Herman with CBS and Max Desfer of the Associated Press.[25] Impressed, *Life* ordered samples from NK, had them tested by Eastern Optical and followed up the results with an order for 20 sets, including cameras. Nikkors would be available for all their photographers. Not wanting to be left behind, *Look*, *Life*'s rival in the modern picture magazine business, soon had its own order into NK.

The onset of the Korean winter triggered additional interest in the Nikon camera. The Contax's shutter had never had a good reputation for smooth operation in cold weather, but the sub-zero temperatures were even stopping some of the Leicas. Seeing their cameras breaking, photographers began buying Nikons as rough'n ready "temporary" replacements. They soon discovered that the new Nikons, heavy and solid as bricks, could take the abuse of ice and mud, and that they kept on working, even in the worst cold.

NK took quick advantage of this interest. The company invited these journalists to stop by the factory at any time. When they did, Dr. Nagaoka made sure that they got the best of service, including rapid repairs and cleaning for their equipment. Mydans, in particular, reported that NK's president would say, "Sit down. Tell me what you like, but particularly tell me what you don't like."[26]

The bright brushed chrome covers were too visible and were attracting enemy gunfire. NK offered their camera with a black lacquered finish. Jun Miki, *Time-Life*'s Japanese contract photographer, was one of the first of the journalists to get such a finish. He described how "In Korea I remember being in a foxhole with an American soldier taking pictures when I heard a loud bang and the soldier slumped over dead. I knew at that moment that the bullet had my name on it. The Chinese were using my camera to aim at and it was too close for comfort. On my next trip back to Tokyo I paid a visit to Nippon Kogaku and had them paint my camera black!"†[27]

Rewinding film took too long and the rewind knob was too hard to grasp in the bitter cold. NK supplied Nikons with large rewind cranks. Soon NK was building a

---

**Duncan's photographs of Japanese art, the reason he went to Tokyo in the first place, finally ran as part of a special issue of* Life *on Asia published on December 31, 1951.*

†Miki's camera was a Nikon I and it became the only Nikon I ever to be painted black.

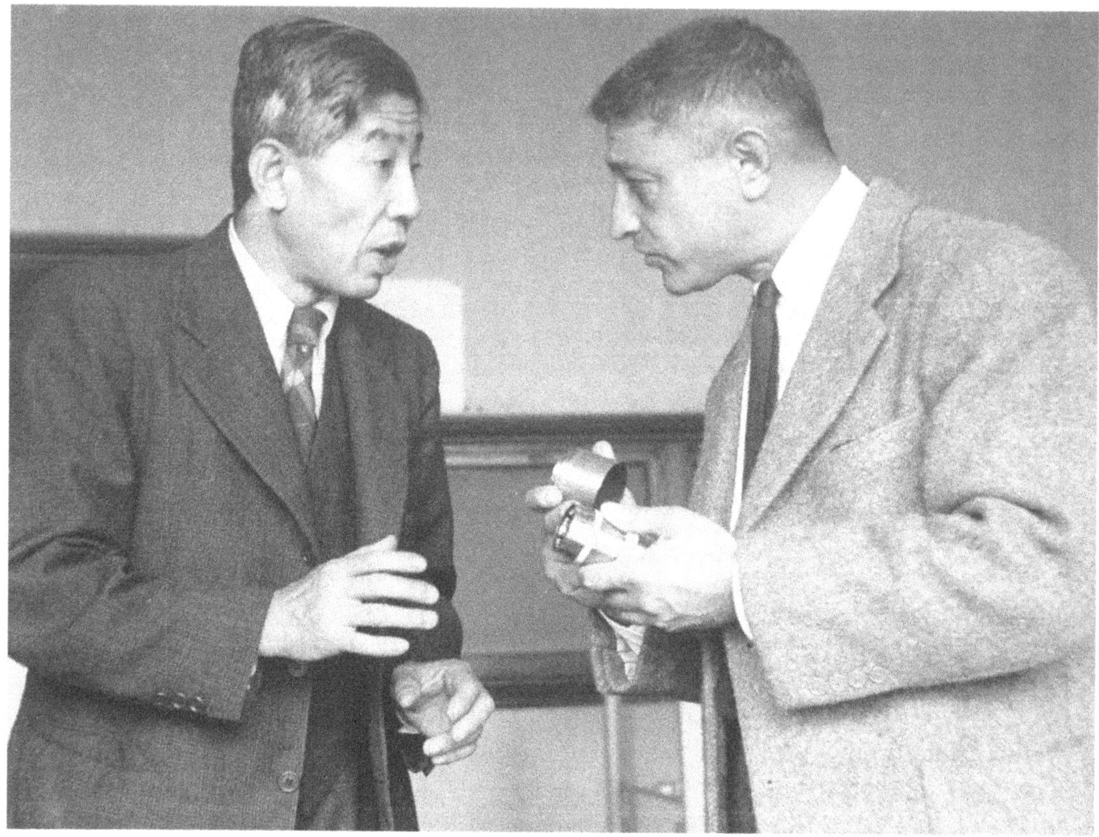

Dr. Masao Nagaoka (left), president of NK, in conversation with Carl Mydans. Mydans is holding a 135mm Nikkor and its sunshade in his hands (Tatsuhiko Arakawa photograph, courtesy Nikon Historical Society).

reputation as a company willing to listen and willing to do whatever it took to help the photojournalist get his or her pictures.

By October, the war coverage of all these photojournalists, particularly Duncan, had received widespread recognition. But, outside of a small circle of New York–based photojournalists, few people knew about the role that Nikons and Nikkors were playing. The most important American magazine devoted to photography, the Ziff-Davis publication, *Popular Photography*, now would get involved.

Up until then, the American press had generally ignored Japan and Japanese products. This was particularly true of the photographic press. Four major magazines were competing for attention in the newsstands during this period: *Popular Photography*, *Modern Photography*, *U.S. Camera* and *American Photography*. All four offered monthly summaries of news events relating to photography and cameras — including small reviews of new equipment, regular columns in areas of specialization, tips for beginners and showcases of photographs. *Popular Photography*, one of many hobby-oriented periodicals that the Chicago-based Ziff-Davis would promote over the years, had the largest circulation. The

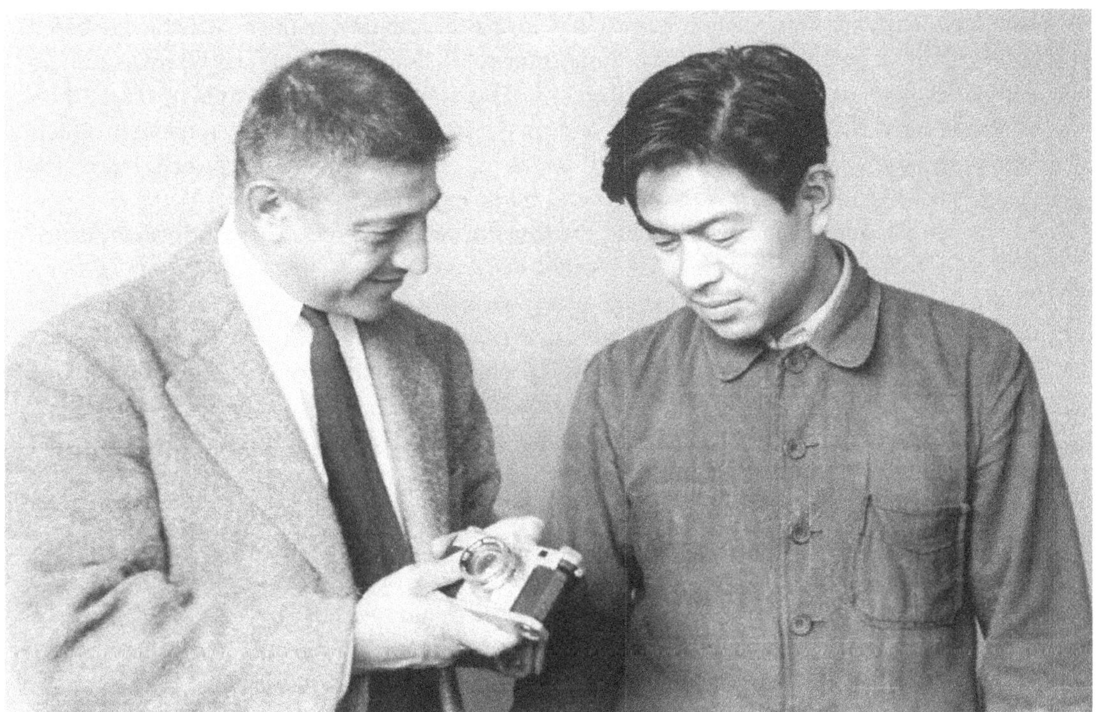

Carl Mydans looking at an early Nikon with Mr. Watanabe, the NK employer who signed off on all Nikkor inspections (Tatsuhiko Arakawa photograph, courtesy Nikon Historical Society).

then Cincinnati-based *Modern Photography* had started in the 1930s as *Minicam*,* only changing its name in 1948 in order to reach a wider range of format users. Its editorial approach was almost exactly the same as *Popular Photography*'s with possibly a little less fluff and a little more interest in equipment. *U.S. Camera* remained the poor cousin, always a little late and a little behind in its technology and editorial approach. For example, by the early 1950s, stereo photography, which had been a fad in the late 1940s, was rapidly fading, yet *U.S. Camera* continued a monthly column devoted to this genre until 1958. The Minneapolis-based *American Photography* was the oldest of the four publications, and the most literary, tracing its roots all the way back to the 1880s. But by 1950, its circulation was fading. Despite the efforts of its editor, George Wright—later to gain fame as the author of the *Nikon Manual—American Photography*'s text-heavy "How-to" articles and photo essays were no longer catching the eye of an increasingly equipment and innovation-oriented public. By the mid–1950s, *American Photography*, without ever seeming to have recognized the photo technology revolution taking place, was gone.

All four of these magazines remained heavily dependent on advertising revenue paid for by the major players in the camera industry, particularly Eastman Kodak and various

**The term "minicam" like miniskirts and minicomputers originally meant small. In this case, it meant cameras that took 35mm film or even smaller formats. Initially a derogatory term, as the use of 35 gained status, slightly larger formats, such as 6cm × 6cm tried to piggyback on the term.*

American manufacturers such as Argus. The mail order houses, many of which were based in New York and Chicago, were also important to *Pop* and *Modern*. The German camera companies, just getting back on their feet, were buying increasing amounts of space, their ads extolling their products' versatility and quality. Only a few ads for Japanese products were peeking out of the back pages, little items that hawked accessories or gadgets, or the cheap "Hit" type still cameras that were still being exported.

In late October, Michael Froelich, the director of Ziff-Davis's eastern division, called a meeting that included Norman C. Lipton, eastern editor of *Popular Photography*, Lynn Phillips, Jr., an advertising director who had worked for *Life*, and Duncan, then in New York reporting to his editors. Phillips was apparently the instigator of the meeting. He had gotten word from his former associates at *Life* about what they were doing with Nikkors and he felt that this might be important for *Popular Photography* to cover.

Duncan talked and showed the others his pictures. They were impressed, and Lipton began working on an item on the Nikkors for his regular "Tools & Techniques" column. The group decided that he could fit it into the February 1951 issue.[28] Duncan's work was continuing to gather rave reviews and in early November, *Popular Photography* decided that it would also do a story just on Duncan's Korean work as well. Arthur Bursch, a freelance writer and contributing editor who wrote under the pseudonym of "Bruce Downes," would interview Duncan and prepare a feature story complete with extensive illustrations.[29]

As these arrangements fell into place, Lipton happened to tell Jacob Deschin about *Popular*'s plans.* To quote Lipton in Goldsmith's story: "He said to me, 'Gee, that's a wonderful story! Do you think I could write about it? Or maybe you want to keep your scoop to yourself?' Well, Jack was a dear friend and a mentor of mine, and besides was working for a newspaper, not a magazine. I also figured it might reinforce my story rather than eclipse it. So I gave it to Jack, and it broke in the December 10th, 1950 issue of the *Times*."[30]

Jacob Deschin was writing from his position as camera editor at the *New York Times*. Just as the *Times* was the "Newspaper of Record" for the United States, and widely read throughout the country, so was Deschin's Sunday column a must-read for thousands of camera enthusiasts. Deschin wielded an enormous amount of influence nationally. The seal of approval he now gave the Nikon was the kind of publicity that NK and OFITRA could only have dreamed of obtaining. This would prove to be the moment the glass slipper fit, proof that the Nikon, the Nikkor lenses and the Japanese optical industry they represented were capable of standing up and being recognized among the best.

The first sentence of Deschin's December 10, 1950, column made it clear immediately that photographic equipment manufacturers everywhere had been challenged. "The first post-war camera to attract attention in America has created a sensation among magazine and press photographers following the report by Life photographers in Korea that a Japanese 35mm camera and its lenses had proved superior to the German cameras they had been using. The camera is the Nikon...." The third sentence drove the point home. "The

---

Deschin is best remembered today as the camera editor for the New York Times, *a position he held from 1941 until 1970, but he also was a contributing editor to* Popular Photography *from its founding in 1937 until shortly before his death in 1983.*

lenses ... are Nikkor, to which American experts give a higher accuracy rating than the lenses available for the German miniatures."[31]

Who were these "experts?"

"Mitch Bogdanovitch of Eastern Optical ... put the Nikkors through a series of rigid tests and found that the average quality was much higher than that of the German lenses."

"Frank Schershel ... said the f/1.4 was sharper than the Sonnar f/1.5."

"Martin Forscher ... described the Nikon as 'a combination of what I feel are the better components of the Leica and the Contax. ... [T]he Nikons are made to close tolerances of accuracy and are well finished.'"

Such a contrast to the Marjoram report from just two years earlier! And all these testimonies were coming from the same experts that Gasser had met and primed the previous winter. Now all of his efforts to win acceptance of this company and the products that he had come to believe in were bearing fruit at last.

Portrait of Jacob Deschin from 1950s period (photographer unknown. From the dustjacket of Deschin's book on the Canon rangefinder cameras. Copyright 1957, Camera Craft Publishing, San Francisco. Courtesy Nikon Historical Society).

"'There is no reason why the Japanese should not be able to keep producing these lenses," Bogdanovitch was quoted by Deschin as saying. "They have the tradition of skill ... and are basically perfectionists. Their lenses have excellent color correction ... and perform better at wide apertures than do Zeiss lenses. I saw these lenses a year ago and said ... they were as good or better than Zeiss lenses, but people thought I was crazy."

In the midst of this love feast, Deschin did not neglect to add the essential mobilizing information. He added that "Lenses and cameras will be available in limited quantities throughout the country about January, according to H.W. Liholm of the import firm, Overseas Finance and Trading Company, Inc., of San Francisco...."

The only sour note lay in the last paragraph. "Spokesmen for Carl Zeiss, Inc. ... and E. Leitz ... said ... that they had not yet had an opportunity to study and evaluate the Japanese cameras and lenses."* In reality, the reaction of the Germans — particularly Dr. Karl Bauer, the president of Carl Zeiss, Inc., USA — was volcanic. For even to *suggest*

The above quotes from the December 10 Deschin column are copyright 1950 by the New York Times. *Reprinted with permission.*

that any lens or camera could be better than a German lens or camera had to be "Absolutely a lie!"[32]

Within days, Deschin was on the phone with Lipton, nearly in tears. Bauer had not only screamed over the phone at Deschin, but he had also threatened to pull all of Zeiss's advertising from the *New York Times*. Having thoroughly flamed Deschin, Dr. Bauer then calmed down and, the next Sunday, Deschin gave him space in his column to make a statement: "We have not furnished any factory new Contax lenses for many years until we started distributing them in 1949–50 with the Contax cameras. ... It is, therefore, improbable that the Zeiss lenses compared in these tests were new, whereas the Nikkors were new lenses. ... Fair comparative tests must naturally be made under equal conditions."[33] The first return shots had been fired, and the German camera industry was now joined in a competitive battle that would last for another 20 years with the Japanese the final and almost absolute winner.

Later, Zeiss would provide new lenses for a rematch. This time the German products beat the Nikkors overall — barely. But the damage to the Germans' reputation had already been done. Thousands of Americans read and remembered the Deschin column, few saw or remembered the later report on new test results.

Nippon Kogaku and the Overseas Finance & Trading Company had now been given a gift more precious than anything a fairy godmother could have granted: free publicity from the most widely read and respected photographic commentator in the country. In addition, the most widely read picture-news magazine had added its endorsement as well through its publication of numerous pictures taken with Nikkor lenses. The challenge both companies now had to face was how to build on that publicity and get enough cameras and lenses into the hands of dealers and the buying public.

5

1951 to 1953: OFITRA's Success and Ultimate Failure

Understanding full well the value of Deschin's December article, Liholm immediately pressed NK to send as many cameras and lenses to the United States as soon as possible. He and Gasser together were developing an ambitious marketing plan for the Nikon, but they needed merchandise for it to work. Both men figured that together they had the time and abilities to make the Nikon a big success. As fate would have it, they had only ten months.

Having sent no Nikons and only a few 50mm f1.4 lenses to the United States since the previous August 1950, NK now found itself in difficulty trying to put together a decent order for delivery to San Francisco by January 1951. It finally managed to ship 100 Nikons — 50 with the f1.4 lens, 50 with the f2 lens — but only by cutting back on its shipments to the CPO. The military exchanges were indeed proving to be a gold mine for NK, and its sales to the CPO were now averaging better than 300 a month. In November and December 1950, NK delivered more cameras to the CPO alone than it had ever sold of the first Nikon model in the entire year of its availability.

To add to OFITRA's sales hopes, NK added 41 additional f1.4 lenses (probably all in Leica thread mount since all the Nikons were still being sold with lenses), 60 of the new 135mm f3.5 Nikkor, 60 85mm Nikkors and 60 35mm wide angles. OFITRA would be able to supply at least one of everything to its small but growing band of dealers. The long, slow days of knocking on dealers' doors one-by-one and being turned away were coming to an end.

In addition to the growing dealer interest, the December 10 column had resulted in a different kind of recognition. SCAP officials did not fail to note the glowing words that Deschin paid to the Nikon and its company. On January 6, 1951, the chief of the Economic and Scientific Section, Major General William F. Marquart, forwarded a letter to Dr.

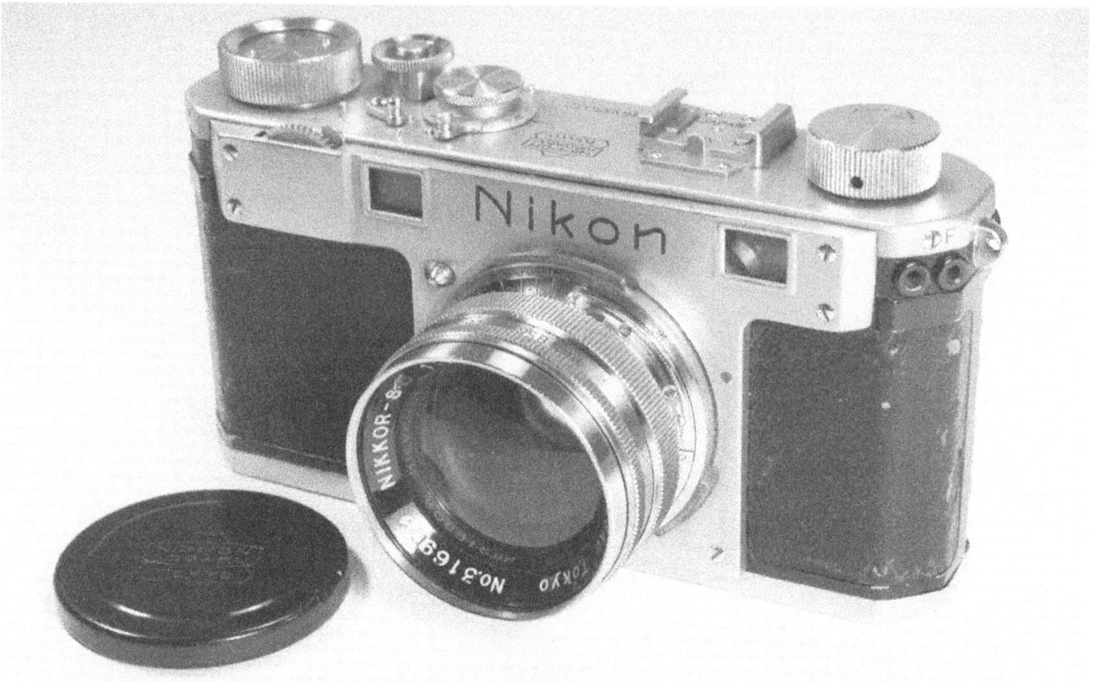

In response to the publicity that Deschin's article in the *New York Times* was generating, Nippon Kogaku shipped 100 Nikons plus numerous accessory lenses to OFITRA in January 1951. This was the biggest shipment that Nippon Kogaku had ever made to the United States up to that time and the first one in months. This camera was part of that shipment. It was purchased by Adolph Gasser for his brother and remained in that family until 2005 when it was purchased by the author. It has factory-installed flash synchonization — a standard feature since the previous November. Nippon Kogaku would refer to this as a "Nikon S" but Americans would call this a "Synched M" or a "Nikon M/S" since the letter "M" still proceeds the serial number.

Although similar in appearance to the Nikon M Hans Liholm had been given in April 1950, the finish is everywhere superior with much less evidence of hand-fitting and adjustment. The normal lens is the 5cm f1.4 Nikkor, the fastest standard, normal lens ever sold for a 35mm camera up to that point.

Nagaoka, adding his own praise for what the company had achieved. This one letter meant almost more than anything else to NK. For over five years, it had been in a constant struggle with the Occupation authorities, trying in any way it could to get the right combination of products, work conditions and paperwork together so that it could stay in business. SCAP had been both friend and opponent, easing the way sometimes, creating barriers at others. Often NK officials must have wondered if it was possible to ever get it right. Now ESC/SCAP was saying:

> ... It is gratifying to note that your company has been accorded world recognition in a most difficult field which demands extensive scientific knowledge and exceptional mechanical skill.... The employees of Nippon Kogaku may take pride in making a substantial contribution toward the rebuilding of the economy of their country.[1]

General Marquart was a career officer with a background in anti-aircraft guns, journalism and boxing. He had no background in either economics or science, but in his letter he got everything right.

The Nikon cameras that would be coming to the United States that January still looked much the same as the first Nikons from 1948, but internally and externally there had been many changes. [See Appendix IV for more details.] The most important change was that since the end of the year, Gasser's flash sync had become a factory standard. On the left end corners two pairs of receptacles now allowed synchronization at either the fast speeds or the slow speeds. These cameras still had the "M" before the serial numbers, but the factory was referring to these as Nikon "S"s, or synced Nikons. Sometime that spring, NK

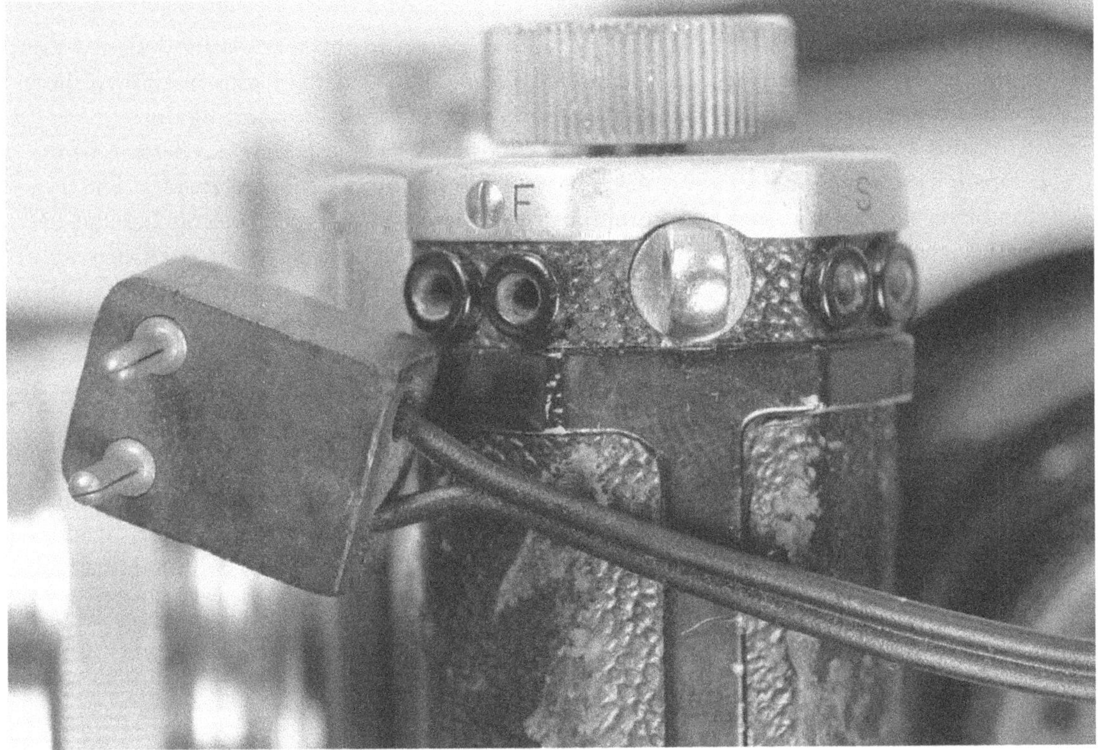

The flash synchronization sockets for the Nikon camera that became standard in November 1950 and the special flash attachment cord these sockets required.

The camera illustrated dates to January 1951 and still has the "M" preceeding the serial number. Synched Ms usually have the "F" and "S" engraved next to their sockets. Nikon S cameras have those letters engraved on the top surface.

The front socket, labelled "F" would have been for use with FP (focal plane) bulbs using the faster, top-dial shutter speeds. There would be a zero or negative delay in the contact in order for the long-burning FP bulbs to peak while the shutter curtains were moving across the film gate. The "S" socket to the back was for the use of bulbs, or electronic flash using the slower, bottom dial shutter speeds. This circuit included a delay of 24 milliseconds to allow the first curtain to complete its travel.

finally used up the last of the initial order of top coverplates. When the factory ordered new plates, the initial "M" no longer seemed necessary, and it was soon dropped.

Latter-day photographers have questioned why Gasser and NK went with these bipost, "nonstandard" flash receptacles. In fact, their sockets were so unusual that every camera came with a flash cord to insure that a user would have some means of attaching a flash unit. The answer has several parts: In 1950, there was still no standard. Leitz, Kodak, Rollei, and even Zeiss, all used flash plugs that were different from the eventual "PC" (Prontor-Compur) standard. The only virtues the PC outlet offered was that it was cheap and compact. It was easily damaged and, with just a friction fit, tended to lose a connection at the most critical moments. NK's engineers were probably wise to seek an alternative. The problem was that their solution was to use the design that Gasser had already come up with, and it never caught on.

The PC receptacle's compactness had been the main reason that Gasser designed the double prong in the first place. He had started adding flash sync to Nikons in his own shop and had found the PC outlet too small for handwork and prone to shorting out.

Other more subtle changes, partly cosmetic, partly practical, were a reflection of the company's growing understanding of American tastes and operational preferences. The thin chrome on the early cameras had a dull finish with details such as the back latches and the shutter release finished with a mirror-polished chrome reminiscent of the Art Deco style that had influenced most industrial design into the 1940s. By the time the Nikon lost the "M," all of the metal work had been changed to a uniform bright brushed chrome of higher quality. The company reduced the diameter of the advance and rewind knobs and raised them to help make them easier to grasp. The accessory shoe also went through several changes, becoming a sturdier, three-piece unit in the process.

The top speed of $\frac{1}{500}$ of a second was still slower than either the Leica or the Contax offered, and the small, reduced view of the finder was not the best, but otherwise, feature-for-feature, the Nikon now compared favorably with the finest 35s made anywhere. In addition, it had two extra selling points: Its lenses were being acknowledged as among the best and fastest in the world, and the camera's handling characteristics were superb.

The Follow-up Press Reports

With the new year, the February 1951 issue of *Popular Photography* began appearing in the newsstands with Lipton's promised commentary on the Nikon and Nikkors. Whereas Deschin had concentrated on the reports of experts concerning the quality of the Nikkor lenses and the Nikon camera, Lipton took a more historical approach. His first three paragraphs detailed the June "discovery" of the Nikkors that was still news to most American readers. Lipton's story included the testing of the 85mm Nikkor and the visit by Bristol and Duncan to NK's factory and their meeting with Dr. Nagaoka.

His next paragraph consisted of a basic description of the Nikon, stating that it "looks like a sturdy facsimile of the Contax II." He detailed the recently added flash sync, then noted that the various Nikkor lenses "seem to have been put together with more than reasonable care."[2] As had Deschin a month earlier, Lipton concluded with the hope and promise that "Overseas Finance and Trading Company of San Francisco will have several hundred cameras and accessory lens outfits to distribute among key camera stores throughout the country early this year."

On Sunday, February 4, 1951, the *San Francisco Chronicle* would give Liholm its best hometown publicity with an article[3] in the Leisure section that described the camera, gave prices and even indicated which of the local stores were carrying the pictured camera and its lenses.

Michael James had been one of the correspondents who had used Nikons in Korea. He now added the one-two punch to Deschin and Lipton's articles with a news report in the *New York Times* that headlined "Optical Market Bid by Japanese Seen: Stiff Competition Is Reported for Germans Who Once Held Monopoly in the Field." The lead sentence followed up with: "The Japanese are making a bid to take over a large portion of the international precision optical market." Nippon Kogaku was the Japanese company giving the Germans that competition. Again, James retold the story of the discovery of the Nikkors, relying more on Mydans's testimony this time. He went on to describe how the Americans were surprised to find that "the Nikon body was apparently as good as the famous Leicas or Contaxes. Second and the bigger surprise was that Nippon Kogaku's lenses, tested mainly out of curiosity, were noticeably better than those from Germany. As a result virtually every picture made in Korea by magazine photographers has been made with Japanese lenses."[4]

Stating that it was the discovery of the Nikon camera that led to the discovery of the lenses was not quite true, but a quote from Hiroshi Hairama [*sic*, should possibly be Shirahama], whom James identified as "Nippon Kogaku's chief of manufacture and principal designer of the Nikon"—thereby depriving Hirishata Fuketa of the credit he deserved—that "shipments to the United States earlier in the year had met with virtually unbending dealer and customer resistance," has the ring of truth.

So also does the quote from Shirahama that followed: "You are justified to look on Japanese goods with suspicion ... before the war, Japan exported some frightfully shoddy goods to the United States. Some of the things going there now, I am sorry to say, are not much better."

James would add additional information in the final paragraphs that hinted at the subtle hand of Lindholm and possibly Sakai. Further tests of the camera and its lenses had been conducted in both the United States and Sweden. The Swedish tests "run on lenses by the Swedish Government's testing laboratories indicated that they were better than the German ones."

"One of the most outstanding facts" James quoted the Swedish report as saying, "is that the Japanese optical glass industry apparently has succeeded in manufacturing complicated glass compositions of a type used in Sonnar (German Zeiss) but without the flaws and bubbles which the Germans so far have not yet been able to eliminate."

Having once more put down the German optical industry, particularly Zeiss, the press let up. The next technical report would not come until May and, while positive, it would be more careful and thoughtful.

Downes's feature article on Duncan—with 14 photographic illustrations drawn from

Duncan's work taken the previous fall — appeared as planned in the March issue of *Popular Photography*. While the focus of the pictures was on men in combat and the focus of Downes's text was on Duncan himself, he did find room to have Duncan comment on his equipment.[5] Downes described Duncan as "...for most of his work he used a 50-mm f/1.5 Japanese Nikkor lens, but carried with him and used also 85-mm f/2 and 135-mm f/3.5 Nikkor lenses. They were recommended to him by photographer Horace Bristol in Tokyo, and tests showed their superior resolving power. When the negatives began arriving in New York, according to Frank Scherschel, Life's assistant picture editor, they turned out to be the sharpest 35-mm negatives the lab had ever processed."

Duncan followed up his photo essays in *Life* with a book published by Harper & Brothers in 1951 titled *This Is War!* A combination of four very personal narratives and three uncaptioned, extended photo essays, the work cemented Duncan's fame and authority. It remains one of the most forceful and intimate looks at armed combat ever published.

Duncan included a three-page description titled "Photo Data" in the back of this book. In it he noted that "Every photograph in This is War! was taken with a Leica camera, but equipped with Nikkor lenses ... made in occupied Japan."[6] He went on to say that "...Horace Bristol ... and I began experimenting with the whole new line of Nikkor lenses ... and discovered, to our utter amazement, that their three standard lenses for 35mm cameras were far superior, in our opinions, to any standard 35mm lenses available on the open market — British, American or German." They had, indeed, replaced all their lenses for their cameras with Nikkors, "Except for our wide-angles and extreme telephotos — over 135mm." Duncan also noted that all the part's for the Nikons and Nikkors were made with Japanese materials except "The spring for the focal plane shutter of the company's Nikon camera — it is Swedish because the manufacturer consider it superior to any steel yet made in Japan."* Duncan concluded his description of his equipment by noting the many other photojournalists in Korea were also using Nikkors and Nikons — just as Lipton and others had done.

As good at marketing as he was at taking pictures, Duncan continued to let the photo industry promote his book through its feature articles. In August 1951, *U.S. Camera* would reprint the photo data pages from *This Is War!* virtually unchanged — giving more free publicity to the Nikkors as well as to Duncan.[7]

James L. Collings, the photography columnist for *Editor & Publisher*, the newspaper publishing industry's weekly magazine, also gave Duncan and his new book a full page's coverage, including extensive descriptions of the Nikkor lenses.[8] Unlike the photographers working for the picture news magazines, American newspaper cameramen were still firmly wedded to the 4 × 5 Graflex Speed Graphic camera with its cut film backs and large flashguns. Yet 35mm was making inroads and coverage like this would soon allow the Nikon to reach into newspaper offices as well.

Three months later, John Wolbarst in *Modern Photography* would provide an extended review of Duncan's book under the title "Do These Pictures Need Captions?"[9] Duncan's refusal to number his book's pages or provide captions had become a major source of

This use of Swedish steel for the springs would show up again as a sales feature in a Nikon Camera Inc. brochure dated 1952.

controversy — and publicity. True, the verbal information was there — if one read the written essays that preceded each set of illustrations — but that was apparently too different for most reviewers. Wolbarst strongly defended Duncan's presentation decision — a formatting that would, in time, become commonplace. *This Is War!* was ahead of its time. By forcing readers to view his photographs without words and within their own context, Duncan was pioneering a visual vocabulary that would become commonplace in thousands of yearbooks and other picture collections by the 1960s.

American publicity and Duncan's continuing testimony were having a major impact in the United States, but its effect on the Japanese was even more profound. In late June 1951, Duncan, once more taking pictures of Japanese art, took time off to address the Circle of Confusion Camera Club in Tokyo. On July 2, the English language *Nippon Times* quoted from his talk. He told the club members that "Since [the discovery] the Nikkor lens has become probably the most desirable lens in the world, rated next to none. Optically the Nikkor lens are really something extraordinary."[10] For the Japanese, by now long used to having the world despise anything they manufactured, the positive reception of the Nikkors had become a revelation. Duncan praised not only the Occupation authorities who had worked so hard to turn Japan around, but also the Japanese themselves. "...and I think even more gratifying is the fact that Japanese are coming up to other cameramen and exclaim 'Aha — Nikkor lens.'

"It is a great source of pride to the Japanese too. They feel that they have put something on the market at this particular time that other people of the world have a lot of respect for, and we certainly do."[11]

Awed by this praise, the *Japan Camera Trade News* would reprint the *Nippon Times* article in its entirety in its August issue a month later. Here is another point to remember concerning what the Nikon and Nikkor lenses did. For not only did they help create a future for all Japanese products overseas, but they helped the Japanese regain some of the self-respect that had been lost in defeat six years earlier.

Encouraged by both his own experiences and faith in NK's products, Jun Miki would show his own support by helping found the Nikkor Club in Tokyo that year. This new photography club was open to users not only of Nikons, but

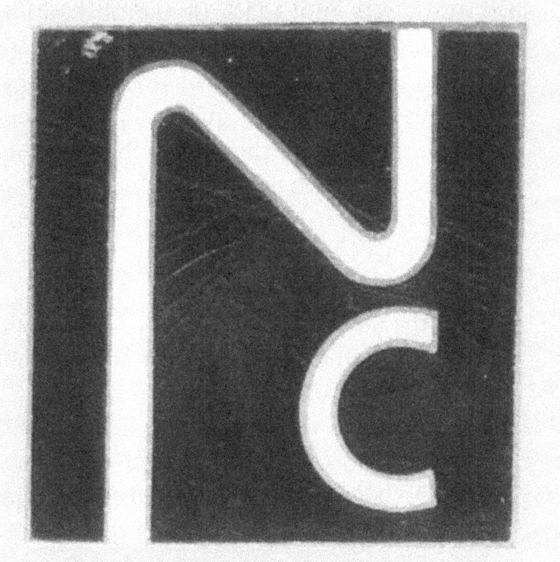

First NIKKOR CLUB Pin. Jun Miki founded the Nikkor Club in 1951. It soon boasted a worldwide membership of photographers wanting to support NK and its products. Robert Capa, the famous photojournalist and cofounder of the Magnum Photo agency, was an early member. When he fatally stepped on a landmine in Indochina three years later, he would have a Contax around his neck, but a Nikon by his side (Tony Hurst photograph).

Nicca and Airesflex owners as well. Dedicated to the improvement of photography using NK products, the Nikkor Club soon had a following that added its own enthusiasm and interest to promote the Nikon and Nikkor optics in Japan.

All of the various stories and articles described above would lead any researcher into confusion trying to determine when the various Nikkor lenses that NK was now producing were actually introduced. None of these writers — Deschin, Lipton, James or Downes — seemed to be entirely sure as to whether Duncan, Mydans or any of the other photojournalists were using 135mm f4 or f3.5 lenses, whether they were using the 85mm f2, or whether they had the 50mm f1.5 or the newer f1.4 normal lens. Part of the actual answer might be found by reading the SCAP export production records carefully. According to those monthly reports, the first 135mm f3.5 Nikkors went out in January 1951, while the 135mm f4 Nikkor remained in production for at least another three months. How could someone like Mydans or Duncan have gotten a hold of the newer lenses months before they were available? How did Deschin get the impression in December that the 135mm f3.5 Nikkor had already been tested in New York and had come through with such flying colors?

The answer is that NK had a huge development and testing lead time for all their lenses. For example, their 85mm f1.5 high-speed telephoto was first prototyped in 1950. It did not go on sale until 1953. By then it had gone through seven different designs! NK had the 135mm f3.5 in its final development stage by June 1950, but it did not actually start regular production until late that fall, with the first specimens reaching marketing in January. But NK was quite willing to send out early samples to persons like Mydans and Duncan because they knew that testimonies from these users could only help them make more sales later. Duncan had the 135mm f3.5 in his kit by September. Pictures of Duncan taken in Korea clearly show him carrying a 135mm f3.5 Nikkor mounted on one of his Leicas. That was the lens that Lipton saw and which Downes and Deschin wrote up.

In the meantime, Gasser was a busy man. At some point during the previous year, he and Liholm had shaken hands on an agreement to share the camera marketing part of the business. OFITRA would import the Nikon and its lenses, and Liholm would handle all the financial and correspondence details, while Gasser would act as a consultant working on distribution, sales, servicing and checking the new equipment as it came into the United States. OFITRA and Gasser would split the proceeds fifty-fifty. Both men understood that they had to bring in product and had to get it out to dealers if they were going to continue to enjoy the interest and support that Deschin's article had triggered.

With so many endorsements in hand, Gasser was finding that many dealers' doors were finally opening. He and Liholm criss-crossed the country, showing off the Nikon and Nikkors to any dealer willing to take a look. Sellable cameras, however, continued to be in short supply. NK had its new 135mm f3.5 in full production, but was still making the 135mm f4 and shipping almost all of them to the CPO to meet demand. France was now an open market as well, and Western Trading was getting a share of the cameras and lenses for that country.

In 1951, the premier trade show for America's photographic and optical industries was

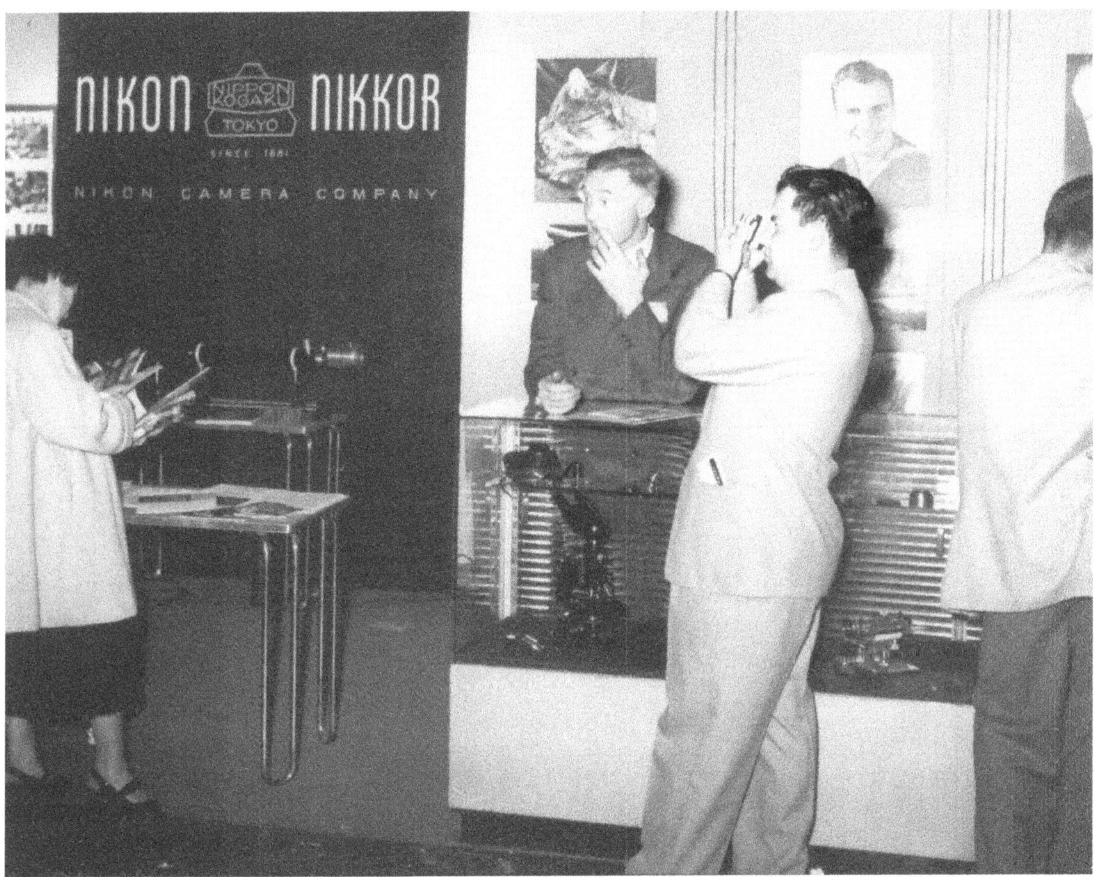

Adolph Gasser manning a Nikon Booth at the April 1951 regional convention of the Master Photo Dealers and Finishers Association in San Francisco. The display to the left includes an "optical column meter which showed [attendees] the sharpness of the Nikkor lenses and how they did not vary in back and front focus." The "Since 1881" is slightly misleading. It refers to the founding year of the Iwaki Glass Seisaku-shoo — one of the three glass companies that combined in 1917 to form Nippon Kogaku. The customer at the counter is examining a Nikon. In the display case can be seen a case for a Nikon camera, a variframe finder, the front cap and lens hood for the 85mm Nikkor, a microscope and a construction level. Note that the display identifies the booth as belonging to the "Nikon Camera Company." This new name would soon move to the forefront, replacing OFITRA as the public face for Liholm and Gasser's venture (photographer unknown, courtesy John Gasser).

the Master Photo Dealers' and Finishers' Association (MPDFA) national convention held that year in Atlantic City the second week of March. Reporting on the convention in his column, Deschin featured OFITRA and the Nikon in his second paragraph. "The show witnessed the formal debut of the Nikon miniature cameras and Nikkor lenses in the booth of the Overseas Finance & Trading Company, Inc. The display drew particular attention because of the possibility that the lenses might in the future offer a serious challenge to the former German supremacy in this field. Adolph Gasser, representative, said the Tokyo

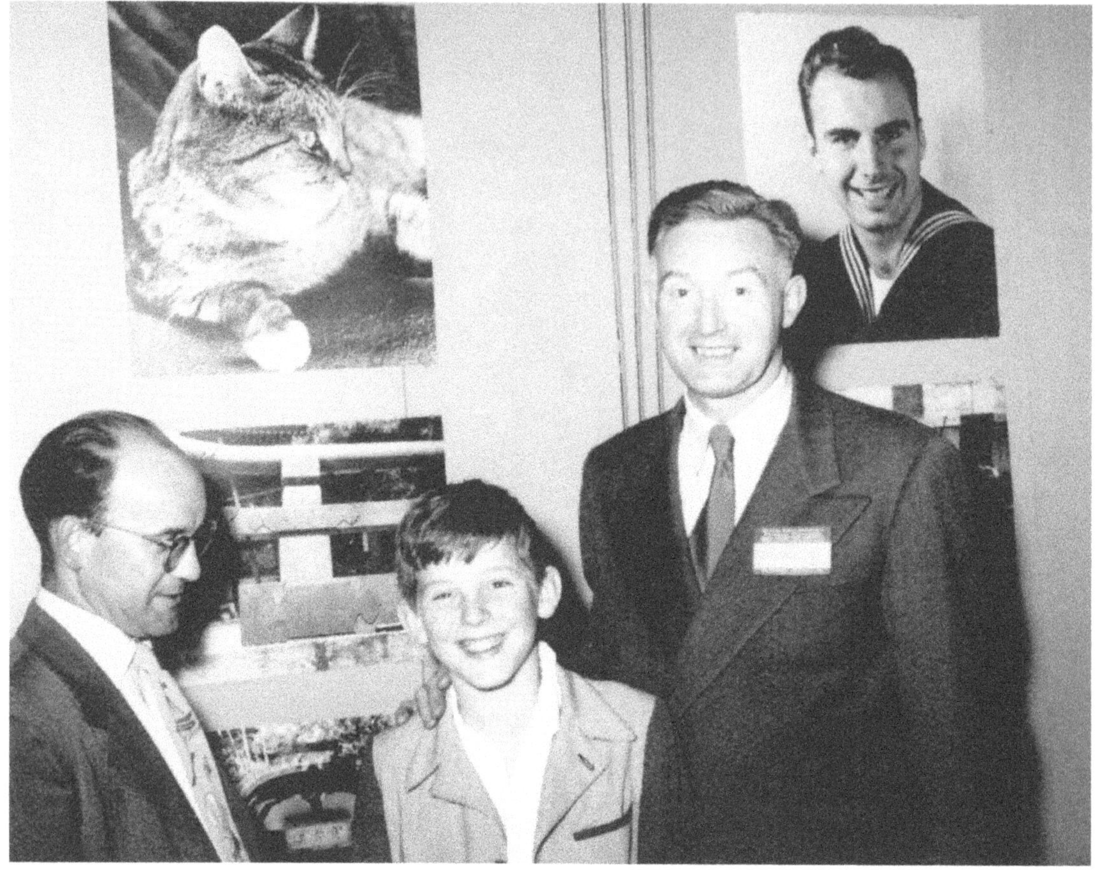

Adolph Gasser and his then eight-year-old son, John, standing in the Nikon Camera Company booth in April 1951. The identity of the other man is uncertain. The enlargements hanging behind Gasser were designed to show off the sharpness of Nikkor lenses (photographer unknown, courtesy John Gasser).

factory was now in full production of the equipment, turning out about 300 complete camera units a month."[12] Deschin went on to quote Gasser on prices both for the cameras and for the lenses. A Nikon camera with the 50mm f1.4 lens would sell for $349.00. This was a lot of change in 1951, but still less than either Leitz or Zeiss were asking for their top-of-line cameras.

Dr. Bauer must have at least dampened Deschin's enthusiasm. By using the words "in the future" Deschin was being a bit more cautious than he had been two months earlier. Also, by calling the 1951 MPDFA convention the Nikon's "formal debut" — while not entirely inaccurate — meant effectively dismissing the more than 100 Nikons that had already gone to the United States and to dealers in the previous two years.

The next month Deschin would have his own 85mm f2 Nikkor, courtesy of Liholm, who had responded to a personal request by shipping Deschin the last one he had in stock at that moment — at a discount. Deschin was appropriately grateful, sending Liholm a personal letter dated April 19 along with a check, and stating how he was "eagerly looking forward to using [the lens] at a ballet tomorrow."[13]

Suggestive of the winds of change that were blowing, *Popular Photography*'s annual roundup of cameras and accessory lenses in its May issue now listed dozens of Japanese-made cameras. The Nikon is there, framed by the Nicca and the Olympus 35 (still using the 24 × 32 format). They share their page with the Minolta 35, a Petri and two models of the tiny 16mm Mycro and the Opema (another 24 × 32 35mm camera). Nikkors also made the photographic lenses list, although prices were not available.

These listings would soon be followed with the release of the first price list from OFI-TRA. The Nikon camera was listed as available with either a 50mm f3.5, a 50mm f2 or the 50mm f1.4. A body only was also available. Prices ranged from a low of $152.00 for the body (including the federal excise tax) up to $349.00 when equipped with the 50mm f1.4. The three normals and the three accessory lenses and a "universal finder" followed with prices for lenses ranging from a low of $54.50 for the 50mm f3.5 all the way up to $198.00 for the 50mm f1.4. The company was shown as the Overseas Finance & Trading Company, Inc. with the address at 465 California Street. Cameras included a leather case, lens cap and a flash attachment cord. Lenses included carrying cases and lens caps. Telephoto lenses also included a lens shade. The final fine print reminded readers that all Nikkors were also available in Leica thread mount at the same prices. In reality, the 50mm f3.5 Nikkor, even though it would remain on the price lists for that year, was already out of production and never would really be available, even though all the early ads for Nikkor lenses showed it in the illustrations.

The Nikon camera and the Nikkors would get two more pieces of free publicity that spring. *Modern Photography* had been scooped by its larger rival, but it was determined not

Price List for NIKON CAMERA and NIKKOR LENSES

	Minimum Fair-Traded List Price	Excise Tax	Total
NIKON CAMERA WITH f/3.5 50mm NIKKOR LENS	168.00	21.00	189.00
NIKON CAMERA WITH f/2 50mm NIKKOR LENS	235.00	24.00	259.00
NIKON CAMERA WITH f/1.4 50mm NIKKOR LENS	316.00	33.00	349.00
NIKON CAMERA BOX ONLY	136.00	16.00	152.00

All Nikon cameras include synchronization for flash and strobe, ever-ready leather case, lens cap and flash attachment cord.

	Minimum Fair-Traded List Price	Excise Tax	Total
NIKKOR LENS f/3.5 50mm	50.00	4.50	54.50
NIKKOR LENS f/2 50mm	98.25	8.75	107.00
NIKKOR LENS f/1.4 50mm	180.00	18.00	198.00
NIKKOR TELEPHOTO LENS f/2 85mm	160.00	15.50	175.50
NIKKOR TELEPHOTO LENS f/3.5 135mm	140.00	14.50	154.50
NIKKOR WIDE ANGLE f/3.5 35mm	82.00	7.50	89.50
UNIVERSAL FINDER	42.00	4.00	46.00

All Nikkor lenses are available in Leica type mount at the same price. Prices include carrying case and lens-cap. The Telephoto lenses are supplied with lens shade.

OVERSEAS FINANCE & TRADING COMPANY, INC. · 465 California Street, San Francisco

Overseas Finance & Trading Company's first price list for the Nikon camera and its lenses, 1951.

to be left behind. In its May 1951 issue, it also reported on the March MPDFA show and noted that for the first time there was a booth "...entirely devoted to a top-grade Japanese miniature, the Nikon, made by Nippon Kogaku. This shows both Contax and Leica design influence, plus a number of additional features." Before moving on to German and American products, the writer noted that "...the Japanese optical industry was well represented also by numerous binoculars and opera glasses, which showed a very high standard of finish and performance."[14]

Modern then followed up with the most extensive coverage that any periodical would ever offer the Nikon during this period. The June 1951 issue (on newsstands in early May) featured an in-depth, six-page review of the Nikon and its lenses written by John Wolbarst.[15] The article led with a full-page blowup portrait of the actress Nancy Marchand in her role as Queen Elizabeth in a Kraft Theatre TV show. The reason? *Modern* wanted the readers to know how really sharp the Nikkors were.

Taking an in-depth, historical approach, Wolbarst again recounted the saga of Deschin's article and the "discovery" by *Life* photographers of the Nikkor lenses the previous year, including the part played by Bristol and Duncan. But then Wolbarst showed that he had done his research, tracing the history of the camera back to 1949 and the early 24 × 32 format. As noted in this book's introduction, he described the meeting of Liholm with Gasser and the resulting withdrawal of the first Nikons from the market. He gave Gasser full credit both for showing how the camera could be redesigned so it would advance the film eight sprocket holes and for designing the flash synchronization system.

This was the first article to note many other details, such as noting that the Nikkors were available in either Leica or Contax mount and the fact that the 50mm f1.4 lens had click stops. Wolbarst then went on to report on a series of careful tests that had been done on the Nikkors and their Zeiss counterparts. He concluded that both the two 50mm f1.4 Nikkors and a 50mm f1.5 Sonnar that he tested offered the same amount of sharpness and contrast. Again, Bagdonowicz [*sic*] and his Eastern Optical Company were called on as experts. This time, Bagdonowicz measured "T" stops — the actual amount of light the lenses passed through to the film, rather than the nominal "focal" stops, which only indicate an aperture to focal length ratio. The results indicated that, although the Nikkor was rated as an f1.4 lens, its actual T rating wide open was no better than the Sonnar at f1.5! Unfortunately, Wolbarst did not list the serial numbers for any of the lenses he tested, so it is impossible to know if the 50mm Nikkors were in the earliest 505XXX series or the slightly later 316XXX series. While this might not have made a difference, NK may have changed the optical formula slightly to include a larger front element that should have had better light-gathering capacity.

The 85mm f2 Nikkor fared a bit better. Wolbarst reported that "Resolving power was very high; there was no noticeable flare and contrast was excellent wide-open."[16] Generally, Wolbarst was impressed, and other than the fact that these lenses weighed considerably more than the German equivalents, he gave the Nikkors an "A" rating, stating that "The verdict was that the Nikkors which were *tested* [magazine italics] were equal to the best of the miniature camera lenses of any make. They were not super lenses — they were simply extremely well made lenses of the Sonnar type." Wolbarst concluded by echoing the thoughts already expressed by Deschin and Lipton: "The Nikon and its lenses indicate the beginning of a new era in the optical industry." and "…it is a direct challenge to the long dominant Leica and Contax. It will be interesting to see how serious the challenge is and how it is met."[17]

Advertisements and the End of the Gasser-Liholm Partnership

The history of the Nikon in the United States now enters a period in which documents are few and far between. Almost the only evidence available appears to be the advertisements that OFITRA and its affiliate, and later successor, the Nikon Camera Company, Inc., ran in the three major photography magazines starting in April 1951. SCAP was winding down its involvement in the Japanese economy and was no longer interested in keeping the detailed records that had marked the early Occupation. The earliest export-production records were compiled weekly. In May 1949, they changed to monthly. The last month in the archives of camera production records is April 1951. These record that NK was easily producing over 300 Nikons per month and continuing to expand the numbers for accessory lenses as well.

The Japanese economy, spurred by rapidly rising exports and the demands of the Korean conflict, was finally booming. There was little more that the Economic and Scientific Section of SCAP could do to help. Soon the designation of "Made in Occupied Japan" would disappear from Japan's exports. On March 8, 1952,* the Occupation officially came to an end, and Japan was its own master once more.

If SCAP can no longer be a source, the advertisements that OFITRA bought can be used to trace many of the changes that were occurring both with the camera and the company responsible for its importation and marketing. *Popular Photography*, benefiting from its early advocacy of the Nikon, ran the first ad for the camera on page 80 of its April 1951 issue. Taking advantage of three months of free publicity, the two-column, half-page ad proclaimed: "The camera that was DISCOVERED by photographers of a great picture magazine! The Nikon f/1.4." A small illustration of a Nikon S equipped with the 50mm f1.4 Nikkor was framed by text referencing the "American newsmen in Korea." While *Life* is not mentioned by name anywhere in the ad, no knowledgeable reader could fail to make the connection. The ad concluded by boasting that the camera and lenses were made by "Japan Optical Company, one of the world's largest optical institutions" and that "Independent experts have found NIKKOR coated lenses to be the finest 35mm lenses made anywhere! And the NIKKOR f/1.4 the fastest 35mm lens." Readers were invited to send in a coupon to receive a free booklet that would provide "full information." "Own the camera used by top professionals!"[18]

Customers who responded to this ad probably received one or two of the orange-and-white brochures that NK was printing, along with a form letter from Liholm that repeated

---

Or April 28, 1952, depending on different sources. The treaty with the United States to end the Occupation had been signed in San Francisco on September 8, 1951.

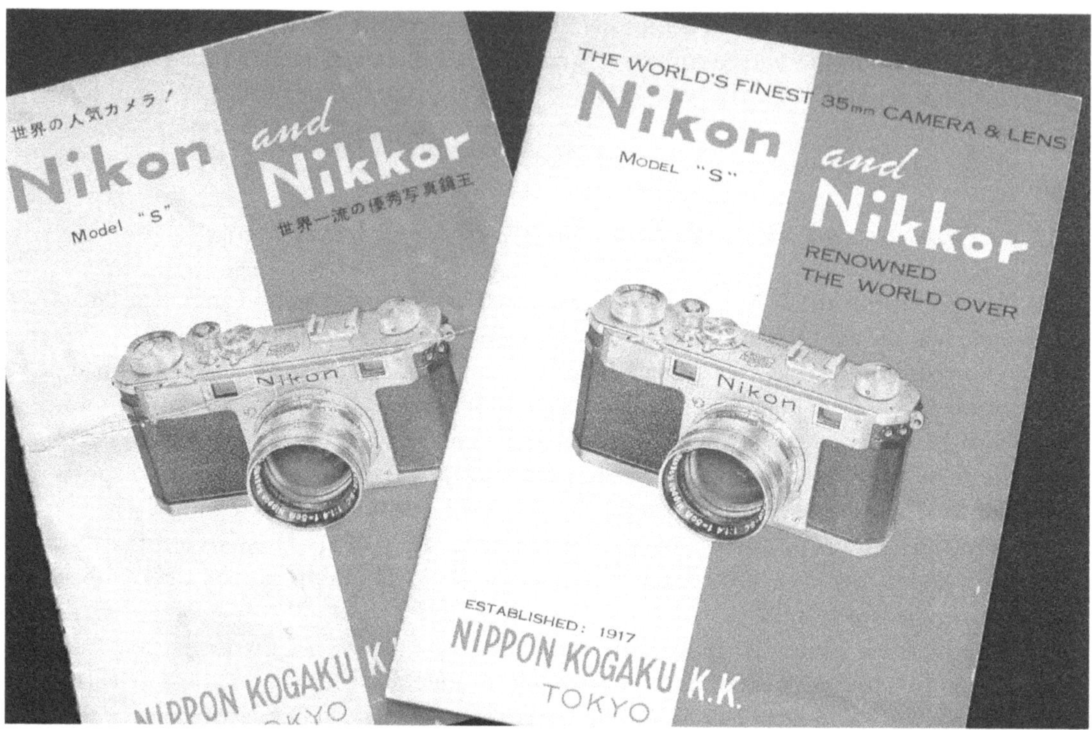

Two early Nikon brochures from 1951 or 1952, one in Japanese, one in English. These were typical of the literature that Nippon Kagaku provided to early dealers and customers (courtesy Nikon Historical Society).

some of the praise that had already come from other writers, including a direct mention of Bruce Downes's article on Duncan that had appeared in the March 1951 issue of *Popular Photography*. "Your camera dealer may have a small supply of NIKON cameras and NIKKOR lenses by now, and will be glad to show them to you," Liholm wrote. "If he hasn't, please send us his name and we will endeavor to make the necessary arrangements with him. Or, you may order directly from us."[19]

While this sales approach may not seem that different from the puffery and appeal to outside testimony that are still stock-in-trade today, other details pointed toward what was happening. First of all, although the reports in the press had all made reference to the manufacturer as "Nippon Kogaku," in these first ads, the English version, "Japan Optical," was the only company name given. Also, the importer was listed as OFITRA and "Overseas Finance & Trading Company, Inc." The address was 826 Merchants Exchange Building in San Francisco — the same building where Liholm had set up his office back in 1948. All these details were soon to change.

Having also decided that the Nikon and the Nikkors were worth considerable coverage, *Modern* got its first ad for the Nikon in the same June issue that had featured the Wolbarst article. This ad is exactly the same as one that had appeared in the April and May issues of *Popular Photography*, and discussed above.

A two-month lull was broken only by a small ad in the July *Popular Photography* placed by Alfred Bass, Inc. of San Francisco, which promised that "WE HAVE THEM! SENSATIONAL NEW NIKON."[20] Bass was an early supporter of the Nikon and would promote the camera on its own throughout this period.

Note in these ads the clearly stated support for dealers. By insisting that sales had to proceed through specialty camera stores, instead of general catalogue companies, OFITRA was insuring that the Nikon would be seen by and sold to the same class of customers who were buying the top German-made miniatures.

This marketing decision by Liholm also resonated with the photographic press. Dependent for much of their subscription revenue on readers who bought their equipment from camera specialty houses, these magazines had to watch again and again as the major catalogue companies, like Sears & Roebuck, would make the sales that the dealers and specialty importers had worked so hard to create. In a letter dated June 11, 1951, to Noboru Hamashima,* Norman Lipton, now the managing editor of *Popular Photography*,† made the point that "There is a basic antagonism between the photographic industry in this country and the large mail-order houses like Sears-Roebuck and Montgomery Ward that works to the disadvantage of professional precision-type products like yours."[21] Liholm and Gasser's success in enlisting press support for their products can be read in the next sentence. "You made a wise choice in selecting such a conscientious and technically sound partnership as Messrs. Liholm and Gasser to introduce your product to the American photographic trade. These gentlemen, with their personal representations in behalf of your company and your products, have overcome anti–Japanese prejudice here to an unbelievable extent."[22]

Lipton's anger at the mail-order companies had come to the forefront because Sears was now importing the Nicca camera under its "Tower" label, and running ads that stated that this was the camera and lens "...used by the leading magazine photographers with special reference to Life Magazine."[23] A month later, Sears had not yet given up on that campaign, and in a letter dated July 30, 1951, Lipton would express his personal concern directly to Liholm. Apparently the ad campaign had been the dream child of a Mr. Seeger of Jardin-Matheson (of Hong Kong fame, and the first buyers of Nikons), and Lipton was determined to kill it. He even wrote to David Douglas Duncan, then back in Tokyo, to enlist his personal intervention with Nagaoka and Hamashima.§ Lipton's personal concerns, friendship and admiration for both Liholm and Gasser come out clearly in the last paragraph of that letter.

**Hamashima had been in charge of NK's civilian sales before the war. He became a member of NK's board in 1947 and head of the board in 1951. He replaced Hiroshi Shirahama as president of NK in 1963.*

†That spring, Ziff-Davis had made the decision to relocate all of Popular Photography's *editorial offices to New York. As managing editor, Lipton was now in charge of the country's major photographic magazine.*

§Duncan would also write to Liholm at this time. In a letter sent from Tokyo and dated July 16, 1951, he thanked Liholm for the binoculars Liholm had sent him, but complained about the new 50mm f1.4 Nikkor, which he felt exhibited too much flare and was not as good as the discontinued 50mm f1.5 Nikkor. Whether NK was able to resolve that problem to Duncan's satisfaction is not clear. NK did change the formula of the rangefinder f1.4 several times over the 14-year production run of this lens.

Please convey my greetings to Mr. Gasser and my hopes for a successful outcome of his negotiations in Tokyo. It is hard to tell anyone why I have become personally interested in your product and your personal marketing problem. Part of it is a professional admiration for a fine product and the desire to see a good story come out right in the end. The rest is the open and refreshing manner with which you and your associates have conducted your relations with the people in our industry. You have set a fine example for others to follow.[24]

Sakai had personally invited Gasser to come to Japan. Eager to work directly with NK's engineers and technicians, Gasser was willing to make the trip and that summer he got his chance. He brought with him a considerable amount of his own testing equipment. One item was the optical bench that Mitch Bagdonowicz had designed for him. With this bench, he could accurately determine the exact focal length of a lens, and tell where its focus was falling — in front of, on or behind the focal plane. He sent copies of the design for this optical bench to NK and they built one of their own to his specifications.

He also packed and took with him his "Strobotac," a potentiometer that consisted of a repeating strobe light with settable RPM in its gas tube. This allowed a technician not only to test the actual speed of a shutter, but also to check the width of the slit opening in a focal plane shutter. The Strobotac could also be used to check the accuracy of movie camera shutters and projectors.

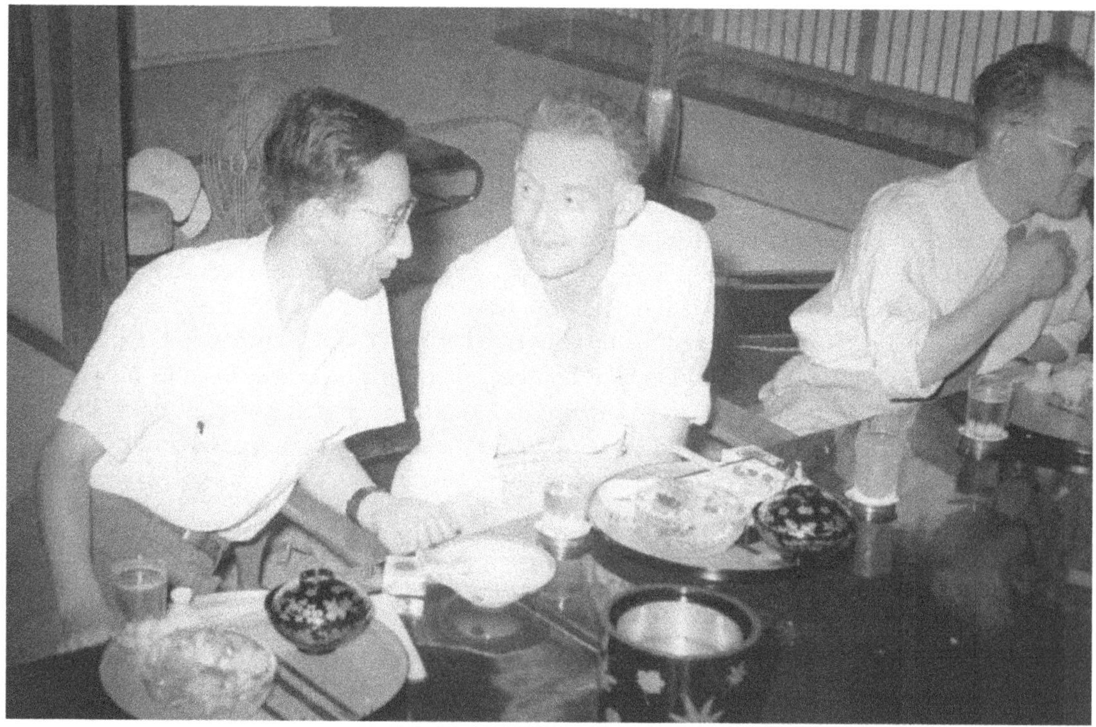

Adolph Gasser in Japan. He is speaking with Sanetoshi Kuratsuji, Nippon Kogaku's sales manager (photographer unknown, courtesy John Gasser).

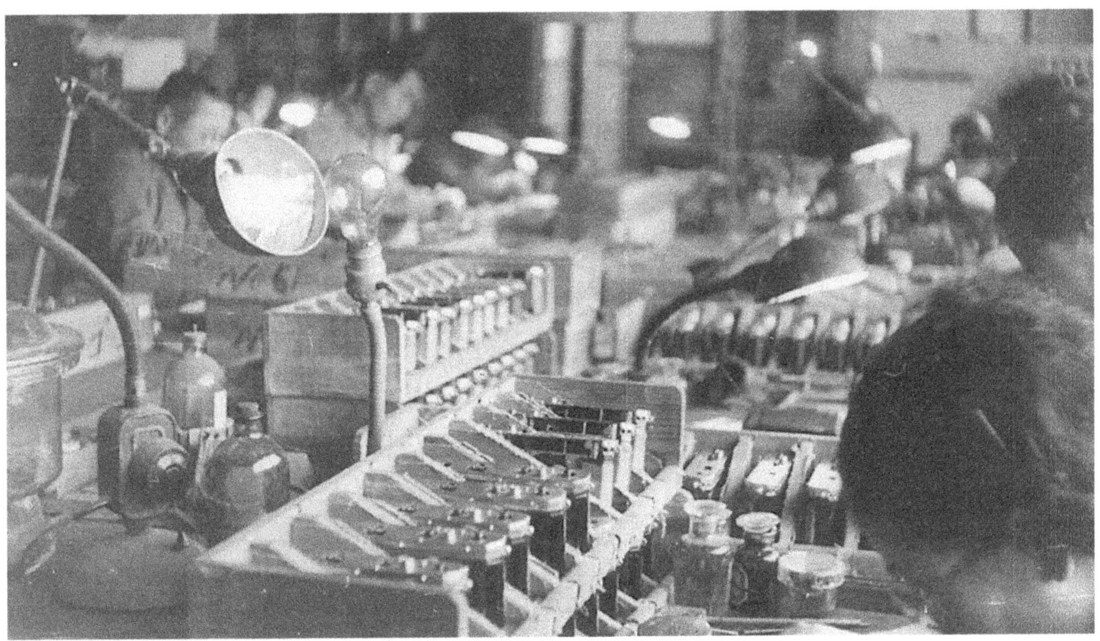

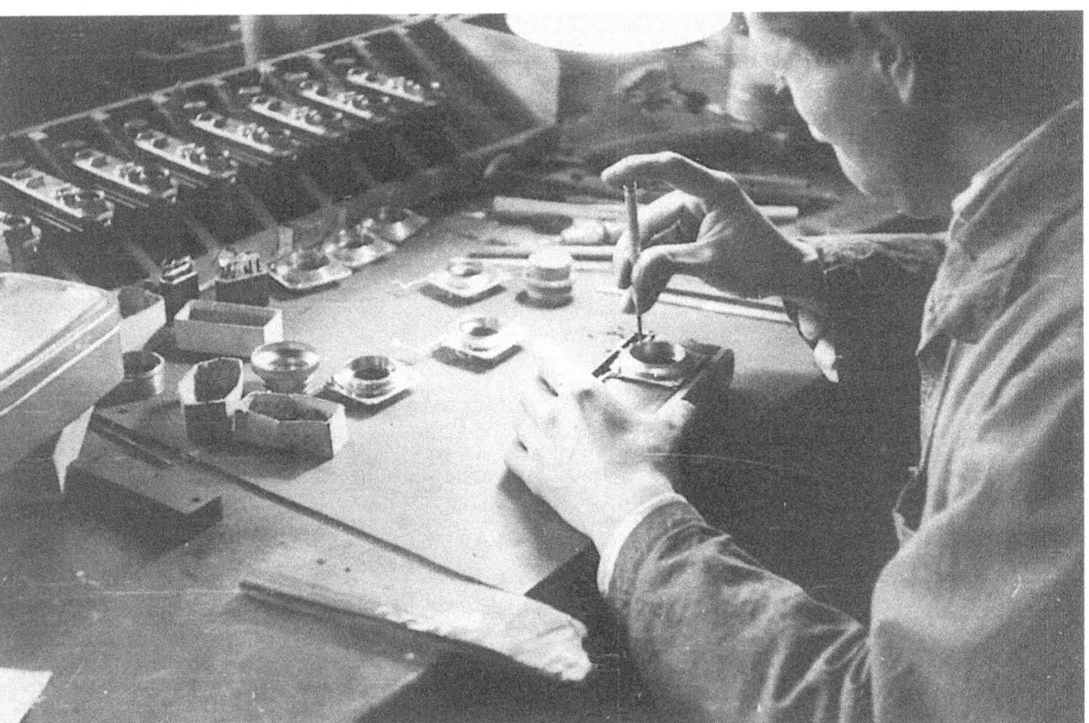

Interior scenes in the Ohi factory's camera assembly room in 1951. The system of bench manufacture clearly shows in these pictures taken by an American sailor who had just bought his own Nikon S at the factory. Cameras moved through the system in sets of ten, each with its own slot in a long, open, wooden box. NK was still using this method as late as 1954 (Danny Husta photographs, courtesy Adriana Husta, Nikon Historical Society and Tony Hurst).

This tool was to prove invaluable to NK's engineers. One of the major problems that Marjoram had pointed out was the poor timing of the Nikon's shutter. Gasser had started testing every camera in his shop as it arrived in America and was still having to adjust and correct every one. NK had elaborate equipment for testing shutters but they were not very accurate. Gasser showed them how to use strobes to check shutter openings and convinced them that their $\frac{1}{500}$ of a second shutter speed was not within tolerances. They had to build a shutter that would allow for the acceleration of the curtains and varying of the opening so as to get even exposure across the width of the film gate.

Gasser spent a month in Japan, first staying in a "luxury" hotel before moving to more modest accommodations, and working with NK technicians every day. Sakai was "extremely nice" to him, but NK's engineers were to be the real beneficiary from Gasser's stay.

But more important for the Nikon, Gasser brought an enthusiasm and knowledgeable interest to the camera design teams at a time when they were experiencing a crisis mode. By July 1951, the Nikon camera was already more than four and a half years old. The company had sunk thousands of precious yen into its development and yet its sales were still far behind those of rivals such as Canon. Perhaps, the engineers suggested, they should abandon the Contax bayonet and redesign the camera to take Leica thread mount lenses like all the other 35mm rangefinder cameras that the American soldiers were so eagerly buying. This would also allow the company to offer its lenses in only one mount. NK may have shown Gasser several prototypes for such a Nikon "L."* It is also possible that they showed him an early prototype for the next model of the bayonet-mount Nikon. Whichever prototype Gasser saw, he was not impressed. "This is not a Nikon," he told NK's engineers. The prototype was too big, too high, the cover plate was "all wrong" and this camera did not resemble the current model at all. No, Gasser told them. Stay the course. You have a good product and its mount sets it apart. If NK changed to a Leica thread mount camera now, the Nikon would be lost in a sea of Leica copies, and it would only hurt the sales of the thousands of Nikons that had already been sent to dealers. Keep what you have, Gasser advised them, and start working on designing a new camera that has a better rangefinder and viewfinder, is still compact like a Leica, but looks like a Nikon.

Gasser also discovered that Sakai had become concerned about OFITRA's sales levels. As a result, Sakai had been working privately on a possible arrangement for OFITRA to sell Nikons through Sears & Roebuck. Gasser was appalled. This was the very approach that he and Liholm had been fighting, and by their efforts, earned Lipton's compliments. But Gasser realized that his host had no understanding of the position that "Tower" labeled cameras held in the hierarchy of American camera quality. He advised against such a contract, insisting that Sears & Roebuck was not the best place to gain a reputation in America. Real income and sales would come in time through gaining a high reputation in the

---

*There were apparently at least four of these Nikon Ls. Nikon Inc. still owns three of them. The fourth, an earlier one, ended up in the hands of Joseph Abbott, Joseph Ehrenreich's righthand man and vice president of Ehrenreich Photo-optical Industries. He, in turn, sold it to a New York collector. Along with one other prototype Nikon, it sold for more than £36,000 at Christies Auction in June 2005. It is now in the Westlicht Museum in Vienna, Austria.

trade. He was able to convince Sakai and Nagaoka to stay with dealers, even dictating the letter that Nagaoka then sent to Sears, and that threat receded.

The Nippon Camera Company and its Nicca were to be the real beneficiaries of that decision, although, in the end, it did not hurt NK either, because every accessory lens Sears sold to go with a 35mm Tower was a Nikkor. Turned down by NK, Sears continued to import Niccas under its "Tower" label, and would do so for the rest of the life of that camera. Liholm did allow the small Mikron binoculars to be sold through the Sears catalog, but Sears did not prove to be a good market for these either.

In August 1951, new two-column, half-page advertisements reappeared in *Popular Photography*. The picture of a Nikon camera was the same, as was the layout, but the ad was quite different in many ways. This time the text failed to make any reference to the discovery or the Korean conflict except for the phrase "...chosen by famous news photographers." Instead, the lead began with "The world is talking about the NEW NIKON CAMERA! for its unequaled QUALITY and its REASONABLE PRICE — a rare combination." Instead of calling on readers to write for a brochure, this ad instructed those interested to "Ask to see the NIKON at your dealers. Examine it. Try it. Your real enthusiasm for the NIKON and NIKKOR lenses will begin when you see the pictures YOU can take with them!"[25] Not only was the word out, but Gasser had by now signed up enough dealers, and Liholm had been able to bring in enough stock that an ad could now act to assist dealers. Liholm and Gasser had insisted from the beginning on uniform pricing and uniform distribution — policies that the better dealers liked.

The final difference hinted at other changes. The importer was now listed as "Nikon Camera Company," an "Affiliate of Overseas Finance & Trading Company, Inc." If this seems a bit confusing, the company's address provides a clue. It was now 278 Post Street, which happened to be the address of Gasser's shop.*

What was going on? All that spring and summer, Gasser and Liholm had been pushing for more deliveries from NK in order to service the accounts the two were creating. At the same time, Gasser was having all the new equipment delivered to his shop for checkup before shipping out to dealers. It only made sense that the importer use the address where all the orders went anyway. But this change was also indicative of the increasingly important role Gasser was playing in the Nikon importation business, particularly since his return from Japan.

One can also read the hand of Gasser in the new name. When Liholm had set up OFI-TRA, it was still not clear what products he would be handling, how much banking would be involved, or even where some products would be coming from. It made sense to adopt a generic name that could cover all of the possibilities. Now NK's products were the only thing Liholm was handling. Why not use a name that would leave no doubts in anyone's mind as to what Liholm and Gasser were doing?

By choosing the name of the camera for the name of this new affiliate company, Liholm and Gasser would be inadvertently "wagging the dog," for in this case, the name of a

Originally Liholm used Room 733 at the 465 California Street address. Later he would move to Room 826 with more space.

single product would be taking over an entire range of manufactures. Within a quarter of a century, that same single product would be lending its name to every product that NK made and Nippon Kogaku would, in time, change its very name to "Nikon, Inc."

If OFITRA and its affiliate Nikon Camera Company were doing everything possible to build and service a market in the United States, by contrast, virtually no activity was occurring in Europe. The enthusiastic reports of the American photojournalists, particularly Duncan, did not go unnoticed, but it was not until November 1951 that Dutch photographic magazine *Focus* carried an article on the Nikon and Nikkor lenses.[26]

What was the Western Trading Company with its franchise for Scandinavia doing? Apparently little, except for the importations mentioned earlier. A small advertisement would appear in a Swedish magazine in June 1952,[27] but beyond that, we have found no evidence of further activity. Western Trading's sole agency agreement ended in 1953, the same as OFITRA's did, and it was not renewed.

Two factors were playing out in Europe and working against NK. One was the enormous power and prejudice of the revived German optical manufacturers, clearly evident in Zeiss's response to Deschin's article. German firms would do everything possible to cast aspersions on all Japanese optical goods throughout the 1950s, discouraging venders from taking a chance on selling what were perceived to be inferior products.

Price was the other problem. While Japanese cameras sold for noticeably less than equivalent German goods in the United States, the opposite was true in Europe, particularly in Germany, where import duties forced Japanese prices to levels higher than those of domestic products. In the end, Lindholm may have decided that creating a market in Europe was something that was just not going to happen. A few sales occurred, particularly in Switzerland, but Nikon would remain a distant nonproduct throughout much of Europe until 1961 when NK established Nikon AG as its own subsidiary for European marketing and sales.

As sales of Nikons and other NK products continued to grow in the United States, so did the demands on the new Nikon Camera Company. In response, Gasser and Liholm began expanding their management team. By that July, Liholm had a man named Sam Locker servicing the account with *Life*. Ross Goodman, an accomplished and experienced pioneer 35mm photographer, became marketing manager, taking over the duties of promoting and signing up dealers from Gasser. He had been a sales representative for Leitz for 11 years prior to coming to the Nikon Camera Company. The stores that carried Leicas were the same stores that Gasser and Liholm were targeting for NK's camera. These stores did not discount, thereby guaranteeing that profits for both the dealers and the Nikon Camera Company would remain at the proper level. Goodman — a "knowledgeable and pretty good man" according to Gasser — was able to use his extensive friendships and contacts to open doors and built a network of dealers willing to carry the Nikon and its lenses. Goodman, in turn, retained Al Levin to be the company's sole salesman for the entire East Coast. Next, Gasser hired Gary Lehman as lead salesman for the West Coast. All three of these men would survive the changes that would occur in the next several years and all three would continue selling NK's products into the Ehrenreich era.

But this first Nikon Camera Company — and the Gasser-Liholm partnership — was

NIKON CAMERA COMPANY

278 POST STREET
SAN FRANCISCO 8, CALIFORNIA

TELEPHONE
YUKON 6-1764

CABLE ADDRESS
NIKONCAL

— REPRESENTATIVE —

TO
Mr. Albert Levin
836 West 26th Street
New York, N.Y.

SHIPPED TO Same

DATE 12 Nov. 1951

Memo Invoice No. 0001

YOUR ORDER NO.

SALESMAN

SHIPPED VIA R.R. Exp.

QUANTITY	DESCRIPTION	UNIT PRICE	TOTAL
1	Nikon Model S #6094080, Nikkor f:1.4 #316401		
1	Zoom Finder #323351		
	(Above delivered by R.J. Goodman)		
1	Nikkor 50mm f:1.4 #320131 — Leica mount		
1	Nikkor 35mm f:3.5 #426423 — Nikon mount		
1	Nikkor 85mm f:2 #287135 — Nikon mount		
1	Cine-Nikkor 50mm f:1.9 #323421		

MEMO
PACKING LIST

Al Levin's first invoice from November 1951 (courtesy Nikon Historical Society).

fragile, based on a handshake, mutual trust and a willingness on Liholm's part to let Gasser do whatever he felt needed to be done to make the Nikon a success. In late fall 1951, the partnership collapsed.

On his 1950 trip to Japan, Liholm had reached an understanding with Nagaoka that he would visit the factory at least once a year. True to that promise, Liholm left for Japan in August or September 1951, going east this time with stopovers in Europe in mind. In Sweden he examined precision "centerless" grinders for potential importation to the United States. Then in October, while in Hamburg, Germany, he suddenly became seriously ill with a lung infection that was to leave him bed-ridden for two years. Unable to work, or do much of anything, he left OFITRA and never worked for Nikon or Uno Lindholm again.

Lindholm now had to pick up the pieces. He soon learned everything he needed to know about the business arrangements that his manager in North America had made, including the fifty-fifty split of profits with Gasser and the separate Nikon Camera Company. This was not the way Lindholm did business. He contacted lawyers in San Francisco and had them write up a letter voiding Gasser's contract effective December 31st!

Gasser was stunned. While he still had his shop and camera repair business, for the last two years he had put his heart and soul into making the Nikon a success in the United States. It had been his efforts and contacts that had gotten the camera and its lenses tested, convinced experts to endorse the products and moved dealers he knew to the point where many were willing to stock and sell a Japanese product. He sued Lindholm for breach of contract. Lindholm used his larger resources to delay, and eventually Gasser settled for a payment of $12,000. In an announcement that December that he sent to all "our customers and representatives" he informed them "with regret" that his Nikon Camera Company was "being dissolved" and that all future

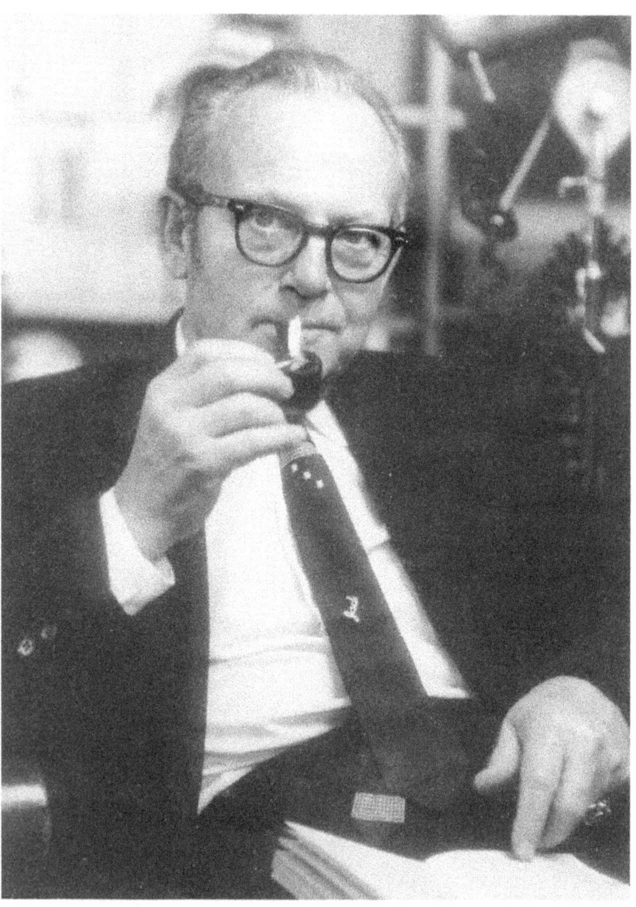

Ross Goodman, the Nikon Camera Company's first marketing manager. A former Leitz sales rep, he was hired by Hans Liholm and Adolph Gasser to set up accounts with dealers nationwide (courtesy Adolph Gasser and John Gasser).

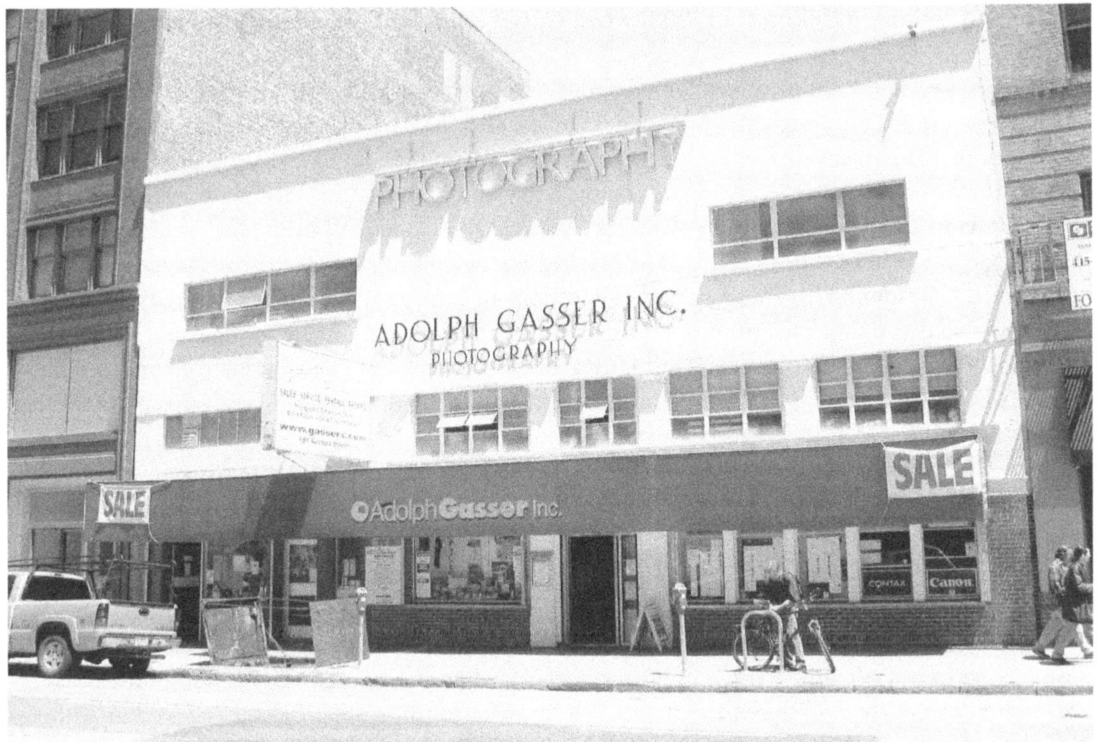

Exterior of Adolph Gasser's store in San Francisco as it appeared in 2005 (Theodore C. Loder IV photograph).

queries and orders would be "once more handled by Overseas Finance & Trading Company."[28] Such was the sad end to the historic and successful personal relationship that had made the Nikon in America happen.

Gasser took the award and used it to expand the retail camera business he had started in 1950. It would prove to be as successful as his repair shop had been, and eventually "Gasser's Camera" would become one of the largest photographic retailers in the Bay area. In 1973, Gasser's bought its present location with 18,000 square feet. In the store's best year, the business would do over $15 million worth of sales. Gasser carried Nikons in his new store and continued to promote them in that way, but he never worked for Nikon, Inc. again.

In 1969 Gasser made one more trip to Japan when Lions International held its convention in Tokyo. NK's then head of sales (Sanetoshi Kuratsuji) took him out to dinner and thanked him for all his efforts.

Gasser would have one more brush with history. By the early 1950s he had become personal friends with the famous photographic writer and outdoors photographer, Ansel Adams. He had even convinced Adams to buy one of the early Nikons in April 1951. Adams had his in-town studio at the end of 24th Avenue in the Sea Cliff District, which was located only four blocks from Gasser's shop. Gasser serviced all of Adams's cameras and, when Adams moved his home and studio to Carmel, he hired Gasser to design the lab and darkroom facilities. In 1962, when Gasser remarried, Adams would serve as his best man.

As for Hans Liholm, after a long recovery, he spent six months convalescing in Spain studying Spanish. Satisfied with his additional linguistic skill, he then planned to return to the United States in 1954. Instead, while visiting his remarried mother in Bremen, he met Dr. Walter Hoffman, a financial expert who ran a consultancy in Hamburg. Dr. Hoffmann had been president and CEO of the Hamburg-America Line (HAPAG)—one of the world's leading passenger and cargo lines—until 1945. HAPAG had lost its entire fleet as a consequence of World War II. Considering his standing and connections in Europe and Liholm's international commercial and banking background, Hoffmann thought that it might be to their mutual advantage to get acquainted business wise. He suggested that Liholm spend some time in his office in Hamburg prior to Liholm's planned return to the United States. Two weeks later, Dr. Hoffman suffered a stroke from which he never fully recovered. Liholm took over the consultancy business, concluded some important agreements and ended up settling in Hamburg where he would live and work for the next 44 years before finally retiring at the age of 74.

The Coming of a New Franchise

It is easy to conjure up "might have beens" when looking at what Liholm and Gasser each accomplished after both men left the importation business. Gasser enjoyed an enormous success in the photographic retail business. Liholm became one of the most important players in the rebuilding of Germany's merchant marine fleet. But neither man was directly involved with Nippon Kogaku again.

But, although Gasser's letter in December 1951 clearly stated that the Nikon Camera Company was no more, it did not die. Lindholm had forced Gasser out, but he had second thoughts about also destroying the company name that the camera-buying public now associated with NK's products in America. Nor did it appear prudent to discharge the experienced team that Gasser and Liholm had assembled. Lindholm ended up retaining both the Nikon Camera Company and most of its management.

In January, all activity was once more being conducted by OFITRA back at 465 California Street. But running a business that involved not just finances and record keeping, but also the receiving, handling, shipping and servicing of dozens of precision optical goods on a daily basis proved impossible to fit back into the smaller offices of the Merchants Exchange Building.* Soon all operations would move to 25 California Street where, once more as the "Nikon Camera Company, Inc.," Lindholm's enterprise would stay for the rest of its California existence. No reference to Liholm's Overseas Finance & Trading Company ever appeared in any advertising or publications again.

Robert (Bob) Evans took over as the general manager for the Nikon Camera Company—a position he would retain for the rest of the Nikon Camera Company's existence.

*Al Levin's first invoice is dated November 13, 1951. By February 29, 1952, he was already up to invoice #122 and shipment #157.

May 1, 1952

Price List for NIKON CAMERAS and NIKKOR LENSES

Minimum
Fair-Traded List Price
Including Excise Tax

NIKON CAMERA WITH f/3.5—50 mm NIKKOR LENS	Not Available at Present
NIKON CAMERA WITH f/2—50 mm NIKKOR LENS	259.00
NIKON CAMERA WITH f/1.4—50 mm NIKKOR LENS	349.00
NIKON CAMERA BOX ONLY, without case	152.00

All Nikon cameras include synchronization for flash and strobe, ever-ready leather case, lens caps and flash attachment cord.

NIKKOR LENS f/3.5—50 mm	Not Available at Present
NIKKOR LENS f/2—50 mm	107.00
NIKKOR LENS f/1.4—50 mm	198.00
NIKKOR TELEPHOTO LENS f/2—85 mm, with leather case and shade	175.50
NIKKOR TELEPHOTO LENS f/3.5—135 mm, with leather case and shade	145.00
NIKKOR WIDE ANGLE f/3.5—35 mm, with leather case	89.50
CINE-NIKKOR f/1.9—38 mm telephoto for 8 mm cameras	59.50
UNIVERSAL FINDER, with leather case	43.00
ZOOM FINDER, with leather case	37.00

All Nikkor lenses are available in Leica type mount at the same price.

NIKON CAMERA COMPANY, INC.   **25 California Street, San Francisco 11, California**

The second price list for the Nikon camera and its lenses, dated May 1, 1952. Note that all reference to OFITRA is gone.

Evans remains somewhat of a controversial figure. A contemporary handout from the Nikon Camera Company states that he had "13 years [experience] in the photographic technical and managerial field,"[29] which would seem to indicate that he was well qualified to lead NK's importing firm, but Gasser denied that when interviewed in 2005. Yes, Evans was one of Gasser's six employees and he "talked a good line," but he "only worked the front counter," and was not a repairman. Gasser regarded Evans's leaving to take over the managerial position in the reincarnated Nikon Camera Company as a betrayal, and he still retained bitter memories of Evans 53 years later.

Liholm's memories of Evans were also mixed, and in correspondence in 2006, he found it difficult to imagine this guy who drove a Morris Minor car to "be different, or the like" would have had the capabilities to be an effective manager. Regardless of Evans's true abilities, the personal connections and friendships that Liholm and Gasser had carefully built with both NK's management and the American photographic press had been broken. The Nikon Camera Company would be unable to repair the damage before the three-year franchise would expire in 1953.

Only a few records relating to the Nikon Camera Company's operations appear to have survived from this period. Even as the reputation of the Nikon and Nikkor lenses continued to grow, the company remained small with everyone apparently filling in as needed.* As noted at the beginning of this chapter, the only published evidence of the camera's

One clue to the size of the operations comes from noting that a letter to Al Levin from J.R. Adams in the "Optical Division" dated September 22, 1952, and a later letter from Bob Evans dated February 4, 1953, were both typed and signed by the same secretary!

progress are the advertisements for the Nikon and Nikkor lenses that appeared at closer and closer intervals in the three major photographic magazines. Not only did these ads appear more frequently, but they also became increasingly sophisticated and gradually moved from the back of the magazines to the front and from small inserts to full-page spreads. The Nikon was now a member of a quartet of 35mm interchangeable lens rangefinder cameras considered the choice of professionals (Leica, Contax and Canon were the other three) and its ad positioning reflected that growing status.

In April 1952, the "Nikon Camera Company, Inc.," located at 25 California Street, took out its first ad in *U.S. Camera*. Still located in the back (page 102), the ad was the largest of any the company had run so far: two columns and three-quarters of a page in length. "Quality" in fancy script was the lead. Again, the reader was urged to "See your camera dealer today," although interested persons could also send in a "postal to address below for free brochure."[30] The picture of the camera was a new one and much larger, and it was accompanied by a second illustration showing six different Nikkors, including the defunct 50mm f3.5.

In June, Nikon would once more be advertising in *Modern Photography*. This ad would be the same size as the one that had appeared in *U.S. Camera*, but it would focus on the "FASTEST NEW 35MM CAMERA LENS NIKKOR F/1.4." The next month *U.S. Camera* would be favored again, this time with a full-page ad on page 27. "Masterpieces in Miniature!" was the headline and this time both the Nikon and the Mikron center-focusing "aristocrat" binoculars were featured. Pictures of the camera and the binoculars were set off against a background of circling and overlapping lines. Within a year, these lines would become a grid, part of an advertising theme that would persist until the introduction of the Nikon S2 in December 1954.

The ads for Nikon would go through two more evolutions during the Nikon Camera Company's tenure of the franchise. The first would revolve around the slogan "From sand to lenses...." A full-page ad on page 75 in *U.S. Camera* in November 1952 reinforced this emphasis on control and quality with a background of photographs taken in the Ohi plant that covered the entire process of lens making from loading crucibles to the testing of the final lenses.

By 1953, *Popular Photography* had renamed itself just *Photography*. This name would last only two years — just long enough to sow confusion among researchers. In March, Nikon was back in that magazine with a two-column ad on page 115. In this ad the various themes all came together: The background lines, now a ⅛-inch square grid and the slogan "From sand to perfect lenses." coexisted with the charge to the reader to "see your Nikon dealer today." The Nikon Camera Company must have liked this ad because it would reuse it again and again for the last nine months it would market the camera. The company complimented this generic workhorse with a series of more specialized full-page advertisements with specific goals in mind. The first, appearing on page 14 in the April issue of *Photography*, demanded "*Don't be misled! KNOW THESE NAMES." The names were, of course Nikon and Nikkor, but the Ciné Nikkors and the Apo Nikkors for industrial process cameras were also featured. "...KNOW THESE FACTS ONLY Nippon Kogaku makes the Nikon...."

The Nicca and Sears & Roebuck were continuing to be the problem. As far back as November 1951, Dick Price, the Nikon Camera Company's new sales manager, had felt forced to remind all his representatives that even though the Nicca came with Nikkor lenses, that camera was not a product of Nippon Kogaku, nor were the Niccas with the Sears "Tower" label. NK was making only one camera: the Nikon, and the Nikon Camera Company would only recognize, service or stand behind Nikons or Nikkors, not other cameras that just happened to have Nikkor lenses.[31]

In May 1953 Nikon would run another full-page ad in *Photography*, this time on page 99. The theme this time would be the company's growing selection of accessories, including the third model of its flashgun, its second model gadget bag, a closeup device, finders, filters and, of course, the accessory lenses, including its new 35mm f2.5 wide-angle Nikkor that had been introduced the previous year — all set off against the ⅛-inch grid. In layout and feel this ad is similar to an ad that had appeared in *Popular Photography* the previous year, but which had featured only the camera.

In July 1953, the last of these special ads would appear on page 111 of *Photography*. It is the strangest of the lot. "Style" was the lead in huge script. "The Nikon and Richard Marx..." was the line that followed. In between, a woman in a girdle and slip stands in her bare feet before a small mirror on a tiny table. Apparently this was high-fashion, and Marx was a high fashion photographer. Peter Gowland, a photographer known for his attractive nudes or semi-dressed glamour shots, also appeared in an advertisement with a similar approach, but I do not have enough bibliographic data to tell where it was actually published. Whether these really made the connection between the camera and professionals remains an unanswered question.

Despite these evidences of success and a steadily growing business, NK was increasingly unhappy with the new Nikon Camera Company of 1952–53. At the time Liholm had negotiated OFITRA's three-year contract, NK still knew little about overseas sales. The exclusive deal the company had granted to OFITRA was NK's way of temporarily solving the problem of what to do about exports to its potentially largest market. Nagaoka and his board had liked Liholm. The photographic press had liked Liholm and Gasser. Liholm and Gasser, in turn, had, in effect, moved mountains in creating a market and a positive attitude toward the Nikon. But once these two men were gone, that personal connection was also lost.

Despite its strong growth and increasing prosperity, NK remained cash poor. It needed sales and cash receipts. It was sending 70 percent of its lenses and cameras to the United States, but it did not have enough to show for this commitment. If it had firm orders in hand, the company could go to a bank and get loans to pay for expansion and the purchase of raw materials. Nikon sales in the United States were increasing, but not at the rate that NK thought they could and not compared to its increasingly successful competitors, particularly Canon.

Canon had built its initial strength based on sales through the military exchanges. It had sold thousands of cameras to military personnel in Japan long before the first Nikon shipments to the CPO in April 1950. By 1953, the Canon Camera Company was shipping hundreds of cameras to the United States through the import firm of Balfour, Guthrie

Company and attempting to go head-to-head with the still more prestigious Nikon and its better-selling, but similar, German rivals. While customers could buy only one version of the Nikon, Canons came in many varieties, some with flash sync, some without, some with a top speed of $\frac{1}{500}$ of a second, others with $\frac{1}{1000}$ of a second. The top model, the Canon IV S2, offered flash sync via a hot shoe plate located on the left end of the camera, a three-setting finder that could be used to gain more rangefinder accuracy, or frame a 100mm or 135mm lens, and outstanding quality at a lower price compared to what Nikons were selling for.* As noted earlier, Canon had standardized its mount on the 39mm Leica thread, making the purchase and mounting of accessories an easy task. The Canon-made Serenar lenses had developed an excellent reputation and the company was catching up to NK in terms of focal lengths and speed offerings. Canon was taking sales away from what had been the Nikon's exclusive niche — those American customers willing to take a chance by purchasing a Japanese-made, professional-level photographic product.

Liholm stated that Uno Lindholm never touched any of OFITRA's income while he was the manager. Instead, Liholm was allowed to plow OFITRA's profits back into the company to allow its expansion. But with OFITRA beginning to move from a startup company to an established institution as the Nikon Camera Company, Uno Lindholm's hold-off attitude may have changed.

When a customer walked into a store and asked to see a Nikon camera, it was because he or she was prepared to buy. If the store did not have any in stock, there was a good chance that store would lose a sale. If that customer then went elsewhere and bought a Canon or a Leica, everyone from the salesman all the way back to the worker in Ohi were losers. If a salesman could promise delivery within a few days, that shop might salvage a sale. But a "few days" meant (and still does today) that the distributor had to have the camera in stock and be prepared to ship immediately. To succeed, the Nikon Camera Company had to maintain a large enough stock of all NK products to be able to fill any order quickly. But that meant that Lindholm would have had to tie up a lot of his capital in inventory and this Lindholm was unwilling to do.

Lindholm's entire business model was based on avoiding at all cost maintenance of an inventory. Goods were ordered only when a customer had already agreed to buy and had delivered the money. The camera shops were not willing to play the game that way and, ultimately, NK was not either.

Since Lindholm discouraged the Nikon Camera Company from placing orders to NK until it had firm dealer orders in hand, the whole system could not expand or work effectively. NK also began to suspect that Lindholm was keeping much more of the profits to himself than the company felt proper.

NK's management had learned a lot about civilian and retail sales in the years since its camera had first come on the market. It pressed Lindholm and Evans to increase their orders. When the Nikon Camera Company failed to do so, and the three-year contract expired, NK decided to go looking for someone else who would.

In 1952, a top-of-the-line Canon IV S2 with a 50mm f1.8 Serenar listed for $295. By contrast, a Nikon S offering a top speed of $\frac{1}{500}$ of a second, but with the f1.4 Nikkor, listed for $349.

In the winter of 1953, NK informed OFITRA/Nikon Camera Company that it would not renew the importation and marketing agreement. NK had decided to create its own wholly owned subsidiary to handle the importing of all of its products into North America. This would be called "Nippon Kogaku (USA), Inc." It, in turn, would contract with a new American-owned firm to handle distribution, marketing and servicing. Sakai, perhaps acting as a middleman, perhaps trying to salvage something for Lindholm, came to the United States and first approached Gasser. Gasser wanted the franchise, but with all of his funds tied up in his new store, he could not meet the startup costs. But in New York City, there was someone who could. That person was Joseph P. Ehrenreich, and when NK sent Hamashima to New York to find a new distributor, Ehrenreich jumped at the chance.

Ehrenreich had been in the photographic retail business since 1931. In 1953 he and his brother, Irving, were the prosperous joint owners of the Penn Camera Exchange in New York City. They enjoyed a high reputation throughout the camera retail business, but Joe wanted to move out of retail and into wholesaling. When E. Leitz, Inc. (New York), the importers of the Leica camera, had briefly disbanded, Joe had attempted unsuccessfully to pick up that franchise. He was not about to pass up the opportunity Hamashima was offering, and he was prepared to sell his interest in Penn Camera to finance the purchase

of the distributorship. That March Ehrenreich reached an understanding with NK. He then spent the next nine months quietly setting up the business to his own liking while the San Francisco-based Nikon Camera Company continued publicly to be the importer.

One of the first things Ehrenreich did was convince NK to send a team of technicians to the United States to train a full corps of repairmen to handle any and all problems that could possibly arise. This team, led by Tsutomu Wada, would stay for two to three years in the United States establishing service centers in New York, Chicago and San Francisco. Ehrenreich traveled to San Francisco where he interviewed Gasser — and hired away one of Gasser's repairmen to work only on Nikons. Ehrenreich wanted Gasser to work for him also, but he realized that to get Gasser, he would have to buy out Gasser's business. This he was not willing to do. He did reach an understanding with Gary Lehman. Lehman would set up his own independent company,

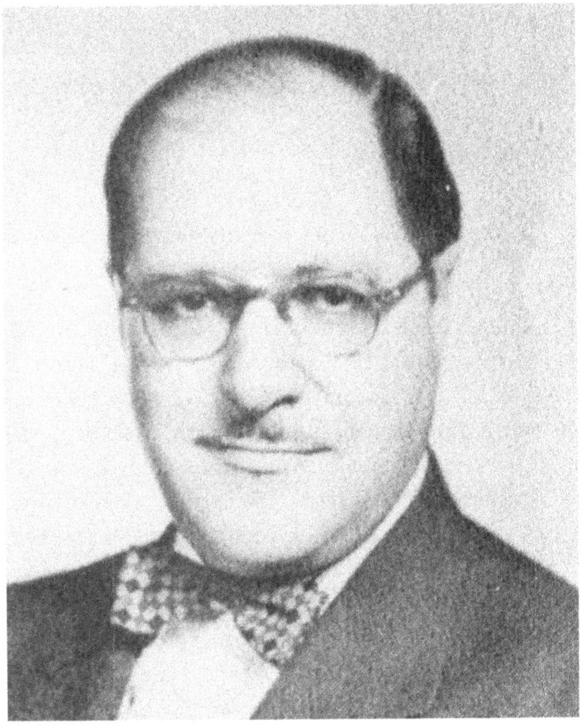

Joseph Ehrenreich, as he would have appeared shortly after he set up Nikon, Inc. (from a 1958 Nikon, Inc., annual report. Courtesy Nikon Historical Society).

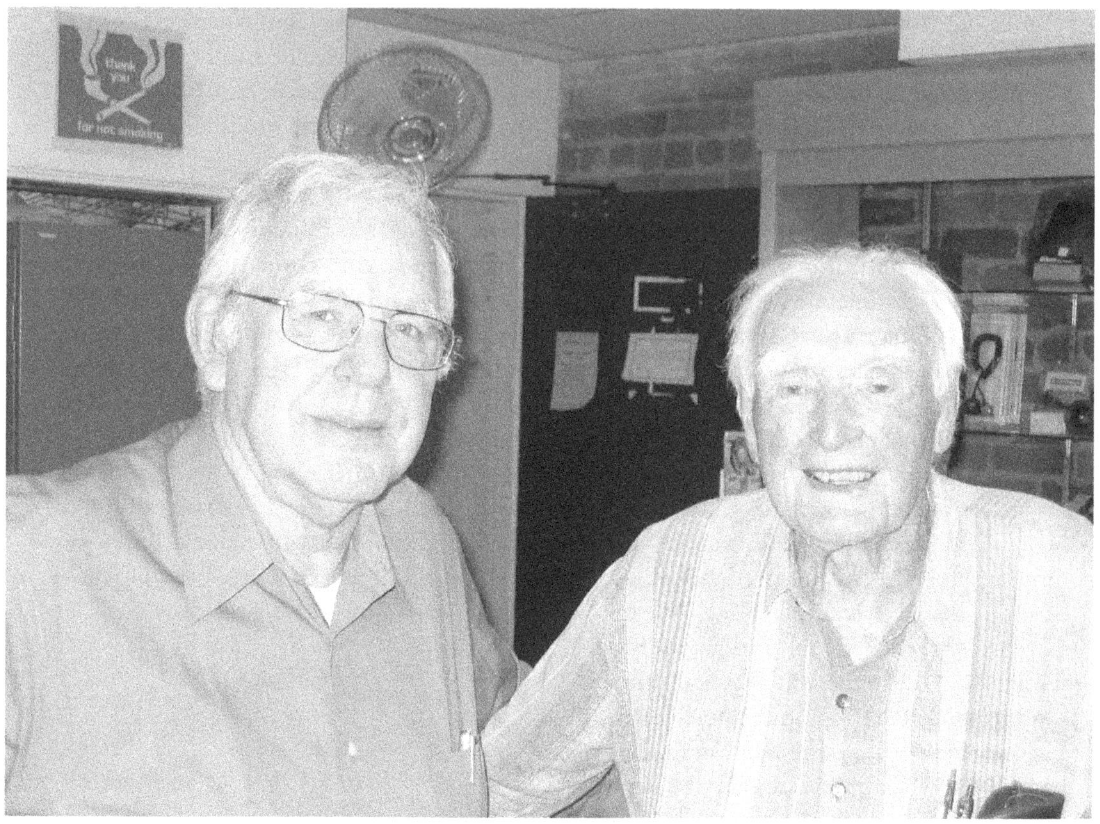

Adolph Gasser, age 93, with his son, John Gasser, in 2005 in their store in downtown San Francisco (Theodore C. Loder IV photograph).

Gary Lehman, Inc., which would continue to distribute NK products on the West Coast, but he would be getting these products from Ehrenreich.

On January 31, 1954, the *New York Times* announced that: "Nippon Kogaku, seventy-year-old Tokyo camera and optical factory, makers of the Nikon cameras and Nikkor lenses, have established an American agency here. It is Nikon, Inc., at 277 Fifth Avenue, headed by Joseph Ehrenreich, formerly of Penn Camera Exchange."[32]

Had the Nikon Camera company and OFITRA without Liholm or Gasser been doing badly? Was NK justified in changing its distributorship? A note in another article that appeared in the *New York Times* 21 months later may be taken as part of the answer.[33] In this piece, the writer quotes Nikon, Inc. officials as stating that when that company took over the distributorship, it had fewer than 75 dealers and was selling only 1,000 cameras per year. Since then, the number of dealers and the number of sales had increased "nearly ten times." These self-serving figures cannot be correct as reported. By the time Ehrenreich took over the American franchise, NK had already manufactured over 20,000 Nikons, and most of these had gone to the United States or sold to the CPO. Nevertheless, Nippon Kogaku had found the right person. Together, Ehrenreich, NK and the Nikon he promoted

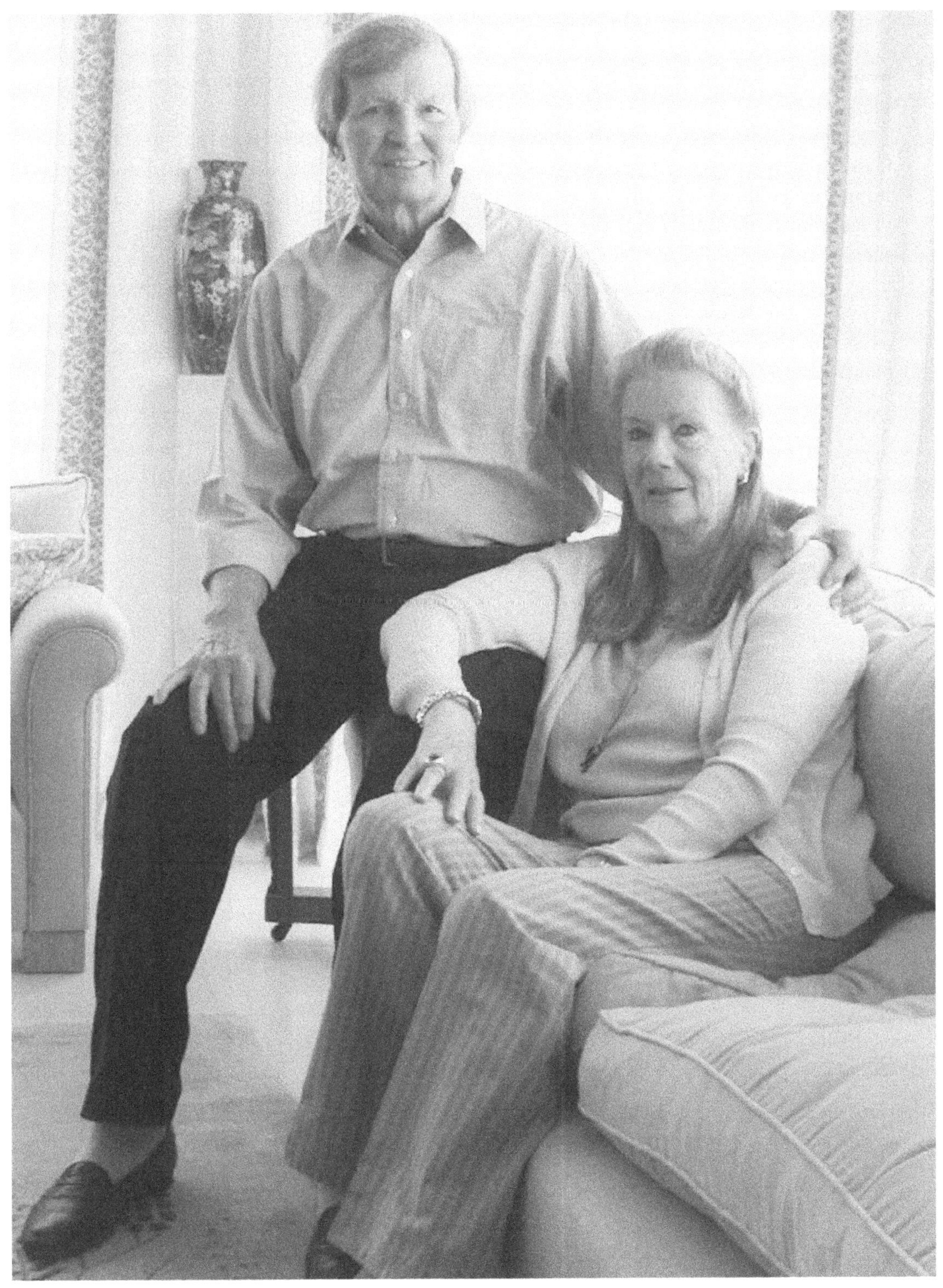

Hans Liholm and his wife, Christiane, in their home in Florida in February 2005.

would ride a wave of success that would continue almost until Ehrenreich's death nearly 20 years later.

Life's photographers and the photographic press had handed Hans Liholm and Adolph Gasser a marketing gift of immeasurable value. For most of 1951, these two had done everything they could to take advantage of that gift. They had continued to face negative attitudes from both dealers and the buying public, but they had the popular press on their side.

They made significant progress, but once both men left the importation business, the growth of the Nikon Camera Company slowed. A new hand was needed, and Joe Ehrenreich provided it. Unfortunately, when he took over, everything that had happened before became lost history.

Epilogue: From the Nikon S to the Nikon F and Beyond

No early history of the Nikon camera in America would be complete without tracing the successful career of Joseph Ehrenreich and his Nikon, Inc. through its end in 1982. What he and his associates and immediate successors, Herbert Sax and Joseph Abbott, did was complete the revolution in camera-buying habits that Liholm and Gasser had started. In 1950, the precision camera market was almost totally controlled by German firms. Many camera specialty shops would not even consider carrying any high-end equipment made outside of Europe. Two decades later, the once all-powerful Zeiss Ikon would be on its way to bankruptcy, and Japanese photographic goods would be dominating the world market and selling everywhere, even in Germany itself.

That this would happen still seemed impossible the first year that Ehrenreich had the marketing and distribution franchise. The Nikon S was outwardly almost exactly the same camera that had first shipped six years earlier. Even the initial ads had a similar feel, carryovers of the campaign that the former Nikon Camera Company had started in 1952. What had changed was the sense of urgency and energy that Ehrenreich now brought to the new company. Joe talked with and listened to working professionals and he insisted that his sales staff do the same. Like Nagaoka in 1950, he wanted to know what the professionals needed, what they liked and what they disliked. He focused on magazine photographers, the men and women who were increasingly using 35mm cameras for their professional work. He catered to them, loaning them lenses and insuring that they got the best repair and support service possible.

Al Levin, working now under Joe, described how he would travel to wherever the "press boys" were working and loan them Nikon equipment to try out. "I let them use the wideangles and the teles. The wides and the teles were things they could not get on their Speed Graphics and Rolleiflexes. They would go back and tell their bosses to buy it because they liked the gear."[1]

Many pros still would not use the Nikon S, particularly disliking its 24 × 34 format, but the new Nikkors that NK was making available helped to break down that prejudice. Up until 1952, only three auxiliary Nikkors had been available: the 85mm f2, the 135mm f3.5 and the 35mm f3.5. Both the 85 and the 135 had received rave reviews and both had proved popular with professionals in Nikon, Contax-specific and Leica thread mounts — despite weights heavier than German equivalents. That year, NK introduced the first of a series of Nikkors that would push the design and speed possibilities to a wider range of focal lengths. This was the 35mm f2.5 W-Nikkor. A full stop faster than the only wide angle that Leitz offered for its cameras, and one-third faster than the Zeiss Biogon for the Contax, the lens yielded excellent sharpness and contrast with little of the edge falloff that plagued most wide angle designs.

The next year, NK would demonstrate its optical leadership even further with its long-delayed 85mm f1.5 Nikkor. An expensive, specialty lens yielding only soft images wide open, it sold in small numbers, but its availability was proof that NK's engineers could match any speed or focal length that the Germans could offer.

So far, NK had not ventured outside the standard 35–135 range of focal lengths expected in offerings by most optical firms. Therefore, the 28mm f3.5 W-Nikkor of 1953 was a real innovation. Considerably wider and with adequate speed, it allowed professionals to consider using a 35 as their "normal" with the 28 as their wide angle.

In 1954, NK would cap its optical progress with two more lenses in new focal lengths, the 105mm f2.5 Nikkor telephoto and a 25mm f4 W-Nikkor. The 25mm owed much of its design to the rare, but similar East German–made Topogon. It remained an uncommon, expensive item, but the sharp 105 — an extension of the proven 85mm f2 — proved popular with both pros and amateurs. The final pieces of this optical feast were the Nikkors for the Nikon's new reflex housing. First came a 250mm f4 Nikkor, then a 500mm f5 Nikkor and, in mid–1955, a fast 180mm f2.5 Nikkor that beat out the Zeiss Olympic Sonnar in speed and sharpness. None of these last three lenses ever proved to be best-sellers. It is likely that fewer than 300 of the nearly 20-pound 500mm Nikkor ever left the factory. With a price of $550 in the mid–1950s, only a few professionals or news organizations could afford such an item anyway. Nevertheless, Nippon Kogaku was proving that feature for feature, focal length for focal length, it could match and surpass anything that Zeiss or Leitz could market.

Throughout 1954 and into 1955, as Nikon Incorporated found its feet, it combined carryover ads declaring "Nikon [:] today's outstanding value in fine 35mm cameras" with single-column ads toting its new focal lengths. In the June 1954 issue of *U.S. Camera*, it promoted the 50mm f1.4 Nikkor with "It's *more* than worth the difference." In the September issue of *U.S. Camera* it was the "NEW ... FAST and PHENOMENAL" 85mm f1.5." In the next month's issue, it would be the "75° COVERAGE AT 3.5" of the 28mm Nikkor. And finally, in March 1955 in *Popular Photography*, it would be the "Longer Faster Sharper..." 105mm f2.5 Nikkor. Pushing the Nikkor optics instead of the camera was to prove a wise decision in 1954, for the Nikon S camera was out-of-date and a new German-made 35 had made it so.

The sensation of the 1954 Master Photo Dealers' and Finishers' Association Convention had been a new model Leica camera: the Leica M3. So novel and revolutionary were its features that all other rangefinder cameras immediately appeared obsolete. Leitz had been working on a new version of its camera since the late 1930s. This "Leica IV" would have a combined viewfinder-rangefinder like the rival Contax and incorporate many other new, advanced features.* World War II had forced the project to be put on hold, but now Leitz had completed its work and could proudly display its masterpiece. A single shutter speed dial with all speeds set at equal distances not only was easier to operate, but also allowed the addition of a light meter that coupled to the dial. A new combined and bright rangefinder-viewfinder not only gave a near-life size image, but also included projected bright frames that changed to match the focal length of a lens and automatically shifted to correct for parallax as the user focused the lens. A double-stroke lever advance, a swing-up back to ease loading film and a quick-change bayonet mount for the new M-series lenses were great features as well.

Where did this leave Zeiss, Canon and Nikon with their knob-advance 35s? None of these formerly equivalent cameras had any of the M3's new features. The reactions of these three manufacturers were to prove fateful.

Zeiss "blinked." The company had already begun to place increasing emphasis on its amateur-oriented line of single-lens reflexes, the Contaflexes. It improved the flash sync on the Contax and provided a superb extreme wide angle, the 21mm Biogon, but otherwise, the company did nothing. The sales of the Contax soon declined. By 1959, the market for its former flagship camera was gone, and, in 1961, the company would cease all Contax production.

Canon, which had been enjoying brisk sales of its many models of Leica lookalike cameras both in the United States and in the military exchanges, had nothing new even planned. Caught by surprise, the company would take two years to prepare a response.

Nippon Kogaku was also surprised, but it had been working on a new camera model since 1950. Most of its redesign efforts had been concentrated on developing a larger and brighter viewfinder. Now it had to decide how much of that model to keep and how much it had to change to respond to the M3 challenge. The company turned to the market-savvy Ehrenreich for advice. His response was to instruct the company to differentiate the Nikon as much as possible from the new Leica, but, more importantly, get it out. Nikon sales were doing well, but once the Leica M3 reached stores in quantity, it would eat the Nikon for lunch.

The NK engineers did what they could. They gave the new Nikon a single-stroke rapid advance and a crank rewind. They included a life-size finder with an albada bright frame for the 50mm lens. The back still came off, but only one latch needed to be turned. The flash sync system became usable at all speeds and included both a hot shoe and a PC terminal within a locking socket. The shutter speeds were still on two dials, but the highest speed was now a thousandth of a second, and speeds could be set either before or after the film was advanced. In the process of redesigning its camera, the frame expanded to the full standard 36mm width, the body became a die casting, and it lost six ounces of weight.

**See Web site April 22, 2006 http://fotomuveszet.elender/0212/nagykepek/jpg_kepek_021217/nagykep.02121701. htm for a picture of what this Leica prototype looked like.*

In December 1954, barely eight months after the Leica M3's introduction, Nikon, Inc. was able to announce this new "Nikon S2" to the press.

While an excellent camera with nice, fit-in-the-hand handling characteristics and with superb optics, the Nikon S2 was still not on the same level as the Leica M3. But neither was it as expensive, and for the mid–1950s, it was good enough. The S2 was to become the most successful of all the Nikon rangefinder cameras with over 56,000 being sold over a three-and-a-half-year period. These sales remained below those of the Leica, but Ehrenreich would sell every one he could get his hands on. The limits were set by NK's manufacturing capacities.

In 1954, Canon's top-of-the-line Leica copy, the Canon IV-S2, had offered sharp optics, precision construction and a range of features equal to or better than its main competitors. Perhaps the only poor design decision that Canon had made was limiting its flash synchronization to the hot plate that interacted only with a special Canon-branded flashgun.

The Canon Camera Company had nothing new ready, nor did it have anything in the pipeline, such as NK had with its S2. Its engineers set to work, determined to manufacture a new 35mm camera that would be innovative and competitive with both the Leica M3 and the Nikon S2, a camera that would go beyond what the Nikon had just managed.

Throughout 1955, as the Nikon S2 began appearing in American camera shops all over the country, Canon continued to promote and sell its Canon IV-S2 and cheaper kin. It ran its last ad for the Canon IV-S2 in January 1956. It had to get something out there — something to remind buyers that Canon too was a leader and innovator — but its new top-of-the-line model was still not ready.

Perhaps Canon tried to do too much with the new Canon Vt. It kept the dialable magnification viewfinder but set it for 35mm, 50mm and RF magnifier. It changed the markings on its dials to white on black. It installed an auto-parallax compensating pin in the accessory shoe, which required special Canon finders. Since a flash would no longer mount there, it added a custom bayonet mount for its new flashgun on the left end, but it put a standard PC connection inside. But the biggest changes were a swing-open back and a bottom-mounted trigger advance — features that none of its direct competitors offered.

Overly eager to get the word out about this new model that Canon was sure would be a success, the company ran a full-page, two-color ad in *Popular Photography* in March 1956. The ad proved a great success, but not in the way Canon had envisioned. Thousands of eager customers headed to their nearest stores only to discover that "coming next month" really meant May or even June or later. The new model was simply not ready or available. Dealers, with plenty of Nikon S2s on hand and unwilling to watch money go back out the door, redirected many of these customers to what they did have in stock. A lot of Nikons got sold because of that ad. It was one of the most successful ads Nikon never ran.

But for NK, Canon must have seemed the least of the problems the company and Ehrenreich were facing. Of even greater concern was the increasing public interest in single-lens reflex cameras (SLRs). The Exakta Camera Company had been building excellent, if eccentric, 35mm SLRs since the 1930s. The East German Praktina, with its SLR camera designed around a system of interchangeable finders, semi-automatic lenses and add-on motor drives, was drawing interest from some professionals. The Japanese-made Asahiflex and Miranda were also garnering public attention. Tokyo Kogaku would soon be introducing its Topcon, a heavy, but rugged SLR that used the Exakta bayonet mount. Minolta would be dumping its interchangeable lens rangefinder camera and going with a SLR as its flagship camera. More and more SLR models were appearing in trade shows and in stores, and the public was buying.

SLRs offered many advantages over a viewfinder-based camera, even one with a coupled rangefinder. Since the photographer framed and viewed through the same lens that would take the picture, the coverage was always on the optical axis. Closeups and telephoto work were easy to accomplish.

Still, until the mid–1950s, many problems remained. Push the shutter release, the mirror popped up, and one's view disappeared. The mirror flopping up was noisy and when one stopped the lens down to shooting aperture, the view was often so dark a photographer could no longer focus the picture. One by one, these problems were being solved. A pentaprism-equipped finder allowed the user to view the ground-glass image right-side up and correct left to right. Frescal lenses and condensers under the focusing screen brightened the view. Spring-loaded levers on the backs of lenses would transfer the action of the shutter release to the aperture so that the lens could remain open until the moment of exposure. And mirrors that dropped back into place immediately after exposure cut the blackout time. Advances in optics were also making SLRs more attractive. Reverse-telephoto designs permitted manufacture of wide-angle lenses that could clear the SLR's mirror box yet still provide the wide-angle coverage more and more photographers were seeking.

The Nikon S2 was barely out the door when NK ordered its engineers to begin work on a new rangefinder model camera that would meet or exceed the feature set of the Leica M3 in every way. At the same time, NK determined to design a new SLR that would incorporate all of this new rangefinder camera's best features and would be the most innovative SLR available.

While all this was happening, NK's optical leadership continued, and from the S2 introduction on, NK would no longer be looking to Germany for any of its optical inventions. By contrast, Leitz was actually dropping focal lengths from its lineup during this same period. In 1956, NK upped the ante with a 35mm f1.8 wide angle, a 50mm f1.1 high-speed normal and a special high-resolution normal lens it called its "Micro-Nikkor."

In September 1957, NK introduced its answer to the Leica M3: the Nikon SP. Ehrenreich and his salesmen had been listening to the requests of professional photographers and photojournalists for three years, and everything they had said they needed had been passed on to NK. It was not by accident that the "P" in the Nikon SP's name stood for "professional." The photographic press responded to the new model with interest and enthusiasm. New Nikons now received the same or better coverage than German cameras, and Nikon sales increased correspondingly.

Not only did the Nikon SP offer a single-shutter-speed dial as did an M-series Leica, it synced strobes at a higher speed and also took a coupled exposure meter. Not only did it offer parallax-correcting bright frames for lenses from 50mm through 135mm, but it offered coverage for the 35mm and 28mm lenses as well. In addition, it could even take an electric motor drive, allowing remote and high-speed picture taking.

NK wanted its new reflex camera to share the same dimensions as the SP. This proved impossible to achieve within the design limitations of the late 1950s. The body had to be longer to accommodate the mirror box. This would delay the Nikon F's introduction until the MPFDA Convention in the spring of 1959. Nevertheless, the Nikon F would offer the same shutter, the same layout of controls and the same feel and handling as the SP. Designed with working professionals in mind, the Nikon F was to prove the most flexible and versatile 35mm camera ever marketed. With truly automatic-aperture lenses, interchangeable finders and focusing screens and backs, the Nikon F could be modified or upgraded into any camera a professional or serious amateur wanted. With it came lenses ranging from 21mm through 1000mm, four with fully automatic apertures and coupling to a separately mounting light meter that allowed a photographer to adjust for both shutter speed and aperture. Within a year, NK would add three more automatic lenses, a 28mm, 58mm f1.4 and an innovative 85–250mm zoom.

The Leica M3 had caught its rivals by surprise in 1954. Now it was NK's turn to take the lead in 35mm photography. Zeiss Ikon had first shown what it believed to be the future choice of professionals in a 35mm SLR, the Contarex, at the German trade show, Photokina, in 1958. Its biggest features were interchangeable backs and a built-in meter that coupled to an aperture control built right into the lens mount. But, while its lenses were excellent, the camera was big, heavy and awkward to use.

Leitz refused to believe that the SLR was the wave of the future. It soon introduced a new reflex housing for its Leicas, the Visoflex II. Compact and easy to handle, it proved popular among scientists and field photographers prepared to work in a leisurely fashion. Not until the mid–1960s did Leitz, faced with fading sales and market loss, introduce its own answer to the SLR challenge. The first Leicaflex, like the Contarex, was expensive, heavy, equipped only with an external meter and, additionally, burdened with a unique viewing screen that only allowed focusing in a center spot. Leitz would, in time, correct these design errors, but its reflexes were never to prove a challenge to the Nikons.

Like NK, Canon had also introduced its answer to the SLR challenge in 1959, the first Canonflex. Instead of a motor drive, it opted to go with a bottom-mounted trigger advance that made tripod work difficult and needed three hands for truly fast operation. Its rangefinder cameras, particularly the less-expensive Canon P, had proved popular, but the Canonflex was a commercial failure. Part of Canon's problem may have also stemmed from difficulties with its U.S. distributors. Scopus had taken over the importation by then, but its ads were few and marketing was languishing. Bell & Howell Company, an established audiovisual equipment company known for its film projectors and 16mm movie cameras, was the next to try and make the Canon a success in America. But B&H was not Ehrenreich, and sales of its top-of-the-line Canon SLRs remained well below those of the Nikon F throughout the 1960s.

Within two years, the Nikon F would be outselling all other serious SLRs. Between 1959 and 1974, NK would manufacture over 860,000 Nikon Fs and easily sell every one. The Nikon F would prove to be the final plank in the platform of quality and features that NK had been struggling to build from 1946 on.

Nikon, Inc. had been successful since 1955 and the introduction of the S2, but the rise of the SLR meant extinction for others. As long as Leitz had continued to make a thread-mount Leica and rangefinders remained popular, the Japanese companies making Leica lookalikes had been able to survive. The year 1959 would see all but Canon disappear. The most notable victim was the Nicca, long NK's biggest customer for thread-mount Nikkors. Yashica bought Nicca out and soon after stopped RF camera production. That fall, NK stopped production of its thread-mount Nikkors.

Japan's domestic camera market had began to boom in the mid–1950s, but few Japanese could afford an expensive camera like the Nikon SP. Wanting to reach more of its own home market, in 1958, NK made its first attempt to reach a lower price point with the Nikon S3, an RF camera with all the features of the SP except the finder, which offered only fixed albada frames for the 50, 35 and 105. A year later, faced with a major economic downturn throughout Japan, NK tried again with the S4, which had even fewer features and sold for even less. But the SLR revolution was already here. Customers, both in the United States and in Japan, were no longer buying interchangeable-lens rangefinder cameras in enough numbers to meet the manufacturing costs.

It is unclear whether Ehrenreich or NK anticipated how sudden and complete this change would be. While Nikon ads certainly pushed the new Nikon F from the moment of its introduction, the Nikon SP continued to be actively marketed until 1961. NK even continued to add new RF accessories and upgrade the RF lenses. Still, as the demands for the Nikon F continued to grow, and sales of the rangefinder Nikons declined, the company was forced to shift more and more of its production lines to the reflex. Temporary RF production stoppages soon became permanent. The SP hung on until 1964, then slowly faded from the price lists.

From Nikon, Inc. to EPoI and Beyond[2]

The enormous success of the Nikon F gave the ambitious Joseph Ehrenreich the resources to expand his photographic goods business into non–Nikon products. In September 1961, he moved Nikon, Inc. to larger headquarters at 111 Fifth Avenue in New York. A year later, Joe created a new, publicly traded company, Ehrenreich Photo-optical Industries (EPoI) and made Nikon, Inc. a subsidiary. Using the EPoI name instead of Nikon gave Ehrenreich the flexibility to import and distribute photographic equipment that had no connection to Nikon at all.

While Nikon, Inc. had been the official distributor of Nippon Kogaku's products in the United States since 1954, as noted earlier, West Coast operations had remained under the control of Gary Lehman in San Francisco. In September 1962, Ehrenreich bought out Lehman and made his firm a subsidiary of the new EPoI. Ehrenreich now had full control of all of Nikon's U.S. operations.

Ehrenreich started the expansion of his import business with the Zena Bronica line of 2¼ square, 120 roll film SLRs. The success of the Swedish-made Hasselblad had made this a growth area, and since the Bronicas used Nikkor optics, including some of the same optics that fit the Nikon 35mm cameras, this system was a logical choice. In time, the EPoI line of products grew to include (at one time or another) the Durst line of amateur and professional enlargers; the Kindermann, Jobo and Capro lines of photo-processing equipment, including tanks and reels; Fujica, the Mamiya line of medium-format cameras, including their press cameras; twin-lens reflex and medium-format single-lens reflexes but NOT their 35mm reflex; the Komura line of lenses; the Sinar line of large-format view cameras; Metz electronic strobes and Unitron Instruments.

All this expansion could not fit into the company's Manhattan headquarters. In 1965 the company moved out to the open spaces of Long Island where they occupied new quarters on Stewart Avenue in Garden City.

Until the 1970s, most overseas photographic equipment manufacturers relied on American companies to import and distribute their products. In the early days this was due, in part, to legal restrictions that discouraged foreign corporations from operating in the United States. Foreign companies that did use their own solely owned distributors could not prevent private individuals from importing their products. Such companies found that they were often competing with themselves. Individuals would import directly from Japan or Germany, crow about the deals they had gotten and then go to the American subsidiary for service when something went wrong. At least one company repackaged every piece of equipment they sold in the United States in order to determine whether equipment needing service had been a domestic sale or not. The foreign manufacturers who used American-owned companies for marketing and distribution could grant those companies exclusive rights to distribute and sell the names of their products. These American companies could block importation of the names they had rights to. This protected the foreign companies, but gave their American-owned distributors greater control of product than a foreign-owned subsidiary could have at that time. Many foreign firms believed that an American distributor would have a better feel for what products Americans would buy and could advertise those products more effectively — a belief the American companies encouraged.

The American importers and distributors fell into two categories. A number of them were photo companies in their own right. Graflex, Charles Beseler, Bell & Howell and Heiland (later Honeywell) were all companies with established reputations in the photography field. Other companies manufactured no products of their own, but acted only as importer/distributors. These included such firms as Ponder & Best, Berkey, Allied Impex (AIC), Hanimex, Karl Heitz and Burleigh Brooks. Some of these companies were so strong that they bought out other importers as well as earlier companies that the foreign manufacturers had set up.

Minolta resisted, setting up its own company in the United States to import, advertise and distribute its own products and only its own products. It kept at it, but most foreign manufacturers were unable to resist the lure of having an American distributor. By the mid–1960s, most of the small, single-product importers were gone. The big American importers grew and succeeded until the mid–1970s when all the major surviving players dropped their American distributors and set up their own subsidiaries.

Nippon Kogaku had pursued a middle path. It decided that it was strong enough to use its own import subsidiary. NK had set up such a company on paper, Nippon Kogaku

(USA), Inc. (later Nippon Kogaku Photo-optical Inc.), back in 1954 when OFITRA/Nikon Camera Company's original exclusive contract had expired. But this company acted only as an import agent. Ehrenreich's firm did all the advertising, publicity, repairs, shipping and sales. In this way, NK gained the best of both worlds. It had control of its own import business, but still had the strength of Ehrenreich's experience and dedication. Besides, NK liked Joe and felt honor-bound to support the man who had fought so hard to establish their company's reputation in North America. It did not hurt that after 1973, EPoI was a major stockholder in Nippon Kogaku.

EPoI grew and prospered until the early 1970s. In 1971, NK entered into a ten-year agreement to continue Ehrenreich's exclusive rights to sell Nikon products in the United States. With his cash cow secure, Joe tried to expand EPoI further by pumping up demand for his non–Nikon products. Unfortunately, this operational expansion came at a time when the United States was entering an economic contraction as the Vietnam War wound down. The weakening American dollar made importing less profitable. In addition, many of EPoI's other products had little reputation or limited demand. Nikon, Inc. remained the only profitable division. The Jobo and Capro lines did particularly poorly and simply could not compete with Kodak and Nikor. Almost every non–Nikon division began to show losses and EPoI stock dropped from a high of over $25 per share to the single digits. Remembering how Ehrenreich had helped NK in the early 1950s, NK agreed to bail EPoI out. It purchased enough shares to make itself the second-largest shareholder.

Worse events soon followed. Canon finally decided to address the need for a professional 35mm single-lens reflex in its product line and in early 1971 introduced the Canon F-1. Some argued that this was simply the camera that Canon should have offered a decade earlier. Nevertheless, it made the Nikon F, with its cumbersome add-on meter finders, finally out of date. The Canon F-1 offered $\frac{1}{2000}$ shutter speed, faster flash sync, high-quality motor drives and other accessories. While press photographers — already heavily invested in Nikon — took mostly a wait-and-see attitude, the photography magazines all turned and asked, "What are you going to do now, Nikon?" Here was a direct threat to EPoI's successful pro line, but what could Ehrenreich do? Except for the unsuccessful, Nikkorex-branded products of the early 1960s, NK had always stayed away from the low-end, amateur market. Nikon's products were all high-end. As long as no other camera manufacturer produced a high-end SLR equivalent to the Nikon F, NK had that market to itself. Now this was no longer true. NK did not have a new professional model ready, and it had to finish developing one under pressure. In its 1971 annual report, EPoI offered a tantalizing glimpse of just such a new camera, but it was still only an idea, a postage stamp–sized photograph barely mentioned in passing.

In October 1971, the company formally announced the new Nikon F2, but it was almost the photographic equivalent of vaporware.[3] EPoI had only a few samples to show the press. A special diode-equipped meter finder was promised that would couple to a servomotor that would automatically set aperture. A Nikon rep readily admitted to the author that a picture of this device was no more than a wooden dummy. The product did not even exist.

The Canon F-1 was available in large quantities, and it was cutting into Nikon's sales.

In an effort to salvage the 1971 Christmas season, NK shipped EPoI a major order of cameras in late November. The shipment disappeared between the Kennedy International Airport and Garden City. Someone hijacked an 18-wheeler full of Nikons. The equipment was never legally recovered.* At first, EPoI put a brave face on it, stating that the shipment did not include any of the new F2s that the dealers were so desperately demanding. This was not true. That shipment apparently included enough F2s for most dealers in the country to get at least one. What happened to these hot cameras and lenses? Again, conversations with sales representatives indicate that they slowly found their way into dealers and private individuals' hands via backdoor transactions. Whatever happened, EPoI did not have them for Christmas 1971 and neither did the dealers. For months, the Nikon F2 would be no more than an image sitting on red rocks in some desert. People could see it, but they could neither buy nor touch it.

By the fall of 1972, the shortage of F2s eased, but Ehrenreich did not get a chance to make the new model a success. On February 7, 1973, while on his way to a business meeting in Los Angeles, Joe suffered a severe heart attack and died. He was 65.[4]

Herbert Sax took over as president, but the company never regained the sense of personal urgency that Joe had given it, nor did NK regain the market dominance that the Nikon F had enjoyed. An easy answer as to why might be that NK had been making and selling nothing but Nikon Fs and the less-expensive Nikkormats for so long that it found the retooling and the creation of a new assembly line more difficult than it had thought possible. Another answer might be that NK and EPoI had grown complacent and too used to success.

EPoI did make it through that period and the F2 did become a success, although not on the same relative scale as the F had been. Part of the reason was that Nikon's competition — and not just Canon — was now promoting features that Nikon did not have. Olympus led the way with its compact and light-weight, full-system, full-frame SLR in 1973. Pentax would soon follow and add a new bayonet mount and its multicoated lenses to the mix — an innovation Nikon had pioneered with its 24mm lens years earlier but never promoted. Canon was touting its compact telephoto optics with low-dispersion fluoride glasses. Minolta also decided to produce a full-system SLR.

Nikon had never offered any noninterchangeable lens rangefinder cameras to compete with the numerous, profitable offerings from Canon and Minolta. It was the last of the five major Japanese camera manufacturers to produce an automatic camera. Nikon got back in the SLR game with the compact Nikon FM and automatic Nikon EM and FE and advanced internally focusing, ED telephotos, but the days when it could sell one camera body as the be-all for any professional or serious amateur were gone.

Other factors were weighing in. The popular view of photography as the next big thing, the "fourth R" as promoters liked to say, was waning. By the late 1970s, personal computing was the new hot thing and photography was losing its image as the leading edge of technology. Prices, fueled by high inflation and increasing labor costs worldwide, were

*News of this incident appeared in either the Rochester, New York, newspaper or, more likely, in Herbert Keppler's weekly photographic industry newsletter, both of which the author had access to at that time.

moving quality photography out of the high-end, amateur market. Nikon could not produce enough of the professional equipment that there *was* demand for — such as the new F3 (introduced in 1980) — yet EPoI was having trouble liquidating huge inventories of old, lower-end equipment that would not sell. Ehrenreich might have had an instinctual sense for the marketplace, but EPoI did not. (Then again, maybe nobody did, as the late 1970s saw many formerly big players in the photography business disappear such as the Topcon, the Mamiya-Sekor and Petri.) Amateur point-and-shoot 35mm photography was booming, but public interest in serious photography was declining. The fortunes of the photography press declined with it. In 1980, this meant higher advertising costs as the publishers raised rates to compensate for inflation and declining subscriber revenues.

As early as 1978, business commentators, such as Robert Metz of the *New York Times*, were offering public speculation as to EPoI's future.[5] The weak dollar compared to the Japanese yen was making investment in American operations potentially lucrative. With its weakened financial position, EPoI was an increasingly attractive target. Takeover rumors fueled a rise in EPoI stock prices, which climbed back up to over $11.00 per share. The biggest factor preventing such a takeover was NK's ownership of 17 percent of EPoI's stock. The Ehrenreich family still owned 23 percent. As long as these two maintained a common interest, no outsider would step in. Besides, the Japanese did not like to "chase stock."[6] In July 1979, NK extended its contract with EPoI until 1983. This would seem to have indicated satisfaction on NK's part with what EPoI was doing. An NK official had been a member of EPoI's board since 1970. In August 1979, a second official from NK moved onto the board as the board's membership dropped from nine to seven. Eiichi Suzuki and Shigeo Miyahara would serve on the board until the company's end.

On June 14, 1979, the relationship of NK to EPoI changed dramatically when NK's stock ownership of the company increased to 40.6 percent. It did this by purchasing all the shares owned by Amelia Ehrenreich, Joe's widow, and shares owned by trusts set up for the Ehrenreich children and the company itself. The Ehrenreich family got a special deal, receiving $15.625 per share.

By April 1980, EPoI's financial picture had changed considerably. In contrast to the profitable 1979 fiscal year, EPoI was admitting net nine-month losses of over $8 million on sales of $113,061,000. Over $5 million of that loss came in the third quarter ending January 31, 1980.[7] The company, faced with defaulting on large loans, sold its shares in Nippon Kogaku (2 percent of total) on the open market, generating a net of $2.3 million. NK, in turn, agreed to help EPoI cover some of its escalating advertising costs, gave EPoI better wholesale prices on its equipment, and backed some of the loans EPoI was in danger of defaulting on. But now a strong NK began to seriously consider whether running importing and distributing as two separate operations made sense in light of the changing economic times. Would it save money if it purchased EPoI and combined operations?

By this time, EPoI had already dumped most of its non–Nikon product lines. Sax got control of costs and, by that fall, the company saw modest balance sheet improvements in its Nikon division and a 20 percent improvement in its instrument division. Belt-tightening, subsidized advertising costs and a smaller debt load put EPoI back in the black. Still, NK concluded that the time had come to take over. EPoI was back in the black only because of NK's help. NK could not see how EPoI would ever be able to function independently again. It proposed to buy all outstanding EPoI stock at $13.00 per share. Six months of negotiations followed. The final (May 15, 1981) report of the company traces EPoI's success and problems. In 1976, it had net sales of $77,997,000, or an income of $1.24 per share. It had a loss in 1977, a small profit in 1978 and a larger profit in 1979. In 1980, despite sales of $152,621,000, it had a loss of $4.16 per share.

NK proposed that the old Nikon, Inc. be merged with NK's American subsidiary, Nippon Kogaku Photo-optical Inc., to form a new company to be called Nikon, Inc.—a single company that would be both importer and distributor. A few private stockholders protested (the sweetheart deal between NK and the Ehrenreich family drew several lawsuits),[8] but with a 40.6 percent ownership, NK did not even have to be hostile. In June 1981, the merger was complete, and EPoI ceased to exist. In the end, private shareholders received $14.00 per share.

In the long run, NK probably benefited from taking over the entire operation. For the employees of the old Nikon, Inc. it probably made little difference at the time since Nippon Kogaku Photo-optical, Inc. had never been more than a legal fiction. Sax continued as president of the new Nikon, Inc., and George Gelber, the executive vice president of EPoI, continued in that position. Both continued to serve as directors on the new Nikon, Inc. board. Jonathan Ehrenreich, Joe's older son, retained a position of vice president through 1984. Amelia Ehrenreich had already left the board, but she remained a life-time consultant of the new company. She endowed five scholarships in photojournalism at Columbia University and continued to be active in photographic affairs for some time. She died on June 5, 2002, at age 94.

EPoI had handled every aspect of Nikon in the United States and EPoI employees continued to work under the new name. As late as 1982, repair slips sent from Nikon, Inc. still used the old EPoI masthead. For the smaller divisions of EPoI that had been piggy-backing on Nikon for years, the economic downturns of the 1970s were a disaster and many of those companies soon disappeared into the past.

Eventually Nippon Kogaku K.K. became Nikon, Inc. worldwide and the United States headquarters left Garden City, moving to Melville, New York, and Torrance, California. The American subsidiary continues as Nikon (USA).

Joe Ehrenreich had ridden the tide of success that he had helped create until his death in 1973. By then, what had started as a one-camera, eight-lens product line had grown into a huge importing and marketing firm: Ehrenreich Photo-optical Industries (EPoI), with over 600 employees and over $100 million in annual sales. In 1982, the old Nikon, Inc., Ehrenreich's creation, passed into history.

All this might be of minor interest, a footnote to the struggling years of 1945 through 1953, except that Ehrenreich and his company actively engaged in myth-making throughout EPoI's existence. An undated 13-page summary of EPoI's operations prepared by the public relations firm of Harshe-Rotman & Druck, Inc. in the early 1970s states in its second sentence that "Nikon cameras, introduced to the U.S. in 1954...." A page later, the report begins a paragraph with: "In 1954, the year the Nikon made its American debut, Joseph Ehrenreich organized the company which evolved into Ehrenreich Photo-optical

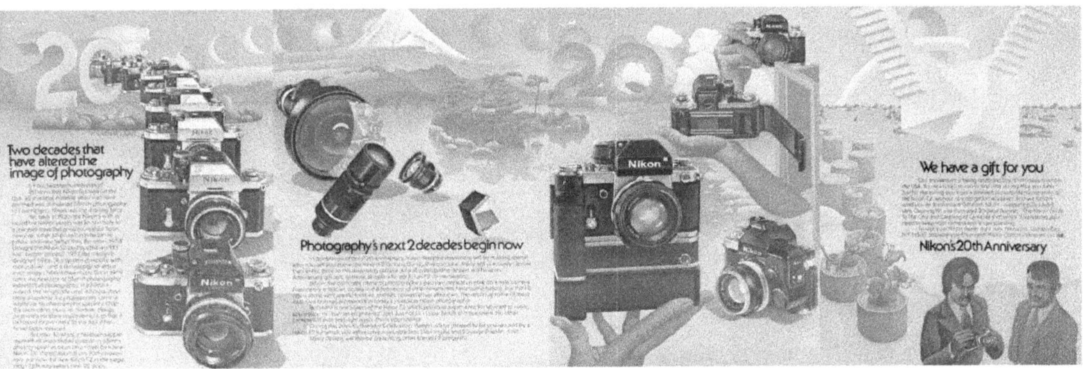

The four-page, full-color 1973 EpoI advertisement that appeared in all the major photography magazines "celebrating 20 years of Nikon in North America."

Industries Inc. (EPOI)...." Even the headline of Joe's obituary in the *New York Times* states that Ehrenreich "...Brought Nikon Camera Here."[9]

EPoI was not only willing to ignore OFITRA and the Nikon Camera Company, but also determined to wipe from memory that company's existence. Even as early as 1957, George Wright's *Nikon Manual*—a work clearly designed to promote the Nikon and its accessories in the same way that Morgan & Lester's *Leica Manual* promoted that camera and its accessories—ignored OFITRA and gave only passing mention of the Nikon models previous to the S.

Any history of the Nikon prior to 1954 ceased to exist once the Nikon F was firmly established as the camera of choice by both professionals and amateurs. Even the older rangefinder models began disappearing. Perhaps the most glaring example of all this self-promotion and rewriting of history occurred in April 1973.

That month, EPoI ran a full-color, four-page ad in all the major photographic magazines to "Celebrate twenty years of Nikon in America." Reading this, it would be easy to assume that the birth of the Nikon — like Athena's popping full-grown and fully armored from Zeus's head — was some kind of instantaneous success wrought by Ehrenreich and his marketing genius. It would be easy to assume that there had been no gestation, no period of labor, no fragile infancy during which Nippon Kogaku had to struggle to conceive and nurture its first camera toward success. It would be easy to assume a "made in Japan" miracle that just needed the right American to produce this business and marketing triumph.

The reality, as we have tried to show in this account, was that the Nikon had a long association with the United States before Ehrenreich officially took the helm in January 1954. The success that Ehrenreich and Nippon Kogaku started to enjoy in 1954 came about because there had been persons all over the world willing to believe in NK's little camera and its lenses and to stake all their efforts on that belief. This account is our thank you to them.

Transcription and Analysis of Nikon and Nikkor Production, August 1948–April 1951

The Occupation of Japan authorities under SCAP maintained a weekly (later monthly) record of all camera and lens production by Japanese optical companies. These records have survived in various forms. I have extracted and transcribed the specific numbers for Nippon Kogaku (Japan Optical Co.) that were recorded and kept in one particular archive that today survives as the records for August 1948 through April 1951. Some of the production records for 1946–1948 have also survived, but they are not as detailed or complete. I used all of these in the text, but felt that the numbers for this particular archive were important to the content of this book because they not only cover production but also state where the finished products sold. The figures appear with commentary below:

Notes

- Official exports initially went out from the *Boeki Kodan* [Trade Corporation], which handled most Japanese camera goods for export in the 1948–early 1949 period. Companies deposited their products with the *Boeki Kodan*, which may have freed the companies from inventory taxes for those items. When the government dissolved the *Boeki Kodan* in the spring of 1949, the column referring to the *Boeki Kodan* was dropped from the reports, which changed from weekly to monthly.

- Many of the early cameras and lenses were exported or given away as "samples." Samples went out directly from the company, not from the *Boeki Kodan*. No destination is recorded for these. Many, like the cameras Hans Liholm and Ludvig Hagburg received in April 1950, were probably given out to traders to stimulate sales and their fate is open to question. Later, some exports go to "E.B.," "Invisibles" and CPO. None of these terms are defined in these records, although we know that the CPO was the "Central Purchasing Office" for the post exchanges, base exchanges and ships' stores that served the American troops in Japan and other Asian locations. Invisibles might refer to cameras or lenses sold directly to American soldiers and sailors at the factory — an apparent practice in the 1950–1951 period.

- The reports may have continued through the end of 1951 but the file in the National Archives contains only the records through April 1951. Figures are not consistent from week to week. Whether this was due to poor math skills or poor reporting is unclear. All entries for the Nikons and Nikkors are under "Japan Optical," not under Nippon Kogaku (NK).
- Only the figures for Japan Optical are given below.

Figures

- Week of August 16–August 29, 1948* (105 f2 Nikons + 70 f3.5 Nikons = 175 total production).
  NK had 105 cameras on hand, 55 with the f2 lens and 50 with the f3.5 lens. They manufactured an additional 70 cameras, 50 with the f2 lens and 20 with the f3.5 lens. They exported four cameras with the f2 lens as "samples." These four are not accounted for in this week's production totals, but they do become part of the totals in October. As a result, production appears to start with 171. This is the earliest record in the file and gives no indication as to when the 105 cameras already in stock were actually produced.
- August 30–September 5, 1948 (101 f2 Nikons + 100 f3.5 Nikons = 201 total)
  NK had 171 Nikon cameras on hand. During that week, the company finished an additional 30 Nikons equipped with the 50mm f3.5 lens. NK does not list any separate lenses. Either they were not in production or they were not available separately from cameras. Since these records only cover equipment available for purchase or export, it may not cover items like the normal lenses that NK was manufacturing for Nippon Camera (Nicca).
- September 6–September 12, 1948 (201 Total)
  The company did not finish a single camera! Perhaps the effort of the previous week was too much?
- September 13–September 19, 1948 (107 f2 Nikons + 100 f3.5 Nikons = 207 Total)
  6 Nikons with the 50mm f2 lens finished.
  Company moves 100 of each model to stock at the *Boeki Kodan.*
- September 20–September 26, 1948 (207 Total)
  No additional cameras completed. Two exported as "samples." No destination given.
- September 27–October 3, 1948 (108 f2 Nikons + 100 f3.5 Nikons = 208 Nikons
  Three additional Nikons finished, all with f2 lenses, but production totals only go up by one. The number of cameras with the 50mm f3.5 lens remains at 100 and all of these are at the *Boeki Kodan.*
- October 4–October 10, 1948 (208 Total)
  Four more f2 cameras finished, but production total figure does not change. Four exported as samples, number on hand in marketing remains at 108. Total production is 108 with f2 and 100 with f3.5. Would one of these samples be the camera that found its way to Kodak that resulted in the Marjoram Report?
- Week missing.
- October 18–October 24, 1948 (116 f2 Nikons + 100 f3.5 Nikons = 216 Total)
  Two Nikons with f2 lens finished. Six sent out as samples for export. Company has 110 on hand, which is an obvious mathematical error since 110 minus 6 should be 104. Nevertheless, the next reports continue to use the 110 figure. 20 Nikons with f3.5 lens exported to Hong Kong,

**This is obviously more than a seven-day period, but these are the dates on the page.*

reducing the number of this type at the *Boeki Kodan* to 80. These were the first Nikons this report indicates as sold.

- October 25–October 31, 1948 (127 f2 Nikons + 100 f3.5 Nikons = 227 Total)
  Company now has 117 Nikons with f2 lens on hand. Another 30 Nikons with the f3.5 lens go to Hong Kong. Company has sent a total of 64 cameras with lenses overseas, 50 of these equipped with f3.5 lens go to Hong Kong. The total production figure is now mathematically correct and even includes the four samples exported but ignored back in August.
- November 1–November 7, 1948 (129 f2 Nikons + 100 f3.5 Nikons = 229 Total)
  Made two f2 cameras. One [or three] f2 camera heads abroad as "sample."
- November 8–November 14, 1948 (229 Total)
  Another f2 camera exported for a total of 18, or 14, depending on whose math we use.
- November 15–November 21, 1948 (229 Total)
  Two f2 cameras exported. Total number of Nikons exported (sold) is 66 [70].
- November 22–November 28, 1948 (229 Total)
  No change.
- November 29–December 5, 1948 (134 f2 Nikons + 100 f3.5 Nikons = 234 Total)
  Five new f2 cameras completed. Ten cameras with f2 lens and ten with f3.5 lens exported to Bangkok, Thailand. The *Boeki Kodan* now has only 40 f3.5 Nikons and 90 f2 Nikons in stock for export. NK did not restock or replace the cameras that the *Boeki Kodan* had shipped. Perhaps the company is already looking for another way to market its products.

- 2 -   Feb 7 — Feb 13

Manufacturer	Name of Camera	Stock on Sunday Preceding Week	For the Week		Stock on Sunday			Export Sales '47–Feb. '49)	Remarks	
			Production	Export	Stock on hand	Stock at Boeki Kodan	Total			
Olympus Optical Co., Ltd.	Olympus Chrome Six I	281	128	72	287	50	337	731	Siam India	76 2
"	" II	1	48	0	49	0	49	5		
"	Olympus 35 I	298	0	2	294	2	296	216	India	2
Fuji Photo Film	Fujica Six 1A	87	0	0	87	0	87	0		
"	" 1B	209	0	0	209	0	209	0		
"	" 1C	266	0	30	236	0	236	509	Siam	30
Tokyo Optical Co., Ltd.	Minion III	337	0	0	260	77	337	408		
"	Minion 35 A	757	0	0	757	0	757	0		
"	" B	250	0	0	250	0	250	0		
Japan Optical Co., Ltd.	Nikon F/2.0	196	0	18	108	70	178	85	U.S.A. Sample	12 6
"	" F/3.5	41	0	12	1	28	29	73	U.S.A.	12
"	Changeable Lens 13.5 cm	121	25	25	121.	0	121	28	India	25
Showa Optical Co., Ltd.	Leotax DIII	294	13	0	259	48	307	57		
"	Semi Leotax 7	84	45	0	129	0	129	680		
Kuribayashi Camera Works.	Petri I	167	0	0	167	0	167	573		

- Continue -

Record of the first shipment of Nikon cameras to the United States (from the *Weekly Report of Camera Production*). NK sent 24 Nikons to OFITRA in early February 1949 —12 had the f2 Nikkor, 12 had the f3.5 Nikkor (National Archives of the United States).

NK manufactures its first accessory lens for the new camera, the **135mm f4**. They make 27 of them. (Good week!) No indication as to the mount these lenses are in.

- December 6–December 12, 1948 [138 + 100 = 238] [135: 27 + 42 = 69]
  Four more cameras with f2 lens produced. Another 42 135mm Nikkors get finished. Two more f2 cameras head out as "samples." This would indicate that the first production "lot" of the 135mm f4 equaled 69 lenses. Note that when it gears up production, NK can complete lenses a lot faster than it can cameras.

- December 13–December 19, 1948 [same] [same]
  A total of 20 f2 cameras shipped to Singapore. One sample exported. Company has now shipped 109 cameras abroad.

- December 20–December 26, 1948 [147 + 100 = 247] [135mm: 69]
  Nine f2 cameras made. One sample exported. No other changes.

- December 27, 1948–January 2, 1949 [156 + 101 = 257] [135mm: 69]
  Nine additional f2 cameras and one f3.5. This one f3.5 camera did not go to the *Boeki Kodan* but stayed at the company. NK is beginning to explore other ways to export and is losing interest in working with the *Boeki Kodan*. It needs to have a sample of the f3.5 camera on hand to show to customers.

- January 3–January 9, 1949 [163 + 101 = 264] [135: 69 + 49 = 118]
  Seven f2 cameras finished. 49 new 135mm f4 Nikkors finished.

- January 10–January 16, 1949 [179 + 102 = 281] [135mm: 118]
  Nine f2 cameras exported as samples; one f3.5 as sample and one 135mm Nikkor as sample.

- January 17–January 23, 1949 [220 + 102 = 322] [135mm: 118]
  Three f2 cameras exported as samples. Two 135mm exported as samples.

- January 24–January 30, 1949 [260 + 102 = 362] [135mm: 118]
  Five sample f2 cameras exported. Forty new cameras made, all f2.

- January 31–February 6, 1949 [263 + 102 = 365] [135: 118 + 6 = 124]
  Three more f2 cameras. Six more 135mm lenses.

- February 7–February 13, 1949 [same] [135: 124 + 25 = 149]
  No new cameras finished. Completed 25 more 135mm Nikkors. Exported 12 Nikons with f2 lens and 12 Nikons with f3.5 lens to the United States. Six more cameras (f2) were exported as samples. A total of 25 135mm Nikkors were exported to India. The company supplied the f2 cameras that went to the USA. The *Boeki Kodan* supplied the f3.5 Nikons — NK had only the one camera in stock and could not meet the request itself. Apparently OFITRA was the importer.

- February 14–February 20, 1949 [278 + 102 = 380] [same]
  A total of 15 additional f2 cameras made. Exported 20 f2s to Belgium and 6 samples.

- February 21–February 28, 1949 [280 + 102 = 382] [same]
  Two new f2 cameras completed. Two f3.5 cameras exported to Hong Kong [original supply all sold or returned?]. Two f2s exported to Sweden and one to Hong Kong.

- March 1, 1949–March 6, 1949 [no record and apparently no change]

- March 7–March 13, 1949 [no change]

- March 14–March 20, 1949 [no change]
  A total of 15 f2s exported to the United States. Hmm. First shipment was not an aberration.

- March 21–March 27, 1949 [no change]
  Two f2s exported to the United States. A total of 26 f3.5's exported to India (last of the f3.5 cameras left in the *Boeki Kodan*). The company has only one Nikon with the 50mm f3.5 Nikkor left. The *Boeki Kodan* still has 70 f2s on hand.

- This week is missing.
  Produced 9 new f2 cameras based on next week's figures. Probably exported two samples.
- April 4–April 10, 1949 [293 + 102 = 395]
  Produced one new f2 camera. Exported two f2 cameras as samples.
- April 11–April 17, 1949 [same]
  No production of new cameras entered. Exported twelve f2 Nikons to USA, and one sample.
- April 18–April 24, 1949 [302 + 102 = 404] [135: 149 + 28 = 177]
  Manufactured nine f2 cameras. Three f2 cameras to USA, one sample.
- April 25–May 1, 1949 [same]
  Twelve cameras with f2 lens exported to USA. One sample exported.
- May 1949* [410 + 102 = 512, but should be 489] [135: 177 + 12 = 189] [85: 29]
  This is the first entry for the **85mm f2 Nikkor** but the chart shows a production of 25 with
  four on hand from previous month, indicating that production had started in April. NK manufactured 85 cameras with f2 lenses in May, and an additional twelve 135mm Nikkors. The
  production total figure for the camera is completely out of sync with previous numbers. The
  company at long last was getting its system of manufacture under control. The camera with
  the f3.5 lens is effectively dead. Four cameras were exported to the United States along with
  four 135mm lenses and two 85mm lenses. Someone was buying these puppies. Four were sold
  domestically to the government office.
  N.B.: The above figures indicate that a total of 72 model 1 Nikons were exported to the United
  States between the second week of February 1949 and the end of May.
- June 1949 [Figure should be a total of 542, but the figures for this month add up to 560] [135mm:
  210] [85mm: 62]
  Exported another 180 cameras to Hong Kong, three to Canada and eleven samples. One 135mm
  exported as sample and two 85mm as samples. Domestic hospital, university and laboratory
  bought five cameras. Made 53 cameras.
- July 1949 [Again, problems with arithmetic. Month-by-month addition yields a total of 592 cameras, but listing shows only 508 Nikons with the f2 lens] [135 figure: same] [85 figure: same]
  f3.5 camera no longer listed. Fifty Nikons manufactured. These would have been the last Model
  1s? Five cameras and one 135mm lens exported as samples. At the end of July, the company
  had 154 cameras in stock. Except for possibly the 12 shipped to Canada in August, these all
  may have eventually been converted to Ms.
- August 1949 [85mm: +5]
  The chart is confusing here. For the camera a zero is typed but someone corrected it in ink to
  50. The entry for the 85mm lens is changed from five to 50. Twelve cameras exported to Canada
  and three samples. Three 135mm Nikkors exported as samples.
- September 1949
  Again, numbers corrected in ink. Camera production is 200 (or 20, if typed number is correct).
  135mm production is 30. 85mm is changed from six to 65. Is this the new "M" camera?
- [No October figures]
- November 1949
  Figures changed by hand in ink. Camera production: 47 (18). The f3.5 Camera shows up again
  with a production of five(!). Ten 135mm and 11 (6) 85mm Nikkors manufactured. University
  bought one camera. Five cameras exported as samples and six went to "E.B." 135mm: one
  sample exported and two to E.B. E.B. also got one 85mm Nikkor. What was "E.B."? Export
  Board? Exchange Board?

Figures now listed only monthly.

- December 1949

    Again, figures changed by hand. A total of 18 cameras produced, and 23 exported: eight to Burma, eight to E.B. and seven as samples. One 135mm lens made and the university bought one. Three exported to Burma and one to E.B. Six 85mm made and two samples were exported. NOW the kicker: NK manufactured 3,550 13mm f1.9 Ciné Nikkors and exported 2,550 of these to the USA. The importation deal with OFITRA to supply lenses for Revere 8mm movie cameras was a major cash source for NK and helped cement the early relationship with OFI-TRA.

- January 1950

    Camera production is 69 or only 12 if the handwritten figure is to be believed. NK exported 115 cameras, all with the f2 lens. A total of 100 went to Switzerland, two to Canada, five to Siam (Thailand), CPO got one, three samples went and four are listed as "invisible." No 135mm lenses were made. Either zero(ink) or 27(typed) 85's were made. Canada got one 135. "Sample" took one 135 and one 85. NK manufactured another 4,440(typed) or 3,550(inked) Ciné lenses and exported 4,000 to the United States.

- February 1950

    Nikon with f1.5 lens [**New product**]: Prod: 14, Export: 8. Samples: 5, Invisible: 3.
    43 f2 Nikon f2: Prod: 43. Export: 17. Venezuela: 6, Invisible: 9. Sample: 2. 135mm: Prod: 0. Export: 14. Venezuela: 4, Invisible: 9, Samples: 1.
    85mm: Prod: 0. Export: 2. Venezuela: 2.
    13mm Ciné Nikkor: Prod: 4,560. Export: 6,000. USA: 6,000.

- March 1950

    Nikon f1.5: Prod: 41, Export: 10. USA: 3, Invisible: 6, Sample: 1.
    Nikon f2: Prod: 97, Export: 25. USA: 5, Philippines: 3, Siam: 4, Invisible: 8, Sample: 5.
    Nikon f3.5: Prod: 12. Export: 12. USA: 12. Hmm. Company still could make a few of these.
    135mm: Prod: 0 15. Export: 15. USA: 5, Siam: 2, Invisibles: 8.
    85mm: Prod: 0. Export: , USA: 5, Invisibles: 5.
    13mm Ciné Nikkor: Prod: 7450. Export: 7450. USA: 7450. Since December the company had built 20,000 of these lenses and exported every one.
    In letter dated March 30, 1950, the Tokyo manager for Western Trading requested a license to sell NK optical goods to "Army personnel and holders of O.S.S. cards." While permission did not come until the end of June, it appears that the company was allowed to start in April. "CPO" immediately becomes the most important source of export sales for NK.

- April 1950

    Nikon f1.5: Prod: 33, Export: 50. Dest: CPO: 31, USA: 5, Invisible: 11, Sample: 3
    Nikon f2: Prod: 55, Export: 61. Dest: CPO: 26, USA: 10, Sweden: 10, Invisible: 11, Sample: 4
    135mm: Prod: 0, Export: 22. Dest: CPO: 10, Invisible: 12
    85mm: Prod: 0, Export: 15. Dest: CPO: 7, Invisible: 8.
    35mm, f3.5 [**new product**]: Prod: 77. Export: 31. Dest: CPO: 7, USA: 5, Invisible: 19.
    13mm Ciné Nikkor: 0

- May 1950

    Nikon f1.5: Prod: 29. Export: 35. Dest: Venezuela: 10, Invisible: 11, Sample: 3, CPO: 11.
    Nikon f2: Prod: 0. Export: 41. Dest: Venezuela: 25, Invisible 12, Sample: 3, CPO: 1.
    135mm: Prod: 0. Export: 24. Dest: Invisible: 16, Sample: 3, CPO: 5.
    85mm: Prod: 0. Export: 12. Dest: Invisible: 7, Sample: 3, CPO: 2.
    35mm: Prod: 21. Export: 15. Dest: Invisible: 7, Sample: 5, CPO: 3.
    13mm Ciné: Prod: 2,000. Export: 2,000. Dest: USA: 2,000.

- June 1950

    Nikon f1.5: Prod: 42. Export: 33. Dest: CPO: 22, Invisible: 8, Sample: 3.

Nikon f2: Prod: 24. Export: 12. Dest: CPO: 3, Invisible: 8, Sample: 1
135mm: Prod: 0. Export: 19. Dest: CPO: 12, Invisible 7.
85mm: Prod: 0, Export: 10. Dest: CPO:8. Invisible: 2.
35mm: Prod: 0. Export: 27. Dest: CPO: 20. Invisible: 7.
13mm Ciné: Prod: 4,000. Export: 2,000. Dest: USA: 2,000.

- July 1950
  Nikon f1.5: Prod: 68. Export: 74. Dest: CPO: 64, USA: 7, Invisible: 3.
  Nikon f2: Prod: 130. Export: 161. Dest: CPO: 118, Africa: 36, USA: 2, Invisible: 5.
  135mm: Prod: 62. Export: 44. Dest: CPO: 23, Hong Kong: 11, USA: 4, Invisible: 6.
  85mm: Prod: 81. Export: 59. Dest: CPO: 22, USA: 4, Hong Kong: 22, Invisible: 11.
  35mm: Prod: 56. Export: 40. Dest: CPO: 31, USA: 4, Invisible: 5.
  13mm Ciné: Prod: 2,000. Export: 4,000. Dest: USA: 4,000.

- August 1950
  Nikon f1.5: Prod: 122. Export: 99. Dest: CPO: 84, Venezuela: 6, Peru: 1, Sweden: 2, Sample: 6.
  Nikon f2: Prod: 28. Export: 29. Dest: CPO: 12, USA: 10, Argentina: 3, Sample: 4.
  135mm: Prod: 37. Export: 26. Dest: CPO: 16, Hong Kong: 5, Sample: 5.
  85mm: Prod: 1. Export: 18. Dest: CPO: 12, Hong Kong: 5, Sample: 1.
  35mm: Prod: 78. Export: 65. Dest: CPO: 62, Sample: 3.

- September 1950
  Nikon f1.4 [**New product**]: Prod: 20. Export:18. Dest: CPO: 14, Sample: 4.
  Nikon f1.5: Prod: 11. Export: 6. Dest: CPO: 2, Yokoto PX: 2.
  Nikon f2: Prod: 69. Export: 74. Dest: CPO: 61, Formosa: 11, Venezuela: 1, Sample: 1.
  135mm: Prod: 19. Export: 23. Dest: CPO: 10, USA: 10, Venezuela: 1, Sample: 2.
  85mm: Prod: 7. Export: 10. Dest: CPO: 9, Venezuela: 1.
  35mm: Prod: 74. Export: 51. Dest: CPO: 36, Venezuela: 2, Sample: 3.

- October 1950 [production figures corrected in ink]
  Nikon f1.4: Prod: 86 (20). Export:74. Dest: CPO: 73, Sample: 1.
  Nikon f1.5: Prod: 68 (11). Export: 6. Dest: CPO: 4, Sample: 2.
  Nikon f2: Prod: 52 (69). Export: 62. Dest: CPO: 52, Sweden: 6, Sample: 4.
  135mm: Prod: 58 (19). Export: 39. Dest: CPO: 34, Hong Kong: 5.
  85mm: Prod: 91 (7). Export: 108. Dest: CPO: 100, Hong Kong: 8.
  35mm: Prod: 175 (74). Export: 223. Dest: CPO: 220, Hong Kong: 3.

- November 1950
  Nikon f1.4: Prod: 153. Export:145. Dest: CPO: 144, Venezuela: 1.
  Nikon f1.5: Prod: 13. Export: 87. Dest:Brazil: 75, CPO:12.
  Nikon f2: Prod: 67. Export: 61. Dest: CPO: 61.
  50mm f1.4 [**New product**]: Prod: 153. Export: 69. Dest: CPO: 69.
  This lens is now being marketed as a separate item.
  135mm: Prod: 141. Export: 153. Dest: CPO: 147, Hong Kong: 4, Sweden: 2.
  85mm: Prod: 139. Export: 146. Dest: CPO:146.
  35mm: Prod: 178. Export: 153. Dest: CPO: 150, Hong Kong: 3.

- December 1950
  Nikon f1.4: Prod: 201. Export: 165. Dest: CPO: 160, Sweden: 2, Indonesia: 1, Sample: 2.
  Nikon f1.5: Prod: 0. Export: 2. Dest: CPO: 2.
  Nikon f2: Prod: 189. Export: 168. Dest: CPO: 150, Iran: 15, Sweden: 1, England: 1, Venezuela: 1.
  50mm f1.4: Prod: 199. Export: 216. Dest: CPO: 203, USA: 12, Sweden: 1.
  135mm: Prod: 231. Export: 160. Dest: CPO: 143, Hong Kong: 12, Venezuela: 4, Sweden: 1.
  85mm: Prod: 153. Export: 104. Dest: CPO:89, Hong Kong: 12, Venezuela: 2, Sweden: 1.

35mm: Prod: 264. Export: 163. Dest: CPO: 150, Hong Kong: 12, Sweden: 1.

13mm Ciné: Prod: 360. Export: 360. Dest: USA: 360.

Note how suddenly the exports change in January. NK had sent no cameras to the United States since the previous August. Now with the new year, suddenly it is their biggest customer besides the CPO.

- January 1951

    Nikon f1.4: Prod: 129. Export:115. Dest: CPO: 65, USA: 50.

    Nikon f1.5: Prod: 0. Export: 0.

    Nikon f2: Prod: 120. Export: 123. Dest: CPO: 73, USA: 50.

    50mm f1.4: Prod: 106. Export: 41. Dest: CPO: 41.

    135mm f4: Prod: 79. Export: 66. Dest: CPO: 91.

    135mm f3.5 [**New product**]: Prod: 79. Export: 66. Dest: USA: 60, CPO: 6.

    Looks like NK was dumping the old 135mm f4 lenses in the military exchanges and sending the new stuff to the United States.

    85mm: Prod: 173. Export: 104. Dest: USA: 60, CPO: 44.

    35mm: Prod: 141. Export: 100. Dest: USA: 60, CPO: 40.

    13mm Cine: Prod: 540. Export: 0.

- February 1951

    Nikon f1.4: Prod: 180. Export: 99. Dest: CPO: 91, USA: 5, Switzerland: 1, Philippines: 1, France: 1.

    Nikon f1.5: Prod: 0. Export: 0.

    Nikon f2: Prod: 178. Export: 96. Dest: CPO: 93, Siam: 1.

    50mm f1.4: Prod: 185. Export: 76. Dest: USA: 54, CPO: 22.

    135mm f4: Prod: 149. Export: 69. Dest: CPO: 69.

    135mm f3.5: Prod: 44. Export: 15. Dest: CPO: 10, USA: 4, France: 1.

    85mm: Prod: 150. Export: 132. Dest: CPO: 99, USA: 32, France: 1.

    35mm: Prod: 279. Export: 204. Dest: CPO: 201, USA: 3.

    13mm Ciné: Prod: 620. Export: 1,100. Dest: USA: 1,100.

    30° Deflecting Prism [**New product**]: Prod: 100. Export: 100. Dest: Feamoom[?].

- March 1951

    Nikon f1.4: Prod: 213. Export: 111. Dest: CPO: 106, Brasil: 2, Indonesia: 3.

    Nikon f1.5: Prod: 0. Export: 0.

    Nikon f2: Prod: 241. Export: 118. Dest: CPO: 89, USA: 27, Italy: 1, Indonesia: 1.

    50mm f1.4 : Prod: 197. Export: 4. Dest: CPO: 4.

    135mm f4: Prod: 50. Export: 13. Dest: CPO: 13.

    85mm: Prod: 62. Export: 19. Dest: CPO:18, Brazil: 1.

    35mm: Prod: 501. Export: 229. Dest: CPO: 229.

    13mm Ciné: Prod: 1,500. Export: 1,501. Dest: USA: 1,500, CPO: 1.

    38mm f1.9 Ciné Nikkor [**New product**]: Prod: 100. Export: 100. Dest: USA: 100.

- April 1951

    Nikon f1.4: Prod: 251. Export: 97. Dest: CPO: 17, USA: 33, Brazil: 45, Other: 2.

    Nikon f1.5: Prod: 0. Export: 0.

    Nikon f2: Prod: 129. Export: 59. Dest: CPO: 57, France: 1, Other: 1.

    50mm f1.4 : Prod: 170. Export: 81. Dest: CPO: 51, USA: 30.

    135mm f4: Prod: 27. Export: 21. Dest: CPO: 21.

    135mm f3.5: Prod: 208. Export: 81. Dest: CPO: 72, France: 1, Other: 5.

    85mm: Prod: 144. Export: 94. Dest: CPO:86, USA: 2, France: 1, Other: 5.

    35mm: Prod: 334. Export: 225. Dest: CPO: 186, USA: 33, France: 1, Other: 5.

    13mm Ciné: Prod: 1,350. Export: 0.

    38mm Ciné: Prod: 95. Export: 0.

The detailing of these records, with breakdowns by focal length and aperture for lenses and the type of lens equipment for the cameras, is particularly useful. There were two copies of this report in the files when I first examined the archives folder in June 2004 — one bound, the other unbound. When I checked the file again in July, the bound copy was missing. Very discouraging. I could not find any clue as to why the records prior to late August 1948 or later than April 1951 were not in the folder. It would have been nice to have been able to photocopy the reports in their entirety to make comparisons with other camera manufacturers during that same period. Unfortunately, my funds and time forced me to concentrate on the pages that showed Japan Optical's production and neglect the other companies.

Several additional points:

- As far as we can determine, these reports cover only equipment that actually made it out of the factory and to marketing. In other words, these production figures cover equipment actually available for purchase. They do not cover equipment that failed inspections nor do the numbers reflect failed equipment, such as the early Nikons than got shipped to Hong Kong, broke and got sent back to Tokyo. Nor would they have covered preproduction units, such as the 21 Nikon prototypes.

- All the cameras sold included a normal lens. It was not possible to buy either a Nikon I or a Nikon M as just a body. It also was not possible to purchase a normal lens separately until late 1950 when the 50mm f1.4 shows up as a separate item.

- The 135mm f4 does not appear in these production reports until December 1948. The 85mm f2 does not appear on the lists until April 1949. The 35mm f3.5 wide angle does not appear until a year later, in April 1950. When these lenses appear on the reports they are listed as "New item." What does this mean in terms of actual dates for these lenses? Traditionally, collectors have referred to these three lenses, along with the two normals (50mm f2 and 50mm f3.5) as being part of the original five lenses available for the first Nikon at the time the camera was announced. Yet, if these dates for introduction are accurate, were any lenses other than normal available for the Nikon initially?

  Remember that these reports are contemporary and primary sources compiled by persons with no business, nor a particular point of view, to promote or alter. They were simply recording the numbers that the various companies sent them. While some of the figuring is erratic, there is no evidence that they are wrong. The serial numbers on the lenses give some indication as to when a series was manufactured. However, that does not mean that a lens starting with, say, 904 was actually made in April 1949. Instead, it might refer to a month when the design was approved, or a decision to manufacture was made. Remember, Nikons start with 609, but the first prototype did not leave the shop until that November.

  The current Nikon Company in its online coverage of the 35mm f3.5 W-Nikkor gives a date of January 1950 for the startup of production. The SCAP reports show April 1950. There may not actually be in conflict because it may have taken NK several months from starting a production line to actually moving a finished and inspected product to marketing where these SCAP records would pick them up.

  With that in mind, it is possible that NK started working on the 135mm f4 in the summer of 1948, which would make that lens a near contemporary of the first Nikons. Giving May 1949 as the first month that the 85mm was available appears accurate and matches the date in Wright's *Manual.* It is possible that when Nikon's archives get the RF telephoto lenses up on the Web that we may have a better sense of where the 85mm fits in. We do not feel that it would be wise under any scenario to regard the 35mm f3.5 W-Nikkor as a contemporary of the first Nikon.

- Production of the 135mm f3.5 started much later than most other sources would indicate. Note that the company continued to make and sell the f4 lens for several months after it had already started selling the newer, faster version. Which version did David Douglas Duncan use? Good question, and the contemporary accounts that appeared in the *New York Times* and the photography magazines are confusing. He was certainly using a 135mm f3.5 Nikkor by September. The first batch of 135mm f3.5 Nikkors start with serial number 50051, suggesting a design approval of May 1950, but actual production beyond prototypes probably did not begin until that fall. Note that the production numbers here closely match the numbers in Rotoloni's 1983 book. They are just later.

- These export figures do give us a number for the 50mm f3.5 in Nikon/Contax mount. Total: 123. Of these, 101 were sold on Nikon Is, 17 were sold on Nikon Ms. That lens in the Nikon mount has to be one of the rarest of all Nikkors. Of course, NK was building hundreds and hundreds of that lens in Leica thread, for the Canon, then for Niccas, so as an *optic*, it is not that rare. My guess would be that the company built a bunch in the late 1940s, then added mounts as needed. Only 123 got mounts for Nikons.

- A point that needs to be made and remembered is that by the time NK actually began the manufacture of its 35mm camera, it probably no longer saw the camera as destined for the domestic market. The purpose was to produce something that would sell overseas in order to generate badly needed foreign currency (although a few of the early Nikons and Nikkors do have distance scales marked in meters!). Overseas, of course, included the American bases' stores and the SCAP records reflect that understanding. The records also clearly indicate that hardly a single Nikon I was sold to Japanese customers. This is easy to understand. The Japanese could not afford professional-level 35mm cameras in 1948 or 1949. The Nikon was not aimed at an impoverished public. It was aimed at the customers with money. If you want to locate Nikon I cameras, the West Coast of the United States would seem to be the best place to start looking. Why not Hong Kong? Hong Kong was an important commercial and trading center, but not a buying center. Most of the Nikons that went to Hong Kong probably moved on to other parts of the British Empire before finding their final owners. So why are so many Nikon I cameras in Japanese ownership today? The answer is that Japanese collectors have been searching for these cameras worldwide, buying them and bringing them back "home."

- Numbers, numbers, numbers ... Why do the export record numbers, the optical production numbers, the numbers from Tatsuhiko Arakawa and the numbers in Rotoloni's book fail to match up, except for certain months? Another good question. Part of the answer may be that it depends on who is doing the counting. For example: The export records indicate a total of 506[642] Nikon I cameras made it out the door and were sold by August 1949. This is quite a distance from the over 700 that serial numbers would give for this first model. But are these figures necessarily incompatible? How many of these serial numbers never made it out of manufacturing? How many failed inspections and got put aside? The 506 figure includes only the cameras that actually were boxed and left the factory. Understanding the manufacturing difficulties NK was having through that period, maybe we should be surprised that over two-thirds made it to stores at all.

- Please do not forget the Ciné Nikkors. NK sold over 28,000 of those little lenses over a seven-month period for use on Revere 8mm movie cameras at a time when its optics for its new 35mm camera were numbering in the dozens. The 13mm Ciné Nikkor was probably more important to NK's survival and success in 1949–50 than anything else it was doing at that time. Even if it was making only $5 to $10 [Gasser states $7] a piece for those optics, that was all hard cash at a time when every Japanese company was desperate for any foreign currency it could get.

Nikon Camera Export Destinations, August 1948–April 1951, Based on SCAP Records (Summary)

Nikon I Sales

August 1948: Sample 4.
September 1948: Sample 2.
October 1948: Sample 10; Hong Kong 50.
November 1948: Sample 6.

December 1948: Sample 4; Siam 20; Singapore 20.
January 1949: Sample 18.
February 1949: Sample 12; Hong Kong 3; USA 24; Belgium 20; Sweden 2.
March 1949: Sample 2; USA 17; India 26.
April 1949: Sample 4; USA 27.
May 1949: USA 4; Domestic 4.
June 1949: Sample 11; Hong Kong 180; Canada 3; Domestic 5.
July 1949: Sample 3.
August 1949: Sample 3; Canada 12; Domestic 2.
Total Nikon I Sales: Sample 70; Hong Kong 233; Siam 20; Singapore 20; USA 72; Belgium 20; Sweden 2; India 26; Canada 15; Domestic 11; Totals 492.

Nikon M Sales

September 1949: Sample 3.
October 1949: Other 17.
November 1949: Sample 5; Domestic 1; E.B. 6.
December 1949: Sample 7; Domestic 2; Burma 3.
January 1950: Sample 3; Siam 5; Canada 2; Domestic 19; Switzerland 100; CPO 1; Invisible 4.
February 1950: Sample 1; Invisible 9; Venezuela 4.
March 1950: Sample 6; Siam 4; USA 8; Invisible 14; Philippines 3.
April 1950: Sample 7; USA 15; Sweden 10; CPO 57; Invisible 22.
May 1950: Sample 6; CPO 12; Invisible 23; Venezuela 35.
June 1950: Sample 4; CPO 25; Invisible 16.
July 1950: USA 7; CPO 182; Invisible 8; Africa 36.
August 1950: Sample 10; USA 10; Sweden 2; CPO 100; Venezuela 6; Argentina 3; Peru 1.
September 1950: Sample 7; CPO 77; Venezuela 1; Formosa 11; Yokota PX 2.
October 1950: Sample 7; Sweden 6; CPO 125.
November 1950: Sample 3; CPO 217; Venezuela 1; Brazil 75.
December 1950: Sample 2; Sweden 3; CPO 312; Venezuela 1; Indonesia 1; Iran 15; England 1.
January 1951: USA 100; CPO 138; France 1.
February 1951: USA 5; Switzerland 1; CPO 184; Philippines 1.
March 1951: USA 27; CPO 195; Brazil 2; Indonesia 3; Italy 1.
April 1951: USA 33; CPO 74; Brazil 45; France 1; Other 3.
Total Nikon M: Sample 71, Siam 9, USA 205, Sweden 21, Canada 2, Domestic 22; E.B. 6, Burma 3, Switzerland 101, CPO 1,699; Invisible 96; Venezuela 48; Philippines 4; Africa 36; Argentina 3; Formosa 11; Yokota PX 2; Peru 1; Brazil 122; Indonesia 4; Iran 15; England 1; France 1; Italy 1; Other 20; Totals 2521.

Nippon Kogaku Production, May 1946–April 1951 (from other SCAP records)

May 1946: binoculars 652; opera glasses 704.
June 1946: binoculars 590; opera glasses 747.
July 1946: binoculars 448; opera glasses 355.
August 1946: binoculars 966; opera glasses 1750.
September 1946: camera prod. 0; lenses 134.
October 1946: lenses 176; binoculars 1273; opera glasses 1867.
November 1946: lenses 101; binoculars 375: opera glasses 1286.

December 1946: lenses 64.

January 1947

February 1947: lenses 43.

March 1947: lenses 142.

April 1947: lenses 34; lense accessories 281.

May 1947: lenses 199.

June 1947: lenses 69.

July 1947: lenses 169.

August 1947: lenses 64.

September 1947: lenses 173.

October 1947: lenses 250.

November 1947: camera prod. 2; *Rotoloni fig '83 2*; lenses 400.

December 1947: camera prod. 2; *Rotoloni fig '83 2*; lenses 361.

January 1948: camera prod. 0; *Rotoloni fig '83 0*; lenses 210; lense accessories 33; binoculars 579; opera glasses 0; telescopes 0; microscopes 0; levels 178; projection lenses 23.

February 1948: camera prod. 0; *Rotoloni fig '83 8*; lenses 210; lense accessories 0; binoculars 406; microscope accessories 200; levels 6.

March 1948: camera prod. 0; *Rotoloni fig '83 2*; lenses 143; lense accessories 0; binoculars 994; microscopes 15; microscope accessories 253; transits 6; levels 118; lensmeters 2; profile projectors 18.

April 1948: camera prod. 0; *Rotoloni fig '83 9*; lenses 211; accessories 32; binoculars 854; microscope accessories 221; transits 6; levels 34; other optical inst 27.

May 1948: camera prod. 0; *Rotoloni fig '83 33*; lenses 172; binoculars 897; microscope accessories 694; transits 11; levels 30; other optical inst 109.

June 1948: camera prod. 0; export prod. 11; lenses 106; binoculars 1125; microscope accessories 1051; transits 29; levels 63; project lenses 3; other optical inst 43.

July 1948: camera prod. 0; *Rotoloni fig '83 4*; lenses 140; binoculars 1076; microscope accessories 809; transits 29; levels 103; projection lenses 58; other optical inst 40.

August 1948: camera prod. 44; export prod. 175; *Rotoloni fig '83 2*; lenses 240; lense accessories 0; binoculars 1139; microscope accessories 713; transits 20; levels 65; projection lenses 3; optical measur inst 14.

September 1948: camera prod. 36; export prod. 39; *Rotoloni fig '83 9*; lenses 207; lense accessories 0; binoculars 1409; microscopes 15l; microscope accessories 485; transits 21; levels 0; optical measur inst 20.

October 1948: camera prod. 46; export prod. 13; *Rotoloni fig '83 76*; lense accessories 468; binoculars 1595; microscopes 202; transits 6; levels 34; other surveying accessories 40; optical measur inst 60; other optical inst 25; other optical inst accessories 21; magnifiers 4300.

November 1948: camera prod. 52; export prod. 2; *Rotoloni fig '83 31*; lense accessories 503; binoculars 1651; microscopes 208; microscope accessories 349; transits 31; levels 30; optical measur inst 11; other optical inst accessories 4163.

December 1948: camera prod. 61; export prod. 28; *Rotoloni fig '83 121*; x-ray camera 2; export lenses 69; lense accessories -; binoculars 741; microscopes 6; microscope accessories 101; transits 19; other surveying accessories 50; optical measur insts 37; other optical insts accessories 6.

January 1949: camera prod. 68; export prod. 105; *Rotoloni fig '83 40*; export lenses 49; lense accessories 602; binoculars 1979; telescopes 37microscopes 180; microscope accessories 433; transits 35; levels 103; other surveying accessories 100; optical measur inst 8; spectacles 2159.

February 1949: camera prod. 58; export prod. 20; *Rotoloni fig '83 85*; export lenses 31; lense accessories 319; binoculars 2250; microscopes 139; microscope accessories 1094; transits 32; other surveying accessories 48; optical measur inst 14; other optical inst 1; spectacles 2668.

March 1949: camera prod. 2; export prod. 12; *Rotoloni fig '83 85*; export lenses 0; lense accessories 389; binoculars 1971; microscopes 150; microscope accessories 770; transits 30; levels 114; optical measur inst 18; spectacles 3397.

April 1949: camera prod. 22; export prod. 10; *Rotoloni fig '83 42*; export lenses 28; lense accessories 305; binoculars 1974; microscopes 279; microscope accessories 322; transits 38; levels 47; other surveying accessories 99; proj. accessories 10; optical measur inst 21; other optical inst 16; spectacles 1654.

May 1949: camera prod. 116; export prod. 85; *Rotoloni fig '83 91*; export lenses 37; lense accessories 612; binoculars 2703; microscopes 145; microscope accessories 650; transits 46; levels 42; optical measur inst 11; other optical inst 11; spectacles 2244.

June 1949: camera prod. 113; export prod. 53; *Rotoloni fig '83 60*; export lenses 25; lense accessories 910; binoculars 2868; telescopes 47; microscopes 221; microscope accessories 922; transits 36; levels 10; other optical inst 128; spectacles 2771.

July 1949: camera prod. 31; export prod. 50; *Rotoloni fig '83 44*; lense accessories 744; binoculars 3371; telescopes 7; microscopes 342; microscope accessories 872; transits 30; levels 41; other surveying accessories 55; projection lenses 58; other optical inst 162; spectacles 1089.

August 1949: camera prod. 44; export prod. 0; *Rotoloni fig '83 34*; export lenses 50; lense accessories 698; binoculars 2689; microscopes 144; microscope accessories 516; transits 24; levels 5; proj. accessories 3; other optical inst 49; spectacles 2684.

September 1949: camera prod. 36; export prod. 20; *Rotoloni fig '83 27*; export lenses 95; lenses accessories 641; binoculars 3962; microscopes 80; microscopes accessories 820; transits 30; levels 114; other optical inst 46; spectacles 5451.

October 1949: camera prod. 46; export prod. 26; *Rotoloni fig '83 49*; export lenses -; lense accessories 653; binoculars 4063; microscopes 159; microscope accessories 322; transits 34; levels 19; projection lenses 40; spectacles 4200.

Novembr 1949: camera prod. 52; export prod. 18; *Rotoloni fig '83 53*; export lenses 21; lense accessories 554; binoculars 2111; microscopes 139; microscope accessories 647; transits 35; levels 1; optical measur inst 11; other optical inst 11; spectacles 2244.

December 1949: camera prod. 61; export prod. 12; *Rotoloni fig '83 70*; lenses 3550; export lenses 16; lense accessories 289; binoculars 3198; opera glasses 569; telescopes 47; microscopes 118; microscope accessories 1008; projection lenses 50; spectacles 3272.

January 1950: camera prod. 24; export prod. 69; *Rotoloni fig '83 108*; lenses 4440; export lenses 27; lense accessories 766; binoculars 3371; telescopes 7; microscopes 162; microscope accessories 872; transits 30; levels 41; other surveying accessories 55; projection lenses 58; other optical inst 162; spectacles 1089.

February 1950: camera prod. -; export prod. 57; *Rotoloni fig '83 101*; lenses 1440.

March 1950: camera prod. 97; export prod. 150; *Rotoloni fig '83 103*; x-ray camera 15; lenses 7450; export lenses 0; lense accessories 698.

April 1950: camera prod. 88; export prod. 88; *Rotoloni fig '83 136*; export lenses 77; lense accessories 597.

May 1950: camera prod. 29; export prod. 29; *Rotoloni fig '83 87*; lenses 2000; export lenses 51; lense accessories 600.

June 1950: camera prod. 66; export prod. 66; *Rotoloni fig '83 170*; lenses 4000; export lenses 0; lense accessories 830.

July 1950: camera prod. -; exprot prod. 198; *Rotoloni fig '83 200*; lenses 2000; export lenses 199; accessories -.

August 1950: camera prod. 151; export prod. 150; *Rotoloni fig '83 50*; export lenses 116; lense accessories 114.

September 1950: camera prod. 100; export prod. 100; *Rotoloni fig '83 230*; export lenses 100; lense accessories 1129.

October 1950: camera prod. 206; export prod. 206; *Rotoloni fig '83 200*; export lenses 334; lense accessories 1217.

November 1950: camera prod. 233; export prod. 233; *Rotoloni fig '83 26*; export lenses 601; lense accessories 5418.

December 1950: camera prod. 390; export prod. 390; lenses 360; export lenses 847; lense accessories 2210.

January 1951: camera prod. 250; export prod. 249; lenses 540; export lenses 513; lense accessories 1707.

February 1951: camera prod. 358; export prod. 358; lenses 620; export lenses 807; lense accessories 2300.

March 1951: camera prod. -; export prod. 455; lenses 1500; export lenses 1054; lense accessories -.

April 1951: camera prod. -; export prod. 380; lenses 1350; export lenses 883.

Totals: camera prod. 2884; export prod. 3846; *Rotoloni fig '83 2401*; x-ray camera 17; export lenses 6030; lense accessories 25619; binoculars 53280; opera glasses 7278; telescopes 145; microscopes 2704; microscope accessories 14124; transits 578; levels 1198; other surveying accessories 447; projection lenses 293; lensmeters 2; proj. accessories 13; profile projectors 18; optical measur inst 218; other optical inst 838; other optical inst accessories 4190; spectacles 34922; magnifiers 4300.

APPENDIX II

The Fate of Nippon Kogaku's Factories

List of Nippon Kogaku's wartime plants and their post-war fates as of early 1947. (From chart in folder 12 in box #2679 in National Archives of the United States, College Park, Maryland [ARC # 366684].)

Note: Head office was in Shiba in 1917, moved to Oi [Ohi] in 1918, moved back to Shiba in 1923, moved to Oi in 1933, moved to Omori in 1942, to Marunouchi in 1944 and back to Oi in 1946.

Note: Spellings used are those used on chart.

Shiba (Tokyo) made photo lenses, binocular, microscope, measuring instruments, astronomical instrument. Sold to Teikoku Printing Company in 1946.
[Nothing noted concerning NK's willingness to dispose of their oldest location.]

Fukui (Fukui): Operated in 1945. "Returned to former owner. Machines burnt."

Shiojiri (Nagano): Opened in mid–1943. [Still operating in 1947. Closed 1950. One of two locations in that prefecture located in the mountains north of Tokyo. See *Matsuo* below.]

Kashiwa (Chiba): Opened in early 1944. Closed in early 1947 but still owned by NK. [Former race track owned by Kashiwa Horse Race Courses. Turned over to Chiba Horse Owners Association in June 1947 according to records in ARC #367467.]

Akita (Akita): Operated only in 1945. Returned to former owner. Serving as Honja Middle School.

Kawasaki (Kanagawa): Opened in 1940. Manufactured Sighting telescopes and predictors. Closed after war but still owned by NK [No. 2 factory owned by Japanese government. No.1(?) plant was turned over to company that manufactured noodle-making machinery on May 19, 1947. See ARC #458126].

Matsuo (Nagano): 1945 only. "Returned to former owner." Motsuo elementary school.

Kawaguchi (Saltamu): Open only in 1945. Returned to former owner. Takahaski Ironworks.

Shimada (Shizuoka): Opened in mid–1944. Made sighting telescopes. Closed and sold to Kawa Musical Instruments Company in early 1947.

173

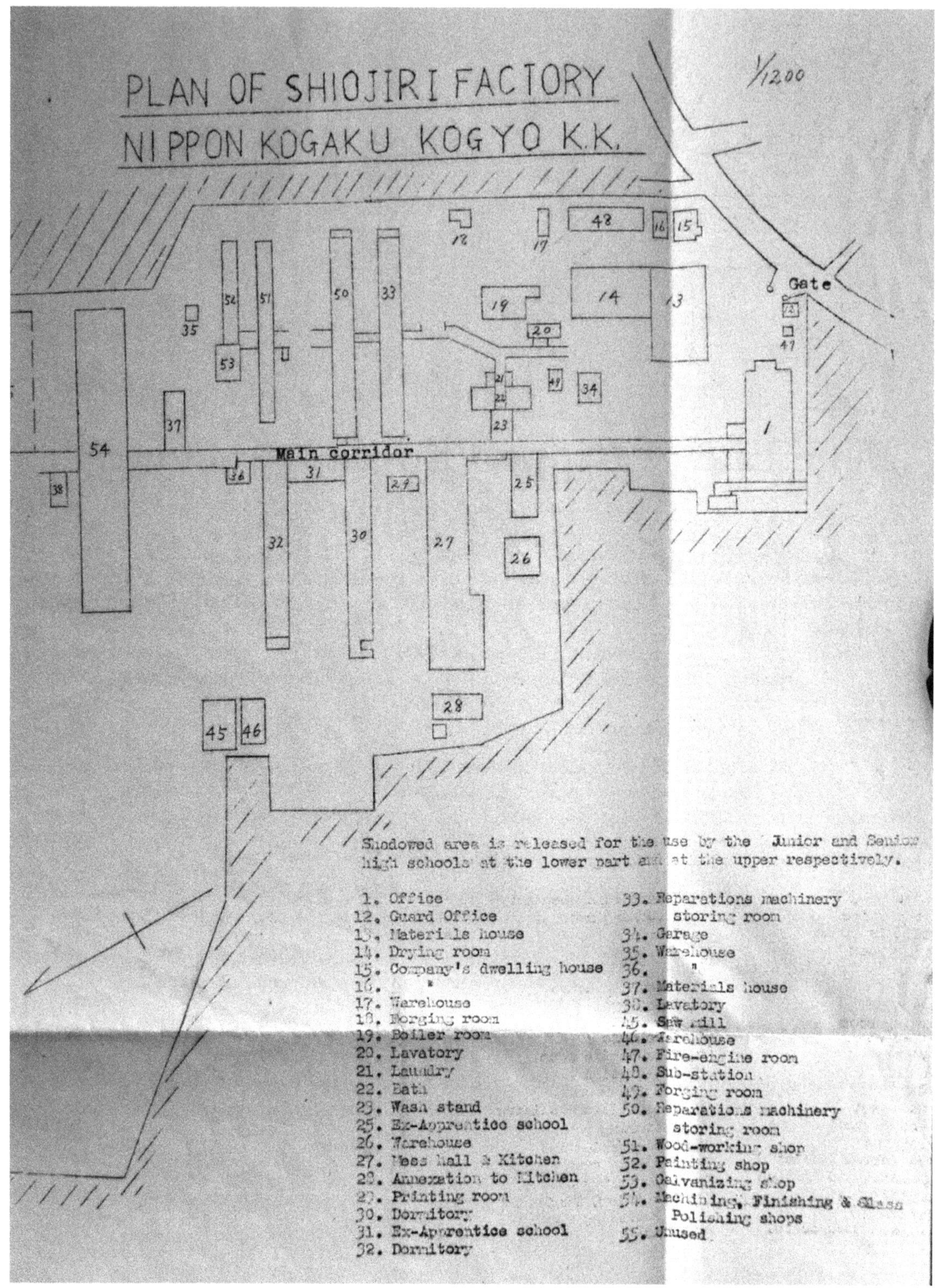

Plan of the Shiojiri plant, Nippon Kogaku's plant in the Nagano district. Note # 45, identified as "Saw Mill." One of the reasons NK retained the Shiojiri plant until 1950 was due to its proximity to forests, which provided wood for tripods and microscope cases (National Archives).

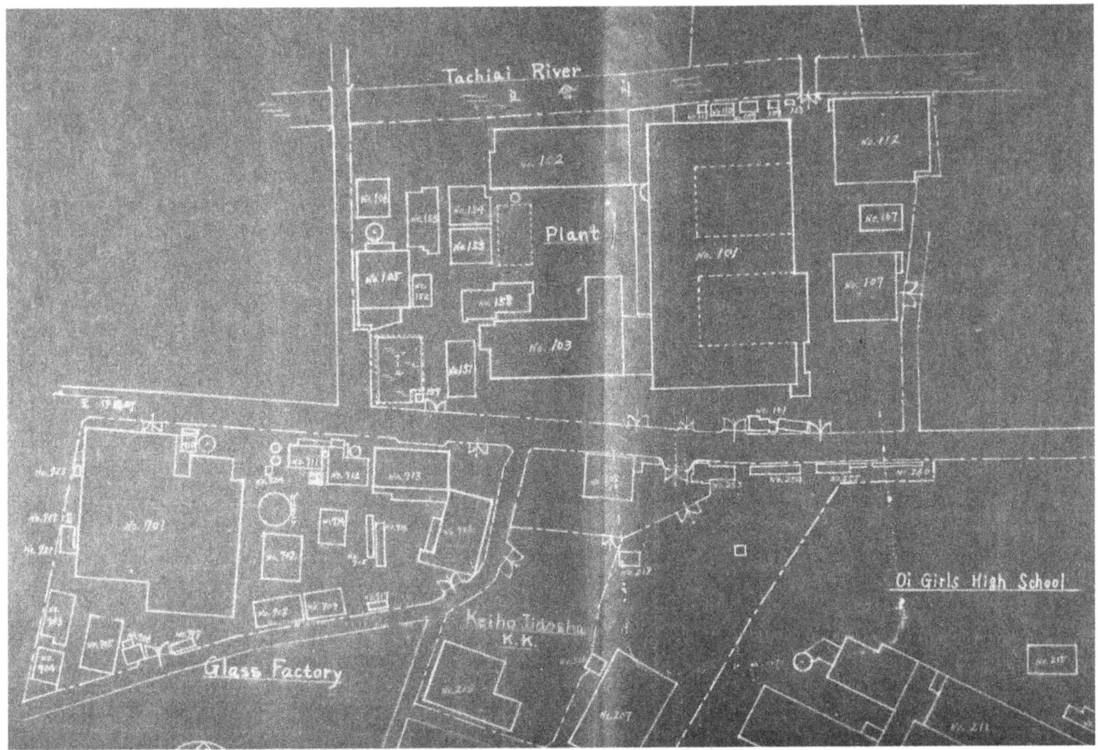

Blueprint of the Oi [Ohi] facilities. The main Oi manufacturing plant is at top. The glass works are to the lower left. The buildings identified as the "Oi Girls High School" had been part of NK's facilities until the end of the war (National Archives).

Omori (Tokyo): Opened in 1944. Returned to former owner in 1945. Made telescopes. Tokai Kogyo Co.

Uenohara (Yamanashi): Opened in mid–1945 just before end of war. Returned to former owner. Hufuku-ji Temple.

Oi [Ohi](Tokyo): Opened in 1918 [rebuilt and expanded in 1933]. Made photo lens, binocular, microscope, surveying instrument, measuring instrument, astronomical instrument, rangefinder, periscope, etc. "Operating under permission for reconversion." [Part converted and serving as Oi Girls' High School.]

Nishiyoshida (Niigata): 1945 only. Returned to former owner. Yashida elementary school.

Tsudayama (Kunagawa): Opened in mid–1940. Closed but still owned by NK in early 1947.

Suzugamori (Tokyo): Opened in mid 1938. Manufactured castings. Closed and loaned to Keihin Lumber Works.

Nishiyoshida (Niigata): 1945 only. Returned to former owner. Yashida elementary school.

Higashi-shinagawa (Tokyo): 1945 only. Returned to former owner. Shibaura Foundry.

Totsuka (Kanagawa): Opened in 1937. Made binoculars, telescopes, predictors, etc. "No.1 burnt. No. 2 sold to Nihon Victor Co. No. 4 occupied by U.S. Army. No. 3 closed, but still owned by NK.

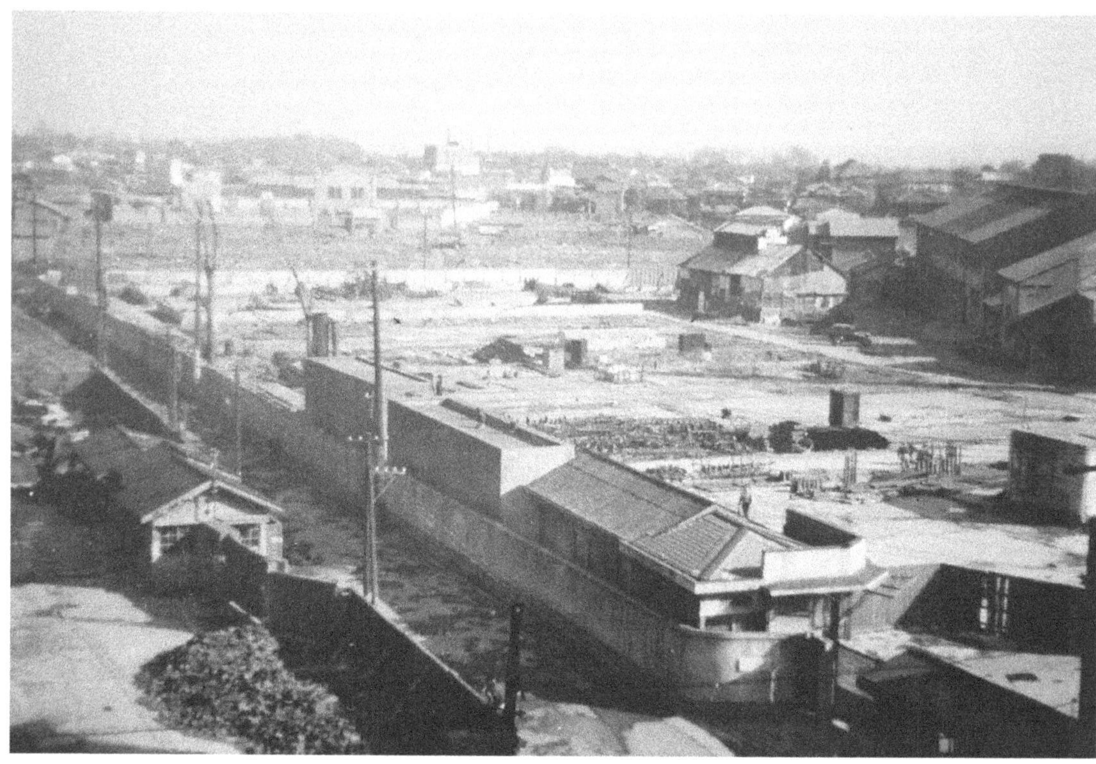

The back of the Ohi plant in the Shinagawa district of Tokyo some time between 1945 and 1948. The street and buildings in the foreground still exist. The buildings in the background became part of the girls' high school (Tatsuhiko Arakawa photograph, courtesy Nikon Historical Society).

Gosen (Niigata): 1945 only. "Factory was not constructed. Machines were loaned."

Kameari (Tokyo): 1945 only. Returned to former owner. Nihon Shigyo Co.

Omiya Glass (Sajtama): Taken over in 1943. Closed but still owned in 1947.

Oi [Ohi] Glass (Tokyo): Opened in 1923. Manufactured optical glass. Operating under permission for reconversion.

The Contractual Agreement Between Nippon Kogaku and the Overseas Finance and Trading Company, April 26, 1950

26 April 1950
Nippon Kogaku Kogyo Kabushiki Kaisha,
5447 Oi Morimae-cho
Shinagawa-ku,
Tokyo.

Gentlemen:

We are submitting below for your approval terms and conditions for an agency agreement between our respective companies as follows:

1. In consideration of the mutual promises and undertakings herein contained, you hereby grant us the sole and exclusive right to offer for sale and to sell all products manufactured by you, in the territories of USA, Canada and Mexico. Your selling prices to us will be mutually agreed upon.

2. You agree to refrain from offering or selling your products directly or indirectly, except through us, to the trade located in said territories and you shall turn over to us all inquiries, orders and other correspondence from trade located in said territories, except in such special cases as we may mutually agree upon in writing.

3. We in turn agree to not handle optical products from any other manufacturer, with the exception of such items which you are unable to supply or do not wish to manufacture or such items as we may mutually agree upon in writing.

4. We agree on our part to do everything possible as we have in the past and are presently doing to promote and increase sales of all your products through travelling of competent sales representatives, advertising, appointing of subsidiary distributors or other suitable means at our discretion.

5. You agree at all times to furnish us all technical data required by us for the sales promotion, maintenance and repair of your products.

6. We agree, at our expense, to design and print circulars, catalogues and operating instructions, necessary for the sale of your products in our territories.

7. You hereby guarantee your products against defects in materials or workmanship and merchandise found to be defective is to be exchanged by you free of charge or the purchase price refunded to us as we may mutually agree upon.

8. Relying on your guarantee, we in turn will unconditionally guarantee your products to our customers and maintain adequate repair and servicing facilities in San Francisco, Chicago, New York and other cities as we may deem necessary, at our expense.

9. To cover the cost of your shipments to us, we shall provide you with an automatically revolving letter of credit in the amount of approximately $20,000 [,] each drawing under this letter of credit to be accompanied by shipping instructions in writing from us. Delivery date, indicated in our signed purchase orders are to be understood as such shipping instructions.

10. If by reason of competition or similar causes the market situation in our territories changes drastically, we shall be entitled to revise prices and production estimates with you, the same as you shall be entitled to similar revisions in the case of cost of labor or raw-materials changes drastically in Japan.

11. This agreement shall be valid for a period of three years from the date it is signed by you. Unless notice is given in writing by either party three months prior to the date of expiration the agreement will automatically be extended for another period of three years.

12. This contract can be cancelled or amended upon mutual agreement between both parties at any time prior to expiration.

OVERSEAS FINANCE & TRADING COMPANY, INC.
[signed]
H.W. Liholm

The foregoing agreement is hereby accepted and approved.
Nippon Kogaku Kogyo Kabushiki Kaisha
[signed]
M. Nagaoka, President.
Dated, Tokyo, Japan,
26 April 1950.

Changes to the First Model Nikons, 1947–1954

Nippon Kogaku considered all Nikons it manufactured between 1948 and December 1954 to be part of the same series. With few exceptions, all contemporary literature simply refers to these cameras as "the Nikon." The Nikon S2, available from December 1954, was the first completely new version and the first Nikon to have a model designation from its introduction.

While identifying a Nikon as being part of the overall 6FB series is easy, the everchanging details can occupy collectors and historians for days. It is almost impossible to find two Nikons made in 1949 or 1950 that are exactly alike in all details unless they are less than a dozen serial numbers apart! Why?

One reason is that virtually all precision camera manufacturers assembled their cameras by hand until well into the 1970s. The complex clockwork shutter timing and film-advance mechanisms required considerable fitting, testing and adjusting—all done manually. Just putting a camera together required enormous amounts of slow, careful handwork to set and tighten each of the numerous screws and many springs. Conveyor belts and breaking down tasks allowed the manufacturers to speed up production, but neither the Japanese nor the Germans nor anyone else were able to avoid the immense and growing labor costs involved with such handwork until the introduction of electronically controlled shutters in the late 1960s. The first Nikons were definitely a "work-in-progress," and they needed considerable upgrading in order to compete effectively against both the established German and other up-and-coming Japanese manufacturers. On the other hand, this hand-assembly and testing process made it easy for Nippon Kogaku to make changes to their camera. As the company received feedback from customers and the workers improved their skills, technicians incorporated these improvements on a continuing basis. Some are easily spotted by experts, others remain hidden under the covers.

Another reason for the variations was due to the materials Occupation-era Nippon Kogaku had available to work with. The shutters in the early cameras were neither accurate nor durable. Inferior metals and the silk for the shutter curtains were major parts of the problem. As the company located better sources for raw materials, it began using them and the cameras reflect those changes.

Other variations, such as whether a synched M had red or black contact insulators, appear to have neither logic nor pattern. Perhaps there were two different suppliers, or two different engineers disagreed and both had their way for a few months.

An examination of Appendix I will show that Nikon camera production peaked in January and again in May 1949 as funds became available to pay NK's assemblers and the workers improved their skills. Production then stopped in August while the engineers redesigned the film gate and film advance mechanism to allow a standard eight-sprocket-per-frame advance. While production resumed the next month, it would take NK another year before its camera production numbers were back up to over 100 per month. From then on, production would climb, peaking at 454 in March 1951. The changeover to the Nikon S the following month brought the numbers down again but, after that, NK never looked back. By 1954, it was easily getting over a thousand cameras finished each month.

Several factors probably contributed to the growth in production numbers that started in July 1950. Sales to the CPO (Central Purchasing Office) mushroomed that July as thousands of fresh American troops poured into Japan in response to the outbreak of the Korean War. These sales provided the cash NK needed to increase production, hire additional workers and invest in new machinery. The conversion to a system of continuous quality control in September speeded up manufacture even further and allowed NK to pass the 200-per-month mark for the first time.

Most of the Nikon's major changes during this period can be associated with these changes in NK's fortunes. But note that many of the changes listed below did not happen once-and-done. For example, it is possible to find early "S"'s with the old "M" style shutter release guard.

The "Made in Occupied Japan" or MIOJ mark, its location and duration of use remain a bit of a conundrum. As noted in the introduction to this book, SCAPIN #1535 directed that all Japanese manufactured goods intended for export be labeled with "Made in Occupied Japan" starting in February 1947. This requirement was removed by SCAPIN #2601, issued on December 5, 1949. Yet all Nikons continued to bear this mark through mid–May 1951 and some MIOJ Nikkors have been found that would have been made even later. The MIOJ mark could not have been a popular requirement, and one might expect that NK would have dropped the mark as soon as SCAP authorized the use of "Japan" or "made in Japan" instead.

Although other possible explanations for the mark's persistence may exist, two immediately come to mind: scarcity of resources and sales to the CPO.

The earliest Nikons, from the first production camera through mid to late summer 1950, had the MIOJ mark engraved on the camera's baseplate. This engraving was done at an early stage of pro-

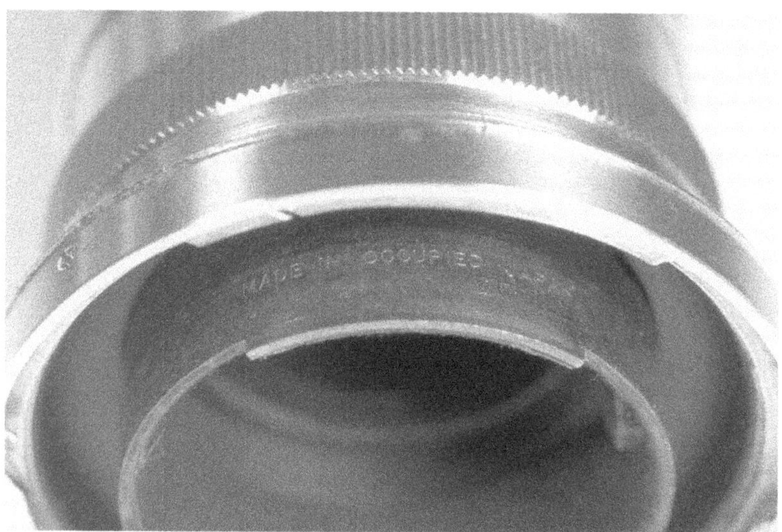

"Made on Occupied Japan" on a 135mm f3.5 Nikkor well into that lens' production, and well past the date when NK had stopped so marking the Nikon. Since 135mm f3.5 Nikkors have been found without this mark that are earlier in the serial number sequence, it is likely that its late appearance here is a simply the result of frugal use of all available parts, rather than a deliberate decision by NK to continue to use the MIOJ mark.

duction, before the plates were chromed. It is possible that NK manufactured 1,000 new backs in the fall of 1949 when the mark was still required, then took until the summer of 1950 to use them up. Even though no longer required, NK simply could not afford to discard so many expensive parts when such a change did not affect sales. It is also possible that the change of the mark to a stamping in the back leather might coincide with the new back with the smaller pressure plate that NK started to use at that time.

But why did NK continue with the back stamp for another ten months? It might be one matter to ship cameras and lenses overseas with just "Japan" as a mark, but sales to the CPO meant sales to Occupation personnel. Perhaps the CPO continued to expect this mark, or maybe NK just felt it prudent to continue to use MIOJ in order not to risk offense.

Both of these explanations might explain why so many of the early 135mm f3.5 Nikkors have the MIOJ mark, even though the lens did not become generally available until January 1951. Starting around January 1950, NK moved the MIOJ mark to difficult-to-see locations on the spring-loaded rings that connected all accessory lenses to the internal focusing mount on the cameras to enable rangefinder focusing. The mark had to have been engraved before these various rings were installed on a lens. Again, NK may have manufactured hundreds or even thousands of these tubes, then continued to use them long after the need for MIOJ ceased to exist. This also might explain why some of the early 135s are marked, while others, even ones earlier in serial number sequence, are not. NK needed to use all the parts it had in stock, whether they were older or newer, as long as they were otherwise the same.

Changes to the Cameras in the Order They Occurred

All Nikons manufactured through the beginning of August 1949 have:

- A frame size of 24 mm × 32mm. Film advance is seven sprockets per frame.
- The manually set frame counter extends to forty.
- The accessory shoe is a simple, one-piece unit.
- The outside of the camera's back is plain and inside has a simple pressure plate.
- Film advance and rewind knobs are larger, but flatter than the models that follow.
- Tripod socket is a simple ⅜-inch thread stamping in the bottom of the camera base plate, although many have a ¼-inch thread insert.
- All Nikons in this series shipped with ever-ready cases. The first ones came with ⅜-inch plugs for securing the case to the camera that matched the camera's tripod socket.

Changes to the Nikon Prototypes (#s 6091–60921), November 1946–February 1948

- The first test cameras have the words "Nippon Kogaku Tokyo" engraved on the top plate. This becomes the NK logo by the start of production.
- The frames around the rangefinder windows become less prominent. This is because the builders had to hand shape the first prototypes. Later front escutcheons were machine stamped.
- The focusing mount gains an infinity lock.
- The "NIKON" on the front plate increases in size.
- Numerous internal changes also occur, and continue to occur through the camera's production.

Changes to the Production Nikon I (#s 60922–609759), March 1948–August 1949

- Upper four screws securing the front escutcheon move from the slanted sides to front.
- The two extra screws used to secure the front escutcheon plate to the camera disappear between serial numbers 60950 and 60970.
- The "Made in Occupied Japan" engraving on the camera baseplates drops to half its former size.
- The collar around the shutter release increases in height so that the button no longer projects above the collar.
- The lens cap for the 50mm f2 collapsible Nikkor changes from a heavy, domed aluminum design with the word "Nikon" to a flat, thinner, plastic design with a raised NKT logo in the center. This will change twice more during early production, first to a chrome-finished aluminum cap and then to a black painted cap.
- The camera case that ships with each camera goes through several versions. Initially, the case is lined with kid leather and features double military-type close straps in the back. Within a few months it changes to a simpler, velvet-lined design with only one closure snap. At first, color of the case is almost an orange brown. By the time the Nikon becomes the Nikon S, the color will have shifted to a darker, more muted tone. The fronts of early cases are blunt, easily accommodating the collapsible lenses that shipped with the cameras. When the noncollapsing 50mm f1.5 Nikkor became available, the cases gained deeper "noses" to allow closure with the longer lens attached.
- The number of snaps that secure the case front to the bottom first number four. This will change to only three by 1949.
- The camera backs are serial number matched to the numbers on the top plates. NK started adding serial numbers to the backs because the mold for the camera body made no allowance for the groove that wrapped around the back opening. The back had to fit into a groove in order to gain a light-tight seal. Workers had to cut and grind out these grooves by hand, individually fitting backs as they worked. NK would continue to engrave matching serial numbers on its camera backs until 1957 when the use of die-castings and a new back for the S2 made such a practice unnecessary.
- A cover plate inside the bottom of the camera conceals and protects the shutter adjustment screws as early as #609209.
- The polished film guide rails increase from two to four and widen after #609213.
- A red dot appears on the top of the shutter release allowing easy monitoring of film advancing. This dot will decrease in size over the next two years. This appears by #609319[?].
- A tang secured with two screws holds the takeup spool in place so that it is no longer removable by as early as 609537. It is uncertain as to when this was added, but Nikons as early as 609209 have been found with this feature. It is possible that in some cases the tang was added later.

Changes to the Nikon M (#s M609759 or M609760–M6092500±), August 1949–November 1950

- The factory adds the letter "M" to the top plates as a prefix to the serial number. This is obviously an add-on since the Ms initially vary in their closeness to the previously engraved serial numbers. On later Nikon Ms, the letter appeared to have been engraved at the same time as the rest of the serial number and it lines up accurately.
- Film advance is eight sprocket. Film frame changes to 24 × 34.

- Camera back gains a raised frame to allow room for heavier blade springs and larger pressure plate that covers half the camera back.

- Camera back's bottom gains a sturdier tripod socket with a quarter-inch insert.

  At that time, NK had at least 137 unsold cameras on hand. All of these were modified with the above changes. The old backs were discarded and new tops and backs substituted. It is probably safe to state that all of the Nikon Ms that show on the production figures for the fall of 1949 were actually preexisting Nikons that were being modified to the new format.

- The eyepiece gains an internal threading but apparently nothing is ever made to screw into these threads. The magnifier on a chain linked to the variframe finder and diopter correction lenses friction fit on the eyepiece.

- The accessory shoe becomes higher, allowing space for a second part that sits below the shoe and projects upward through openings in the shoe, giving the shoe two pressure springs. This occurs by #M60 91280.

- To compensate for the higher shoe, the rewind knob increases in height, making it easier to grasp.

- The lens caps change from plastic to stamped metal.

- The bright, polished chrome latches and shutter release change to a brushed chrome that matches the rest of the camera's finish. This has occupied by # 6091653.

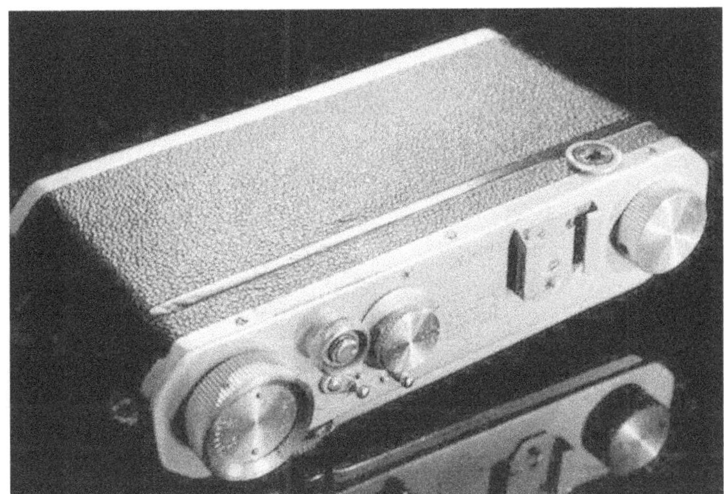

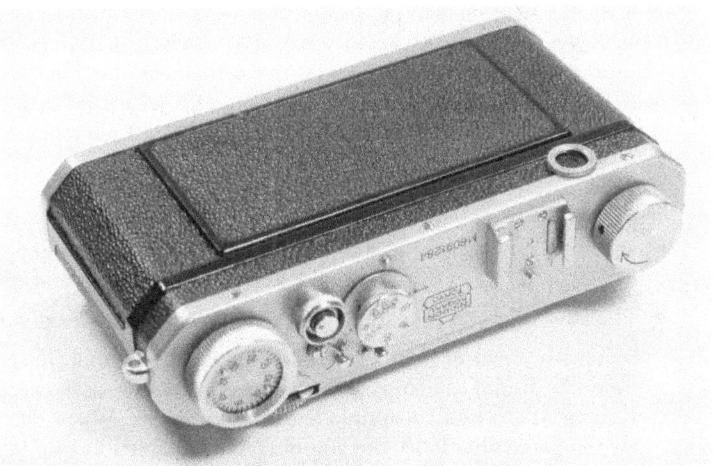

In addition to the format, Adolph Gasser had criticized two other features of the Nikon camera: its film pressure plate and its tripod socket. These pictures show the way that Nippon Kogaku's engineers dealt with those problems.

The plain back of a Nikon I. The back for a Nikon M. Note the rectangular ridge on the Nikon M. This marks the part of the back that were cut and set back to create room for a larger and more substantial pressure plate that not only covered the film gate but part of the takeup spool. All Nikon Ms and Ss have this back ridge. The raised backs were complete replacements since the original backs could not be modified. NK discarded all the backs for the Nikons it had on hand in August 1949, and substituted these new backs. At the same time, the company replaced all the top covers as well, so that serial numbers would continue to match. So, in reality, the first 159 or more Nikon Ms started their lives as Nikon Is (Nikon I photograph by Ling Lee).

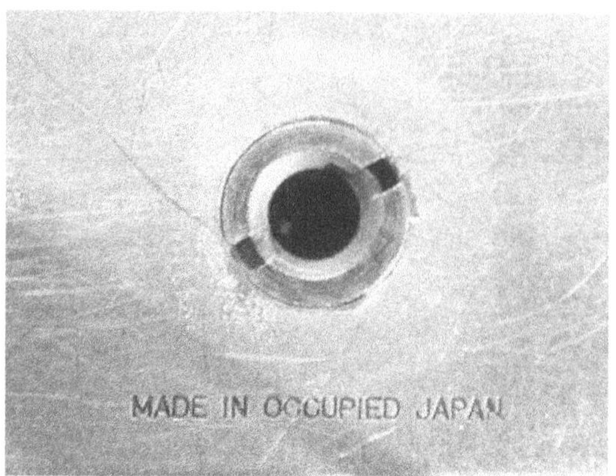
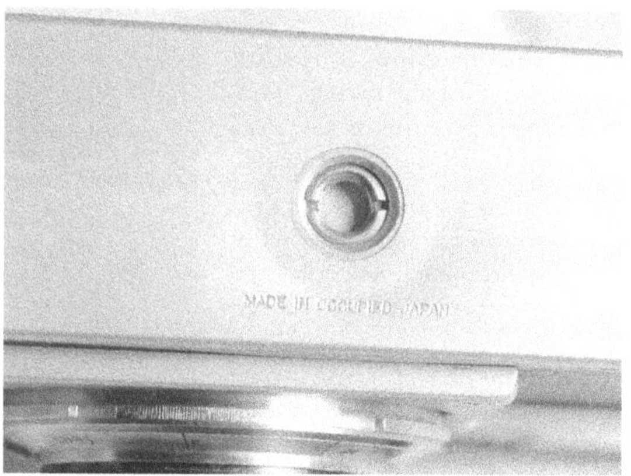

Left: The tripod socket on a Nikon I was a simple ⅜-inch stamping in the bottom's brass cover. It had little strength and could be easily bent or broken out. This Nikon I from July 1949 has a quarter inch plug screwed into the stamping, but the weakness remains. Note the "Made in Occupied Japan" mark. It is smaller than the first production Nikons, but still obvious to anyone taking the camera out of its case. *Right*: The tripod socket on a Nikon M manufactured in late March or early April 1950. Note the reinforcement of the ⅜-inch thread with a permanent plug and the factory-installed quarter-inch bushing. The MIOJ mark is still present but is no longer paint-filled. Four months later it would become an almost invisible stamp in the back leather (Nikon I photograph by Ling Lee).

- The accessory shoe's stop that prevents forward movement of mounted accessories becomes a separate part, secured with its own two screws. This is stronger than the former single projecting pin. The added piece exists in at least two varieties. This change shows up later than #6091680 and from July 1950. #6092011 has this shoe in the earlier three-piece version.

- The advance knob gains some height, making it easier to grasp.

- By mid-summer of 1950, cameras no longer ship with a collapsible 50mm f2 Nikkor. For a brief time, the 50mm lens ships with a chrome cone inserted between the lens head and its mount, preventing what was a collapsible lens from doing so. When the 50mm f1.4 Nikkor becomes available in September 1950, the 50mm f2 Nikkor starts to ship in a new mount that is similar to the one used by the 50mm f1.4.

- The MIOJ engraving moves from the camera's base plate to a small stamping in the leather on the camera back in the lower left-hand corner of the raised frame by August 1950.

- The film pressure plate decreases in size and a raised two-bladed tang to the right of the plate takes over for the plate at that point. However, the raised ridge on the camera back remains the same. Two projecting tangs — one at each end of the back sides — that slotted into deeper slots in a camera's groove change from being separate pieces attached with two screws each to being integral parts of the back itself. These two changes may have occurred at the same time the location of MIOJ changed.

- A red dot behind the serial number is added to the top plate to indicate the location of the focal plane.

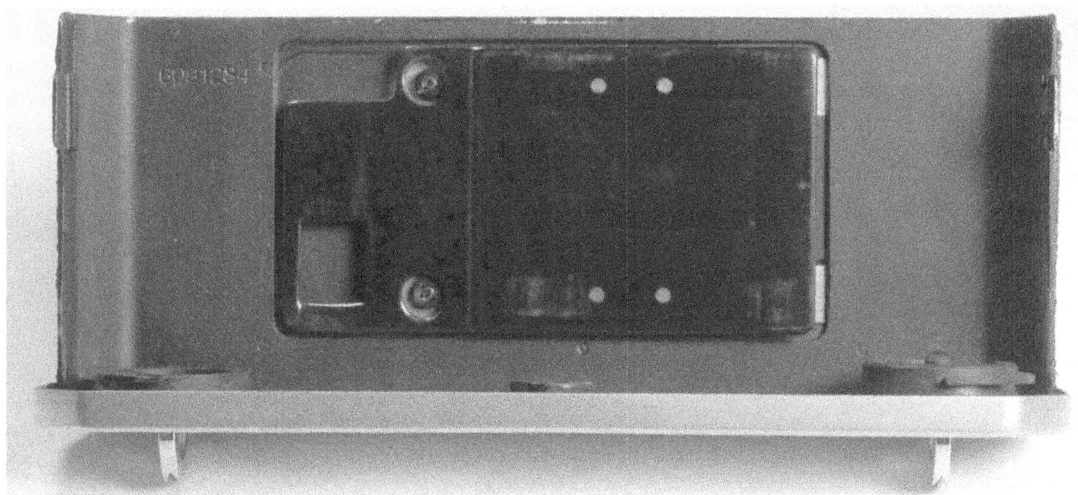

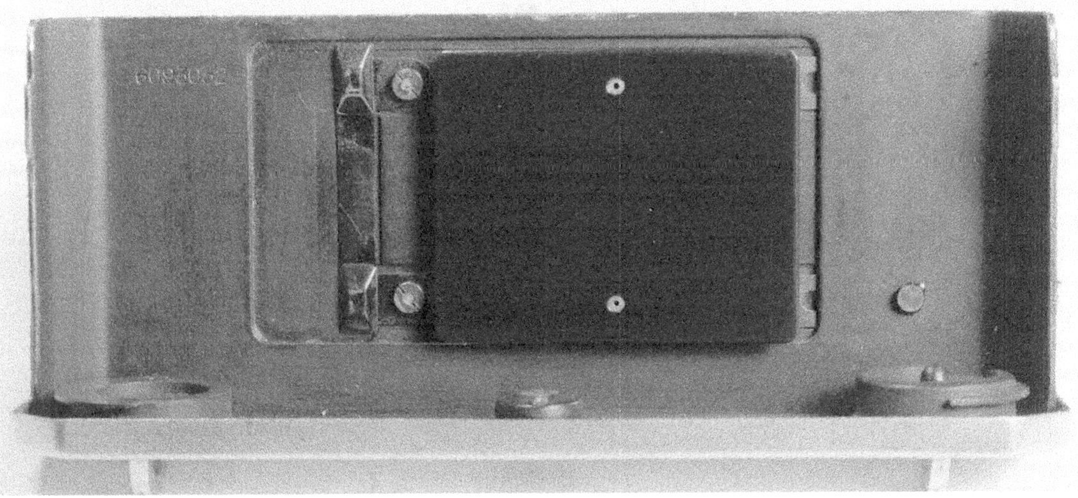

Examples of Nikon M pressure plates. *Top*: Early (manufactured in either late March or early April 1950). *Above*: Late (manufactured in January 1951). The oversized pressure plate which required the cutout in the back of the Nikon camera can be seen in the upper picture. By the end of the year, Nippon Kogaku has switched to a simpler, better-finished pressure plate system. All Nikons would continue to use that system until 1957. Note the back serial numbers which match each camera's number.

Changes to the Nikon MS or Synched M (#s M6092501– M6094125 [at least]), November 1950–March 1951

- Flash sync following the Gasser design becomes standard at approximately number 6092500 (November 1950) [last recorded unsynched number M6092480]. Sync letters are engraved next to the flash sockets on the sides of the top cover.

  Note: Collectors today generally refer to these cameras as "Synched Ms" or "Nikon M/S." However, the factory considered (and still considers) all Nikons with flash sync as "Nikon S." This contributes to the confusion as to exactly when the Nikon "S" started production.

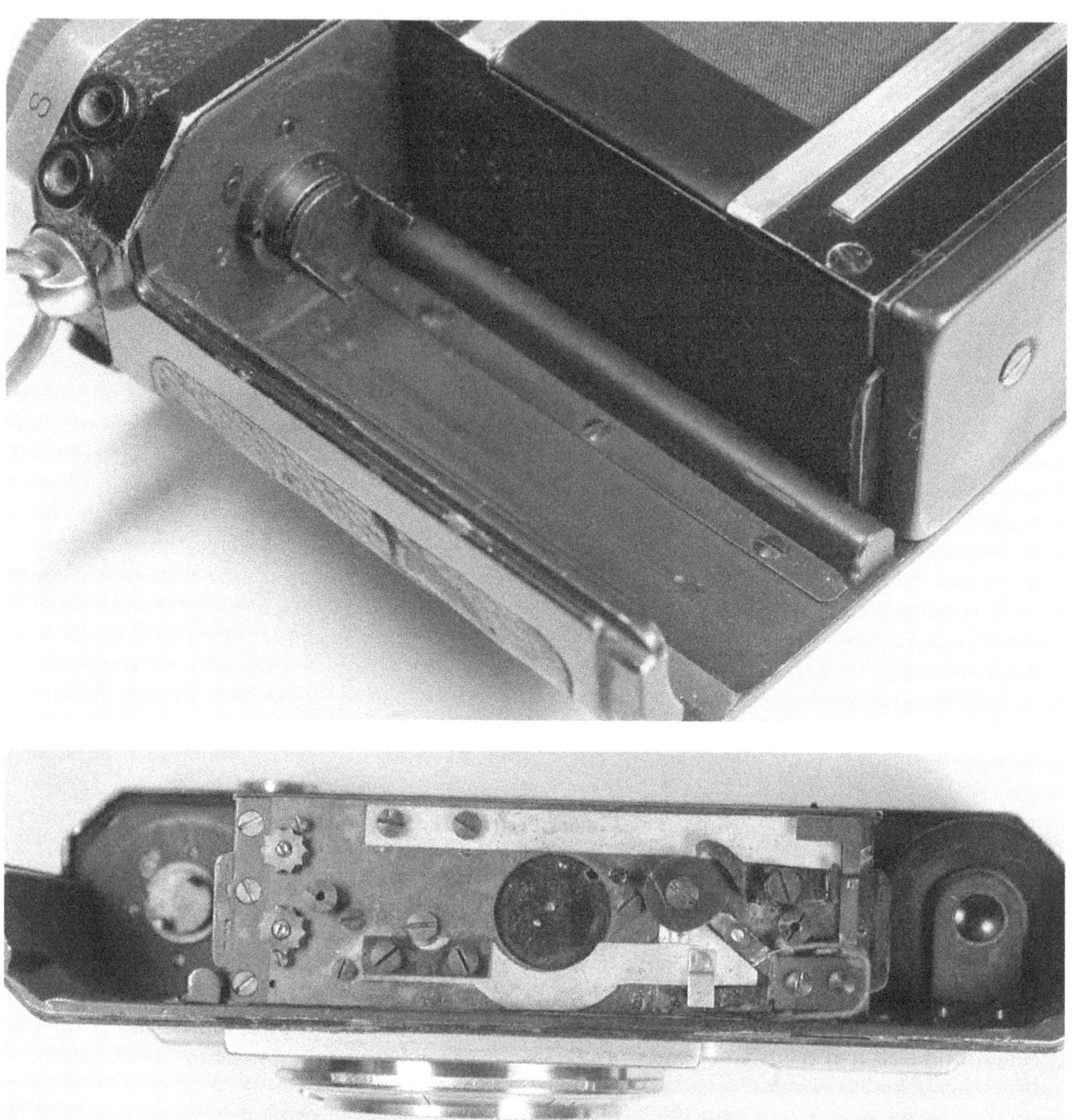

Top: The easy way to add flash synchronization was to place a terminal right next to an internal switch near the shutter speed dial. This was the solution that both Leitz and Zeiss followed, which is why terminals on the Leica and Contax are on their upper backs where the sync cords can easily poke the photographer in the eye. Gasser wanted the terminals to be on the end of the camera next to where a flash gun would go and out of the photographer's way, but this required running wires across the bottom of the Nikon then up to the top and out the left end This was the first solution: a tube screwed in place on the side of the film magazine chamber serving as a wire chase. Later a change in the body casting allowed the wires to be run out of sight within the body casting itself. *Above*: The electrical contacts for the Nikon's synchonization are connected to the two long spring blades screwed to the bottom of the camera body casting under the internal cover plate.

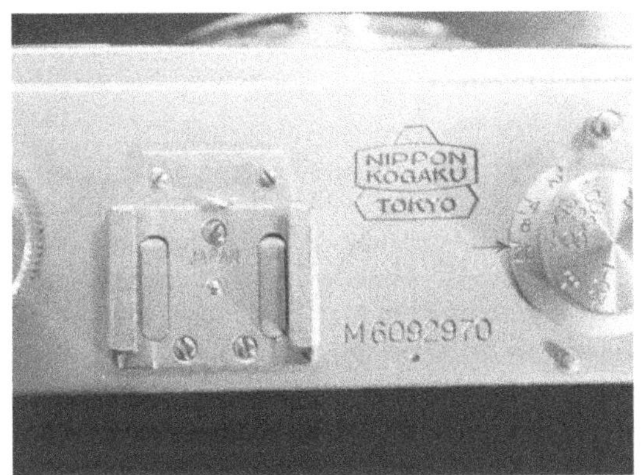 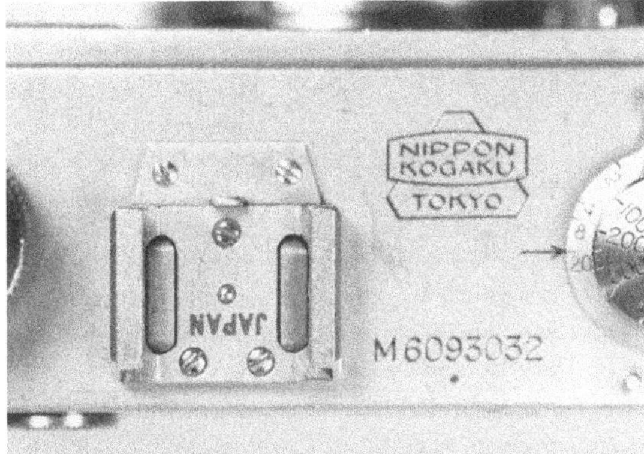

A few late production Nikon Ms have "Japan" engraved on the accessory shoe. This mark was apparently an add-on feature. The letters sometimes face front, sometimes face back, are sometimes set to the front of the shoe, sometimes to the back. Most of the Nikons with this feature appear to be in the #M60926XX to #M60930xx range, which would place their manufacture to between December 1950 and late January 1951. According to Adolph Gasser, the 100 Nikons shipped to OFITRA in January 1951 had this added mark.

It is possible that Nippon Kogaku decided to add "Japan" to the Nikons going to the United States in response to the favorable publicity that Jacob Dreschin's article in the *New York Times* had generated. Dreschin had stated that a *Japanese* product was the best of its kind in the world. Perhaps NK believed that American customers might actually be looking for a camera made in Japan. It proved to be a false hope. American prejudices against Japanese products continued to be strong into the 1960s (left: Ling Lee photograph).

- The shutter release guard changes to a higher, larger pattern. This appears as early as December 1950, but cameras were still being shipped with the older style guard as late as April 1951.

- A few (very few) of the Nikons manufactured during this period have "Japan" engraved in small letters in the middle of the accessory shoe. This mark varies in size, sometimes faces front, sometimes faces back.

- The sync indicator letters move from the sides to the top cover. This is a late change, starting from around M6093508.

- The finish of all Nippon Kogaku products continues to improve month by month throughout this period. In early March 1951, at about #6093544, the camera's chrome changes from a flat-toned chrome to a high luster, brushed finish that is heavier and closer to the Contax in appearance. All Nikon rangefinder cameras will continue to use this finish from then on.

- Many of the synched Nikons made between December 1950 and April 1951 have red plastic sync sockets. Most continue to have black sockets and that soon becomes standard. When the sockets are red, the sync indicator letters, "F" and "S," are also red.

- A new rewind knob becomes standard with a smaller diameter and increased height, making it easier to grasp and turn. The advance knob has already gained height but will keep its same diameter.

Changes to the Nikon S (#s 6094126 ± 6133001), April 1951–January 1955

- In April 1951 at serial number 6094126 ± the "M" is dropped from the serial number. All Nikons from this point on are definitely considered to be Nikon Ss. Within weeks, the MIOJ mark is dropped as well. Only the very first Nikon Ss have the MIOJ stamping. The highest number recorded with MIOJ stamped in the back leather is 6094526[1]. "Made in Japan" is engraved on one of the back latches instead. According to Fuketa, this occurred in May 1951 after 4,470 cameras had been produced, but note that #6094467 lacks the MIOJ mark, so the changeover may not have been clean cut.

- An additional screw appears in front of the accessory shoe to better secure the top plate and help prevent warping.

- NK moves to pressure casting the bodies. Not only do the results require less handwork afterward, but the new body casting incorporates a tunnel for the sync wires, eliminating the need for the screwed-on tube that had been secured against the wall of the cavity for the film magazine.

- In the fall of 1951, the tripod socket changes to a larger internal plate secured by four external screws to the back's baseplate. The two projecting tangs on the back sides disappear about this same time. The raised ridge in the camera backs that once marked a machined recess for the oversized pressure plates becomes little more than the evidence of an ornamental, rectangular groove on the back insides.

- The country mark on the bottom latch is shortened to just "Japan" at the end of February 1952. This is the last obvious change to the 6FB series. From then until the Nikon S ceases production in January 1955, the camera remains essentially the same, although the finish continues to improve.

- Additional number variations should be noted: Serial numbers started at 6091 with the "609" serving as an unchanging preface. When the cameras reached eight digits (60900000), they continued to treat the 609 this way for approximately 1,200 cameras. Then the numbering dropped back to seven digits and continued from 6100001. In addition, a number of early Nikon Ss that should date from before this eight-digit series also have eight digits with the last number always being "1." These particular eight digit Nikons are now considered duplicate numbers, and are not therefore true eight-digit Nikons. While no different from seven-digit Nikons, the eight-digit Nikons generally command a higher price among collectors. A few Nikons start with a serial number of "906XXXX" instead of "609XXXX." These are rare and are considered to be engraving errors rather than later manufactures.

- A few of the early Nikons have their distance scales marked in meters.

- One Nikon I, formerly owned by *Life* contract photographer Jun Miki is black-painted. He requested that the factory do that after the chrome finish had drawn fire in Korea.

- *Life* magazine ordered several Nikon Ss with black finishes for the same reason.

- Nippon Kogaku supplied *Life* and other photo publishers with a few Nikons with large rewind cranks instead of knobs in order to speed up rewinding film back into its magazine.

- The Nikon S was available in black finish as a special order item for photojournalists.

Chapter Notes

Introduction

1. "The Japanese Photo Industry," *Popular Photography,* April 1957, 136.

2. John Wolbarst, "...report on the NIKON." *Modern Photography,* June 1951, 44–45, 82–86. Both Gasser and Liholm confirmed that the account as it appears in this article is what happened.

3. SCAP records. *Camera Monthly Report,* 1945–1950 [ARC #456369] (College Park, MD: National Archives).

4. Adolph Gasser interview. (21 July 2003).

Chapter 1

1. John Baird, *The Japanese Camera* (Yakima, WA: Historical Camera Publications, 1990), 45.

2. Allen R. Greenleaf, *Photographic Optics* (New York: Macmillan, 1950), 57.

3. Hans Braakhuis, "History of Nippon Kogaku 1600–1949," *Nikon Catalogus,* May 26, 2006, 7, http://home.planet.nl/~nikon.catalogus/.

4. Jeff Alexander. "Nikon and the Sponsorship of Japan's Optical Industry by the Imperial Japanese Navy, 1917–1945." *B.C. Asian Review* 13 (Spring 2002): 2.

5. Braakhuis, "History of Nippon Kogaku," 14.

6. Ibid.

7. Baird, *Japanese Camera,* 49–50.

8. Peter Abrahams, *Outline of Japanese Binocular Production,* April 21, 2004, 1, http://home.europa.com/~telescope/japanbin.txt.

9. Baird, *Japanese Camera,* 54.

10. Alexander, "Nikon and the Sponsorship," 4.

11. Baird, *Japanese Camera,* 64.

12. Abrahams, *Japanese Binocular Production,* 2.

13. Richard Lane. "The Nippon Kogaku 'Type 95' Bombsight," *Nikon Journal* 80 (June 30, 2003): 6–7.

14. Brian Long, *Nikon: A Celebration* (Marlborough, Wiltshire, U.K.: Crowood Press, 2006), 17.

15. Robert C. Mikesh, *Japanese Aircraft Equipment 1940–1945* (Atglen, PA: Schiffer Military History, 2004), 146–147.

16. Mikesh, *Japanese Aircraft,* 100–111.

17. Alexander, "Nikon and the Sponsorship," 10.

18. Michael James, "Optical Bid by Japanese Seen," *New York Times,* Sec. 3, February 11, 1951, 7.

19. Alexander, "Nikon and the Sponsorship," 11.

Chapter 2

1. SCAP records. James R. Morrison, "Addition to Reparations List," letter addressed to Commanding Officer, Tokyo-Kanagawa Military Government District, APO 503. Date: October 26, 1946.

2. SCAP records. Headquarters Eighth Army G-1 Military Government Section: Economic division. File M&J [#] 41. Dated October 16, 1945.

3. SCAP records. "Application for Reconversion to Essential Commodities Manufacture." Nagano: December 28, 1945.

4. Tatsuhiko Arakawa, "Birth of the Nikon," *Nikon Journal* 15 (September 30, 1998): 1.

5. Samuel Eliot Morrison. *History of United States Naval Operations in World War II.* Vol. 2. *The Rising*

Sun in the Pacific 1931–April 1942, 25–26 (Boston: Little & Brown, 1963).

6. *See:* Sales Room — CPO —1945–1952 [ARC #309214] for listing of goods available for ordering and prices.

7. Edward Kelleher, in interview with Brian Richter, spring 2001. Part of a class project. published as a Web site, <http://web.mit.edu/bkr/www/jrtfinal/start.htm.>

8. Alexander, "Nikon and the Sponsorship," 13.

9. Nippon Kogaku K.K. Shiojiri, December 1949–April 1951, 1945–1951 [ARC #367504].

10. Kazuo Kawai, *Japan's American Interlude* (Chicago: University of Chicago Press, 1960), 142.

11. Takemae Eiji, *Inside GHQ: The Allied Occupation of Japan and Its Legacy* (London: Continuum, 2002), 109.

12. Tsuyoshi Konno, "Historical Evidence for Nikkor Lenses after World War II," *Nikon Journal* 3 (September 1984): 4.

13. SCAP records. "List of Machinery Required for Oi Factory." Dated January 14, 1947.

14. Japan Optical Production [Folder 14, Box 7230, SCAP Records].

15. Baird, *Japanese Camera,* 87.

16. Morrison, letter, October 26, 1946.

17. Nippon Kogaku K. K., December 1945-April 1951 [ARC #366597] [Inventory of Shimada in preparation for reparations].

18. SCAP records. Letter from Reparation Enforcement Bureau, Ministry of Commerce and Industry dated March 1947.

19. Ibid.

20. Hau Seimiya, SCAP records. Letter to Lt. Col. F.J. Gulley, Commanding Officer, Chiba Mil. Govt. Team. Dated July 7, 1947.

21. Japan Optical, Nippon Kogaku, May 1947–September 1947, 1945–1951. Series: Reparations Status Reports, 1945–1951. SCAP Records. [Box 2726, folder 14. ARC #367467]. Includes memo dated July 7, 1947.

22. Hideo Yoshikawa and Joanne Kauffman, *Science Has No National Borders* (Cambridge, MA: MIT Press, 1994), 5–9.

23. Mikio Itoh [Nikon Inc. Archivist], personal correspondence, 2005.

24. "Masao Nagaoka, 77, Dead; Former President of Nikon [Obit.]. *New York Times,* November 22,1974, 42.

25. Shiojiri Plant. [ARC #367504].

26. Arakawa, "Birth of the Nikon," 1.

27. Ibid.

28. Ibid.

29. Ibid.

30. SCAP records. Camera Production in Japan (Special Report No. 10), 1934–1952. [ARC #478312].

31. *Report No. 10,* 1.

32. SCAP records. [Draft of] Camera Production in Japan (Special Report No. 10), 1934–1952 [1946], 8.

33. Draft Report No. 10, 15.

34. *See* the *Subclub* Web site (http://www.subclub.org/shop/175mm.htm) for a comprehensive listing of the dozens and dozens of "Hit" type cameras manufactured in the postwar years.

35. *Early 35mm Cameras* (http://coropolaris.net/supercameras/early/early_135.html).

36. Tatsuhiko Arakawa, "The Nikon Story," *Nikon Journal* 49 (September 30, 1995): 1–3.

37. Nikon Digital Archives, http://www.nikon.co.jp/main/eng/d-archives/camera/history_e.htm, 3.

38. Ibid.

39. Arakawa, "Birth of the Nikon," 3.

40. Letter from Ministry of Commerce and Industry, Japanese Government. Addressed to Reparation Enforcement Bureau, Ministry of Commerce and Industry [ARC #485136 & #485137].

41. Greenleaf, *Photographic Optics,* 51.

42. Wolbarst, "Report on the Nikon...," 84.

43. Masahiko Fuketa, "Comments on the 50mm f1.8 Nikkor," *Nikon Journal* 10 (December 1992): 7.

44. SCAP records from "Nippon Kogaku file," five pages date-stamped January 14, 1947.

45. "Japan's Export Industries," *The Oriental Economis,* (Tokyo, 1949), 79.

46. Interview with Robert Rotoloni, Nikon Historical Society on June 23, 2005.

47. SCAP records. Masao Nagaoka. "Reports to Holding Company Liquidation Commission" [ARC #485136]. Dated March 8, 1948.

48. Kawai, *American Interlude,* 148.

49. Personal correspondence with Mikio Itoh, Nikon, Inc. archivist, December 10, 2004.

50. Robert A. Fearey, *The Occupation of Japan: Second Phase 1948–50* (Westport, CT: Greenwood, 1972).

51. Mikio Itoh, Nikon Digital Archives, "Archivist's Memo No. 3: In the Early Days of Nikon Camera Brochures," *Nikon Web Magazine,* December 7, 2004, http://www.nikon.co.jp/main/eng/darchives/camera/history_e.htm.

52. Arakawa, "Birth of the Nikon," 4.

53. "The Marjoram Report," *Nikon Journal* 15 (September 30, 1998): 7–12.

Chapter 3

1. John Gunther, *The Riddle of MacArthur: Japan, Korea and the Far East* (New York: Harper, 1951), 95.

2. SCAP file on Horace Bristol. Letter from Economic and Scientific Section, Finance Division,dated March 2, 1949. "FIB" comeback, dated May 15, 1949. Letter to *Fortune* Editorial Department, July 20, 1949.

3. Ibid.

4. SCAP records. Taro Matsuda, letter to GHQ/SCAP: Application for permission of manufacture of additional items by Oi plant, Nippon Kogaku Kogyo K.K. [ARC #457040]. Dated June 2, 1948.

5. T. Yagi, managing director, Nippon Kogaku Kogyo K. K. Letter to Minister of Commerce and Industry. Subject: Application to convert designated reparations plant. [ARC #458110]. Dated February 8, 1949.

6. SCAP records. Brazilian Sisal (Overseas Finance Trading Company, Ltd.) Jl-32178, 1945–1952. SCAPGeneral Export and Import File [ARC #447698].

7. Hans Liholm, personal letter to author, dated December 1, 2004.

8. Wolbarst, "Report on the Nikon," 82.

9. SCAP records. J. Yagi, managing director, Nippon Kogaku Kogyo K.K. Letter to Headquarters, Tokyo Civil Affairs Team. Subject: Application for release of land and buildings, dated August 15, 1949

10. *History of Nikon Cameras, Nikon Digital Archive,* http://www.nikpn.co.jp/main/eng/d-archives/camera/history_e.htm. 7.

11. Mikio Itoh, E-mail correspondence, dated December 10, 2004.

12. SCAP records. Letter to minister of international trade and industry, Subject: Application for increase of authorized production. Dated October 20, 1949.

13. *Bausch & Lomb Optical Co. v. Overseas Finance & Trading Co, Inc.* 112 USPQ6 (Comm'r Pats. 1956)—1213.08 (d).

14. Reparations Inspection Check sheet [for Oi plant], October 24, 1949 [Author's signature is not decipherable].

15. S. Tanaka. "Application for Changes in the Permitted Production Amount of the Reparation Designated Oi Plant, Nippon Kogaku Kogyo Kabushiki Kaisha," November 14, 1949, 2–3.

16. Ludv. T. Hagberg, "Application for Permission to Engage in Business Activity," December 6,1949. Letter addressed to chief, Foreign Investment Board, ESS, SCAP.

17. Arthur Goldsmith, "How the West Was Won," *Popular Photography,* March 1991, 35. Goldsmith implies that Gasser's trip to New York had taken place back in early 1949 before Gasser had met Liholm and while the Nikon I was still in production, but conversations with Gasser — and Deschin's column — would indicate that Gasser started doing the legwork after the Nikon M came out and after he and Liholm had already reached their first understanding.

18. Ludv. T. Hagberg, "Application for Permission to Engage in Business Activity," March 30,1950). Letter addressed to chief, Foreign Investment Board, GHQ, SCAP.

19. Ibid.

20. See illustration of Nagaoka's business card.

Liholm had kept the card ever since receiving it in 1950.

21. Masao Nagaoka, "Dinner Address Given 24 April 1950," Hans Liholm Papers.

22. Ibid.

Chapter 4

1. Robert M. Thomas, Jr., "Horace Bristol, 88, Depicted War & Poverty" [Obit.], *New York Times,* August 7, 1997, B9.

2. Much of the information on Duncan is based on three sources: Roy Flukinger, DDD: "...And Every Day a Fabulous Life," *HRC Online Exhibition,* University of Texas at Austin, December 8, 2004, http://www.hrc.utexas.edu/exhibitions/online/ddd/ddd6.html [5 pages]; Duncan's own eccentric autobiography, *Photo Nomad* (New York: Norton, 2003); and a phone interview with the author on February 16, 2005.

3. Ibid.

4. Peter Lownds. "Mr. Jun Miki ... An Interview." *Nikon Journal* 7 (March 1990): 14.

5. Quoted in the *Nikon Digital Archives* from an article by Jun Miki entitled "Nikkor and I" that appeared in the *Nikkor Club Quarterly Magazine* 26 (30 November 1963).

6. David Douglas Duncan, *Photo Nomad,* 418.

7. Goldsmith, "How the West Was Won," 37.

8. David Douglas Duncan, interview, February 16, 2005.

9. Goldsmith, "How the West Was Won," 38.

10. Duncan, *This Is War!: A Photo-Narrative in Three Parts.* Reprint 1967 (New York: Bantam, 1951. from introduction. Pages are unnumbered.

11. *Life Photographers: Their Careers and Favorite Pictures* (New York: Doubleday, 1957), 62–63.

12. Lownds, "Jun Miki interview," *Nikon Journal,* 14.

13. Dante Stella, *Nikon vs. Leica,* August 24, 2006, (http://www.dantestella.com/technical/nikoleic.htm) [1 page].

14. SCAP records. E.W.G. Letter to Foreign Investment Board. Subject: Security Check on Arkadi M. Grekow, alias Grekof, Representative of Overseas Finance and trading Co., Inc. Dated: June 24, 1950 [ARC #323097].

15. John W. Dower, *Embracing Defeat: Japan in the Wake of World War II* (New York: Norton, 1999), 534.

16. E.W.G. Letter to Foreign Investment Board, June 24, 1950.

17. Ibid.

18. SCAP records. *FTC vs, Nippon Kogaku K.K.* (Hearing notices nos. 82 & 83) 1947–1951. Series Fair Trade Commission File, 1947–1951 [ARC #442262].

19. Perhaps working with Goro Matsunaga,

credited as "Designer of flash system for Nikon M" in *Nikon Journal* [NHS-57] 15, no. 2 (March 31, 1998): 5.

20. *Nikon Digital Archives,* 10.

21. Story related to author by Robert Rotoloni, president of the Nikon Historical Society, June 23, 2005.

22. SCAP records. Masao Nagaoka, letter to Kanto Civil Affairs Region. Dated August 18, 1950 [ARC #366684]. This letter was Nagaoka's appeal to the civil authorities for help in ending the strike.

23. SCAP records. "Report of Inspection of Oi Plant after Twelve Hour Strike." Dated August 22, 1950.

24. Duncan, *Photo Nomad,* 198.

25. Goldsmith, "How the West Was Won," 38.

26. Ibid.

27. Lownds, Jun Miki interview, 14.

28. Norman C. Lipton, "Tools & Techniques," *Popular Photography,* February 1951, 28. October to February might seem like a long lead time, but for all three of these publications "February" really meant the beginning of January. Lipton was giving himself barely over a month to have a story ready to go to press.

29. Bruce Downes, "Assignment: Korea," *Popular Photography,* March 1951, 42–47, 98–100.

30. Goldsmith, "How the West Was Won," 38.

31. Jacob Deschin, "Japanese Camera: 35mm Nikon and Lenses Tested by Experts," *New York Times,* Sec. 10, December 10, 1950, 21.

32. Goldsmith, "How the West Was Won," 39.

33. "A Statement," *New York Times,* Sec. 2, December 17, 1950, 17. Deschin included this as an addendum to his usual column. The quotes are credited to "Carl Zeiss, Inc."

Chapter 5

1. *Nikon Digital Archives: History of Nikon* (http://www.nikon.co.jp/main/eng/d-archives/camera/history_e.htm), 15.

2. Lipton, "Tools and Techniques."

3. "Japan Produces a First-Rate Camera," *San Francisco Chronicle,* Leisure Section, February 4, 1951.

4. Michael James, "The Japanese Are Making a Bid to Take over a Large Portion of the International Precision Optical Market," *New York Times,* Sec. 3, February 11, 1951, 7.

5. Downes, "Assignment: Korea," 47.

6. David Douglas Duncan, *This Is War!* The book has no page numbers but quote is from first page of "Photo Data."

7. David Douglas Duncan, "Camera Data," *U.S. Camera,* August 1951, 52–53.

8. James L. Collings, "Jap Lenses 'Superior' Korea Photog Finds." *Editor & Publisher,* July 14,1951, 36.

9. John Wolbarst, "Do These Pictures Need Captions?" *Modern Photography,* November 1951, 52–53, 96–100.

10. "Life Camera Ace Speaks before Tokyo Photo Fans: Duncan Praises Japanese Lens..." *Nippon Times,* July 2, 1951, 4.

11. Ibid.

12. Jacob Deschin, "Dealers' Show" *New York Times,* Sec. 10, March 18, 1951, 11.

13. Jacob Deschin, "To H.W. Liholm," April 19, 1951. Liholm Papers.

14. "Behind the Scenes," *Modern Photography,* May 1951, 14.

15. Wolbarst, "...Report on the Nikon," 44–45, 82–86.

16. Ibid., 86.

17. Ibid.

18. "The Camera That Was Discovered by Photographers of a Great Picture Magazine!" [advertisement] *Popular Photography,* April 1951, 80.

19. Undated form letter from 1951 signed by H.W. Liholm under the OFITRA masthead. Nikon Historical Society.

20. *Popular Photography,* July 1951, 134.

21. Norman Lipton, "To N. Hamashima," June 11, 1951. Liholm Papers.

22. Ibid.

23. Ibid.

24. Lipton, "To H.W. Liholm," July 30, 1951. Liholm Papers.

25. "The World Is talking about the NEW NIKON CAMERA," *Popular Photography,* August 1951, 100.

26. Robert Bakker, "The 'Nikon' in the Netherlands after World War II," *Nikon Journal* (June 30, 2006): 16.

27. Ibid.

28. Adolph Gasser. "Announcement" *Nikon Camera Company* [December 1951].

29. "The Story of the Nikon Camera Company" [Undated. Presumably 1951]. Single sheet aimed at potential dealers. Includes story about the first Nikons being brought to Gasser for his examination, which would indicate that it dates to 1951 when Gasser was still with the Nikon Camera Company. Includes profiles of Evans and Goodman.

30. "Quality ... You'll Get It with This Great New Camera. Nikon f/1.4." [advertisement], *U.S. Camera,* April 1952, 105.

31. Nikon Camera Company, "Information Copy to Sales Representatives: Relationship of the Nikon Camera and/or Nikkor Lenses to Other Cameras of Japanese Manufacture," November 16, 1951.

32. "Along Camera Row," *New York Times,* Sec. 10, January 31, 1954, 11.

33. Brandon M. Jones, "Japan Challenges Leadership of Germany in Camera Market," *New York Times,* October 3, 1955, 36.

Epilogue

1. Al Levin in interview. "The Levin Tapes, Part II," *Nikon Journal* 39, 10, no. 3 (March 1993): 15.

2. Much of the material covered in the remainder of this chapter appeared in slightly different form in Michael Wes Loder, "The Rise and Fall of EPOI ... When and Why," *Nikon Journal* 80, 20, no. 3 (June 30, 2003): 12–14.

3. "New Camera Planned," *New York Times,* August 10, 1971, 45. A tiny notice in the back of the *Times* was the first public announcement.

4. "Joseph Ehrenreich, 65, Dead; Brought Nikon Camera Here," *New York Times*, February 9, 1973, 38.

5. Robert Metz, "Marketplace: A Takeover of Ehrenreich?" *New York Times,* July 31, 1978, D4.

6. Ibid.

7. Herbert Sax, *Letter to Stockholders,* April 25, 1980, 1.

8. "Court Test for Ehrenreich," *New York Times,* June 10, 1981, D15.

9. Harshe-Rotman & Druck, Inc. "Marketing Strategy behind Nikon Cameras Changed 'Made in Japan' into Quality Image," 1974.

Bibliography

Introduction

Researching a topic first investigated 30 years ago lends a perspective to the enormous changes that have occurred in scholarly procedures. While I discovered more information this time around, in many ways the quality of that information is no better than the information that was available in 1973–74. And, with time, some of it has declined.

Background: Between 1971 and 1974, I read extensively and collected a variety of texts ranging from clippings and corporate brochures to books on the Nikon rangefinder series of cameras. In 1975, the growing demands of family and work ended this work and much of this material got put aside.

In 2003, a casual search of the web resulted in the discovery of a "Nikon Historical Society" (www.nikonhs.org/index.html) where an ongoing discussion group dealt with many of the questions I had sought answers to a generation earlier. I quickly discovered that I had far more knowledge than many of the discussion group participants. This was partly due to having actively worked with Nikons when many of the questioned events were happening, but also because I had already done much of the research. Now questions came up that I "knew" the answers to, but I had no sources I could cite to back up what I knew. I am an academic librarian. I wanted to be able to back up what I knew with scholarly citations.

Challenged, I began to replicate the earlier research I had done. I quickly discovered that while a lot more information was accessible today, areas of business history and some aspects of popular culture remained as poorly documented as ever. For example, I wanted to write up a brief history of Ehrenreich Photo-optical Industries, the parent company that imported the Nikon cameras from the early 1960s through 1982. The *New York Times*—available in both index and full-text—turned out to be almost the only readily available source. Yet its coverage was far from complete. Fortunately, as a stockholder in "EPoI" for much of that period, I had received many mailings directly from the company, which I was able to draw on to complete a picture of what went on in this long-defunct company, particularly during its last four years of existence.

I was particularly interested in the history of Nippon Kogaku Kogyo Kabushiki Kaisha (Japan Optical Industry Company, Limited), the manufacturer of the Nikon Camera and Nikkor lenses, during the period of the Occupation of Japan and immediately afterward, 1945–1953. Here I discovered that very little had been written, and what had been written was not necessarily accurate. Technical information, such as film format size, dates and even names of persons involved seemed almost impossible to track down. Even historical information contained in the present-day Nikon, Inc.'s own Web site seemed suspect to me.

After a year of intermittent research using all the modern tools available, I had a lot of information, but I was no closer to the final answers to many of my questions than I was when I started. In fact, I probably have far more questions now than I did in 1975.

What research methods had I used in the 1970s? Everything — sources and indices — was paper or microfilm then. I used the *New York Times* index and read articles on microfilm. I went through *Reader's Guide* but found little of use then or now. This raises a serious issue concerning research into popular culture — a category which photography certainly falls into. For much of the period I was interested in, the H.W. Wilson Company's *Reader's Guide to Periodical Literature* remains the only easily accessible index. Yet its coverage is limited to fewer than 200 titles and during the period of the early 1950s, it did not cover either *Popular Photography* or *Modern Photography*—the two most important magazines covering the photographic field in the United States. Effectively, there was no index, on-line or off, for that time period. As a result, I had to do the same legwork I did back in the early 1970s: I went into the stacks, located bound volumes of these periodicals and went through every issue, page by page.

While my technique ended up the same, and the articles I located were the same, time has resulted in changes — none for the better. In 1974, I could count on a major academic library — such as at the University of Oregon where I was studying — to house complete runs of past issues of important and widely read magazines. I also expected that these issues would be in fairly good condition. This is no longer true. I had to visit both Lehigh University's and Penn State's libraries to find most of what I was looking for. Even then, I found many issues and volumes missing. Even in the issues that were there, numerous cuts with knives or razors had removed articles or pictures. Fortunately, I was not looking for glamour shots of semi-nude women, or I would have been even more frustrated, for that seemed to be what were mostly gone. Penn State's bound copies of the long-defunct *U.S. Camera & Travel*—the other, less-well-known photographic magazine sold during the 1950s and 1960s — had been relegated to high-density storage in an annex. No one seemed to have issues of *Camera 35*. I have yet to find an index that covers these publications either. Time had also taken its toll on the paper. While these publications used relatively high-quality, glossy stock, the condition in every case was noticeably lower than it had been 30 years earlier. Despite my careful paging, I could not avoid leaving tears in almost every volume I examined.

Today's technology is a vast improvement in one area. In 1973–74, photocopying required long waits at service desks, considerable expense and mediocre copies. Hours of research and examination of over ten years of two different magazines resulted in four or five pages of careful notes and two poor-quality photocopied pages. This year's research yielded over 200 photocopied pages, all of a quality approaching the original (except no color) at a cost a fraction of what I would have spent in 1973 once I adjusted for inflation.

The page-by-page examination also allowed me to locate ads for the Nikon and its accessories and more notable business rivals. I could not have located any of these via an index or Web-based search. Sometimes there is simply no substitute for getting in the trenches.

The Web was a mixed blessing. To be able to search the *New York Times* index online, call up the articles I wanted and print them from PDFs out at my desk certainly made life easier, but, as I noted above, other indexes proved to be a disappointment. Search engines yielded a great deal of information, but many of the histories were written by enthusiasts relying on secondary sources. A lot of the information was simply plain wrong.

The Web is not alone in this regard. I have a copy of a major article on the first successes of the Japanese cameras in the United States written by Arthur Goldsmith, a well-known writer in the photographic press. It appeared in a 1991 issue of *Popular Photography*. Goldsmith's article provided me with the names of several persons active during that period and provided the most detailed account that I have read on the "discovery" of the Nikon in 1950—and I have cited this article several times in my account. But the story was also riddled with technical errors such as what the format of the Nikon S was, what date the

Nikon M was introduced and when flash sync was added. These are the same kinds of errors that I came across at Web sites regularly, but finding them in a magazine coming from a writer with the standing of Goldsmith was discouraging.

Yet the Web proved a blessing in two unexpected ways: first of all, I discovered, to my surprise, that two of the most significant players in the early importation of the Nikon were, in fact, still alive. I was able to contact Adolph Gasser — age then 92 — in San Francisco via e-mail. He phoned me several times and graciously gave me almost three hours of his time answering my questions about his involvement with the importation of the Nikon. Hans Liholm, the other important early player, proved harder to track down, but eventually I was able to contact him. He phoned me many times, lent me historical photographs and, finally, after reading my first draft, invited me to his home where I spent three, immensely valuable days going over the manuscript with him page by page.

The second valuable Web source proved to be the index to the National Archives of the United States. But here personal contacts and the "Auld Boy Network" were essential to get me started, for it would never have occurred to me that such records were in the Archives. I had contacted the U.S. Army Heritage and Education Center in Carlisle, Pennsylvania, in hopes that some of the Occupation records might be located there. After some time, the staff graciously replied with a note that the Occupation records were in the National Archives. My contact also provided a nice "working bibliography" of items concerning the Occupation that I promptly mined for several likely looking items. I had no idea how one searched the National Archives. Instead, I turned to a friend who was a military historian and asked him for his thoughts. He, in turn, contacted another historian who basically answered "No problem!" He let me know that the records from the Occupation of Japan had been indexed and were available on-line!

Now, I could have eventually figured this out myself—maybe. But how many researchers would know that the SCAP records had been indexed, when many of the Archives records have not? The Web page included searching instructions and I was able to locate many citations for original documents from that period—probably the most important primary sources located in the United States for this time period in Japan's history. Unfortunately, the index was the only way in, and it covered only general document titles. It did not cover content. For example, searching under "Nikon" yielded nothing! A search under "Nippon Kogaku" was more rewarding, but finding citations could be of no benefit without viewing the entire document. Fortunately, the National Archives in College Park, Maryland, were "only" three hours away by car. I made seven trips there before I was able to view all the information that place is likely to have. Again, a source unavailable and inaccessible 30 years ago is, via the Web, at least searchable.

I have divided my sources into several categories: Periodical articles, books, miscellaneous (including Web sites and interviews) and SCAP records in the National Archives. Each category is organized in a slightly different way to facilitate the reader's understanding of the materials. Most entries are annotated.

Periodical Articles and Advertisements, in Chronological Order

Untitled [Diagrams of the then-current five Nikkor lenses for 35mm cameras] *Kohga Gekkan* (April 1948). Unnumbered page shows the lens formulæ for the 5cm f3.5, 5cm f2, 5cm f1.8, 8.5cm f2 and the 13.5cm f4 Nikkors. At that time only the first two optics were in production and the 5cm f1.8 never got beyond the prototype stage. [Courtesy of the Nikon Historical Society].

"Japan: New Door to Asia." *Time* 52 (May 9, 1949): 32–36. Overall coverage. Editorial position that Japan is critical to stopping the spread of communism in Asia and needs support.

Deschin, Jacob. "Japanese Camera: 35mm Nikon and Lenses Tested by Experts." *New York Times*, sec. X, 21, December 10, 1950. N.B. Probably the most important article ever published on the Nikon and Deschin's most famous column. It created the necessary stamp of approval from the most influential figure in American photography at the time.

"A Statement." *New York Times*, Sec. II, 17, December 17, 1950. A follow up to Deschin's previous column in which Dr. Karl Bauer, the head of American Carl Zeiss, Inc. challenges Deschin's statements from the previous week.

Lipton, Norman C. "Japanese Lens Progress" under Column "Tools & Techniques." *Popular Photography*. February 1951, 28. Recounts much of the same information that Deschin had already reported.

"Japan Produces a First-Rate Camera." Leisure Section. *San Francisco Chronicle*, February 4, 1951. [page unknown], courtesy Nikon Historical Society.

James, Michael. "Optical Market Bid by Japanese Seen: Stiff Competition Is Reported for Germans Who Once Held Monopoly in the Field." *New York Times*, Sec. III, 1, 7, February 11, 1951. James was an early Nikon and Nikkor lens user. This news report is hardly unbiased.

Downes, Bruce [pseud. for Arthur Bursch]. Illustrations by David Douglas Duncan. "Assignment: Korea." *Popular Photography*, March 1951, 42–51, 98–100.

Deschin, Jacob. "Dealers' Show: New Cameras and Changes in Others Presented." *New York Times*, Sec. X, March 18, 1951, 11. Includes information on OFITRA and Gasser as the company's representative.

"MPDFA's Big Show." *PTN Photographic Trade News*, April 1951 [reprint]. Similar information to that provided in other publications in the magazine aimed at the industry rather than the consumer. [Courtesy, Nikon Historical Society].

"The Camera That Was DISCOVERED by Photographers of a Great Picture Magazine! The Nikon f/1.4." OFITRA Overseas Finance & Trading Company, Inc. 826 Merchants Exchange Building, San Francisco, California [Advertisement]. *Popular Photography*, April 1951, 80. First advertisement in a major American magazine.

"Latest Equipment Unveiled at Photographic Trade Show; More 35mm Cameras." Behind the Scenes: News of the Photo Industry. *Modern Photography*, May 1951, 14.

Annual Equipment Listing. *Popular Photography*, May 1951, 94, 149. Lists Nikon Camera and Nikkor lenses — including 8mm Ciné-Nikkors.

Wolbarst, John. "...report on the NIKON." *Modern Photography*, June 1951, 44–45, 82–86. The most complete story of the "discovery" of the Nikon and an in-depth evaluation of the camera and its lenses as they existed in early 1951.

The "discovered" ad appears on page 107 of the June 1951 *Modern Photography* issue.

"Life Camera Ace Speaks before Tokyo Photo Fans: Duncan Praises Japanese Lens..." *Nippon Times,* Monday, July 2, 1951, 4 [reprint]. A report on a speech David Douglas Duncan gave to the Circle of Confusion Club. Includes small portrait of Duncan. [Courtesy of Nikon Historical Society].

Collings, James L. "Jap Lenses 'Superior,' Korea Photog Finds." Photography Column. *Editor & Publisher* 84, no. 29 (July 14, 1951): 36.

"Life Camera Ace Speaks before Toyko Photo Fans." *Japan Camera Trade News* (August 1951) [reprint]. A verbatum reprinting of the earlier article that had appeared in the *Nippon Times*[see above]. Includes illustrations of the Nikon camera and a Nikon equipped with a 85mm Nikkor and the varifocus finder. [Courtesy of Nikon Historical Society].

"The World Is Talking about the NEW NIKON CAMERA! For Its Unequaled Quality and Its Reasonable Price — a Rare Combination." Nikon Camera Company. 278 Post Street San Francisco 8, California. "An affiliate of Overseas Finance & Trading Company, Inc." [advertisement]. *Popular Photography,* August 1951, 100. Also appeared in September 1951 issue. 278 Post Street was the address of Gasser's camera repair agency.

"Famous Nikkor Lens for Your Leica, Canon, Contax, Nicca, Nikon" [advertisement]. Nikon Camera Company. *Modern Photography,* January 1952, 102.

"Quality...: You'll Get It with This Great New Camera. Nikon f/1.4" [advertisement]. *U.S. Camera*, April 1952, 105. First ad in *U. S. Camera.*

"Masterpieces in Miniature" [advertisement]. *Popular Photography,* May 1952, 119. This same ad would also appear in the July 1952 issue of *U.S. Camera* on page 27.

"Fastest New 35mm Camera Lens: Nikkor F/1.4." [Advertisement]. *Modern Photography* June 1952, 99.

"Nikkor: World's Finest 35mm Lens" [advertisement]. *U.S. Camera*, August 1952, 74. Small, half-column ad featuring a picture of six Nikkor lenses clustered together. Points out that they are available in mounts for "Nikon, Leica, Contax and Canon camera."

"The Nikon" [advertisement]. *Modern Photography,* October 1952. This is a full-page ad with the background grid covering the entire page. Shows the camera from top, back, front and ends.

"Perfect Christmas" [advertisement]. *Popular Photography,* November 1952, 123. Christmas ornaments, each with a different accessory for the Nikon hang in this full-page ad. A single column version of this same ad would also appear in the December 1952 issue of *U.S. Camera* on page 109.

"The Nikon" [advertisement]. *Photography,* March 1953, 115. Also appears in April 1953 issue of *U.S. Camera* on page 136, and on page 71 of its May 1953 issue, and in the December 1953 issue of *Photography* on page 195. This would be the last advertisement that the Nikon Camera Company would run.

"Don't Be Misled! Know These Names: Nikon, the Camera; Nikkor, the Lens" [advertisement]. *Photography* April 1953, 14.

"The Nikon, accessories, The Nikkor lens" [advertisement]. *Photography,* May 1953, 99.

"Style: The Nikon and Richard Marx..." [advertisement]. *Photography,* July 1953, 111.

"Peter Gowland and the Nikon" [advertisement], circa July 1953. [Publication and page uncertain.]

Deschin, Jacob. "Along Camera Row: Japanese Firm Sets Up Agency Here For Its Cameras and Lenses." *New York Times*, Sec X, January 31, 1954, 11. Deschin's announcement of the establishment of Nikon, Inc. under Ehrenreich — replacing the San Francisco–based "Nikon Camera Company, Inc."

"They've got to be good" [advertisement]. *Photography.* April 1954. 15. The first ad I have been able to locate run by the new Nikon, Inc.

[Same advertisement] *U.S. Camera.* April 1954. Inside front cover.

"Nikkor 50mm f1.4: It's more than worth the difference" [advertisement]. *U.S. Camera.* June 1954. 30. The first of a series that ran until the spring of 1955 extolling the Nikkor lenses without mention of the Nikon camera.

"Nikon: the 35mm Camera That Was Built to Optical Standards" [advertisement]. *Photography.* June 1954. 25.

"Nikon: Today's Outstanding Value in Fine 35mm Cameras" [advertisement]. *U.S. Camera.* August 1954, 12.

"NEW ... FAST and PHENOMENAL! Nikkor 85mm f1.5" [advertisement]. *U.S. Camera.* September 1954, 34.

"75° COVERAGE AT f3.5: Nikkor 28mm f3.5 EXTREME WIDE ANGLE LENS" [advertisement]. *U.S. Camera.* October 1954. 10.

"*Longer Faster Sharper* ... THE NIKKOR 105mm f2.5" [advertisement]. *Popular Photography.* February 1955, 84.

"The Japanese Photo Industry" [Special advertising Section]. *Popular Photography,* April 1957, 129–176. Text gives overview of history and development of Japanese photographic industry. A nice summary of the problems that Japan faced in the postwar period and the importance of the camera industry to its successful creation of an overseas market for its manufactured goods.

"Sam Briskin Dies, Revere Founder, Retired Chairman of Revere was a Philanthropist." [Obituary] *New York Times*, May 16, 1961, 43.

"Joseph Ehrenreich, 65, Dead; Brought Nikon Camera Here" [Obituary] *New York Times*, February 9, 1973, 38.

"Masao Nagaoka, 77, Dead; Former President of Nikon" [Obituary]. *New York Times*, November 22, 1974, 42.

"Jacob Deschin, Camera Editor" [Obituary]. *New York Times*, June 21, 1983, A26.

Konno, Tsuyoshi. "Historical Evidence for Nikkor Lenses after World War II." *Nikon Journal* 3, no.1 (September 1985): 2–4.

Lownds, Peter. "Mr. Jun Miki ... An Interview." *Nikon Journal* 7, no. 3 (March 1990): 13–15.

Goldsmith, Arthur. "How the West Was Won." *Popular Photography*, March 1991, 34–39. A thorough description of the "discovery" of Nikkor lenses in 1951 with additional details concerning the early importations. Good illustrations. Repeats many inaccuracies. Does not cover the 1951–53 period.

Fuketa, Masahiko. "Comments on the 50mm/f1.8 Nikkor." *Nikon Journal* 38, 10, no. 2 (December 1992): 7.

Meyer, "Cy." "MIOJ: From When to When?" *Nikon Journal* 38, 10, no. 2 (December 1992): 13.

"The 'LEVIN TAPES' Part I." *Nikon Journal* 38, 10, no. 2 (December 1992): 15.

"The 'LEVIN TAPES' Part II." *Nikon Journal* 39, 10, no. 3 (March 1993): 15.

Cording, Clemens. "Dating the End of 'MIOJ': A Research Project." *Nikon Journal* 39, 10, no. 3 (March 31, 1993): 14–15.

Arakawa, Tatsuhiko (Translated from the Japanese by Kyoko Saegusa and George Landon). "The Arakawa Trilogy." *Nikon Journal* 45, 11, no. 4 (September 1994): 5–9. Information on Arakawa and his three books on the early history of Nikon.

_____. "Excerpts from the Nikon Story." *Nikon Journal* 46, 12, no. 1 (December 1994): 4–7. Considerable information on the early history of the Canon 35mm camera and its relationship with Nippon Kogaku during the 1930s.

_____. "Excerpts from the Nikon Story." *Nikon Journal* 47, 12, no. 2 (March 1995): 6–8. More information on the design of the Canon lens mount and Nikkor optics in the 1930s.

_____. "Excerpts from the Nikon Story." *Nikon Journal* 49, 12, no. 4 (September 1995): 1–3. Information on the Nikon L.

Rotoloni, Robert. "MIOJ! 50 Years Later." *Nikon Journal* 55, 14, no.2 (March 31, 1997): 14–15.

Thomas, Jr., Robert M. "Horace Bristol, 88; Depicted War and Poverty" [Obituary]. *New York Times*, August 7, 1997, B9.

Arakawa, Tatsuhiko. "Birth of the Nikon: An Historical Perspective." *Nikon Journal* 61, 15, no.4 (September 1998): 1–5.

"The Marjoram Report: The Complete Document from November 1948..." *Nikon Journal* 61, 15, no.4 (September 1998): 6–12.

Alexander, Jeff. "Nikon and the Sponsorship of Japan's Optical Industry by the Imperial Japanese Navy, 1917–1945." *B.C. Asian Review* 13 (Spring 2002): 1–21. This is based on Alexander's doctoral dissertation. Another version of this appears in the on-line periodical *Gateway: An Academic Journal on the Web*, Issue no. 5 (spring 2003) (http://grad.usask.ca/gateway/archive17.html).

"Amelia Ehrenreich" [Obituary] *New York Times*, June 7, 2002, B12.

Millard, Max. "Staying in the Picture" [Bio on Adolph Gasser and his store]. *San Francisco Examiner,* October 18, 2002 [reprint].

Classic Camera (Special Issue Rangefinder Nikons) Issue 26 (May 2003). Milan, Italy: *Editrice Progresso.* Includes color pictures of the early Nikon prototypes.

Loder, Michael Wes. "The Rise and Fall of EPOI ... When and Why." *Nikon Journal* 20, no. 3 (June 30, 2003): 12–14.

_____. "The Object at Hand ... A Historic Camera from a Time of Transition." *Nikon Journal* 22, no.3 (June 30, 2005): 3–6. Article describing and featuring pictures of Liholm's Nikon M.

Bakker, Robert. "The 'Nikon' in the Netherlands after World War II." *Nikon Journal* 23, no.3 (June 30, 2006): 16–17. A report on the results of examining coverage of Nikons by the Dutch photographic press during the 1940s and 1950s.

Loder, Michael Wescott. "At the Beginning of Nikon in America ... Adolph Gasser 1912–2006 [Obituary]." *Nikon Journal* 23, no. 4 (September 30, 2006): 18–20.

_____. "The Object at Hand ... A Second Historic Camera from a Time of Transition." *Nikon Journal* 24, no.1 (December 31, 2006): 14–15. Describes the Nikon M purchased by Adolph Gasser for his brother in January 1951.

Books, in alphabetical order

Baird, John. *The Japanese Camera*. Yakima, WA: Historical Camera Publications, 1990.

Braakhuis, Hans. *Nikon Catalogus* [Netherlands] 2003. Dutch text. Braakhuis's compilation of information on all Nikon cameras, which he prepared for the 2004 Nikon Historical Society Convention in Tokyo. See also entry under Web sites for English-language alternatives.

Braczko, Peter. *The Complete Nikon System: An Illustrated Equipment Guide*. Rochester, NY: Silver Pixel Press, 2000.

Condax, Philip L., Masabiro Tano, Takashi Hibi, and William S. Fujimura. *The Evolution of the Japanese Camera*. Rochester, NY: International Museum of Photography at George Eastman House. 1984. Record of an exhibition on Japanese cameras.

Dower, John W. *Embracing Defeat: Japan in the Wake of World War II*. New York: Norton/Free Press, 1999. Book posits the thesis that much of the Japanese behavior in the immediate postwar period can be seen as a reaction to being released from preparation for dying in defense of the homeland. A revisionist, cynical look at what happened to both the Japanese and SCAP during this period.

Duncan, David Douglas. *Photo Nomad*. New York: Norton, 2003.

_____. *This Is War!: A Photo-Narrative in Three Parts*. New York: Bantam, 1951. Reprint, 1967.

Fearey, Robert A. *The Occupation of Japan: Second Phase,1948-50*. Westport, CT: Greenwood, 1972. First published by Macmillan in 1950. Important information on the Japanese economy and reparations during this period.

509th Composite Group History/Pictorial Album (Staff: Paul W. Tibbets, Jerome J. Ossip et al.). Columbus, OH: Mid Coast Marketing, 2002. A history of Adolph Gasser's unit during World War II.

Great Life Photographers, The. The Editors of Life. New York: Bulfinch Press, 2004. Capsule biographies of almost all of *Life*'s many photojournalists, including Bristol, Mydans and Duncan, but not Miki, who was considered only a "contributing photographer."

Greenleaf, Allen R. *Photographic Optics*. New York: Macmillan, 1950. Greenleaf covers the entire spectrum of lenses then available from American and European firms while ignoring the Japanese, which is unfortunate since most of the real innovation was by then occurring in Japan. Still, a good review of optical designs and the problems faced by lens designers.

Gunther, John. *The Riddle of MacArthur: Japan, Korea and the Far East*. New York: Harper, 1950-1951. Important information on role and status of "traders" in Japan during the Military Occupation of Japan.

Kawai, Kazuo. *Japan's American Interlude*. Chicago: University of Chicago: 1960. An overview of the occupation period that is more positive and optimistic than the Dower book above.

Lewis Gordon, ed. *The History of the Japanese Camera*. Translated by William Fujimura and Amy Fujimura. Rochester, NY: Rochester Museum of Photography at George Eastman House, 1991. Coverage of period from the 1850s through 1991. Details about many other companies other than Nikon. Good perspective.

Life Photographers: Their Careers and Favorite Pictures. New York: Doubleday, 1957. Biographical sketches of 40 of *Life*'s photographers, including Robert Capa,

who had died in 1954. However, does not include coverage of David Douglas Duncan.

Long, Brian. *Nikon: A Celebration*. Marlborough, Wiltshire, UK: Crowood Press, 2006. A "coffee table" feast full of numerous color pictures of various Nikon products, dating from the company's beginnings through the then-current offerings in digital technology. Long had full access to the Nikon Company archives and his uncritical account reflects the Nikon Company's own view of its history. Early historical information is useful, but with no references or bibliography, the information must often be used with caution.

Mikesh, Robert C. *Japanese Aircraft Equipment 1940–1945*. Atglen, PA: Schiffer Military History, 2004. Chapter 4 "Aerial Cameras" by Richard Lane is of particular value with excellent pictures and descriptions, including units made by Nippon Kogaku (pages 100–111). Chapter 6 (pages 140–182) covers gunsights and bombsights, many made by Nippon Kogaku.

Morrison, Samuel Eliot. *The Rising Sun in the Pacific: 1931–April 1942*. Vol. 3 of *History of United States Naval Operations in World War II*. Boston: Little & Brown, 1963. Part of a classic series. Writing from more than a dozen years' perspective, Morrison was respectful of the Japanese armed forces' technology and abilities.

Mydans, Carl. *Carl Mydans, Photojournalist*. With interview by Philip B. Kunhardt, Jr. New York: Abrams, 1985.

Oriental Economist. *Japan's Export Industries*. Tokyo, Japan, 1949.

Pont, Patrice-Herve. *Nikon Saga*. Neuilly, France: Fotosaga, 1997.

Rayfield, Stanley. *How Life Gets the Story: Behind the Scenes in Photojournalism*. Garden City, NY: Doubleday, 1955. Includes contemporary pictures of many of the famous *Life* photographers mentioned in the text.

Rotoloni, Robert. *Nippon Kogaku and the Nikon Camera: The History of the Japanese Camera* Monograph Collection. Yakima, WA: Historical Camera Publications & Nikon Historical Society, 1989. Covers much of the same ground as Rotoloni's Hove-published book cited below, but only covers the cameras. More up to date than the Hove title.

_____. *The Nikon Rangefinder Camera: An Illustrated History of the Nikon Rangefinder Cameras, Lenses and Accessories*. 2nd edition. East Sussex, UK: Hove, 1983. Hove Collectors Books series. Although now dated, this was for many years the "Bible" for Nikon rangefinder camera collectors and historians. Best source for serial number ranges. Essential illustrations. One must treat with caution the startup and ending dates Bob had access to when he wrote this book. Replaced by the title below.

______. *The Complete Nikon Rangefinder System*. Farington, Oxon, UK: Hove Foto, 2007. This is the replacement for Rotoloni's 1983 work.

SCAPINS: Supreme Commander for the Allied Powers' Instructions to the Japanese Government from 4 September 1945 to 8 March 1952 (Not including administrative Instructions designated as SCAPIN-A's). General Headquarters, Supreme Commander for the Allied Powers, March 20, 1952. Includes instructions to the Japanese government on the role the *Koedi Eidan* and *Koedi Kodan* (government-sponsored trade corporations). The *Kodan* were dissolved in the spring of 1949 except for two for government exports and imports, and their functions were taken over by private contractors. Also records giving the Japanese government the responsibility for export decisions.

Steichen, Edward. *A Life in Photography*. Garden City, NY: Doubleday, 1963. Information on Steichen's wartime photography program with navy aviation.

Takemae, Eiji. *Inside GHQ: The Allied Occupation of Japan and Its Legacy*. London: Continuum, 2002. Detailed description of SCAP and its activities from a Japanese viewpoint.

Tydings, Kenneth S. *The Nikon Guide*. New York: Greenberg, 1956. One of the earliest "How to" handbooks. It went through several editions until replaced by Wright's *Manual*.

Wright, George. *The Nikon Manual: A Ccomplete Handbook of 35mm Technique*. New York: Universal, 1957. The introduction (pages 11–15) covers the early history of Nippon Kogaku and the 1950 "discovery" of the Nikkors in as much detail as was available anywhere in the 1950s. Wright's citations remain as good a guide as any to the contemporary accounts on the Nikon published in 1950 and 1951.

Yoshikawa, Hideo, and Joanne Kauffman. *Science Has No National Borders: Harry C. Kelly and the Reconstruction of Science and Technology in Postwar Japan*. Cambridge, MA: MIT Press, 1994. A biography of one of the many SCAP administrators.

Interviews

Note: Much of the information, including quotes included in chapter 3, is based on the interviews cited below with Gasser and Liholm.

Duncan, David Douglas. 2005. Phone interview by M.W. Loder. February 16.

Gasser, Adolph. 2003. Phone interview by M.W. Loder. July 21.

______. 2004. Phone interview by M.W. Loder. November 2.

______. 2004 Phone interview by M.W. Loder. December 21.

______. 2005 Personal interview by M.W. Loder. October 19.

Kelleher, Edward. In interview with Brian Richter. Spring 2001. Part of a class project. Published as a Web site. <http://web.mit.edu/bkr/www/jrtfinal/start.htm.> It is possible that the camera that Kelleher owned was an early Nikon, although if purchased in 1948, it was more likely a Canon. He used it extensively in Japan and, according to his grandson, won several prizes for his work. He was a member of a group of officers who formed an informal camera club in Tokyo between 1948 and 1950.

Liholm, Hans W. 2004. Phone interview by M.W. Loder. February 16.

______. 2004. Phone interview by M.W. Loder. November 22.

______. December 4, 2004. Personal letter to M.W. Loder.

______. 2005. Personal interview with M.W. Loder. February 23–25, at his home in Longboat Key, Florida.

Rotoloni, Robert. 2005. Personal interview with M.W. Loder. June 23, at his home in Dyer, Indiana.

Correspondence, Web Sites, Miscellaneous

Abrahams, Peter. *Outline of Japanese Binocular Production*, April 21, 2002, http://home.europa.com/~telescope/japanbin.txt.

Adams, J.R. *From Nikon Camera Company, Inc. to Al Levin*, September 22, 1952. A response to a letter from Levin concerning the status of an order for microscopes from Peerless, a major photographic products dealer in New York. [Copy courtesy of Nikon Historical Society.]

Anderson, Jr., L.E. *To Al Levin from Ship's Store Officer*, February 20, 1952. Officer requesting the status of an order for a Nikkor lens in Leica mount. [Copy courtesy of Nikon Historical Society.]

Anonymous. *From Nikon Camera Company, Inc. to Al Levin*, July 22, 1952. Routine correspondence covering commission rates, new sales arrangements, equipment for sale and difficulties the company was experiencing with Japanese prices. It is possible that a second page is missing. The letter may have come from either Robert Evans or Ross Goodman. [Copy courtesy of Nikon Historical Society.]

Bowman, Becky [Chronicle staff writer]. "Adolph Gasser — S.F. Photography Shop owner" [obituary]. *SFGate*, April 6, 2006, http://www.sfgate.com/

cgi-bin/article.cgi?file=/c/a2006/04/02/BAGEUI24 RL1.DTL. Obituary for Gasser that appeared in the *San Francisco Chronicle*'s Web site.

Braakhuis, Hans. *Nikon Catalogus*, "History of Nippon Kogaku 1600–1949," May 26, 2006, http://hpme. planet.nl/~nikon.catalogus/. Braakhuis's online history of optical manufacturing in Europe and Japan. Excellent background material. He had access to NK's official histories, which were published in limited editions in Japan and have never been translated.

______. Visits to Europe: Presentation for NHS Con 10, Vienna, Austria, May 21, 2006. [CD with PDF format]. The text with pictures for Braakhuis's talk. In English. Excellent information on the early connections between Nippon Kogaku and various European optical firms.

______. Web page on history of Nikon company and its connections to Mitsubishi *Zaibatsu*, October 27, 2004, http://hpme.planet.nl/%7Ebraakl17/). [6 pages].

Baird, John. *Nippon Kogaku, the Early Years from 1908–1950*. [proceedings] Nikon Historical Society Convention (1988).

Bausch & Lomb Optical Co. v. Overseas Finance & Trading Co. Inc., 112 USPQ 6, 8 (Comm'r Pats. 1956), http://www.bitlaw.com/source/temp/1213_09.html. "(noting that "Kogaku," the transliteration of the Japanese word for "optical," was properly disclaimed). If non–English wording which is translated must be disclaimed, the actual non–English wording should be disclaimed, not the English translation. The applicant must disclaim the wording which actually appears in the mark, not a translated version which is not technically part of the mark."

Brief History, 17 December 2004, http://www.nikon. co.jp/main/eng/portfolio/ history.htm [4 pages]. Outline by year of the Nikon company's history.

Deschin, Jacob. *To H.W. Liholm*. April 19, 1951. Liholm Papers. A letter from Deschin thanking Liholm for promptly providing him with an 85mm f2 Nikkor.

Duncan, David Douglas. *To H.W. Liholm*. July 16, 1951. Liholm Papers. A thank you note to Liholm for providing Duncan with Nikon binoculars, followed by a complaint about the new f1.4 Nikkor lens, which Duncan felt was too flare prone.

Evans, R.V. *Letter Addressed to Al Levin from the Nikon Camera Company's General Manager*. February 4, 1953. In this letter, Bob Evans follows up on earlier correspondence dealing with Nikkors mounting on Contax cameras. Levin had wanted to promote Nikkors to Contax owners, but apparently Nikon could not supply enough Nikkors in the Contax mount at that time. [Copy courtesy of Nikon Historical Society].

Fotómuüvészet online. *Schwanner Endre: Nikon 1917–1997*, December 17, 2004, http://fotomuveszet.elender.hu/9734/973410_eng.html [13 pages].

Flukinger, Roy. DDD: "...And Every Day a Fabulous Life" [Introductory Essay: David Douglas Duncan]. *HRC Online Exhibition*, University of Texas at Austin, December 8, 2004, http://www.hrc.utexas. edu/exhibitions/online/ddd/ddd6.html [5 pages].

Gasser, Adolph. "Announcement." *Nikon Camera Company* (undated but presumedly from December 1951). Gasser's letter to "our customers and representatives" announcing the end of his Nikon Camera Company and the turning over of all operations to OFITRA effective December 31, 1951. [Copy courtesy of Nikon Historical Society].

Harshe-Rotman & Druck, Inc. "Marketing Strategy behind Nikon Cameras Changed 'Made in Japan' into Quality Image." [1974?]. An undated paper from a public relations firm that combines an unofficial history with biographical profiles of Joseph Abbott and Herbert Sax, the two men who replaced Joseph Ehrenreich after his death in February 1973. Contains a lot of company promotional material. Much of the information from the early years is misleading if not simply untrue.

Hennig, Peter. *When Japan took over*, April 21, 2004, http://www.photodo.com/art/ When3.stml [6 pages.]

"Invoice number 001." *Nikon Camera Company*, 12 November 1951. Al Levin's first invoice in his new job as Nikon representative for the East Coast. It records six items: a Nikon S with 50mm f1.4 lens, a zoom finder, a 50mm f1.4 in Leica mount, a 35mm f3.5 and an 85mm f2 in Nikon mount and a 38mm f1.9 Ciné-Nikkor.

"Invoice No. 122." *Overseas Finance & Trading Company Inc*, February 29, 1952. Record of the shipment by A.B. Padilla of four research microscopes and four binocular attachments to Al Levin in New York. [Copy courtesy of Nikon Historical Society.]

Itoh, Mikio. Nikon Web Magazine. *Nikon Digital Archives*. "Archivist's Memo No 1 'Serial No 6091,'" February 17, 2005. http://www.nikon.co.jp/main/ eng/darchives/memo/m01_e.htm [1 page]. A discussion of the discovery and recovery of the first prototype Nikon. Includes a brief chronology of the development of the camera.

"Archivist's Memo No.3: 'In the early days of Nikon camera brochures,'"December 7, 2004, http://www. nikon.co.jp/main/eng/darchives/camera/history_e. htm [4 pages]. Itoh traces the changes in NKT's advertising brochures for the new Nikon camera as it tried to get a handle on its new market.

Liholm, H.W. "We now are submitting for your approval..." [Contract] dated April 26,1950. Liholm Papers. A copy of the contract written and signed by Liholm and Nagaoka granting OFITRA exclusive importation rights to North America for three years.

______. "Now you will discover the Nikon..." [1951]. Undated flyer from early to mid 1951 put out by the Overseas Finance & Trading Company as a follow-up to its early advertising. It appears to be the coversheet Liholm sent out with brochures. [Courtesy of Nikon Historical Society.]

Lipton, Norman. *To N. Hamashima.* June 11, 1951. Liholm Papers. Details changes in *Popular Photography's* headquarters, including Lipton's becoming managing editor. Contains strong protest against Sears & Roebuck's attempt to piggyback on the positive publicity that the Nikon and Nikkors were getting.

______. *To H.W. Liholm.* July 30, 1951. Liholm Papers. Further discussion of the Sears marketing controversy. Lipton was looking forward to meeting Liholm when he stopped in New York on his way to Europe and Japan.

Nagaoka, Masao. *Dinner Address Given 24 April 1950.* 2 pages. Liholm Papers. Speech Dr. Nagaoka gave at dinner for Liholm, Hagberg and Sakai toward the end of their negotiations.

Nikon Web Magazine, *Nikon Digital Archives.* "History of Nikon Cameras," December 17, 2004, http://www.nikon.co.jp/main/eng/d-archives/camera/history_e.htm [26 pages]. The official and most comprehensive history of the Nikon on the Web.

Price List for Nikon Camera and Nikkor Lenses [1951]. Overseas Finance & Trading Company, Inc. 465 California Street, San Francisco. [Lists cameras with 50mm f3.5, f2 and f1.4 lenses, also lists 85mm f2, 135mm f3.5, 35mm f3.5 and universal finder]

Price List for Nikon Cameras and Nikkor Lenses — dated May 1, 1952. Nikon Camera Company, Inc. 25 California Street, San Francisco 11, California. [Same listing as above, but 50mm f3.5 is "not available," Additions: 38mm f1.9 Ciné-Nikkor and "Zoom finder."]

"Relationship of the Nikon Camera and/or Nikkor lenses to other cameras of Japanese manufacture," November 16, 1951. Damage-control mailing from the Nikon Camera Company to its sales representatives intended to set the record straight as to the status of Nikkor lenses that were appearing on other Japanese cameras. [Courtesy of Nikon Historical Society.]

Small, Marc James. *Post War Camera & Lens Design Thievery.* April 12, 2001.http://teachnet.edb.utexas.edu/~leica/thievery.htm [2 pages]. A prejudiced and strongly worded attack on both Nippon Kogaku and Canon in reference to their usage of many German optical and mechanical designs in the immediate postwar period. [From a photocopy courtesy of Nikon Historical Society.]

Stella, Dante. *Nikon vs. Leica Lenses,* December 5, 2004, http://www.dantestella.com/technical/nikoleic.html [1 page].

The Story of the Nikon Camera Company & Notes on the Makers of the Nikon Camera. Two single-page flyers produced by Gasser's Nikon Camera Company in the fall of 1951. The "story" sheet cov-

ers the company's major employees and their credentials. The "Notes" piece describes Nippon Kogaku and its many products. It was later published in a printed form complete with an illustration of the Ohi plant. [Courtesy of Nikon Historical Society.]

The Sub Club, June 30, 2006, http://www.subclub.org/index.htm [14 pages]. A fan site for subminiature cameras and photography. Offers in-depth information and pictures of the many different Japanese subminiature format cameras manufactured in the postwar period.

Tateno, Yokoyuki. *History of Nikon Cameras,* May 23, 2003, http://www.nikon.co.jp/main/eng/d-archives/camera/history_e.htm [9 pages]. Part of Nikon, Inc.'s official Web site. Lots of history, in both English and Japanese.

"This is Nippon Kogaku K.K." 1954 [advertising brochure]. Brochure published in Japan in English for use of Nippon Kogaku, U.S.A., Inc. — the paper company that actually imported Nikon equipment for Nikon, Inc. to sell. Includes listing of NK's officers and portraits of the Board of Trustees. Lens page shows and lists lenses from 28mm f3.5 through 250mm, including the then-new 105mm f2.5. Illustrates and lists 25cm but no other short-mount lenses. Reflex housing appears to be a prototype.

Verlangieri. December 6, 2006. http://www.calpots.com/sp_exhibits/camera_exhibit/25_camera.html. Comments on Sam Briskin by his grandson, Philip Briskin.

Original Records from the American Occupation of Japan, 1945–1952

(Records viewed in 2003–2004 and 2006 are listed by ARC number when available; by date, otherwise)

Note: Identification of records in the U.S. National Archives College Park, Maryland, is by ARC number. Each ARC number refers to a specific file folder. However, a file folder may hold more than one item. The relationship of the contents in a folder, the record title in the online index and the title on the folder may be tenuous at best. In addition, often useful items would turn up in adjacent folders for which no ARC number would be known. Dates appear in bold face below when they are critical to the identification and location of documents cited in the text.

The following folders in the National Archives were found to be useful, or somewhat useful:

(1) ARC Identifier Number and Title

309187— CPO — Misc[e]llaneous (1 Jan.— 30 June, 1950), Folder #19, 1945–1952

Creator: SCAP, Office of the chief of Staff. Office of the Comptroller. Audit Division (05/14/1949–04/28/1952)

Audit of inventory in the ship's store located at Subic Bay in Philippines. Notes 2 Nikons, 2 finders and 1 lens on hand, all damaged.

309214— Sales Room — CPO, 1945–1952 [also ARC #309215, #309217].

Creator: SCAP, Office of the chief of Staff. Office of the Comptroller. Audit Division (05/14/1949–04/28/1952)

Inventory of the CPO Sales Room for December 31, 1950. Lists the Nikon with f1.4 lens, 135 f4 tele lens, 8.5cm f2 lens, wide angle and univ. viewfinder. These would all have been samples that buyers could examine before placing an order.

321669— FIB-30, Horace Bristol, 1949 —1951.

SCAP. Legal Section. Administration Division. (10/02/1945–04/28/1952?).

This folder and the five which follow all contain records and correspondence relating to Bristol's work and status in Japan.

321670— FIB-30A, Horace Bristol, 1949–1952.

322322— Fl-82, Horace Bristol, 1947–1949.

322386— FL-131, Horace Bristol, 1947–1949.

322589—#99, Horace Bristol (Suspense), 1948–1950.

322590—#99A, Horace Bristol, 1948–1950.

323097—#552, Overseas Finance & Trading Co, Inc., 1948–1950.

The dossier kept by SCAP on the company.

Note: Western Trading Co., Ltd. is file #358 in the same container box. Files on Horace Bristol's files are also in the same box.

Folder #358

- Letter from Ludv. T. Hagberg dated **December 6, 1949**, to chief, Foreign Investment Board. His request to import special foods for children.
- Letter from Hagberg to Foreign Investment Board dated **March 30, 1950**, requesting permission to sell NK products to "Army personnel and holders of O.S.S. Cards."
- Letter of approval to sell to CPO, **June 28, 1950.**
- Other letters dated: May 16, 1950, July 7, 1950, July 15, 1950, July 29, 1950.
- Letter notifying Western Trading that after **January 1, 1952**, permits will no longer be needed.

Folder #552

- The series of letters between A. Grekow and

the Chief, Foreign Investment Board are in this folder. Letters are dated **May 16, 1950**, May 19, 1950, May 26, 1950, June 24, 1950, June 29, 1950, July 5, 1950, July 12, 1950, and July 17, 1950.

366478— List of Authorized Use — Oi [Ohi] Plant, Nippon Kogaku K.K. (Japan Optical Industry Co., Ltd.), **May 1948–1951**. [208 pages]

This report includes a complete inventory of everything NK had on site, including wheelbarrows and bicycles! Includes a blueprint of the factory keyed to the inventory showing the location of items in the inventory. Lists "20 hand cameras."

Includes reparations inspection check sheet dated **April 30, 1948.**

Includes **May 1948** monthly production report. NK managed to finish 35 f2 and f3.5 lenses "for Nikon Camera."

By contrast, it managed 111 f3.5 lenses "for Leica Camera" but no lenses for "Canon camera."

[Is this the transition away from supplying lenses for Canon, or does the separate listing indicate the old "J" mount or different Canon thread?]

366597— Nippon Kogaku K.K., December 1945– April 1951, 1945–1951.

Inventory of the Shimata plant in preparation for reparations dated **January 15, 1947.** Building to be released to Kawai Musical Instruments Co. Part of the plant had burned.

366683— Nippon Kogaku, Oi Plant, December 1947–March 1951, 1945–1951.

Series: Plant Reproduction Data, 1945–1951. Several records, including production authorization for **March 7, 1949.** Application to move newly purchased machinery (vacuum pumps) for use in coating lenses and binocular prisms dated June 13, 1949, and a reparations status report for March 31, 1951.

366684— As above, except January 1946–October 1947, 1945–1951.

Part of Plant Reproduction Data, 1945–1951.

Letter dated **July 24, 1948**, authorizing use of nonreparation machinery to increase production. Allows up to 500 cameras per month for Oi [Ohi] plant.

Photographic & Optical Equipment Production Data for **March 1949**. Japan Optical was making 15 tons of optical glass per month! Fuji was managing a bare 750 kg and Chiyoda Optical an average of one ton. On the other hand, NK's lens production and camera production were far below its competitors.

Request dated **August 15, 1949**, for release of

land and buildings at Ohi factory so that more precise lathes could be used.

Another request dated **September 20, 1949,** asking for release of buildings and grounds.

Permit issued by GHQ/SCAP dated **January 3, 1950,** permitting the expansion of production.

Reparations Status Report dated **March 31, 1951.** Second page lists production for February through March 31, 1951. During this period, the company manufactured 620 cameras, 1,490 "Camera gadgets" and 2,514 photographic lenses. While not up to the 7,000 asked for in 1948, it is a considerable improvement.

Includes correspondence dealing with the **August 1950** strike.

367132—As above, **April 1951,** 1946–1951.

Part of Reparations Plants File, 1946–1951 Series.

367453—Reparations Status Records, 1945–1951.

367467—Japan Optical, Nippon Kogaku, **May 1947–September 1947,** 1945–1951.

Series: Reparations Status Reports, 1945–1951. [Box 2726, folder 14].

Memo dated **July 7, 1947,** acknowledging that company has requested permission to use equipment in place until reparations take place.

367503—Japan Optical, Kawasaki, 1945–1951

SCAP. Civil Affairs Section. Kanto Civil Affairs Region. (1950–1952).

Series: Reparations Status Reports, 1945–1951.

Most of the "Reparations Status Reports" are records on facilities made by SCAP inspectors concerning the condition of buildings and equipment. Most of NK's plants have a separate folder. See other status reports which follow below.

367504—Japan Optical, Tsudayama, April 1947–April 1951, 1945–1951.

Series: Reparations Status Reports, 1945–1951.

367529—Nippon Kogaku K.K., December 1949–April 1951, 1945–1951

Series: Reparations Status Reports, 1945–1951.

Report on Shiojiri plant dated **November 20, 1947,** signed by Dr. Nagaoka for Reparations Section. Includes brief history of company and the Shiojiri plant including number of workers and production. Plant had been silk factory, purchased by NK in 1943 to provide a facility away from bombing raids and close to forests. It was closed after the war but reopened and manufactured farm machinery [!]. Wood sources were used to build tripods and levels for

optical equipment, then production moved back into optical precision instruments. Includes inventory of machinery and lists workers by class and sex. Submitted by Nagaska [Dr. Masao Nagaoka], the NK president.

A sheet of Japanese optical goods production for 1947

367530—Nippon Kogaku Kogyo, Matsumoto, April 1950–April 1951, 1945–1951.

Series: Reparations Status Reports, 1945–1951.

370190—Nippon Kogaku Kogyo, January 1947–September 1947, 1945–1951.

SCAP. Civil Affairs Section. Tokai-Hokuiku Civil Affairs Region. (01/01/1950–04/28/ 1952).

Series: Reparations Status Reports, 1945–1951.

383029—Eastman Kodak Co., July 1948–November 1951, 1950–1951.

Series: Patent Files, 1950–1951. Files of letters of complaint over misuse of Kodak name, includes photos of marquee in violation.

397759—Leica Camera, 1946–1951

Series: Subject Correspondence File, 1946–1951. Includes letter from Netherlands government trying to reclaim Leica camera looted in the Dutch East Indies.

403033—Nippon Kogaku K.K., Totsuka Kojo, 1945–1951.

Series: Plant Records 1945–1951. Handwritten draft of application to dispose of Takuta plant. Part of the plant had been destroyed by fire, part was in use by the U.S. Army. Nippon Kogaku was trying to sell the unused part that had not been destroyed.

403034—19-92 Nippon Kogaku Kogyo Kawasaki Kojo, 1945–1951.

Series: Plant Records, 1945–1951.

40303519-93 Nippon Kogaku Kogyo Tsudayama Kojo, 1945–1951.

Series: Plant Records, 1945–1951.

403150—Mun 26-43 Disp Area Nippon Kogaku, 1945–1951

Series: Plant Records, 1945–1951.

403151—26-43 Mun Nippon Kogaku Kogyo K.K., Shiojiri Kojo, 1945–1951.

Series: Plant Records, 1945–1951.

403153—26-44 Nippon Kogaku Kogyo K.K. Matsuo Koyo, 1945–1951.

Series: Plant Records, 1945–1951.

403154—26-46(a) Mun. Nippon Kogaku Kogyo K.K. (39-179) Nishimura Chokokukk, 1945–1951.

Series: Plant Records, 1945–1951.

403339—34-65 Nippon Kogaku Kogyo K.K. Kawaguchi Kojo, 1945–1951.

Series: Plant Records, 1945–1951.

403492 — Munitions 39–179 Nippon Kogaku Kogyo (Japan Optical), 1945–1951.
  Series: Plant Records, 1945–1951.
403706 — Nippon Kogaku Kogyo, 1945–1951.
  Series: Plant Records, 1945–1951.
403707 — Same as above.
403822 — 39–180 ... Same as above.
403823 — 39–181 ... Same as above.
403824 — 39–182 ... Same as above.
403937 — Munitions 2–11(a) Nippon Kogaku Aikita Kojo, 1945–1951.
  Series: Plant Records, 1945–1951.
403938 — Same as above.
406481 — 004A Eastman Kodak Co. Ltd., 1945–1951.
  Series: Decimal File, 1945–1951. Charges brought against a Japanese company going by name of "Kodakara." Charges copyright-trademark infringement.
436281 — Bulk Enclosure No. 63: Optical and Spectacle Industry Data, 1945–1951
  Series: General Subject File, 1945–1951. Dated **May 23, 1948**, NK had 30 workers engaged in "finished spectacle lenses." No current production but planned to make 5000 per month.
436518 — Bulk Enclosure No. 336: Reconversion Permit for Reparations Plant — Nippon Kogaku Kogyo K.K., 1945–1951.
  Series: General Subject File, 1945–1951.
44226 — 2FTC vs. Nippon Kogaku Kogyo K.K. (Hearing Notices Nos. 82 & 83), 1947–1951.
  Series: Fair Trade Commission File, 1947–1951. Records of the charges brought against NK for entering into exclusive export agreement with OFITRA and Western Trading.
446371 — Japanese Government Export List, 1945–1951.
  Series: General Export and Import File, 1945–1951.
446644 — Export Catalog (1946–1949) 1945–1952.
  Series: General Export and Import File, 1945–1952. Japan was shipping lots of fish oil and agar-agar to the United States in 1952. Lots of Binoculars but few cameras and no brand name listings.
447055 — Export Inquiries, 1945–1952.
  Series: General Export and Import File, 1945–1952.
447698 — Brazilian Sisal (Overseas Finance & Trading Co., Ltd.) JI-32178, 1945–1952.
  Series: General Export and Import File, 1945–1952.
  Wheelin' & Dealin' in **August 1949**.
456368 — Business Record, Camera Department, Export Bazaar, 1945–1950.
  File Unit from Record Group 331: Records of

Allied Operational and Occupation Headquarters, World War II, 1907–1966.
456369 — Camera Monthly Report, 1945–1950. [Box 7230, folder 15].
  Series: Topical File, 1945–1950. Covers weekly, later monthly, production for export by various Japanese Optical and Camera companies from **August 1948** through **April 1951**. Covers cameras and accessory lenses. **This is the main source for Appendix 1.**
457040 — Japan Optical Co. (Tokyo), 1945–1950. [Box 7258, folder 2; see also Box 7230, folders 15 and 16, which covers overall optical production for 1946 and 1947.]
  Series: Topical File, 1945–1950.
  Directive dated **December 28, 1945**, to Shiojiri factory permitting the manufacture of "items you have hitherto handled."
  Letter dated **December 24, 1946** (received **January 14, 1947**).
  A cover letter from NK's secretary thanking a "Mr. Tate" of the Economic & Scientific Section of GHQ/SCAP for its support in the previous year and outlining NK's production plans for the coming year.
  Binoculars were the only product of note that NK was able to produce in any numbers in 1946. An attached chart traces the growth in production of binoculars and opera glasses from November 1945 through December 1946. In addition, the company began manufacture of spectacles in March 1946 and resumed the manufacture of "photographic lenses" in February 1946. The company states that it made 772 of these in 1946. Most of these would have gone to either the Canon Camera Co. or the Nippon Camera Co. (manufacturers of the Nicca).
  A production schedule called for the Nikon camera to be in full production by March of 1947 along with wide angle and telephoto lenses. "Leica" normal lenses — already in production — were projected at 200 per month and rising to 300 per month by April. The Nikoflex was also scheduled for production in June of 1947. These projections proved to be much too optimistic.
  A list of equipment needed for the Oi [Ohi] plant. NK had brought in a lot of the equipment that had been in its other plants, concentrating them in its Ohi location. It then had "loaned" what it did not need to various "friends" who needed the equipment in order to convert their companies. NK was requesting permission to sell that equipment

and in a chart projected its needs by type of equipment for the coming year.

Some Outstanding Facts about Nippon Kogaku Kogyo K.K. [1947?]

A year-by-year history of the company going all the way back to the founding of the Iwaki Glass Mfg. Co. in 1881. The focus of the narrative is on the company's interest and focus on civilian products and how it was "forced" to provide support for the military against its own aims and desires.

Photographs of Products "collected by Technical Department," Japan Optical Industry Co. Ltd. [1947?]

Pages of photographs of actual products or engraved drawings of products from vertexmeters, eyeglasses, microscopes and levels to even fisheye lenses. The number of past, present and potential products is impressive, although no images of periscopes or rangefinders are included. An important view into what NK was capable of manufacturing in the way of civilian products.

Letter dated **October 16, 1950**, concerning a contract to provide 1,000 7X50 and 5,000 6X30 binoculars to the National Police Reserve.

Letter from Taro Matsurda, director of General Affairs Bureau to GHQ/SCAP concerning *application for permission of manufacture of additional items by Oi plant ...* dated **June 2, 1948**. Includes indication of interest by various American companies in NK's new camera.

An **undated**, handwritten note listing military hardware that NK had manufactured for the Imperial armed forces including "Anti-aircraft and torpedo predictor" and "bomb sight for army (Norton type)." While these items had been manufactured elsewhere, NK was in trouble with the Occupation authorities because they had moved the machinery to make these items to the Ohi plant. "Reports Rosenberg" written in margin.

Letter from Peter deLeeuw, Head of Ceramic Group, dated **January 13, 1948**, addressed to Campbell Osborn recommending the removal of Nippon Kogaku from reparations list. Writer points out that NK is only supplier of Precision levels and other such instruments which are essential for the reconstruction of Japan.

Letter from SCAP dated March 23, 1948, granting the "temporary use of the pumps, boilers and electrical equipment" belonging to NK for the buildings being used as a girls' school.

A Table dated **December 22, 1947**, showing the export destination by American company of binoculars being exported to the United States and the CPO. Companies included Manhattan Novelty Company and Park Instrument Co., among others.

457387 — Niigata: Nippon Kogaku Kogyo K.K., 1945–1950.

Series: Topical File, 1945–1950.
Lists of facilities and status, **April 30, 1947**. SCAP was concerned about the shifting of machinery for reparations.

457540 — Saitama: Nippon Kogaku Kogyo K.K., 1945–1950.

Series: Topical File, 1945–1950.
Includes records for Shinagawa plant, May 15, 1947.
Includes a reconversion permit from Lt. Col. Timothy Ryan for Takahashi (Kawaguchi factory) authorizing the use of machines for the manufacture of wooden axles for oxcarts and carriages.

457698 — Tokyo: Nippon Kogaku, 1945–1950.

Series: Topical File, 1945–1950. Request for Reconversion Permit that would allow increase in production of cameras, telescopes and other optical instruments. Two items, dated July 24, 1948, and March 7, 1949.

458110 — Nagano: Nippon Kogaku Kogyo K.K., 1945–1950. [Box 7291, folder 36].

Series: Topical File, 1945–1950. [Correspondence relating to Shiojiri Plant.]
Includes a booklet showing range of precision instruments.
Includes letter of application for release from reparations, dated **May 19, 1947**.
Letter of approval signed by Lt. Col. B. Shafer, dated **October 10, 1947**.
Includes a request dated **February 8, 1949**, to add binoculars to the list of items permitted to be manufactured at Shiojiri plant.
Second letter, same topic, dated **March 10, 1949**.
Third letter, same topic, dated **April 4, 1949**.
Permit issued, **June 15, 1949**.

458126 — Kanagawa: Nippon Kogaku Kogyo K.K., 1945–1950.

Series: Topical File, 1945–1950. Status of Industrial Facilities, **May 19, 1947**.
The Kawasaki facility was being converted into a plant for manufacturing noodle-making machinery.

458307 — Nippon Kogaku Kogyo K.K., 1945–1950. [Box 7298, folder 17].

Series: Topical File, 1945–1950. Request that the Shiojiri plant be released from reparations, dated **May 29, 1949**. Includes

approval by J.A. O'Brien CWO, USA. "Currently manufacturing microscopes & tripods for surveying instruments."
Includes a detailed description of Shiojiri plant and equipment holdings.

459040 — Camera Industry, 1934–1952 [Box 8098, folder 4].

40 variously numbered pages detailing the history of Japan's photographic industries. Includes tables of manufacturers, including NK. No date appears on the report, but statistics run through 1948, suggesting a date of sometime in late 1948 or early 1949.

462567 — Smaller Enterprise — Nippon Kogaku Kogyo K.K., Goto Optical Co., 1946–1947.

Series: General File, 1946–1947. This file includes a "Brief overview of Japanese Optical Industry," a profile of the Goto Optical Company — a small cooperative firm that made telescopes, which Nippon Kogaku was buying out — and a brochure on the Nikon M camera and its lenses.

468987 — Nippon Kogaku Kogyo (10–027–00), 1946–1950.

Series: Zaibatsu Corporation File, 1946–1950.

468988 — Nippon Kogaku Kogyo (10–027–00), 1946–1950.

Series: Zaibatsu Corporation File, 1946–1950.

477876 — Exports from Japan Reported during Month, Year by Country of Destination, in Quantity and Value, 1934–1952.

Series: Price, Production and Distribution File, 1934–1952.

478312 — Camera Production in Japan (Special Report No. 10), 1934–1952.

Series: Price, Production and Distribution File, 1934–1952. Report on the condition of Japanese Camera Industry dated **June 25, 1946.** 7 pages. Cover title: "GHQ-SCAP Economic and Scientific Section Research and Statistics Division Special Report No.10: Camera Production in Japan 25 June 1946."

[Copies of this report turned up in other folders as well.]

478313 — Production, Stocks on Hand and Exports between Japan and US, 1934–1952. Series: Price, Production and Distribution File, 1934–1952. Another copy of "Special Report No.10."

479038 — Camera Industry, 1934–1952.

Series: Price, Production and Distribution File, 1934–1952.

479040 — Camera Industry, 1934–1952.

Series: Price, Production and Distribution File, 1934–1952.

The Camera Industry in Japan. [40 unnumbered pages]. **May 1946.**

480270 — Nippon Camera (99–004–24), 1946–1950.

Series: Zaibatsu Corporation File, 1946–1950. One of the series on the attempted breakup of the Zaibatsu — this one deals with the manufacturer of the Nicca Camera, which used Nikkor lenses.

485136 — Nippon Kogaku Kogyo K.K. (HCLC No. 154), No. 1, 1947–1949.

Series: Fair Trade Practices Law 207, 1947–1949. Report prepared by President Nagaoka and Seihachi Karasawa (Chief-director of Union of Nippon Kogaku) to the Holding Company Liquidation Commission. **March 8, 1948, April 7, 1948.**

Total of 21 pages including a listing of all of the company's trademarks and response to a questionnaire.

September 17, 1947, Report on general information on reporting company. "Cameras, photographic lenses, movie projecting lenses and reflectors..." are among items mentioned that the company manufactures. Two plants out of a total of 14 are in operation. This is the report for the liquidation and turn-in of shares as part of the dismantling of the Mitsubishi holding cartel.

Includes a map showing plant locations dated **April 21, 1948.**

Letter [Copies also found in ARC #485137] dated **March 26, 1947,** from: Ministry of Commerce and Industry, Japanese Government. Addressed to: Reparation Enforcement Bureau, Ministry of Commerce and Industry. Signed "K. Tauiaki" (sp?).

Subject: "Application for Exemption from Designation of Reparation Control to the Oi Factory and the Oi Glass Factory of the Nippon Kogaku Kogyo K.K. (The Japan Optical Industry Co., Ltd.) as Privately-owned Munitions Plants."

This is a protest of "private munitions" designation of NK and seeks to avoid reparations for NK. "Nature and object of this particular company are entirely peaceful ... [military] demands were overwhelming and compulsory." Writer makes case that NK's products will "Make lucrative export goods for Japan."

Includes a list of products and schedules of manufacture for 1947. Cameras are mentioned with a planned production of 300 per month to meet 5.8 percent of perceived domestic demand. This level to be reached by May 1947.

Includes outline of history of company.

485137 — Nippon Kogaku Kogyo K.K. (HCLC No. 154), no. 2, 1947–1949.

Series: Fair Trade Practices Law 207, 1947–1949.
Letter dated May 20, 1948, giving background for antitrust action.

488408 — Raw Film Situation in Japan, 1945–1949.
Series: Central File, 1945–1949. Report on the extreme shortage of film stock in Japan which was affecting the ability of film industry to make movies.

501042 — Nippon Kogaku Kogyo K.K., Koriyama Plant (Ferro-Alloy) — Fukushima Prefecture.
Series: Mine Reports, 1946–1951.

501043 — Nippon Kogaku Kogyo K.K., Miharu Plant (Ferro-Alloy) — Fukushima Prefecture.
Series: Mine Reports, 1946–1951.

(2) Other Archives Records without ARC number, in chronological order

16 October 1945
Directive from the U.S. Eighth Army permitting the immediate resumption of manufacture of "spectacles, binoculars, photographic lenses, microscopes, magnifying glasses, etc." Under lenses, the specific optics listed include only "f— 5cm 1:2.8" and "F — 38cm 1:8."
[The 38mm lens was a telephoto for 8mm movie cameras.]

25 June 1946 [No ARC number, but in Box 8098, folder 2].
Copy of "Special Report #10. Camera Production in Japan." Copies of this same report can be found in other folders.

26 October 1946
Letter from Military Government District, Tokyo Detachment, APO 181
James Morrison, 2nd Lt. recommends that entire company be placed on the list of private munitions plants subject to reparations.

13 November 1946
Letter from Lt. Col. R. Shafer approving the placement of Nippon Kogaku on reparations list as a privately owned munitions plant.

21 December 1946
SCAP memo designates NK as a reparation factory [no copy] referenced below 7.
[This was potentially disastrous. Munitions plants were to be dismantled and all manufacturing equipment was to be removed and awarded to Allies — most likely China.]

14 January 1947
List of machinery required for Ohi Factory.

15 January 1947
Shimada factory listed for reparations

29 April 1947
Directs the machinery for reparations be taken under custody and control.
[Employees were required to tag and seal (coat with oil and grease, i.e., "moth-ball") equipment identified for reparations. A third or more of NK's main plant in Oi [Ohi] was so sealed and shut off.

9 June 1947
Memo directing NK to submit list of machinery for reparations [no copy, referenced below]

24 February 1948
Report on general company data. Cameras are listed as 2% of total production. Photographic lenses are 5%. Optical glass (50%), precision optical measuring instruments (16%) and binoculars (15%) are way ahead.

27 February 1948
Draft of a letter describing current NK and noting that the company seeks to dispose of unused plants. [By the end of the war, NK had been operating more than 20 plants at up to 16 different locations.]

24 March 1948
List of actual production of binoculars and opera glasses. [see 4 August 1948 below].
At that time, almost all of NK's binoculars were going for export. As the remarks point out, export figures include shipment to the CPO.

12 May 1948
Indicates a production of seven cameras for Nippon Kogaku between January 1948 and March 1948. Had nine cameras on hand as of March 31, 1948.

1 July 1948
Reparations inspection check sheet.

24 July 1948
Authorization to use nonreparations machinery to increase production. Allows 500 cameras per month. For Oi plant [Ohi]

4 August 1948
List of "Actual Production and Distribution of Binoculars and Opera Glasses." A report from the Optical & Precision Instruments Manufacturers' Association. NK is first on list and apparently competing well in numbers with the other major players, including Tokyo Kogaku.

5 March 1949
Report on Shiojiri plant equipment.

7 March 1949
Revision of the reconversion permit of July 1948 for Oi plant. Increases production level for photographic lenses to 1,200 per month but does not mention cameras at all. Perhaps no change in status.

4 April 1949

Granting request from Reparations Board to permit NK to manufacture binoculars at Shiojiri plant. [See 8 February 1949 above.]

20 October 1949

Request for increase in production limits of measuring instruments and photographic lenses. [See 7 March 1949 above.] Limit would go from 1,200 to 7,000. Instruments would increase from 160 to 700. These new limits would be reached in seven months [i.e., May 1950].

24 October 1949

Reparations inspection check sheet for Ohi plant.

14 November 1949

A letter from the chief of the Procurement & Reparation Division supporting Nagaoka's request for the increase in photographic lenses and instruments noted under 20 October 1949 above. He specifically mentions that "An export contract was concluded between the United States of America."

13 December 1949

Request from Reparations Agency to allow Ohi plant to increase maximum production limits for photographic lenses and precision measuring instruments. No numbers given.

Summer 1950

An undated spreadsheet, but probably dating from this period, lists products exclusive to NK — perhaps a defense against charges made against the company. The spreadsheet points out that virtually all these products had to be imported before the war. Items include apochromat lenses for printing, "high quality photographic lens, f1.5," Precision level, transits, optical parts for physical laboratory and measuring instruments. In optical glass, NK accounted for 83 percent of domestic production.

5 July 1950

Memo causing problems for company over removal of warning siren.

22 August 1950

Report of inspection of Ohi plant after 12-hour strike.

21 April 1951

List of equipment released from reparations by that division. Mostly lens grinding machines. [The Occupation is starting to wind down and the likelihood that any of this equipment would ever go elsewhere is no longer a priority.]

1946–47

Overview of Japanese optical industry.

Index

Numbers in *bold italics* indicate pages with photographs.

www.ingramcontent.com/pod-product-compliance
Ingram Content Group UK Ltd.
Pitfield, Milton Keynes, MK11 3LW, UK
UKHW051853150726
7214IPUK00021B/404